The phrase "economic system" refers to the organizational arrangements and processes through which a society makes its production and consumption decisions. In this book, Professor Conklin explores the diversity of economic systems and the choices societies must face in determining the economic systems best suited to their needs. He discusses the alternative objectives and alternative decision modes that are available to societies. Objectives such as efficiency, growth, liberty, and equality – though themselves desirable – frequently involve trade-offs; the more complete attainment of any one objective may involve the partial sacrifice of another. In pursuit of its objectives, each society uses a combination of decision modes. Professor Conklin examines six of these: free enterprise, price controls, subsidies, taxation, non–price regulations, and public enterprise. He ends with a discussion of the processes societies use to make their choices among objectves and decision modes.

Professor Conklin has painted a vigorous and extensive picture of the limitations and possibilities that economic systems present for societies. This book will serve as a valuable tool for all who wish to understand the nature of economic decision making and to participate more effectively in their own society's choice of economic system.

Comparative economic systems

Comparative economic systems

Objectives, decision modes, and the process of choice

DAVID W. CONKLIN

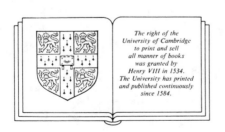

The right of the
University of Cambridge
to print and sell
all manner of books
was granted by
Henry VIII in 1534.
The University has printed
and published continuously
since 1584.

CAMBRIDGE UNIVERSITY PRESS

Cambridge
New York   Port Chester   Melbourne   Sydney

Published by the Press Syndicate of the University of Cambridge
The Pitt Building, Trumpington Street, Cambridge CB2 1RP
40 West 20th Street, New York, NY 10011, USA
10 Stamford Road, Oakleigh, Melbourne 3166, Australia

First published 1991

Printed in Canada

Library of Congress Cataloging-in-Publication Data
Conklin, D. W. (David W.)
Comparative economic systems / David W. Conklin.
p.   cm.
Includes bibliographical references and index.
ISBN 0-521-34439-5. – ISBN 0-521-34889-7 (pbk.)
1. Comparative economics.   2. Decision-making.   I. Title.
HB90.C658   1991
338.9—dc20   90–42541
                                                            CIP

British Library Cataloguing in Publication Data
Conklin, David W.
Comparative economic systems.
1. Economic systems
I. Title
330.12

ISBN 0-521-34439-5 hardback
ISBN 0-521-34889-7 paperback

Contents

Acknowledgements

This has been written as a textbook, and its structure is the outcome of discussions with students in several universities. In recent years, the economic systems of many societies have changed dramatically. Students in my comparative economic systems courses came to feel that traditional textbooks were no longer as relevant and helpful as they might be in stimulating and directing their studies. I would like to thank the many students who used manuscript drafts in their courses and whose suggestions have led to this book.

The reader will quickly realize that this book is built upon detailed references and quotations from a very large number of authors. Their insights and analyses provide the content for this textbook, and I would like to acknowledge their contributions. In many cases, their writings have not yet been incorporated into the traditional comparative economic systems literature, but I believe that this literature is enriched by their contributions. An advantage of the structure of this book is that it facilitates the integration of contributions from other specialized fields.

My early interest in this subject was stimulated by several professors, in particular Evsey Domar, Charles Kindleberger, Simon Kuznets, Max Millikan, Paul Samuelson, and Robert Solow. This textbook draws upon research projects that I have undertaken in collaboration with many whom I would also like to thank, including Thomas Courchene, Adil Sayeed, France St-Hilaire, and John Whalley. Many have provided research and secretarial assistance including Linda Bamber, Andy Baziliauskas, and John Mitsopulos.

I would like to take this opportunity to thank my family, in particular my mother Ida, my wife Marilyn, and my children David, Jamie, and Lauretta, who often provided secretarial and research assistance. I would also like to thank Baela and Sidney Sanders for their encouragement, and David Laidler for suggesting that I write this book.

CHAPTER 1

Introductory overview

The phrase *economic system* refers to the organizational arrangements and processes through which a society makes its production and consumption decisions. In creating and modifying its economic system, each society chooses among alternative objectives and alternative decision modes. Many objectives may be seen as desirable, and we shall focus in Part I on efficiency, growth, liberty, and equality. An underlying theme is that these objectives frequently involve inconsistencies and trade-offs. The more complete attainment of any one objective may involve a partial sacrifice of another. The emphasis placed on various objectives has differed among societies, and for each society the emphasis has changed over time.

In the pursuit of its objectives, each society uses a combination of decision modes, and we shall analyze six of these in Part II: free enterprise, price controls, subsidies, taxation, non–price regulations, and public enterprises. Each society leaves some economic decisions in the hands of individuals or groups, while establishing laws and incentives that govern such decentralized decision making. Each society also owns and operates some economic activities collectively. Some communist societies have created substantial planning structures to coordinate the activities of vast public enterprise networks; yet even within such systems individual initiative is expected and rewarded. For each society, the reliance upon different types of decision modes has varied from one economic activity to another, and for each society these choices have varied over time.

The procedures for choosing objectives and decision modes have also differed among societies, and Part III examines these. Reform of the economic system occurs continually, as each society evaluates its experiences, and frequently the modifications are so substantial that they are referred to as revolutions. With the closer integration of the new world economy, international trade and investment relationships constrain each society's choices in regard to modifying the economic system. An underlying reality is the limitation of human knowledge about the implications of alternative modes of decision making. Today, many so-

1

cieties are changing their economic systems in response to new judgements and new predictions about these implications. Consequently, a
purpose of this book is to enable readers to participate more intelligently
in their society's choice of economic system.

In pursuing the objective of efficiency, a central concern is the nature
and extent of unemployment. Modifications in an economic system may
be advocated in order to reduce unemployment, and people have often
been critical of free enterprise on the grounds that it can entail considerable unemployment. Also of concern is the failure of certain markets,
as a result of cost patterns that lead to monopoly, or as a result of
externalities that have positive or negative impacts on those outside of
the market relationship. Other decision modes, such as subsidies, taxation, or public enterprises, are often seen as useful in these situations
of market failure.

The objective of growth places emphasis on innovation, entrepreneurship, and productivity improvements. A society may decide that a
certain collective action would stimulate these features, and so would
enhance its overall growth rate. Again, this collective action may take
a variety of forms, such as subsidies or tax concessions for education,
retraining, and research, or the development of public facilities for these
purposes. Concerns for the environment may influence a society's objective in regard to growth. For some societies, the depletion of natural
resources may create limits to growth, and so the renewal of resources
and the development of alternative resources may also be an element
of the growth objective.

For most societies, ideological objectives and value judgements are
concerned with individual liberty and an acceptable degree of inequality.
For some societies, individual liberty may be perceived as equality of
opportunity, with the freedom to maximize personal income and to
acquire property. For other societies, the maximization of personal income and the acquisition of property may be seen as the exploitation
of people who are less fortunate. Hence, the choice among alternative
economic systems may be dependent upon the society's ideological
objectives.

In the pursuit of these objectives, each society has adopted a variety
of decision modes. Programs of subsidies and tax concessions can alter
private economic decisions, and can modify the distribution of income
and wealth. Price controls and non–price regulations can permit some
decentralized decision making within centrally determined guidelines.
Public ownership and operation of particular activities provide a more
direct instrument for the achievement of social objectives.

The choice of decision mode can vary from one economic activity to another. Each of the alternative models for organizing economic activities presents advantages as well as problems. Consequently, the choices of economic system components involve trade-offs among social objectives and governing instruments. For each society, these choices have varied over time. The economic system of each society is continually changing and so one may compare different time periods for a particular society, and evaluate the impact of reform movements, as well as compare different societies at the same point in time. The perspective and structure of this book assist the reader not only in traditional comparisons of capitalist, socialist, and communist economies, but also in comparisons within each of these broad categories. In some societies, decisions are taken at each of several government levels, and so the individual may be a member of several economic systems, each with its own set of decision modes. In comparing systems, one may consider the province or state, the nation, or even international communities. In these ways, the book's perspective and structure extend the relevance and usefulness of a course in comparative economic systems.

The literature of public choice examines the processes through which individuals and groups influence their society's choices of objectives and decision modes. Each society's political structure is of central concern in regard to these processes of choice. Although each society is continually modifying its economic system, there are times when the changes are so significant that the word revolution is used to describe them. A dramatic and abrupt alteration in a society's economic system may occur peacefully. However, many societies have experienced conflict as part of the process for choosing and modifying the economic system. Furthermore, relationships with other societies may constrain a society's choices. Of particular interest today are the globalization of markets and the growth of multinational enterprises. Linkages of trade and investment may limit the extent to which a society can create an independent economic system. Political relationships, such as trade agreements, may also limit the freedom of a society to make these choices.

Part I: Objectives

Chapter 2: Efficiency and growth

Karl Marx felt that unemployment would be a key element in the self-destruction of the capitalist system, as the accumulation of capital and its substitution for labour would result in an ever-increasing *reserve army of the unemployed*. For some, the Great Depression of the 1930s lent credence to this view. On the other hand, the 1930s experience led John Maynard Keynes and his followers to advocate an increase in collective expenditures so as to stimulate the economy through deficit financing. The devastation of the 1930s, together with the new Keynesian theory, meant that many societies did accept a collective responsibility for ensuring full employment. Demand management became an important focus of economic policy. Many came to believe that by raising or lowering taxes and expenditures, a society could maintain full employment without inflation.

Yet in the late 1970s, much of the world was once more mired in an economic environment of high unemployment. Furthermore, inflation persisted at an unacceptably high level in spite of this unemployment, and so this period is often referred to as a time of *stagflation*. Not surprisingly, stagflation led to the development of new economic theories to explain it and to the advocacy of new policies to deal with it. Monetarism gained new respectability with its explanation of inflation as the result of overexpansion of the money supply and with its recommendations for restraint in monetary policy. Some economists have expressed a belief that society is unable to vary the rate of money expansion in a way that would appropriately modify business cycles, and that consequently, money supply should be expanded in accordance with a predetermined rule rather than relying upon the discretion of planners in the central banks. Fiscal policy is seen by some as of little usefulness because of rational expectations. A view propounded by Robert Barro is that citizens will see a current deficit as a future tax liability on their part, and so they will reduce private expenditures and increase private savings by the amount of the deficit. Consequently, the net impact of deficit financing may not be the stimulation that Keynes and his followers had expected.

Analysis of less developed countries has led to the theory of the dual economy and structural unemployment. While some sectors may be fully employed and progressing well, others may have severe unemployment and few growth prospects. Workers are not able to shift easily from the latter to the former. Special skills and improved education may be a prerequisite. A physical migration from one region to another may be necessary. More plants and equipment may have to be built before more jobs can be made available. Recently, similar concerns have arisen in the economically advanced nations as well. Persistent unemployment is seen by some as not a general problem of inadequate aggregate demand, but rather as a set of structural problems that require massive worker retraining, significant geographical mobility, and policies that will assist in the adjustment towards a new mix of economic activities. For "supply-siders," this adjustment will depend upon entrepreneurial initiative, which may be retarded by excessively high levels of taxation. In this view, only by cutting marginal tax rates can a society release the creative exertions necessary to create full employment without inflation. In an extreme position, Arthur Laffer has even argued that a reduction in tax rates may stimulate economic activity so much that the total revenue of the government may actually increase.

The objective of efficiency also may include concerns about particular market structures. In certain markets, marginal costs may continually decrease with larger outputs, and so a monopoly may be able to supply the entire market at a lower cost than could a number of producers. Having attained a position of market dominance, however, a monopolist will be inclined to set prices above a socially optimal level. Market structures of oligopoly with a few producers, or imperfect competition with many differentiated producers, can also lead to socially undesirable distortions. In addition, markets can fail because of externalities where a production or consumption activity impacts individuals or businesses that are not involved in the production–consumption relationship. These impacts may not be considered by the participants when they make their economic decisions. Consequently, the interests of others may be affected either negatively, as in the case of pollution, or positively, as in the case of research. These situations of market failure can be seen as a cause of inefficiency, and choosing the appropriate decision mode for these markets can be seen as an important objective.

The adoption of new processes in production and distribution, or the creation of new and improved goods and services, are of particular interest to modern societies for whom the achievement of economic growth is determined to a large degree by innovation. The linkages among entrepreneurship, innovation, and economic growth deserve special attention in evaluating economic systems. In calculating the net advantages of an innovation, the entrepreneur must be able to quantify the relative values of inputs and products. A price system provides the basis for such calculations of cost and revenue. Even in a centrally planned economy, where relative prices may not reflect costs and scarcities, entrepreneurship requires the utilization, at least implicitly, of a set of relative values. In these computations, the difference between costs and revenues — usually referred to as *profits* – provides a guide as to the desirability or usefulness of the innovation as well as a personal reward for the entrepreneur. The behaviour of competitors will affect this probability, and so anticipations concerning their possible reactions will influence the entrepreneur's investment decision. The possibility that competitors may copy the innovation can limit its profitability, and yet it is the competitive adoption of innovations that underlies a society's productivity improvements.

The process of growth can eliminate some jobs and, at the same time, can create new opportunities; and it can alter the social structure as successful entrepreneurs gain wealth and status. Yet the rigidity or openness of the social structure can, in turn, inhibit or stimulate entrepreneurship and economic change. A society may choose to share some of the uncertainty and risk involved in this process, both as a means of encouraging innovation and also as a commitment to assist those who may be hurt. For a society, the relationships involved in entrepreneurship may add to the forces which naturally encourage the agglomeration of economic activities, and so may lead to significant differentials in growth rates among the various geographical regions of a country. In this sense, a society may be seen as consisting of a number of different regional economic systems.

Innovation affects people other than the entrepreneur — whether employees or customers — and these externality impacts mean that society as a whole has a strong interest in the process. Private rates of return may vary substantially from social rates of return. The attempt by a society to ensure that the latter are the basis for entrepreneurial decisions involves government employees in the decision-making process itself, as they manipulate prices, create special financial incentives, impose regulations, or intervene with public enterprises. Hence an important issue concerns the ability of government employees to make these types of decisions. In recent years, concerns have been expressed that growth may be limited by the quantity of natural resources available to each society. Related to these concerns has been the realization that the ability of the environment to cope with pollution is also limited. Consequently, many societies are tempering their growth objective with a desire to maintain an acceptable quality of air, water, and aesthetic attributes.

Chapter 3: Liberty and equality

This chapter first discusses the concept of liberty and the relationship between the individual and the economic system of which he or she is a member. Throughout the literature on this subject, one frequently encounters the issue of property ownership. Karl Marx, for example, emphasized a sharp division between those who own property and those who do not. The latter are compelled to become wage labourers, and they may be paid less than the value of their output. The capitalists are thereby able to accumulate surplus value, and the wage labourers are exploited. It is clear that the terms and conditions of private ownership are a central element in the pursuit of liberty. Nevertheless, this issue is not as clear-cut as many authors have suggested, because these terms and conditions can take a myriad of forms. The meaning of private ownership can be transformed significantly through the tax system, effectively confiscating part of the ownership through taxes directed at a particular activity. It can also be transformed through both price and non–price regulations. Rent controls, for example, can significantly reduce the right of property ownership, and changes in rent control legislation can alter the meaning and value of ownership. Non–price regulations can alter the freedom of an individual or firm to choose its production technology or the characteristics and quality of its products. On the other hand, a communist society may prohibit private ownership of the means of production, and yet at the same time it may delegate decision-making authority to the individual operators, and it may provide material compensation, differentiated according to the results achieved. Consequently, the manager in such an economy may enjoy many of the benefits of private ownership even though he or she cannot purchase or sell any ownership equity. Property ownership is thus seen as a far more complex issue than many writers have recognized.

Many European and North American commentators have emphasized a linkage between free enterprise and Western democracy. It has been argued, for example, that only a society based upon the individualism of the competitive market will have the determination to reject totalitarianism. In fact, a society that sees itself as a homogenous unit and an egalitarian comradeship may see democracy as less desirable than a dictatorship in which the elite leadership is able to choose and implement the policies that will be in the best interests of the community. Clearly, the division of economic decision-making between people as individuals and people as a collective is intimately related with the choice of political system. At the core is one's judgement as to the nature of human fulfilment and the degree to which individual decision making is part of the personal development of individuals. Does the person find fulfilment as part of the society's achievement, as the result of his or her individual achievement, or as the result of some combination, perhaps with the balance shifting over time?

A central concern of each society is the degree of inequality that results from its economic system. A myriad of alternative combinations of decision modes can be used to alter the income distribution. To the extent that it values consumer sovereignty, a society may place greater emphasis on the redistribution of cash, leaving individuals free to choose their own consumption patterns. Economic theory suggests that, with perfect knowledge and wise judgement, this approach should maximize consumer utility. In his seminal commentary on this subject, John Kenneth Galbraith in *The Affluent Society* expressed his view that people do not exhibit these characteristics. Manipulated by advertising and ignorant of the attributes of many of their prospective purchases, they become snared in a reflexive pursuit of material acquisitions, which is not optimal in terms of the true enhancement of their well-being. A more thoughtful elite leadership could make better consumption decisions. Subsidization of health care, education, and housing is an important decision mode for many societies. Inherent in many such programs is the belief that every member of society should receive a prescribed minimum amount of such goods and services, and that collective intervention is necessary for this to be achieved.

Substantial theoretical debate has developed over the actual incidence of particular types of taxes and, therefore, the degree of their progressiveness. In many instances, the answers are unclear, and the income redistribution thought to exist in certain tax systems may not actually be attained. Furthermore, many societies have created such a hodgepodge of expenditure subsidies that the achievement of the underlying redistribution objectives may be unclear in this sphere as well. Apart from the uncertain impact of these redistribution policies is the important issue of their impact on private incentives. Progressive tax structures may reduce private effort and innovation; social pension programs may result in a reduction in private savings; and expenditure programs may discourage low-income people from working.

Part II: Decision modes

Chapter 4: Free enterprise

With free enterprise, production and distribution decisions are made by individuals in free markets where prices fluctuate so as to equilibrate the demand and supply for each good and service, and for each factor of production. People are free to spend their income as they wish, including the purchase of property. The acquisition and inheritance of capital are usually considered essential attributes of the free enterprise mode, and so economic systems where this mode is predominant are often referred to as capitalist. Theoretical analyses emphasize the efficiency of this decision mode, whereas interpretations of human motivation stress its incentives to work, save, invest, and innovate. However, critics point to various types of market failure. Imperfect competition may result from increasing returns to scale or barriers to entry. Externalities may cause discrepancies between private and social rates of return, and hence between the optimal private and social patterns of investment and production. Individual consumers may lack the knowledge or wisdom necessary for them to make choices that are in their own best interests. Furthermore, the free market's distribution of income, wealth, power, and opportunity is considered by some to be excessively unequal and unfair. Also of importance is that adjustments in free markets may not occur smoothly or quickly, and some individuals may be hurt by fluctuations in prices and output. In particular, unemployment may be prolonged and severe.

At various points in time, even communist nations have adopted this decision mode for some of their economic activities. In the Soviet Union, for example, during the 1921–8 period, the New Economic Policy (NEP) relied upon it heavily. Even during the Stalinist period of detailed central planning, this mode was applied to farmers for their private plots, which produced a significant share of Soviet agricultural output. Debates over USSR decentralization reforms in the 1960s and again in the 1980s resulted in some sectors adopting modifications of it; and China in the mid–1980s experimented with it. At the end of the 1980s, reform movements in many European communist nations have sought to extend the scope of this decision mode, thereby significantly altering their economic systems. This mode seems to be more appropriate for some types of economic activities than for others. However, judgements about its advantages and shortcomings have varied among individuals, often on the basis of ideological objectives. Among the critics of the free enterprise model, Karl Marx deserves special attention.

Chapter 5: Price controls

With the use of price controls, an attempt is made to maintain some of the efficiency and incentive attributes of decentralized decision making while society collectively decides upon prices. In the past, most societies have applied this mode to some of their economic activities. Motivations have included: the desire to reduce the price fluctuations sometimes found in free markets; the belief that reducing certain prices will make it easier for low-income people to purchase the necessities of life; or the judgement that raising certain prices will stimulate the growth of important economic sectors. The imposition of tariffs on imported goods has often been seen as a means of raising the prices received by domestic producers, and hence of encouraging domestic expansion, particularly of manufacturers. Some societies have imposed across-the-board price controls as a means of restraining inflation. For many communist nations, decentralization reforms have involved the retention by government of the right to set prices.

The analysis of this model reveals a series of shortcomings. With a price set below the free-market equilibrium level, shortages can lead to black markets with various supplements provided by the purchaser over and above the set price. Shortages can also lead to formal rationing procedures which may be inefficient and may be susceptible to illegal evasions. Faced with a predetermined price, producers will be inclined to reduce the quality of their products. Innovations that could improve quality may be neglected. Furthermore, when prices change in a free market they are reflecting changes in demand and supply conditions, and in turn, they lead to adjustments necessary for efficiency. The inflexibility of collectively determined prices may retard or inhibit these adjustments, leading over time to inefficient distortions in a society's production and consumption.

Chapter 6: Subsidies

This mode retains decentralized decision making, but society collectively provides special financial incentives for particular types of economic activities. Society decides which activities should be encouraged to expand more rapidly than would otherwise occur, and these are given subsidies. Most societies have felt that cultural activities should be treated in this manner. In the post–1930 period, most societies have also provided special assistance to the economic activities of their more backward or depressed regions. They have often promised financial incentives for new investment and bailouts for firms that otherwise might cease operations. With the stagflation of the 1970s, many societies extended such financial incentives beyond particularly depressed regions with the hope of reducing unemployment and stimulating growth in the economy as a whole. Research and development expenditures have been considered a key to productivity improvements which may benefit society as a whole, and so private enterprises are frequently the recipients of special assistance. Exports are seen as a creator of jobs, and so many governments offer programs through which they guarantee the payment by foreign purchasers and through which they provide loans at subsidized rates to finance the transactions. Subsidy programs are incorporated into the industrial policies of some societies in order to engineer economic growth and international competitiveness.

Critics point to the political influences and corruption that may develop in such a decision mode, as well as the waste in lobbying costs as firms attempt to gain access to the financial subsidies or to encourage the creation of new programs for which they might qualify. Most significant, perhaps, are the analytical difficulties facing a society as it seeks to determine the appropriate size and conditions for such programs, and also the administrative difficulties facing the civil service as it seeks to implement society's wishes. This process tends to centralize individual economic decision making, shifting the investment and production functions away from individuals and firms and towards governments. In general, subsidies require that the society as a whole be aware of the results of such decisions, calculating the value of altering free-market outcomes, and then offering sufficient incentives to maximize society's welfare. Subsidies alter price ratios, and so they change the patterns of specialization and exchange.

Most societies provide consumption subsidies to reduce the price of certain goods and services below the price that would prevail in a free, competitive market. The production of these goods and services is left to the marketplace, rather than being undertaken directly by the government. However, the amount that is produced and the distribution among individuals are affected by the terms and conditions of the subsidy programs. In most cases, the subsidy programs are designed so that the producer receives financial assistance in return for fulfilling certain requirements. For health care, for example, subsidies may be geared to the number of patients treated and to the nature of each treatment. For education, subsidies may be based upon the number of students and the completion of a specified curriculum. For housing, subsidies may depend upon renting to people whose incomes are below a stipulated level. Consequently, with this decision mode, we already encounter some of the difficulties of communicating information and coordinating decisions that will appear most clearly in the detailed centralized command structure discussed in Chapter 9.

Chapter 7: Taxation

Through taxation, a society can alter the economic decisions made by individuals and enterprises. Within each economic system, taxes can be imposed on a wide variety of categories or bases, including the factors of production, goods and services, individuals, and businesses. The use of multiple tax bases exists for political and social, as well as economic, reasons. The well-being, or ability to pay, of individuals cannot be adequately reflected by one single indicator, and so reliance on a single type of tax may be considered unfair. Circumstances, such as health, and marital and family status, can vary substantially among individuals, and directly affect the benefits they receive from public expenditures.

Individuals also vary in terms of the utility they derive from work and leisure, and from consumption and saving. Many regard the small business sector as a disproportionate creator of new jobs, and so tax rates are often set at a lower level for small businesses than for large businesses. Certain types of activities, such as R&D, are similarly stimulated through tax concessions. Hence, there are arguments for taxing people or enterprises differently, in accordance with their particular circumstances.

The mixture and incompatibility of the society's objectives also can result in the application of a mixture of various types of taxes. Furthermore, different taxes offer different mechanisms to achieve the chosen objectives, and the use of a variety of tax bases provides additional flexibility to pursue competing objectives simultaneously. On a more practical level, levying all required revenues through one tax would compound the inequities and distortionary effects of this particular tax, and would result in severe compliance problems.

The choice of tax base will also be influenced by certain economic characteristics of the jurisdiction involved. The mobility of factors may result in tax shifting. For instance, the burden of factor taxes may be shifted onto the less mobile elements of the economy, such as land and unskilled labour. Revenue stability may also be a concern for governments. To the extent that incomes fluctuate more than consumption over time, the latter will be a more stable source of tax revenues. The relative importance of household production that results in imputed incomes could also be an issue in determining the proportion of revenue to be derived from income taxes versus other taxes such as those on sales or property. In a political federation, the choice of tax base may also be related to the legal and constitutional division of taxing powers among political jurisdictions.

Chapter 8: Non–price regulations

With the use of non–price regulations, society responds to the perceived shortcomings of the free enterprise model by establishing a myriad of rules that instruct individual decision makers to do specific things. Often these rules are imposed on a case-by-case basis, requiring that civil servants examine all prospective decisions of a particular type and pass judgement as to whether certain aspects of these prospective decisions would be in society's interests. Often the behaviour of the private sector must be monitored by civil servants to ensure that society's wishes are being followed. For example, construction of an automobile requires the manufacture of hundreds of components. Each of these components may have its own production technology, its own geographical location, its own transportation processes, and its own advertising and marketing programs. Governments can choose any of these elements as the object of regulation. The goals of non–price regulation could include, for example, the working conditions of employees; the impact of production facilities and waste materials on the purity of air and water, or on the aesthetic appearance of the community; the appropriateness and accuracy of advertising and marketing programs; the health and safety of customers who use the product; and the financial obligations of the producer to its suppliers, employees, customers, and government. For any aspect of any economic activity, a society may conclude that private decision making could be contrary to the best interests of the society as a whole. Through non–price regulations, a society is able to make any particular economic decision collectively. Furthermore, for many of those decisions that it leaves to individuals and firms it is able to restrict freedom of choice.

In designing such regulations, a society can institute many kinds and degrees of legal standards, and can enforce its regulations in a variety of ways. Because of the wide diversity of non–price regulations, this chapter examines five examples individually, seeking to explain the rationale for their imposition, and the advantages and shortcomings of each. These examples illustrate general themes. Non–price regulations frequently take the form of laws, and so the relationships between law and economics are particularly significant in this decision mode. The processes for evaluating costs and benefits of a regulation are not clear-cut or straightforward, and they often encounter difficulties in quantifying certain attributes such as cultural sovereignty, clean air, and public safety. Recently, some countries have adopted deregulation programs on the argument that efficiency and growth are reduced by the compliance costs and distortions caused by regulations. Throughout these examples, another central theme is the tendency for changing circumstances to render some regulations obsolete. A regulation that appears to be appropriate at a certain time may later be seen to encounter practical difficulties that limit its usefulness. As indicated by these themes, this mode for collective decision making is complex, and it is subject to considerable uncertainty and frequent change.

To develop specific sets of regulations and to ensure that they are being followed by individuals and firms may require the existence of a large bureaucracy. Many observers question the ability of such a bureaucracy to fulfil its responsibilities successfully, and some even question the criteria for judging success in this model. An interesting phenomenon that has gained increasing attention and that appears to hamper the functioning of this model is the tendency for those being regulated to capture the regulatory process and use it for their own purposes, rather than in society's interests. Apart from this, the individual decision-making process may experience higher costs due to the additional uncertainty and risk created by non–price regulations (and the threat of additional regulations) as well as the expenses incurred in presentations to the regulators and the search for alternative ways to conform to regulations.

Chapter 9: Public enterprises

Faced with the difficulties of price controls, subsidies, taxation, and non–price regulations – and yet unwilling to accept the shortcomings of free enterprise – many societies have turned to the collective ownership and operation of some types of economic activities. This has frequently been the case when the number of producers is limited for technological reasons and when the other decision modes would result in monopolistic behaviour. Certain activities may be considered essential for the growth of the economy, and yet private operators may not be able to capture all the benefits. Existence of externalities may mean that an investment will not be undertaken, or if the activity is undertaken, it will not produce as much output as would be socially optimal. Historically, canals and railroads provided important nineteenth century examples of the struggle by societies to decide whether subsidies to private owner–operators formed the optimal mode or whether collective ownership and operation was more appropriate. Today most societies own and operate a vast array of activities ranging from roads and public utilities to steel and aircraft manufacturing – many of which exhibit the characteristics of monopolies, scale economies, and externalities.

Yet it can be argued that collectively owned and operated activities seem unable to introduce innovations as readily as individuals or private firms, and that their production costs are higher. Furthermore, it appears to be difficult to balance the variety of social objectives that citizens may advocate, and a collective enterprise may be buffeted by changes in perceptions about these social objectives. The quality of service may also be criticized. The United States, in particular, has rejected this decision mode, and in the 1980s many nations have chosen to privatize some of the activities that had previously been collectively owned and operated.

The shortcomings of the free enterprise model are seen by some as so severe that only a few economic activities should be left to the free market. They see the private return to investment and production as deviating so far from the social return that only a thorough collective involvement in economic decision making can result in an optimal economic system. Of major concern is the economic inequality that results from the other decision modes – an inequality which not only is seen as unjust, but also which divides society into unacceptable class distinctions. Profit maximization is thus perceived to be not only less than optimal but also ideologically unacceptable.

However, the mechanics whereby all economic decisions can be made collectively – or by central planners who represent the collective and make decisions in its interest – have proven to be faulty as well. Extensive production information must be conveyed from each individual and enterprise to the central planners, and this transmission of information has proven in practice to be extremely difficult and to involve innumerable errors and misunderstandings. Since each economic activity requires inputs from many others – and, in turn, provides its products to many others – the central planners must coordinate the production information that they receive from each economic activity with the information from many others. This coordination exercise, referred to in the Soviet Union as material balances, has also proven, in practice, to be extremely difficult. Changes in production conditions – due to anything from equipment breakdowns or poor harvests to inventions that could improve product quality or reduce necessary inputs – cannot be dealt with easily in this decision mode. That is, an inflexibility appears to be inherent with central planning. Distortions arise with shortages of some items at the same time as excesses of others, and with an inability to make the appropriate adjustments.

Of particular significance is the difficulty of conveying and analyzing information about potential innovations and their usefulness. Consequently, it appears that productivity improvements may be slowed seriously in this model. Individuals and enterprises may lack incentives to innovate quite apart from the fact that they may not have the responsibility and authority to do so. Material incentives would result in an inequality which may be rejected as inappropriate and unjust. Furthermore, without a market it is not clear what the value of any particular innovation may be. Of course, this difficulty in dealing with material incentives affects daily activities since human beings can choose to alter the intensity of their work. A complete monitoring of every individual seems not to be possible. Without such monitoring, the lack of material incentives appears to retard the care and effort that people apply to their jobs.

The severity of these shortcomings seems to vary with the economy's level of development. Modern products consist of more components than the simpler versions of earlier times or of less developed countries. The increasing specialization of production facilities means that interfirm transactions must increase if potential cost reductions are to be realized. Scientific advances have become more sophisticated requiring large laboratories and complicated research programs. The problems of this decision mode – of transmitting information between economic units and central planners, of coordinating this information, and of adjusting decisions in response to new developments – all seem to become more significant as an economy becomes more developed. Yet it is conceivable that future advances in computers, telecommunications, and information management could enhance the relative desirability of this decision mode.

Part III: Choosing objectives and decision modes

Chapter 10: Reform and revolution

A basic theme of this chapter is that the choices of various decision modes – and their modifications and combinations – involve trade-offs among social objectives. Arthur Okun's well-known book *Equality and Efficiency: The Big Trade-off* propounds that society's attempts to impose more equality inevitably cause more inefficiencies. The attainment of one of these objectives must always be sacrificed in order to get more of the other. In the 1980s, scholars have attempted to estimate the precise nature of this trade-off. We shall see that many trade-offs, in addition to this one, must be faced by a society in creating and modifying its economic system. Equality of opportunity conflicts with equality of outcomes, and a society must clarify its economic interpretation of basic concepts, such as justice and fairness. The pursuit of national unity, national culture, or national independence can each involve some sacrifice of per capita income. The pursuit of environmental protection or a shorter work week, or other attempts to improve the quality of life, may similarly involve some sacrifice of per capita income. The act of saving and investment requires a choice between present consumption and future consumption, and for society as a whole it may involve an intergenerational transfer of per capita income. Somehow, a society must rank its conflicting objectives, and it must develop combinations that appear to be most appropriate. For each society, this process has involved changes. Reversals and modifications have occurred frequently. A relatively new body of literature, called *the theory of public choice,* considers how democratic societies, consisting of many different interest groups, manage to arrive at public policies, when these involve trade-offs and conflicts.

Public choice is complicated by the fact that a society can utilize a variety of instruments, types of policies, or modes of decision making. Each has advantages and shortcomings. The type of government intervention that is most appropriate for one economic activity may not be the most appropriate for others. At issue then is not only a choice among social objectives, but also a choice among decision modes for achieving the desired mix of objectives. As indicated earlier, this process has involved considerable learning on the part of each society, since theoretical analysis can rarely, by itself, provide much precision in regard to predictions about the outcomes, over time, of any particular set of choices.

The word *revolution* is frequently used to describe a significant change in an economic system. Subjective judgement is involved in determining whether the system has changed enough to warrant the use of the word revolution. Historians have referred to the broad adoption of new and improved technologies as agricultural or industrial revolutions. Walter Rostow, in his book *Stages of Economic Growth,* has presented the view that most societies pass through distinct phases of development. Each of these stages has its own set of characteristics, such as the rate of savings, the degree of technological sophistication, the nationalism and centralization of the state, and the values and success criteria of the members. A central feature of Rostow's analysis is the takeoff into self-sustaining growth. Throughout these stages, the economic system is continually changing.

Karl Marx developed an interpretation of revolution which has remained the focus of debate for over a century. The economic conditions of a society, and its production technology in particular, determined social and political relationships. Capitalism and the bourgeois owners of business were the inevitable result of the new industrial technology. Their achievement of phenomenal economic growth would be marred by their constant introduction of new labour-saving machinery which would create even larger numbers of unemployed and depress wage levels. Business cycles were inherent in capitalism and would exacerbate these problems to such a degree that the impoverished, having nothing to lose but their chains, would rebel and overthrow the system. A dictatorship of the proletariat would create the ideal society. This new organization of production and consumption was described by Marx's phrase *"from each according to his abilities; to each according to his needs."* Interestingly, the first successful communist revolution occurred not in one of the most economically advanced nations but in the largely agrarian Russia of 1917. Furthermore, many noncommunist societies have instituted programs of income redistribution to reduce the incidence of the poverty which Marx felt would destroy the system.

Modern sociologists have presented various theories concerning the nature and causes of revolution, particularly about the degree of violence involved. Some emphasize political aspects, often with the focus on the personalities and abilities of individual leaders or on the technical mechanics of military manoeuvres and the seizure of power. Lenin's concept of the revolutionary party consisted of dedicated professional revolutionaries with strong ideological commitment and with oratorical and writing skills that could move the masses. Other writers emphasize *relative deprivation* or the personal loss of previous economic and social status which leads individuals to reject the economic system. In considering these theories, this chapter emphasizes that each society does alter its economic system over time, frequently in ways so significant that they deserve to be called revolutions. Even the Soviet Union has shifted its system dramatically. The NEP in 1921, Stalin's central planning system in 1928, or post-Stalin reforms could each be described as revolutionary.

Chapter 11: Constraints imposed by the new world economy

For each society, the choice of an economic system is affected by that society's relationships with other economic systems. This can be seen clearly in cases of military or political domination, where both the ruler and the ruled adjust their economic systems in accordance with the realities of the domination. For example, the existence of the British Empire in the eighteenth and nineteenth centuries meant that, for the many member societies, the choice of economic system was severely circumscribed. The Soviet Union extended its power over Eastern Europe after the Second World War in a manner which limited the options facing societies there. In recent decades, the United States has actively sought to influence the choices of many societies throughout the world, particularly in Central and South America. These cases of military and political intervention illustrate the necessity, when comparing economic systems, to consider each society's choices in the context of that society's relationships with other economic systems.

Relationships that are not military or political can also affect a society's choices. Of special importance are trade and investment. The development of trade relationships can strongly influence a society's economic system, particularly as the domestic structure adjusts to the provision of exports. The characteristics of a principal export, and its production requirements, may affect many features of the economic system, including the role of government, as well as the nature of employment relationships. The *staple theory,* for example, describes the reliance of some colonial societies in the nineteenth century on exports of wheat, timber, and cotton, and it explains how their economic systems were shaped by these exports. Even in recent decades, many societies continue to rely on the export of a narrow range of natural resources, with significant repercussions on their choice of economic system.

Foreign investment can further restrict a society's options by transferring important decisions out of the hands of local citizens. Many societies today fear the possibility of such foreign influence, and so they look to their governments to play a larger role than they otherwise would as a means of counteracting that foreign influence. In recent decades, foreign investment has increasingly occurred within multinational enterprises (MNEs), and it has increasingly been motivated by international differences in technology. Today the multinational enterprise links societies in ways that affect the economic systems of its host countries. At the same time, many societies perceive that their growth and prosperity depend upon their international competitiveness, and they look to their governments to stimulate the technological progress upon which that competitiveness is based. From this perspective as well, a society's choices concerning its economic system are not made in isolation from other societies, but rather are shaped by the realities of their relationships.

Although political and military domination have circumscribed many societies' choices concerning their economic systems, the perspective of this book relates more closely to the role of economic relationships. In view of the purpose of this book, this chapter deals exclusively with economic forces, particularly the growing significance of technology as a determinant of trade and investment, and hence government policies, and the growing significance of the multinational enterprise as a vehicle through which these economic impacts of technology are transferred among societies. Within the new global economy, these relationships among societies are important determinants of each society's choices concerning its economic system. Of particular importance are international trade agreements, which may explicitly restrict each signatory's choices in regard to decision modes. The imposition of tariffs, the provision of subsidies and tax concessions, the establishment of regulations, and the operation of public enterprises can each be seen as unfair competition for foreign suppliers. Consequently, international agreements may place limits on their use.

The structure and perspective of this book enable the student to compare alternative economic systems in a manner that is new and, hopefully, more interesting and useful. Common problems are examined so that common solutions are highlighted as well as contrasting behaviours. In this process, we can learn from each other's systems. Underlying this approach is the belief that many government programs and policies cannot be thoroughly and satisfactorily analyzed on a theoretical basis alone. Theory must be supplemented by concrete experience and the evaluation of actual outcomes. It is not appropriate or helpful for the student to see communist nations as monolithic command economies with all decisions made by central planners, or to see capitalist nations as free enterprise economies with prices, production, and consumption determined through individual decisions in the marketplace. Such simplifications hide the essential fact that all societies are wrestling with the optimal rôle for collective decision making in a variety of different kinds of economic activities, and are continually adopting, rejecting, and modifying alternative decision modes.

PART I

Objectives

CHAPTER 2

Efficiency and growth

Introduction

Most twentieth century societies have been concerned with the objectives of efficiency and growth. Generally, people hope that their economic system will provide full employment, and an increase over time in both aggregate and per capita production. Arguments for changing the economic system have often been based on a belief that the current economic system is resulting in inefficiencies, or that it is not adequately stimulating increases in productive inputs or improvements in technology or the skills of the labour force.

Macroeconomic textbooks discuss a *production possibilities frontier,* representing the maximum amounts of alternative outputs that the society can produce, given the current levels of its inputs and given the technology which is available. Efficiency can be seen as a concept related to a society's production possibilities frontier, in that a society functioning inside of its production possibilities frontier is inefficient. Some of its inputs may be unemployed. Price inflation may impede the decision-making process. The technology being used may not be the best available. Certain markets may not be operating efficiently due to a *market failure* such as monopoly, externalities, or the public nature of certain goods and services. Along the production possibilities frontier, a free enterprise society will produce at a point where relative prices reflect consumer preferences, and this point can be seen as representing efficiency in consumption. For centrally planned economies, where relative prices may not reflect consumer preferences, production may be criticized as inefficient, in that the particular combination and qualities of goods and services produced may not be the combination and qualities that could maximize consumer satisfaction.

Growth can be seen as a shift outward of the society's production possibilities frontier. Growth can be the result of an increase in the quantity or quality of inputs, or an advance in the technology underlying their use. The distinction between the supply of inputs and any improvements in their quality and use is particularly important if the growth objective is seen as growth in production per capita rather than growth in total production. Simon Kuznets, in his book *Modern Economic Growth,* has pointed to differences between the causes of growth in aggregate output and the causes of growth in output per capita.

The enormous addition to population must have meant a large increase in the labour force, and the rise in total product must have led to an appreciable rise in the volume of capital accumulation and hence at least of reproducible capital. A significant share of the rise in total product must therefore be statistically allocable to an increase in inputs of labour and capital. The interesting question relates to the growth of product per capita. . . . [1]

In this connection a brief reference to the analysis for the United States by Denison is in order. Setting aside the depressing effects of a reduction in hours almost completely offset in Denison's analysis by resulting improvement in productivity per hour, we find that of the total growth in real national income per person employed, 1.44 per cent per year for 1909–57 (or 15.4 per cent per decade), capital and land contributed only 0.18, or about 12 percent; while the increased education of the labour force and the increased output per unit of input, due largely to economies of scale and spread of technical knowledge, contributed together 1.25 (0.58 and 0.67, respectively), or over 85 per cent. Since education and economies of scale are results of additions to and spread of the stock of useful knowledge, the dominant role of the latter – compared with the increase in input of resources – in the rise of product per capita is apparent.

The conclusion that increased input of man-hours and capital, as such, plays a minor role in the rise of production per capita reflects some key features of modern economic growth. [2]

Although the objectives of efficiency and growth can be separated for some theoretical purposes, they are too closely linked to be analyzed separately for all purposes. Employment opportunities may be created through improved efficiency or through increased growth, and the critics of an economic system may choose to advocate either improved efficiency or increased growth as the appropriate solution to an unemployment problem. Furthermore, improvements in education and skills can be seen as a more efficient use of society's labour force and also as a cause of growth.

Increasingly in recent years, the number and nature of a society's employment opportunities have depended upon the ability of the economic system to adjust its mix of products and its production technology. Changes within other societies have altered each society's comparative advantage and trade patterns, creating unemployment in certain activities and requiring production adjustments. This process of adjustment may be seen as related to *dynamic efficiency* rather than the *static efficiency* represented by a static production possibilities frontier. The need for continual adjustment means that a society's unemployment rate and growth rate are linked in a number of important ways. In particular, adjustment means that certain activities may suffer increased unemployment, even though the society as a whole may achieve increased growth and employment. A society may even suffer an overall increase in unemployment during the transition time involved in adjustment. Adjustment may also be more successful in certain geographical regions than in others, resulting in the possibility that a society may be seen as a number of economic systems rather than a single homogeneous economic system.

In 1972, *The Limits to Growth* was published by the Club of Rome. This book reports the results of mathematical calculations concerning the long-term impact of five global trends: accelerating industrialization, rapid population growth, widespread malnutrition, depletion of non-renewable resources, and a deteriorating environment. In a commentary on the report, the Club of Rome stated:

From the response to the draft we distributed, we believe this book will cause a growing number of people throughout the world to ask themselves in earnest whether the momentum of present growth may not overshoot the carrying capacity of this planet – and to consider the chilling alternatives such an overshoot implies for ourselves, our children, and our grandchildren.[3]

The problems that continued growth may encounter have given rise to a substantial literature on each of the five global trends analyzed in *The Limits to Growth*. This literature suggests that the objectives of efficiency and growth may have to be supplemented by other, related objectives. For some of these objectives, achievements cannot be readily quantified and compared. How should we measure the overall success of an economic system in minimizing pollution and protecting the natural environment? It is likely that the literature on comparative economic systems will, in the future, devote increasing attention to such questions.

The historical record

James Tobin has compiled data for five countries for the years 1973, 1979, and 1983 to indicate unemployment rates as well as *capacity utilization indexes* for their manufacturing sectors.[4] These data reveal a wide diversity among the five countries, and also a substantial difference in the performance of each economy over the ten-year period. Unemployment rates varied from 0.8 percent for West Germany in 1973 to 11.5 percent for the United Kingdom in 1983. Capacity utilization indexes varied from 100 percent for Japan in 1973 to 32 percent for the

United Kingdom in 1983. For the United Kingdom, the 1983 experience contrasted sharply with its 1973 experience, when unemployment was 3.3 percent and capacity utilization was 43 percent. For the United States, the 1983 levels of unemployment at 9.5 percent and capacity utilization at 75 percent also contrasted sharply with the 1973 experience when unemployment was 4.8 percent and capacity utilization was 88 percent. Table 2.1 presents Tobin's data.

Some observers may see these unemployment and utilization data as the result of fluctuations in aggregate demand which can be moderated through fiscal and monetary policies. Others believe that high unemployment and low utilization percentages require basic changes in the economic system and its decision-making processes. Tobin, for example, has stated that "[m]acroeconomic expansion is the key to progress against unemployment."[5] Yet, Tobin also warns:

> It will not solve all the problems, to be sure. The pathology of urban neigh-bourhoods that condemns nearly half of black youth to unemployment cannot be cured by monetary and fiscal policy. The same is true of growing youth unemployment in Europe. Macro policies and general prosperity will not restore the old high-wage jobs in smokestack industries in the American Midwest or the Ruhr.[6]

Table 2.1 also indicates growth rates for the five countries. With these as well, wide differences have existed among countries at any point in time, and for each country substantial variations have occurred over time. Some observers have interpreted such differences to be the result of alternative economic systems. In the 1980s, the United States experienced a substantial increase of employment opportunities, while at the same time, most western European countries suffered persistent high unemployment with no similar job creation. Michael Ellman has analyzed this divergent experience in an article entitled *Eurosclerosis*.[7]

> In 1983, those unemployed for over a year accounted for 40 per cent of western European unemployment but only 13 per cent of North American unemployment. Further, whereas in the ten years prior to 1983 there was a net loss of 1.5 million jobs in OECD Europe, there was a net gain of 15.8 million jobs in the United States.
>
> This divergent experience has given rise to the diagnosis of "Eurosclerosis." According to this view . . . the divergent experience results from the lesser free-dom of the market mechanism to operate in western Europe. The downward inflexibility of real wages, the welfare state, restrictions on the right of employers to fire redundant workers, high minimum wages, and a political and cultural climate hostile to enterprise have prevented the price mechanism fulfilling its normal function of matching supply and demand. In the United States, in con-trast, the flexibility of the economy, relatively unhindered by counterproductive

Table 2.1. *Selected macroeconomic data for OECD countries*

	Unemployment rates[a] (%)(average for year)			Capacity utilization indexes[b]		
	1973	1979	1983	1973	1979	1983
United States	4.8	5.8	9.5	88	86	75
Japan	1.3	2.1	2.7	100	90	83
West Germany	0.8	3.2	8.5	87	84	78
France	2.6	5.9	8.3	85	82	77
United Kingdom	3.3	5.6	11.5	43	42	32
Seven summit countries	3.4	5.0	8.3			
Fifteen OECD countries	3.3	5.1	9.0			

	Real growth (% per yr) GNP or GDP			Output gap: % shortfall of 1983 GNP/GDP below 1979, projected to 1983 by	
	1965–73	1973–9	1979–83	1973–9 trend	mean of 1973–9 and 1965–73 trends
United States	3.8	2.8	0.9	7.1	8.9
Japan	9.8	3.7	3.6	0	11.2
West Germany	4.1	2.4	0.5	7.5	10.4
France	5.2	3.1	1.1	7.7	11.3
United Kingdom	3.8	1.4	0	5.3	9.8
Seven summit countries					
Fifteen OECD countries					

	Money wage inflation[c] (%)			Unit labour costs[d] (% Increase over prev yr)		
	1973	1979	1983	1973	1979	1983
United States	7.1	8.4	4.6	3.4	6.9	3.7
Japan	23.4	7.4	4.5	2.3	−2.5	1.2
West Germany	10.7	5.5	2.7	5.4	2.0	−1.2
France	14.6	13.0	11.0	7.2	6.1	8.0
United Kingdom	12.7	15.5	8.0	5.4	12.8	1.2
Total OECD	13.0	9.6	6.0			
Seven summit countries				4.6	5.3	3.5

	Price inflation, GNP/GDP deflator (% rise over prev yr)		
	1973	1979	1983
United States	5.8	8.6	4.2
Japan	11.9	2.6	1.0
West Germany	6.5	4.1	3.0
France	7.1	10.4	9.0
United Kingdom	7.1	15.1	5.2

Table 2.1 (*continued*)

| | Price inflation, GNP/GDP deflator (% rise over prev yr) | | |
	1973	1979	1983
Total OECD		8.4	4.7
Seven summit countries		7.4	5.2

Notes: Except for the United States, figures for 1983 are OECD estimates from incomplete information. The seven summit countries include Italy and Canada. The fifteen OECD economies are the advanced countries, for which employment dates are meaningful.
[a]Unemployment rates are standardized by OECD to US definition.
[b]Estimates of utilization of manufacturing capacity. For Japan, the Ministry of International Trade and Industry index is normalized to 1973. For the United Kingdom, figures are percentages of firms reporting full utilization.
[c]Hourly earnings in manufacturing for the United States and West Germany; monthly earnings for Japan; weekly earnings for the United Kingdom; hourly wage rates for France
[d]Labour costs per unit of manufacturing output, for Germany, includes mining
Source: James Tobin, "Macroeconomic Diagnosis and Prescription," in Morley Gunderson, Noah M. Meltz, and Sylvia Ostry, eds., *Unemployment: International Perspectives* (Toronto: University of Toronto Press, 1987), pp. 13–14.

government regulations, and stimulated by a positive attitude to entrepreneurship and profits, has enabled employment creation to flourish.[8]

Ellman has concluded that the differences in economic systems do explain part of this divergence in performance. Nevertheless, he cautions that unemployment can also be the temporary result of an adjustment process, reflecting the successful pursuit of dynamic efficiency. From this perspective, one might see the high 1983 U.S. unemployment rate as a symptom of the economic system's positive adjustment rather than as an indication of failure.

Some authors have pointed to the Japanese data as evidence of outstanding performance, and have recommended that other countries should adopt elements of the Japanese economic system. Some authors have pointed to the United Kingdom data for the 1970s and early 1980s as evidence of a "British problem" that arose from the excessive use of subsidies, regulation, and public enterprise, and the high tax rates required to finance these. Many such analysts have advocated a radical restructuring of the UK economic system and warned of the dangers for other countries that can accompany a movement towards such a socialist economic system.

At the same time, other observers have emphasized that growth in a modern economy depends upon research, education, and retraining. These are activities where externalities are significant, and, consequently, where collective decision making is becoming increasingly important. These commentators argue that free enterprise will not, by itself, invest in research, education, and retraining to the degree that would be socially optimal. These perspectives will be discussed in later chapters.

Simon Kuznets has developed Table 2.2 to indicate long-term growth rates of various countries over various time periods.[9] These data reveal wide differences among countries at any point in time, as well as substantial differences over time for most countries. Nevertheless, Kuznets's analysis suggests that certain features of the growth process are common among various economic systems, and these common features will be a focus of our discussions later in this chapter.

In Table 2.3, Gregory and Stuart have presented data to compare the growth experiences of the United States and the Soviet Union.[10] Since calculations of growth rates depend upon the prices used, Gregory and Stuart present U.S. growth rates using several alternative sets of prices. Furthermore, there are substantial differences for USSR growth rates between the estimates of American experts and the official Soviet estimates.

In an article concerning the Soviet Union, Hardt and Gold have emphasized the importance of a substantial decline in growth rates as the reason for Soviet reforms in the 1980s.[11] "The economy, which had grown at an average of 5.4 per cent p.a. during Brezhnev's first (the Soviet Eighth) Five-Year Plan (1966–1970) grew at only 2.7 per cent in his last (the Soviet Tenth) (1976–1980)."[12] This perspective is shared by Philip Hanson who has emphasized five aspects of the recent Soviet slowdown in growth rates:

First, for any comparison with Western countries, the Soviet official growth figures are too flattering to the USSR. In terms of Western-style GNP, and with concealed inflation properly allowed for, Soviet real national income has been increasing at 2.0–2.5 per cent a year so far in the 1980s, and not at the 3.0–3.5 per cent indicated by Soviet data. That is roughly equivalent to only 1.0–1.5 per cent growth in GNP per head of population. Estimating Soviet GNP in 1982 rouble prices, instead of the 1970 rouble prices previously used, the CIA in early 1986 produced an assessment of Soviet growth in 1984–5 of about 1.5 per cent per annum against about 2 per cent in their previous assessments. That implies a growth of GNP per head of population of only about 0.5 per cent a year.

Second, the very slow growth of the past seven years is part of a long-run slowdown that goes all the way back to the 1950s. If this tendency continued, the economy would pass through zero growth to absolute decline. Third, the

Table 2.2. *Rates of growth in total product, product per capita, and product per man-hour, developed countries, two long periods, 1870–1913 (I) and 1913–60 (II) (percentage per decade)*

	Total product		Population		Product per capita		Product per man-hour	
	I (1)	II (2)	I (3)	II (4)	I (5)	II (6)	I (7)	II (8)
1. United Kingdom	24.4	20.7	9.2	4.5	13.9	15.5	16.3	19.5 (20.2)
2. France	16.9	15.7	1.8	1.9	14.9	13.6	19.6	23.0 (20.2)
3. Germany, FR (1871)	33.2	28.4	12.4	9.4	18.5	17.4	22.7	21.6 (20.4)
4. Belgium	30.5	15.1	10.0	3.8	18.7	10.8	22.3	18.0 (14.4)
5. Switzerland (1890)	26.7	29.8	11.8	7.2	13.4	21.1	16.7	26.7 (25.0)
6. Netherlands (1900)	24.8	30.1	15.0	14.2	8.5	13.9	11.4	18.2 (17.1)
7. Denmark	37.0	26.1	11.2	9.4	23.2	15.2	28.7	19.4 (18.7)
8. Norway	23.7	32.3	8.3	8.5	14.2	21.9	19.3	30.7
9. Sweden	33.9	27.5	7.2	6.3	24.9	20.0	30.2	25.4 (24.5)
10. Italy	15.0	25.4	6.8	6.8	7.7	17.4	12.9	26.1 (22.1)
10a. Italy (1890)	22.6	25.4	6.9	6.8	14.7	17.4	20.4	26.1 (22.1)
11. Japan (1880)	37.8	45.0	10.9	13.3	24.3	27.9		
12. United States (1871)	52.7	34.5	23.0	14.0	24.1	18.0	26.5	26.8 (28.8)
13. Canada	45.1	34.9	19.1	18.6	21.8	13.7	22.7	24.5 (24.3)

Notes: The entry in brackets in the stub is the initial date of the first period, if different from 1870. The output series for 1960, underlying column 2 were arithmetic means of 1959–61. Per capita product rates were derived from those for total product and population.
Source: Simon Kuznets, *Modern Economic Growth: Rate Structure and Spread* (New Haven, CT: Yale University Press, 1966), pp. 352–3.

Soviet Union is in military competition with the West and China. It already allocates a much larger share of GNP to military purposes than Western countries do. If it were to have slower economic growth than the U.S.A. over a long period, it would eventually be unable to maintain its status as one of the two military superpowers.

Table 2.3. *Annual rates of growth of GNP in the USSR and the United States*

USSR	American estimates		Official Soviet estimates (net material product)
1885–1913	3.3[c]		—
1928–40	5.4[a]		14.6[d]
1950–60	6.0[c]		10.1
1960–70	5.1[c]		7.0
1970–79	4.0[c]		5.3
1928–79	4.5[b]		8.8
1928–79, effective years	5.1[b]		9.7
1950–79	4.9[b]		7.6
United States	1860 prices	1929 prices	1958 and 1972 prices
1834–43 to 1879–88	4.4	—	—
1879–88 to 1899–1908	3.7	3.8	—
1899–1908 to 1929	—	3.4	—
1929–50	—	—	2.8
1950–60	—	—	3.2
1960–70	—	—	4.0
1970–79	—	—	3.1
1929–79	—	—	3.1
1950–79	—	—	3.5

[a] 1950 prices.
[b] Combined index, 1950 prices 1928–50, 1970 prices thereafter.
[c] 1970 weights.
[d] 1926–7 prices.
[e] 1913 prices.
Source: Paul R. Gregory and Robert C. Stuart, *Soviet Economic Structure and Performance* (New York: Harper and Row, 1981), p. 332.

Fourth, the USSR is also engaged in "peaceful economic competition" with the West, China, and Japan. The political leaders want to exhibit faster economic growth than their main competitors. They want this partly for the sake of the Soviet Union's prestige in the world at large and partly to support their authority in their own country.

The final reason why the slow growth is of such political importance has to do with consumption levels. If real GNP per head of population is growing at 1.0–1.5 per cent a year, the competition for resources between defence, investment and consumption is necessarily severe.[13]

A key theory which appears throughout our text is that the prerequisites for growth can vary depending upon the society's stage of development.

Prior to the 1980s, the Soviet Union was able to adopt technology developed previously in other countries. Today, the innovation process and entrepreneurship have a new importance, and consequently public enterprise and central planning may no longer be optimal. Furthermore, a series of basic changes in the nature of production and consumption have also served to retard growth under the centrally planned system: the greater complexity of modern products; the growing significance of quality rather than just quantity; and the heavier emphasis on consumer satisfaction rather than solely industrial or military success. Although the command economy provided rapid growth in earlier years, these changes mean that a radical alteration in the economic system is now necessary if rapid growth is to be achieved again in the future.

Unemployment

Since earliest times, people have sought to increase their material well-being, and throughout history many people have been disappointed in this struggle. Some people have failed to obtain a type of employment that they have considered to be appropriate. For some individuals, employment has not provided adequate scope for their talents, or their hours and conditions of work have not been satisfactory, or the level of remuneration has been too low. Some people at certain times have simply not been able to find any employment. All of these situations may be seen as a failure of the economic system to produce efficiently, on its production possibilities frontier. In discussions about this subject, and in the collection and analysis of data, there has been a tendency to focus on those who have lacked jobs and who can be clearly labelled as unemployed. However, when considering the efficiency of the economic system, it is important to be aware of the various forms of *disguised unemployment,* where people have jobs that do not fully utilize their abilities. Furthermore, it is also important to be aware of the economic system's impact on the incentives of individuals to seek employment and, therefore, its impact on the size of the labour force. For example, a system with generous subsidies may experience little measured unemployment because people who would otherwise be categorized as unemployed have chosen not to join the labour force.

There are many reasons why the unemployed have been a focus of analysis. Unemployment has always been seen as a situation of calamity for the individual and family. Karl Marx pointed to unemployment as an inevitable weakness of the capitalist system and predicted that the number of unemployed would increase over time, leading inevitably to revolution. No doubt Marx's spectre of social unrest caused by unemployment still motivates the concerns of many. In fact, some observers blame unemployment for the rise of Hitler and Nazism in the 1930s in Germany. Some societies, confronted with the 1930s depression and challenged by Keynesian economics, have officially pledged in legislation to minimize the number of unemployed. Since the 1930s, many non-Communist societies have perceived times of high unemployment to be the result of inadequate aggregate demand, and they have often manipulated fiscal and monetary policies in an attempt to moderate fluctuations in demand. Furthermore, many societies have adopted social security programs, such as unemployment insurance, specifically formulated to assist these people. Thus, for many societies, the economic system has been modified in hopes of minimizing unemployment, and in hopes of reducing the personal hardship and social and political unrest that accompany unemployment.

For the less developed countries, unemployment has generally not been perceived as a result of inadequate aggregate demand. Rather, analysis has emphasized inappropriate human skills, backward technology, and inadequate capital stock. Solutions for unemployment have been seen in various policies and programs that could ameliorate these shortcomings. Often, less developed countries are described as possessing *a dual economy* in which a modern and fully employed sector coexists with a traditional sector, based on subsistence agriculture. In the latter, the low incomes and limited prospects have been described as *disguised unemployment*. Although everyone may have a place in the economy, some people are earning so little that they are in effect unemployed. In the 1950s the economic development literature emphasized the need for capital accumulation to expand the advanced sector. The concept of a fixed capital–output ratio added weight to this view. Increased foreign aid was seen as a mechanism for the requisite expansion and as the appropriate solution to this endemic unemployment problem. Recent analyses of the "dual economy" emphasize the barriers that prevent these disguised unemployed from shifting out of their relatively ineffective jobs into the more productive, advanced sector; and they emphasize how these barriers may be breached through education and technology transfer, as well as investment in productive facilities. From this perspective, a society's labour market is regarded not as a single entity but rather as a number of separate and different markets. Wages may vary substantially among these sectors, yet labour may not be able to shift from the subsistence levels of one market to the much higher levels of the modern industrialized sector.

Dynamic efficiency and adjustment

People change jobs; some businesses close their doors; new businesses arise and expand. In this process, some unemployment is inevitable, although such unemployment may vary in significance from one society to another and from one time period to another. In times of rapid and substantial economic change, when the structure of the economy is being altered, some unemployment may take on an additional characteristic. People who were trained for one type of job may find that they can no longer practice their trade; they must be retrained in order to work in a different kind of job. Alternatively – or in addition to this experience – people who have lived in one particular community and who have invested in a home there find that they cannot obtain a suitable job in their community; they must move their family to another city, perhaps in another region of the country. Unemployment in such cases will be of longer duration; its resolution will require substantial investment in education and skills training together with major expenses of geographical relocation. The post–1945 period has been a time of particularly great structural change.[14]

A major impetus for economic change has been the growth of new trade relationships – a growth based on several significant trends. Within the past two decades some of the LDCs (less-developed countries) have become NICs (newly industrialized countries) and have created a manufacturing sector capable of exporting to Europe and North America. Paying extremely low wage rates, they are now able to compete within the markets of the developed nations in a substantial range of manufactured goods. For generations, Great Britain and the United States maintained a technological lead, ahead of other industrialized nations. Within recent decades, this lead has been challenged in many types of production. Most dramatically, Japan has been able to develop new manufacturing techniques and new forms of business organization that have created products desired by North American and European consumers. Technological advance can have a sudden and substantial impact on existing markets, abruptly reducing the sales volumes, prices, and profits of traditional manufacturers. Since the Second World War, political leaders have recognized that reductions in tariff barriers can increase international trade in a manner that will raise average incomes for all trading partners. A search has occurred for new trade agreements that will expand trade flows. Often such arrangements expose traditional manufacturers to a competition to which they are not accustomed and for which they are not prepared.

Within Europe and North America, manufacturers have been exposed to new competition as a result of each of these developments. Rapid shifts in foreign exchange rates have added to the surprising alterations in competitive positions. All of these phenomena mean that business adjustment has become a daily requirement rather than a periodic search for improvement. A nation whose businesses rely on growth of traditional facilities and expansion of current practices may find that its firms are losing sales, profits, and jobs. The importance of entrepreneurship – and the preparedness to innovate and to experiment with new methods – has been amplified by this set of developments. Technological change will affect job prospects not so much by creating large numbers of new high-tech firms offering new high-tech jobs, but rather by enabling traditional industries to adopt new production methods. For many people, technological change will alter the content of their existing jobs, requiring continual reeducation and the acquisition of new skills.

Any one particular innovation may, by itself, hurt specific employees either by reducing their relative wages or even by eliminating their jobs. For the workers who are hurt, technological change may be undesirable. At best, they may have to shift to some other corporation; at worst, they may have to retire early or endure a long period of job search and retraining; they may even have to sell their home and move to a different city, paying relocation costs and possibly losing equity in their home as well as company pension rights. If their community is small or offers few employment alternatives, or if their community is particularly hard hit by job losses, then the suffering may be severe and the number who suffer may form a noticeable and politically powerful group. Hence a society experiencing rapid and substantial technological change will inevitably contain workers whose job losses are painful and who may consequently seek government assistance both in retarding change and in assisting personal adjustment.

What may be true for a society as a whole – that technological change enhances growth, productivity, income levels, and jobs – may not be true for some members of society whose jobs may be adversely affected. This phenomenon – of more and better jobs for most, yet fewer and worse jobs for some – may increase in importance as the pace of technological change quickens. It may give rise to political conflict over the optimal pace of technological change, over specific policies that could retard that change, and over programs for assisting those who are hurt by the change. In this political conflict, the proponents of change usually cannot point to specific new jobs that can immediately make up for the lost jobs that may accompany change. They may point to expected cost reductions, quality enhancement, or new products, but these improvements cannot easily be quantified and balanced against lost jobs. Often the beneficiaries of change cannot be identified ex ante. This is particularly troublesome when the jobs being lost are obvious and when the employees who face severe adjustment problems plead for government obstacles to prevent change. From this perspective, one can see that, within any society, individuals may disagree about the relative desirability of alternative economic systems because of differences in their attitudes towards the changes and adjustments that accompany growth.

Foreign exchange rates and unemployment

The 1970s and 1980s have been a time of rapid and substantial fluctuations in international exchange rates. These fluctuations have altered comparative costs and have disrupted established trade patterns. Adjustments have been necessary in production and employment; and unemployment has been a part of this adjustment process. Of special interest have been cases where a nation's currency has increased in value due to exports of a natural resource or due to capital inflows. In some such cases, unemployment has been substantial and long term. Oil exports, for example, have driven up the international value of many currencies. In those countries, the production of other commodities has been constrained: Exports other than oil have been limited, while competition from imports has increased. The fortunate resource sector whose exports have caused this phenomenon may not be labour intensive to a great enough degree to permit full employment. The unemployed may lack the requisite skills or capital to shift into those import-competing areas where they could survive. Wage comparisons with the export sector may hamper the wage declines that could be necessary for this process to occur. Apart from transitional adjustment difficulties, such situations entail a real risk that the circumstances could again change abruptly, requiring another set of adjustments.

The command economy: disguised unemployment and inefficiency

For the communist countries, detailed central planning promised a way of guaranteeing that everyone would have a job. Each person would be required to work at a job allocated specifically to him or her. At every point in time, there would be some work of some social value that could be done, and so central planners would have no difficulty in finding jobs for everyone. People could be compelled to work, and so wages would not have to be set high enough to entice people into the labour force. Nor would wages have to adjust to equilibrate the demand and supply for each type of labour. In particular, firms would not have to make hiring decisions on the basis of profit maximization. Firms would not have to ensure that any additional workers would create a marginal product greater than or equal to their wage. These views in regard to communist central planning have encountered practical difficulties in actual implementation. It appears that basic human nature is such that material incentives must often accompany the planned directives. Furthermore, it appears that severe shortcomings in the central planning process can result in substantial disguised unemployment under these economic systems. Even for the command economy, economic change brings the need for adjustment. Technological change requires that employees undergo retraining. The depletion of natural resources or the discovery and development of new supplies of natural resources may involve the need to shift large numbers of people from one geographic location to another.

In the post–1945 period, the Soviet Union has engineered a huge expansion of capital facilities, agricultural cultivation, and population in the republics of Siberia and Kazakhstan. Throughout the Soviet Union, a substantial movement of people has occurred from the rural areas to the cities. It is interesting to note that this nation has relied strongly on the financial incentives of income differentials to encourage the requisite population movements. In theory, the decisions to invest capital into new regions and in new enterprises might be thought to be a more flexible process than reliance on the free-enterprise model. In practice, the Soviet Union has encountered severe adjustment difficulties. As part of these, disguised unemployment appears to have been significant. Employees have not always worked in the enterprises or positions where they could be most effective. Agriculture, in particular, seems to have undergone a protracted period of extremely inefficient production, with labour apparently not allocated in an optimal manner.

Since the 1950s, Western commentators on the Soviet economic system have emphasized the inefficiency entailed in an aggregate production that is not based on consumer preferences. Countless anecdotes illustrate the frustration experienced by people who are unable to acquire a desirable mix and quality of goods and services. Shortages result in queues for those goods that are available. However, no index has been developed to convey the extent of this inefficiency.

Inflation, the Phillips curve, and stagflation

In the 1960s and 1970s many countries experienced a significant rise in inflation rates. For people receiving fixed incomes, such as pensions, this phenomenon caused severe personal hardship. For people making economic decisions – whether businessmen in their daily activities or investors considering alternative uses of capital – the increase in inflation brought significant new uncertainties. Inflation rates could vary over time to a degree they could not predict beforehand. Interest rates mirrored these rapid and extreme fluctuations. The magnitude and variability of inflation rates and interest rates could disrupt decision making and cause well-made plans to fail. Both creditors and debtors confronted new and unforeseen problems. A shift from long-term fixed-rate mortgages and term loans to short-term variable-rate demand loans added another new element of instability and uncertainty. Negotiations of wage contracts could fail to provide appropriately for inflation in the cost of living, thereby intensifying strife between employees and employers, in both the private and the public sectors. Expectations of future inflation led to demands for wage increases that appeared to fuel an inflationary spiral. People looked to their governments for new policies that could reduce inflation.

In the 1960s, a concept that caught the attention of governments and the public was the Phillips curve. Phillips found that a close inverse relationship seemed to exist between the rate of inflation and rate of unemployment. Phillips examined data in a number of countries which indicated that inflation rose as unemployment rates fell. Other observers developed a variety of analyses concerning the causal relationships involved in this phenomenon. Many of these stressed a cost-push interpretation. Employees were believed to have greater bargaining power when relatively few were unemployed, whereas their bargaining power was diminished if large numbers of unemployed could take their places. Although union seniority might protect employee jobs in any particular firm, a large number of unemployed would mean that other firms could readily expand their work force and thereby indirectly reduce the sales and jobs in any high-wage firm. Employer resistance to wage increases was stronger in times of high unemployment, not only because of their possible ability to hire cheaper labour, but also because of their fear of competitors who might do so.

This concept led to a dramatic policy prescription. If a close relationship existed between unemployment and inflation, then a society had to face a trade-off between these two evils. A society could only solve its inflation problem by deliberately increasing the numbers of unemployed. Tighter fiscal and monetary policies could restrain aggregate demand, and could increase unemployment so that inflation could be reduced. In many societies, the 1970s and 1980s have seen a public debate over this choice between controlling inflation and increasing jobs.

This choice became more confusing as the 1970s proceeded, in that inflation remained high, even while unemployment levels rose. Throughout the non-Communist world, a new phenomenon of *stagflation* took hold of the economy. Extremely high levels of unemployment, not seen since the 1930s, persisted in the presence of high inflation. Growth in per capita income levels slowed significantly as did the rate of productivity increases. This situation has led to the development of a plethora of explanations and policy prescriptions. Some have emphasized time lags in the process of adjusting wages and prices to the new, higher unemployment levels. Some have modified the Phillips curve. For example, some have added the role of expectations to the relationship, presenting an "expectations augmented Phillips curve." Many observers, however, have not been so sanguine and have presented arguments for significant changes in the economic system in order to modify this trade-off relationship between inflation and unemployment.

Some observers have chosen to emphasize the inflationary expectations in the wage and price setting process. They see wage negotiations as particularly significant, since long-term wage contracts can build future inflation into the system, and so they believe in a greater role for government and collective decision making. Some advocate price controls – including controls over the price of labour – as being necessary in times of low unemployment in order to restrain inflation. Many societies adopted this view in the 1970s and instituted various types of price control programs. Alternatively, as the next section suggests, some have advocated a basic change in the wage-setting process.

The impact of wage inflexibility on unemployment

The functioning of a competitive labour market should automatically result in a movement towards full employment. If unemployment does exist at any particular time, then wages should fall to that level at which firms are prepared to hire all the employees who wish to work. To many observers, the existence of unemployment simply represents the failure of wages to fall immediately to the equilibrium level. Some place a major portion of the blame for unemployment on the mechanics of wage determination. Long-term contracts mean that time must pass before wage decreases can be negotiated. The shortsightedness of particular union leaders might delay these necessary adjustments. Some commentators recommend reforms which they believe could speed up this movement towards equilibrium by increasing the flexibility of wages.

Martin Weitzman in his book, *Share Economy: Conquering Stagflation,* advocates a new basis for employee remuneration. Instead of paying workers a fixed wage, corporations should offer a base pay, plus a share of the value of output, perhaps a share of total revenue or a share of profit.[15] Weitzman points to Japan as an example of this approach. In Japan, twice yearly profit-sharing bonuses can significantly affect the worker's total remuneration. The key, from Weitzman's perspective, is that this bonus is flexible and provides a flexibility in the wage package that is lacking in most capitalist countries.

Under a share contract, if a firm hires more workers, then, ceteris paribus, the remuneration of all employees will fall slightly. This provides the firm with a greater incentive to hire additional workers than that which exists under a straight wage system. The marginal labour cost to the firm is less than the average labour cost. "Any system where a substantial number of big firms are operating with the marginal cost of labour lower than the average cost of labour will have an inherent predilection toward providing more employment and expanding output."[16] The expansion of a share system ends when there is no more unemployment. "At that point each share firm wishes to expand further, but it cannot because there is no more unemployed labour to be found."[17] Weitzman emphasizes that this method for determining remuneration not only constrains wages directly, but also constrains inflation indirectly by increasing total production.

The rise of monetarism

For many generations, commentators on economic affairs have noted the relationship between the money supply and inflation. In earliest times, the debasing of the coinage led to price increases. In the sixteenth and seventeenth centuries, Spanish shipments of silver from Latin America caused inflation in Spain. As long as the money supply was directly linked to quantities of gold or silver, new discoveries of these metals could result in inflation. At other times, some politicians saw a dependence of the money supply on gold as a cause of too slow an expansion in the money supply, and some argued for a severance of this connection as a solution to tight money. Most dramatic perhaps was the slogan of William Jennings Bryan in his 1896 U.S. Presidential campaign, "You shall not crucify this nation on a cross of gold."

In the 1960s and 1970s, some economists pointed to the extremely rapid expansion of the money supply as the cause of inflation. They did not focus on the wage negotiation process, cost-push experience, or the market processes whereby prices were set. Rather they blamed governments themselves, and central bankers in particular. The solution was that governments should cut back on the rate at which they had been expanding the money supply. Monetarists criticized the ability of governments to fine tune the money supply so as to moderate business cycle fluctuations. They doubted the ability of central bankers to forecast accurately. They questioned the bankers' ability to operate independently of political pressures that would consistently advocate monetary expansion so as to stimulate business, even when this approach could be inappropriate and inflationary. Many monetarists argued, therefore, for a constant rate of expansion of the money supply equal to the long-term rate of growth.

In the 1970s and 1980s, many central banks – faced with the monetarist analysis – did significantly reduce the rate of monetary growth, restricting that growth to predetermined "targets." These reductions are often seen as the cause of the accompanying unemployment increases. From an optimistic perspective, one might see this situation of the 1975–85 period as a time of adjustment. Lags were inevitable as economic relationships changed to conform to the new lower rate of money growth. Consequently, some monetarists are among the most sanguine about the stagflation experience. The passage of time, with a continually low expansion of the money supply, will bring about lower inflation. The underlying real determinants of economic growth will then restore satisfactory levels of employment and growth. From this perspective, a policy change is all that is necessary, rather than any basic change in the economic system and its decision modes.

The competitiveness in the market

Critics of the free enterprise model often point to *market failures* as evidence of inefficiencies. It is important to note that market failures can lead to inefficiencies with other decision modes as well. With certain products, marginal cost declines over the relevant range of outputs. A single supplier may be able to produce at an average cost lower than that attainable if many competitors were to exist. However, a single supplier – or even a small number of suppliers who act collectively – may use this market power in undesirable ways. In the free enterprise mode, such suppliers may restrict their output so as to raise prices, with the result that production is not socially optimal. With price controls, where prices are set centrally, we shall see that market power can also cause inefficiencies, particularly through quality deterioration. With non–price regulations, a situation of too few producers can lead to the capture of regulators by those being regulated, with the result that the regulators and their enforcement may not be in the best interests of the public. Also, with subsidies or public enterprise, the existence of market power can enable the producer to influence decisions made centrally. In such cases, central planners are unable to refer to a market and to examine competitors' behaviour as a way of verifying the information provided by the producer.

The degree of distortion in any particular market and the length of time that distortion will persist are important questions in weighing the advantages and shortcomings of alternative decision modes. Yet these questions are not easily answered. Furthermore, the answers will vary from one product to another, and from one time period to another. Consequently, it is not surprising that the choice by societies of a certain decision mode has varied among products and over time.

Public goods

As indicated in the above discussion, the marginal cost of providing an additional quantity of a good or service may be less than the average cost, in the relevant output range. In some cases, the marginal cost may be zero or negligible, and these cases are often referred to as *public goods*. Provision of public goods may entail an initial cost, but once this has been incurred then additional usage may involve little or no additional cost. Examples could include parks, highways, and defence. It is true that a monopolist could own and operate such activities, as in the above discussion concerning market competitiveness. However, when marginal cost is zero the argument for public ownership may seem stronger than when marginal cost is simply below average cost. Furthermore, a monopolist could experience difficulties in controlling access to such goods and services. The features which underlie the cost configuration may also inhibit the process of charging an access fee. This problem may also be an argument for public ownership. The concept of public goods suggests the existence of various degrees of *market failure,* with the need to analyze each situation on its own merits.

Externalities

The production, consumption, and investment decisions of any particular individual can impact other economic activities. It is true that in some situations, private contracts may be developed to deal with such impacts. However, in other situations, contracts may be too complex; interrelationships may be too numerous and their quantification may be too difficult. The individual whose decision is causing the third-party effects will then have no incentive to include these impacts in his or her decision making. Pollution, for example, may severely affect the well-being of others who, without collective regulation through government, may not be able to influence the polluting activity.

Positive impacts may occur as well as negative impacts. Expenditures on research and development for new products or processes may provide benefits to others than the originator. Yet the inability to capture these third-party benefits may limit these expenditures to lower amounts than would be socially desirable. Only subsidies or direct government operation of research facilities may be able to maximize social welfare.

The significance of such third-party effects and the degree to which they can be captured by the private contract process vary among economic activities and over time. Furthermore, people disagree about the ability of governments to deal with such situations, and about the most appropriate techniques for collective intervention. Nevertheless, we can say that the choice of a certain decision mode is often based on the view that third-party effects warrant active government involvement in production, consumption, and investment decisions.

Growth and entrepreneurship: An historical perspective

In the 1920s, Kondratiev analyzed long-term trends in economic activities. Kondratiev suggested that an economic upturn contained forces within it that strengthened each other in a cumulative advance that could go on for several decades. One such force could be the application of inventions which may have been discovered during previous years but which had not been implemented because of depressed economic conditions. With an economic upturn and expanding customer demand, entrepreneurs would have the confidence to introduce these as innovations. Joseph Schumpeter refined these insights of Kondratiev and interpreted economic history largely in terms of the strength of entrepreneurial activity.[18]

Schumpeter focused on a few pathbreaking innovations, each of which cleared the way for many related innovations. The applications of steam power to the manufacturing process provided an important nineteenth century example of this. Once steam technology was understood and after it had been applied in one process, the equipment could be modified quickly and easily to assist many kinds of manufacturing. In this way, all manufacturing costs were reduced within a short period of time. The need for new facilities and equipment created a demand for capital goods which led to new job opportunities. Growth, development, productivity, and jobs – all were enhanced.[19]

The development of railroads greatly reduced transportation costs, thereby reducing the prices of many products. New agricultural areas could be cultivated; competition increased as the scope of each market area widened; and railroads needed substantial quantities of capital goods. Consequently, most businesses were affected by this railroad revolution. The lower costs and new marketing possibilities opened up a wide range of innovations for all businesses. That is, the railroad innovation made possible a long series of other innovations. Furthermore, the railroad innovation meant that new capital investments had to be made to produce specific commodities such as trains, tracks, and steel.

In the period 1900–50, the development of electric power, together with its application in both production and consumption, provided unlimited opportunities for manufacturers to reduce costs. These opportunities also extended throughout the agricultural sector as rural electrification expanded, and as innovations in the processing and storage of food altered traditional marketing procedures. Domestic electrification permitted the creation of a myriad of new appliances. In this way, electric power was an important innovation not only in itself but also by leading the way to countless other innovations as well.

During the period 1900–50, automobiles and trucks also became a major force in most economies. Like railroads, they reduced transportation costs and expanded the scope of most markets. More than the other key innovations, they came to form a large component of many nations' economic activities, directly employing millions of people within vast factories. The expansion plans of the motor vehicle producers could affect a society's growth rate; their location decisions could alter the relative prosperity of entire regions; and their purchases of raw materials and components could determine the success and scale of hundreds of other businesses.

Schumpeter explained the trends and cycles of many aggregate economic variables by relating them to these leading entrepreneurial activities. The latter reduced production and distribution costs throughout the economy, permitted the development of innovations in many other types of businesses, and greatly increased demand for new capital-goods facilities to produce machinery, equipment, and construction materials.

Entrepreneurship and the economic system

In capitalist nations, the desire to attain material success and advanced social status has served as a major incentive for entrepreneurial activities. Entrepreneurship has been intimately linked with social change: It has been able to alter existing social relationships, and some people have seen it as their best means of advancement. Yet social rigidities

and attempts to maintain the status quo can act as strong barriers to
entrepreneurship. In particular, these barriers will be strongest and most
prevalent in economic systems where governments play a major role in
economic decision making.

Many studies of pre–World War II entrepreneurship have examined particular success stories. They have emphasized the fluidity and
openness of social and political structures that permitted the speedy
introduction of new techniques, the rapid growth of new corporations, and the swift acquisition of wealth, power, and prestige by successful entrepreneurs. In the nineteenth century, the United States
stood out as a nation whose social and political structure permitted
economic change to a degree not found in other nations. Many writers have commented positively on the lack of government intervention in the largely free enterprise U.S. system. Some post–World
War II studies of entrepreneurship and growth look at the same subject from a more negative perspective, discussing the obstacles to
change that a government can establish in its efforts to protect vested
interests. Olson, in particular, has investigated this theme, concluding
that the governmental protection of vested interests almost inevitably
ossifies a society. He identifies the lobbying by special interest groups
that leads a government to create barriers to change. In his opinion,
a society that does this slows down its own progress. Only a dramatic
and pervasive shock, such as military loss in a major war, can smash
the rigidity of such arrangements and open a society once more to
economic change and progress.[20]

Studies such as Olson's conclude that the pace of change is largely
determined by the extent to which economic decisions are made by
governments. Criticism of mercantilism, arguments for free trade, and
insistence on the rights of individuals vis-à-vis the state have all touched
upon the relationships between economic change and the rigidity of the
social and political structure. In this sense, the writings of Olson and
his followers are not entirely original. What is new and significant is
that the latter have concentrated on the process of current government
decision making within democracies, making use of the recent literature
on public choice.[21] They examine the impact of vested interests on that
process and the ability of established groups to maintain their income,
wealth, and social status by preventing change. Several of Olson's central
tenets bear on this issue:

> On balance, special-interest organizations and collusions reduce effi-
> ciency and aggregate income in the societies in which they operate,
> and make political life more divisive.
> Distributional coalitions slow down a society's capacity to adopt new

technologies and to reallocate resources in response to changing conditions, and thereby reduce the rate of economic growth.

The accumulation of distributional coalitions increases the complexity of regulation, the role of government, and the complexity of understandings, and changes the direction of social evolution.[22]

Olson explains the "economic miracles" of nations defeated in World War II, particularly Japan and West Germany. Military defeat shattered the protective privileges that governments had established in response to traditional vested interests, and it enabled new groups and individuals to advance unhampered by restrictions. "At least in the first two decades after the war," Olson writes, "the Japanese and West Germans had not developed the degree of regulatory complexity and scale of government that characterized more stable societies."[23]

At the other extreme, Olson describes the calcification of relationships and practices in Britain, detailing the way in which it has retarded economic change. He points out that this is the nation with the longest period of time since suffering from any major national disaster such as revolution, invasion, or dictatorship. He links this political stability with the fact that the economic growth of other large democracies has surpassed Britain's. Olson discusses Britain's calcifying special interest groups, particularly the trade unions, associations of professionals such as lawyers, and producers' organizations such as farmers' groups. "In short, with age, British society has acquired so many strong organizations and collusions that it suffers from an institutional sclerosis that slows its adaptation to changing circumstances and technologies."[24]

A separate literature has argued that entrepreneurship alters social and political relationships, destroying established patterns and replacing them with new arrangements. The editors of *Entrepreneurs in Cultural Context* summarize this argument:

Cultures are ultimately transformed by the actions and decisions of individuals. Perhaps in no area of social science research is this process more dramatically illustrated than in the study of the entrepreneur. . . . The entrepreneur is also able to work within the cultural system while consciously upsetting its state of the equilibrium to his advantage. . . . In many ways then, the entrepreneurs are the movers and shakers of any society.[25]

Schumpeter was a prominent proponent of this view. He explained the economic development of capitalist societies as a "process of creative destruction" in which the

fundamental impulse that sets and keeps the capitalist engine in motion comes from the new consumers' goods, the new methods of production or transportation, the new markets, [and] the new forms of industrial organization that capitalist enterprise creates.[26]

Schumpeter described the

process of industrial mutation . . . that incessantly revolutionizes the industrial structure from within, incessantly destroying the old one, incessantly creating a new one. This process of creative destruction is the essential fact about capitalism.[27]

Landes has linked these two perspectives, noting that "economic theory has traditionally been interested in one-half of the problem – the determinants of economic change – rather than its non-economic effects; and it has long vitiated that half by holding non-economic variables constant."[28] Landes stresses the fact that economic development is a process that "affects all aspects of social life and is affected in turn by them."[29] Referring to specific economic achievements, he has concluded that these "material advances in turn have provoked and promoted a large complex of economic, social, political, and cultural changes, which have reciprocally influenced the rate and cause of technological development."[30]

This combination of the two perspectives suggests the self-reinforcing nature of change and the self-reinforcing nature of ossification. Rapid entrepreneurial advances alter relationships, thereby preventing the codification and regulation of conduct that could hinder future advances. But a society that falters in its economic development will automatically lose the fluidity of structure upon which a revival of development depends. The second perspective, which sees social and political structures as being changed by entrepreneurial advances in a cumulative process, strengthens Olson's warning that governmental protection of vested interests can lead a nation into decline. And this perspective emphasizes the long-term advantages of the free enterprise system with a minimal role for government decision making.

The careers of individual entrepreneurs add another dimension to the relationships between social structure and entrepreneurship. A disproportionate number of entrepreneurs have come from minority groups who are outside the mainstream of society. Wilken refers to many authors who have concluded that

entrepreneurship very often is promoted by social marginality. . . . Individuals or groups on the perimeter of a given social system or between two social systems are believed to provide the personnel to fill entrepreneurial roles. They may be drawn from religious, cultural, ethnic, or migrant minority groups, and their marginal social position is generally believed to have psychological effects which make entrepreneurship a particularly attractive alternative for them.[31]

Hagen has carried this an additional step by focusing not simply on minorities but on minorities who have suffered "withdrawal of status respect." He looks at various situations that lead to such "withdrawal of status respect," and, in particular, has noted the importance of self-selection in immigration and of nonacceptance in a new society.[32] Immigration entails self-selection in that immigrants generally are aggressive and optimistic risk takers. Furthermore, they may find that avenues to success in their new country are blocked: They are not part of the established culture and their professional qualifications may not be honoured. Their only available route for advancement may be through business. Exposure to different production methods in their homeland may spur certain immigrants to take risks and pursue an entrepreneurial career.[33] Wilken has also noted the importance of cohesion within the immigrant community and

the presence of positive attitudes toward entrepreneurship within the group. . . . [A] high degree of group solidarity or cohesion . . . is necessary to counteract whatever opposition may be forthcoming from mainstream groups within the larger social situation.[34]

Some commentators have suggested that innovation today requires group decision making within the corporation that is contemplating innovation. Within each firm, creative and conscientious initiative has become necessary at many different stages of the production process. Entrepreneurial characteristics must be cultivated throughout economic organizations. Some authors argue that this requires a radically new approach to management–labour relations and group versus individual success criteria within each firm. For corporate employees to work together in joint problem solving will require new decision-making procedures and structures, as well as new social attitudes towards consensus building. Reich, whose views have been shaped by Japan's experience, is a proponent of this theory:

The success of modern Japan, in particular, seems to contradict Max Weber, the German sociologist, who attributed the West's economic progress to the demise of traditional relations like guilds, parishes, and clans and to the simultaneous rise of individualism. Japan's emphasis on community, consensus, the long-term security for its workers – based squarely on traditional communal relationships – appears to have spurred its citizens to greater feats of production than has the rugged individualism of modern America. . . .

A social organization premised on equity, security, and participation will generate greater productivity than one premised on greed and fear. Collaboration and collective adaptation are coming to be more important to an industrialized nation's well-being than are personal daring and ambition.[35]

Reich places great emphasis on what he terms *flexible-system production.* The era of standardized mass production is disappearing in the Western world, largely because the newly industrialized countries are able to manufacture at much lower costs. In its place has come a demand for commodities that are unique or that have small production runs. In Reich's opinion, such commodities require innovation as well as special skills. All workers must be involved in the development of the product. The traditional corporate command structure cannot respond quickly or appropriately enough to the customers' specialized needs. New patterns of corporate organization are necessary, Reich argues – patterns that foster entrepreneurial attitudes among workers.

In his book, *How American Business Can Meet the Japanese Challenge*, Ouchi has gone so far as to claim that in Japan "nothing of consequence occurs as a result of individual effort."[36] Similarly, Athos and Pascale state that

for the Japanese, independence in an organizational context has negative connotations; it implies disregard for others and self-centredness. . . . The work group is the basic building block of Japanese organizations. Owing to the central importance of group efforts in their thinking the Japanese are extremely sensitive to and concerned about group interactions and relationships.[37]

The participative approach to decision making requires the exploration of alternative solutions by managers and production workers until a consensus is reached. This process minimizes the role of middle management by bringing senior management into direct contact with the workers.

Currently, many Western corporations are attempting to introduce some elements of the Japanese approach and to imbue production workers with more feeling for their company's objectives and success. The concept of *quality circles,* for example, requires groups of employees to develop new techniques to improve the quality of the product they are manufacturing. The expansion of profit sharing is based on a hope that production workers will be more conscientious and creative so that their firm will benefit.

Some authors, like Reich, believe that a basic change in social attitudes and in government intervention will be necessary to attain Japan's pervasive entrepreneurial initiative. Rugged individualism must be replaced with group decision making and consensus; free enterprise capitalism must be replaced with a much greater commitment to education, retraining, and adjustment assistance. Yet such opinions are not universally accepted. Many observers focus on the achievements of individual entrepreneurs, even within Japan; others note that the Japanese have had more success in imitating the innovations of other nations than in innovating themselves.

The existence of more than one economic system within a single society

A modern economy is far from a homogeneous unit. Rather it consists of innumerable, clearly distinct production sectors, each with its own labour market, technology, and product demand. In theory, a labour market equilibrium could be attained among all of these sectors, with different wages reflecting different levels of skill, education, and experience. In practice, however, changes in any one of those sectors can disturb such an equilibrium and can necessitate labour mobility, retraining, and new capital investment. This process of adjustment involves unemployment. Furthermore, the presence of these innumerable distinct production sectors means that inflationary pressures can exist in some while being absent from others. General macro policies to contain inflation cannot have a uniformly successful impact. Distortions caused by the alternative decision modes will not hit every sector with the same degree of inefficiency. Of particular importance, growth may not occur uniformly throughout a society.

Urban and regional studies have emphasized *agglomeration economies,* which are the special benefits that accrue to individuals and firms simply because of an increase in the size of the community within which they live and work. A wide variety of goods and services provides the consumer with more choice, and the prices of some things may be reduced. This may be true of government goods and services as well as those privately produced. Individuals know that if they lose their jobs, they have a better chance of finding new jobs, and they have more opportunities to move upwards by changing their jobs. Firms may save on transportation and communication costs by locating in a densely populated region. Inventories can be smaller; production schedules may be smoother. Firms have access to a larger work force with a wider variety of skills. Advertising may be more effective, and firms may operate on a larger scale with lower unit costs.

Quite apart from such traditional urban and regional agglomeration economies, there are particular reasons why entrepreneurial activities will be more geographically concentrated. To the extent that innovation is an interfirm process with one company's entrepreneurial activity being linked with that of others, it may be essential for some firms to locate near one another. To the extent that innovation depends upon university research facilities, firms will locate near the leading universities and, consequently, near each other. To the extent that innovation requires highly sophisticated and specialized scientific skill, it may be necessary for an entrepreneurial firm to locate near similar firms, from which it may entice employees.

Earlier, we considered the relationships between entrepreneurship and the social and political structure. A federal nation may contain cities and regions with widely varying social and political regimes, and entrepreneurial activity may find a more welcome environment in some locations than in others. One criticism of Olson's writings, for example, is that he treats nations as homogeneous units. For a federal nation Olson's arguments should be modified so that differences in the entrepreneurial environment among provinces, states, regions, and cities are made clear. These differences in entrepreneurial environment cumulate on top of the reasons cited already for regional concentration, particularly since entrepreneurial success will, of itself, alter the social and political structure in ways favourable to further entrepreneurship. A survey of 250 high technology firms in California's Silicon Valley sought to determine where and how new companies were started, who started them and why. Of the firms examined, 85.5 percent were begun by former employees of existing firms. Researchers concluded that

a tremendous amount of work is involved in starting up a new business. New employees must be recruited, facilities and supplies must be lined up. Founders of new enterprises are less likely to find these in unfamiliar areas than in locations where their own companies were.[38]

The significance of these tendencies can be seen in the postwar growth of microelectronic firms, which have concentrated in a few urban regions. To the extent that the ready availability of natural resources loses its importance as the determinant of investment location, and to the extent that urban and regional concentration is intensified by the special agglomeration economies of entrepreneurial activities, we may expect an increase in disparities based on city and region. In the process of entrepreneurial adjustment, we may expect some cities to forge ahead quickly while other cities and regions will suffer as their growth prospects diminish. It is therefore likely that social and political conflict over the optimal pace of adjustment and over the appropriate role of government will increasingly follow regional lines. In many important respects, a nation may consist of a number of quite different economic systems.

Sharing uncertainty and risk

A distinction is sometimes drawn between government subsidies that are directed to those people who happen to have low incomes and to those corporations that require *bail-outs* to survive, and government subsidies that represent an ex ante social sharing of entrepreneurial risk. The former may result in some reduction of entrepreneurship, whereas the latter may stimulate entrepreneurship. Analysis of risk–return outcomes and the incentives promised by successful innovations will be different if decision makers know that they may receive government subsidies regardless of their success or failure. A substantial and pertinent body of economic literature has examined an aspect of this, referred to as "moral hazard."[39] Furthermore, entrepreneurial efforts may be diverted to trying to maximize the subsidies that can be obtained through government lobbying and public appeals. The economic literature known as *public choice* has dealt with this danger that is inherent in government programs, and that offers financial assistance to particular individuals, groups or businesses. On the other hand, a society may recognize that some of its members could be hurt by economic change occasioned by circumstances beyond their control; and so the economic system may offer a safety net to limit the extent of such individual losses and also an adjustment process to assist individuals and firms who wish to move away from obsolete economic activities.

Nearly everyone in a changing society must make judgements in the face of uninsurable risks. Personal decisions concerning education, career, employer, and private investments all involve such risks. Since modern life has automatically subjected everyone to important risk bearing, an argument is sometimes made for a new kind of government intervention that pools specific risks and rewards so that individuals are less exposed to economic misfortune. That is, government may be able to insure against risks in a situation where citizens want such insurance and where no institution other than government can provide it. The enormity of the risk sharing may be so great and its nature so complex that private institutions may not be able to administer it effectively. Present-day economic activities now involve such new and severe risks for all citizens that the optimal social contract may entail a sharing of many of these risks, as well as a sharing of the concomitant rewards and losses. Arguments for such risk sharing may recommend provision of public funds for many specific purposes: the personal acquisition of knowledge and skills; employment relocation costs, retraining, and the sale of homes; or guarantees of certain investments, such as deposits in financial institutions.

Of particular importance is the view which sees the development of human capital as the result of individual entrepreneurial decisions and which sees risk sharing as an appropriate government purpose. This view has received special attention in an article, "Market Adjustment and Government Policy," in which the authors suggest that

a well-known failure in the market for human capital stems from the inability of workers to diversify their portfolios across alternative skills or professions. As a result, workers are said to be too risk averse from society's perspective. Numerous schemes have been proposed to offset this risk aversion, including the financing of job retraining and other subsidies to promote human capital formation.[40]

Some observers have applied a similar argument to the programs that provide subsidies to corporations. One rationale for a public sharing of uninsurable risk of capital loss is illustrated by the following example:

Suppose that there were 100 R&D projects that could be undertaken in totally unrelated fields, each costing 1 million and each with a 50 percent chance of success. Suppose further that for each successful project, the revenue would be 4 million, thus generating a profit of 3 million; for each unsuccessful project, the 1 million would be lost. If all the projects were undertaken, one would expect about 50 of them to succeed, generating a total profit of 150 million (50 × 3 million). When the 50 million spent on the 50 projects that are expected to fail is subtracted from the amount, there is a net profit of 100 million for all the projects combined. Yet it is quite conceivable that a firm would hesitate to invest 1 million if the 50 percent chance of a 3 million profit were offset by an equivalent chance of losing its investment. If such risk aversion were widespread, most of the 100 projects could remain untackled, and most of the 100 million gain could remain unrealized. This example illustrates all at once that risk-spreading can be a reason for government to assist the R&D process and that it need not be a reason if firms are not especially reluctant to face risks or if the odds are not good enough, even from society's point of view.[41]

The application of this government risk-sharing purpose seems to involve the concept of an acceptable size of downside risk based on the size of the decision-making entity. In the preceding example, a large enough corporation could conduct all the projects, but a corporation of adequate size may simply not exist. This type of market failure, based on the inability of the private market to create a sufficiently large corporation to conduct the necessary number of high-risk projects, may vary in significance over time and among countries. For example, it may be that a large, developed economy may have venture-capital investment firms of greater number and size than a small or less developed country. So this government risk-sharing argument may be appropriate in the latter case but not in the former. Here we see a clear reason for the choice of economic system to differ somewhat among countries and over time.

Other aspects of government risk-sharing also deserve mention. In a modern democracy, some special interest groups will actively try to retard those aspects of economic growth that will inflict hardship on them. Special payments may be necessary compensation in a democracy to purchase the acquiescence of those who will be hurt by economic growth. In this sense, a social consensus may involve an acceptance by society of change and growth because a safety net exists for those who will be hurt. The safety net of government subsidy programs may be seen as a sharing of the risks of economic change. In this view, such programs may enable more rapid economic change than could otherwise occur. Public pensions, for example, can be seen as the only politically acceptable way of forcing older workers to retire, thereby giving way to younger workers who may be more capable of implementing new production methods.

A substantial theoretical literature assesses the effects on society's well-being of changes that improve the welfare of some while reducing the welfare of others, and the concept of compensation payments is a central element. Government may be the most appropriate mechanism to make such payments. In any case, the literature dealing with compensation criteria forms a useful framework for evaluating certain government programs of financial redistribution. From this perspective, one may appreciate that these programs facilitate entrepreneurship and innovation by compensating those who are harmed and by thus reducing their potential opposition. Much government planning and regulation seeks to reduce risk, not in the manner described above – through the social acceptance of risk as a form of insurance – but rather by eliminating spontaneous or unanticipated change. This general desire for planning can lead to greater certainty, but, at the same time, can reduce the opportunity for entrepreneurial initiative. Some regulations can be seen as a form of government planning, by which the scope for individual decisions is sharply restricted, often to the advantage of vested interests. Other regulations seek to enforce social accountability and social obligations on private firms. The post–World War II expansion of planning and regulation may have diminished entrepreneurial activity below the level it would otherwise have attained. The view is often expressed that "a more permissive public policy and attitude – that is, a reduced regulatory environment – would foster both organizational and technological innovation."[42] The long-term implications of many kinds of planning and regulation are relatively uncertain. Consequently, the choice of economic system involves experimentation, together with some degree of willingness to alter the economic system based upon the evaluation of outcomes. Here the lessons that may be learned through comparisons among economic systems can be seen as particularly useful in the process of choice.

Assessing governments as entrepreneurs

A central message of this chapter is that all economic activities will be buffeted by change. Ours is an era of particularly rapid change and adjustment. Established practices, procedures, and products will inevitably be replaced, frequently because of competition from foreign enterprises, but often simply because of the overwhelming pace of technological advances. Entrepreneurial adjustment will be essential for all economic activities, including those owned and operated by governments.

Quite apart from the need for entrepreneurship within government activities is the need for entrepreneurship in government decisions that affect the private sector. When a government decides to give subsidies to individuals or firms in the private sector, the public service becomes a part of the entrepreneurial process: The public service must possess enough perception and creativity to recognize and support perception and creativity; it must evaluate risk–return outcomes and decide which possibilities it will support. Deciding which funding requests should be accepted and which should be rejected are entrepreneurial decisions. Government employees may even attempt to negotiate changes in the applications for funding. To the degree that government employees lack entrepreneurial characteristics, a society may wish to avoid these kinds of decision modes, and it may wish to adopt practices that are aimed specifically at stimulating entrepreneurship within the public sector.

The historical, classical analyses of entrepreneurship are helpful in investigating this issue. Examples of successful entrepreneurs and bureaucrats are believed by some to be at opposite ends of any spectrum of entrepreneurial behaviour. The creativity, spontaneity, individual initiative, and personal risk taking of the entrepreneur contrast sharply with the obedience to bureaucratic rules, concern for proper progress, and reference to chains of authority that mark the government employee. Individuals who seek the financial rewards that accompany successful risk taking and originality probably will not apply for public-service positions, whereas those citizens who fear risk taking and appreciate an occupation that has clear guidelines may be more inclined to apply for government positions. In describing entrepreneurs, Ronen states that rarely does this individual reside in the large, bureaucratic organization. . . . The entrepreneur and the small firm seek each other out. The managerial-type individuals, preferring the executive suites of large organizations, hardly encourage alert entrepreneurs to cast permanent anchor anywhere near them.[43]

As was indicated earlier, marginal individuals who have been raised outside the established social order – for example, members of minority groups and immigrants – may see private entrepreneurship as their only route to wealth and prestige. Such backgrounds and personalities may not be accepted readily into the elite ranks of civil service leadership.

Bureaucracies are endemically resistant to change. Thompson has emphasized that "in the case of the bureaucratic organization, however, there is special need for caution with regard to change."[44] Specialization is part of the bureaucratic structure, and those who have become proficient at one particular activity have a strong vested interest in opposing change. Furthermore, the employees become "specialized in working with one another. . . . Consequently, any suggestion for change must be measured against its effect on the cooperative system as a whole. Bureaucratic organizations must plan and control change."[45] Perception and creativity are not encouraged – and may even be discouraged. Thompson carries this view further: "Many studies attest to the fact that groups, over a period of time, exert powerful conformist pressures on their members. . . . Consequently, there is nothing about groups as such that can be guaranteed to increase individual creativity; they could, in fact, have just the opposite effect."[46]

Thompson's basic theme is that "the literature on problem solving suggests that for some kinds of tasks, groups are more effective than individuals, while for other tasks the reverse is true."[47] This theme is pursued by Arrow in an article on innovation in large and small firms. Arrow bases his analysis on the belief that "entrepreneurial activity, however defined, operates in different ways in large firms than in small ones."[48] Decisions about capital allocation differ because they are based on different decision-making procedures; the internal accounting prices of large firms and government may not reflect relative costs; and information may not be conveyed as readily within large firms as it is through changes in market prices. In some ways, large firms are in the same position as government bureaucracies with respect to fostering entrepreneurship, but in several very important respects government bureaucracies face much greater barriers. The large firm generally does respond to market prices, it pursues profit as a clear success criterion, and it is shaped by and interacts with its competitors. By contrast, government bureaucracies may not respond to market prices, they may not pursue profit as a criterion of success, and they may lack competitors.

Stories are recounted of entrepreneurs selling their prized personal possessions to gain the final small funding necessary to attain success. Many entrepreneurs sign personal guarantees by which their personal wealth is loaned to the capital funds of their companies. In undertaking new and original activities, such individuals recognize the importance of being persistent, and they understand the likelihood of initial losses before ultimate victory. It is easy to look towards government subsidies and public enterprise as simply an extension of this type of persistence. Public funds can enable an enterprise to continue beyond the point at which individuals on their own would have to capitulate. Occasionally, such persistence leads to an otherwise unattainable achievement. However, with these decision modes, the likelihood exists that closure and disinvestment will be delayed excessively, with society being compelled to finance this inefficiency. Government financial support for entrepreneurial activity can alter the natural pace of expansion as well as the natural disinvestment process. Initial smallness and growth based on success in the marketplace can minimize the probability of large-scale losses when new projects fail. Many entrepreneurial activities will fail regardless of the amount of capital that is poured into them. Knowing this, the private sector will generally demand results before providing additional funding. Governments seem much more reluctant to cut their losses and end attempts to innovate.

In order to reach an entrepreneurial decision that involves new production methods, the decision maker must be able to measure, compile, and compare the many changing aspects of these methods using some common scale, so as to ascertain whether the new combination of costs and outputs will be more or less favourable than those yielded by the existing production methods. The price structure is absolutely decisive; it is through price comparisons and combinations that the decision maker can anticipate probable results. The price structure sets the guidelines for entrepreneurial decision. Simple repetition of traditional production processes need not rely on these guidelines nearly as much as do the deliberations over the advisability of adopting innovations.

The implications of the price structure for entrepreneurial activity have attained a new significance. In the past, decision makers, at least those within noncommunist governments, have been able to refer to free-market prices as the basis for their calculations. Now, however, the governments of many societies are playing a major role in determining the price structure, with the result that prices may be influenced significantly by administrators, rather than by the market forces of relative scarcity and demand. Observers who have examined economic practices in communist nations have devoted considerable attention to the implications of government price intervention for entrepreneurial decisions. The concerns about communist price setting expressed in that literature have a growing relevance for those noncommunist nations whose economic systems include considerable reliance on government price controls and subsidies.

An example of such concerns is the literature dealing with a firm's decision to alter a product's quality when confronting prices set by government rather than by the marketplace. Faced with such a possibility, a government may be tempted to establish quality standards as well as to set prices. If central planners desire production of a better quality product, it is not a reasonable solution for them to respond to quality debasement by lowering the market price. The possibility of altering quality severely complicates government price setting. In a market where prices are set by government, the quality issue is intimately linked with possibilities for innovation. Central planners may find it particularly difficult to obtain detailed information concerning the costs and quality changes that potential innovations would entail if implemented; and so the implications of time lags in the price adjustment process are especially important in the realm of technological change. Decisions to innovate will be affected by the existing price structure, and the resulting pattern of innovations may not be the most socially desirable. Central planners may not be able to respond as quickly or as well as could the continual process of price adjustments in a free market. A recent body of literature within Western economics has begun to address these issues. General programs of wage and price controls, implemented to restrain inflation, have been reviewed from this perspective. Studies have also been made of specific programs that deal with individual economic activities, where a government has decided to interfere with market price setting.

A major concern is that price relationships determined by government may have once been appropriate, but may no longer be so, and may be sending wrong signals to agents in both the government and the private sectors. The need to change government regulations as circumstances change is illustrated by the following quotation from the Economic Council of Canada's report *Reforming Regulation:*

Eventually, however, many regulations tend to outlive their usefulness. The conditions that led to their introduction may no longer exist or, even if they do, there may be new and more pressing demands for the employment of the economy's scarce resources. Technological change has substantially altered the structural and competitive conditions in some industries; overall growth and change within the economy have, furthermore, altered the income position of various groups in society. Government regulatory policies, especially those that seem to inhibit the natural dynamics of markets, have very different consequences and meaning in the halting economic environment of the 1980s than they had in the high-growth climate of the 1950s and 1960s. The question that then arises is: how can we offset the tendency in the policy-making process to adopt new regulations uncritically and to maintain existing ones long after they have outlined their usefulness?[49]

Entrepreneurial decisions within government activities can be sensitive to profit both as a success criterion and as a personal financial incentive. Once again, reference to the experience of communist nations is useful. Decision makers must be given some success criterion, and communist countries have experimented with a wide variety, including minimization of average production costs, maximization of output denominated in some physical attribute such as weight or number of units, and several aspects of profit: profit per unit of capital, profit per unit of labour, and the ratio of profits to total production costs. A substantial literature has developed on the distortions fostered by such criteria; this literature may now be relevant in noncommunist nations that have extensive government enterprises. Communist nations have learned that, even within government-owned enterprises, people do respond to personal financial incentives to a degree that cannot be achieved solely on the basis of exhortation or appeals to comradeship and patriotism. As we shall see in Chapter 3, Abram Bergson has drawn together a variety of data that reveal that even the pre-reform Soviet Union relied upon substantial income differentials.

Many authors see entrepreneurship and competition as being intimately linked, with the latter acting as a constant stimulus to the technological advance of all participants. This literature indicates the importance of creating government structures within which separate units can compete. This competition should enable the more successful units to expand and to receive financial rewards as well as social recognition. At the same time, the competition among public institutions should compel the contraction or at least prevent the expansion, of those units that are less successful. The array of possible competitive modes deserves more detailed analysis and experimentation so that entrepreneurship can be fostered within government activities.

Rivlin has emphasized the need to learn more about different ways of providing government services. She has analyzed "three strategies for finding more effective methods of producing education, health, and other social services: (1) analysis of the *natural experiment;* (2) random innovation; and (3) systematic experimentation. The major conclusion was that all three strategies should be pursued with increased energy and greater methodological sophistication."[50] Rivlin has recommended that governments should actively experiment with new, alternative approaches as a permanent entrepreneurial search for improved programs and procedures. The present chapter suggests the value of conducting this search within a competitive environment. It is through competition that firms that deliver goods and services will display their most creative and diligent efforts, and it is through competitive comparisons that choices among alternative decision modes can best be made. In this regard, special mention should be made of an advantage that may accrue to nations with federal structures. Within broad nationally established objectives, it may be possible for the subnational governments to pursue different methods for delivering goods and services. A federal state may thereby provide a natural laboratory for the kinds of experimentation advocated by Rivlin.[51]

Many government programs have been designed specifically to foster productivity improvements in particular sectors of the economy. In referring to "a menu of possible policies," Denny and Fuss warn that "with our current knowledge, we cannot be certain of the size of net benefits of any policy to enhance productivity growth. Any steps taken to improve our productivity performance should be monitored carefully to ensure that the net benefits are positive."[52] Concerns for the environmental impact of growth add to these uncertainties about the advantages and shortcomings of alternative programs and policies. In his book, *The Age of Uncertainty,* Galbraith has suggested:

In the last century capitalists were certain of the success of capitalism, socialists of socialism, imperialists of colonialism, and the ruling classes knew they were meant to rule. Little of this certainty now survives. Given the dismaying complexity of the problems mankind now faces, it would surely be odd if it did.[53]

Essay and discussion topics

1. Discuss the relationship between a society's economic system and the extent and nature of unemployment.
2. Choose an example of market failure and compare the decision modes chosen in alternative economic systems for this type of economic activity.
3. Discuss the relationship between the Soviet Union's rate of growth under Stalin and the Stalinist system of detailed central planning.

4. Discuss the relationship between Britain's rate of growth in the 1960s and 1970s and the British economic system's emphasis on welfare and public enterprise.
5. Discuss the features of an economic system that may stimulate innovation and entrepreneurship.
6. Discuss the relationship between a society's objective of economic growth and that society's concern for the environment.

CHAPTER 3

Liberty and equality

Introduction

In adopting and modifying an economic system, many societies have been motivated by ideological objectives, as well as by the criteria discussed in Chapter 2. Some societies have believed that the attainment of certain ideological objectives may be more important than the achievement of efficiency and growth. Though ideological objectives can be many and varied, the concepts of liberty and equality have been a focus of debate. Philosophers, as well as political leaders, have presented their opinions in regard to these concepts, and they have often disagreed about the nature or definition of liberty and equality. As we have seen in Chapter 2, a society's achievements in its pursuit of efficiency and growth can be measured quantitatively and then compared with the achievements of other societies. However, in regard to ideological objectives, societies may disagree concerning the appropriate measurement process, and a comparison of the achievements of different societies may be much less precise.

For an economic system, the concept of individual liberty involves many issues, some of which are closely linked with the concept of equality. Important questions include, for example, which decisions each individual has the right to make in regard to the production, distribution, and consumption of goods and services. In what ways does the society as a whole circumscribe the scope for these individual decisions? In what ways does the society limit the individual's personal material gain that results from these decisions? Should all members of society share equally in these individual rights? Should equality entail equality of opportunity, with individual freedom to gain in accordance with one's own achievements in competition with others? Or should equality entail equality of outcomes, with a continual redistribution, over time, of income and wealth? If equality of outcomes is considered desirable, is absolute equality necessary? To what degree should redistribution reduce the inequality established in the individual pursuit of economic activities?

For both liberty and equality, the right to own private property is a key element. As we shall see in later chapters, the right of ownership is often modified by society through price controls, and through the establishment of regulations that restrict the individual's freedom to use private property. Furthermore, government can provide subsidies and levy taxes in ways that redistribute incomes and affect the material benefits an individual receives from property ownership. The right of ownership has come to involve much more than physical property and the *means of production*. Today, we are becoming an *information society* where ideas and technology are playing a greater role in economic activities. Individuals are increasingly concerned about government protection of their intellectual property, through patents and copyrights. In many societies, the expansion of government activities has itself created new sets of property rights. Some farmers, for example, have been given quota rights to produce certain quantities of certain products, while practitioners in many occupations own licenses permitting only their select group to work. Many individuals have come to regard subsidies for education, housing, and health care as their right, together with the right to receive welfare payments in the form of cash subsidies.

The concepts of individual liberty and equality form an important part of many noneconomic issues, and are often linked with a society's legal, political, religious, and moral practices. The struggle for equality of women, for example, has focused on a variety of rights, including: equal access to education, equal pay for work of equal value, the implications of divorce for the division of family assets and pension rights, the provision of benefit programs for part-time work, and the right to share jobs. Racial discrimination has involved the alienation of minority groups from the mainstream of the economic system, and so the pursuit of integration has often focused on the rights of minorities to jobs and to special government programs for developing job skills. Even language rights affect the conduct of economic activities, and mobility rights influence the economic opportunities that individuals may enjoy. For many legal contracts, interpretation and enforcement deal with the economic rights of the signatories. A society's standards of fairness may lead it to support weaker parties in contract negotiations, and its concern for moral values may lead it to proscribe certain economic activities such as gambling or prostitution. In ways such as these, a society's economic system and its concepts of liberty and equality are modified through changes in the society's legal, political, religious, and moral practices.

For a society, the objectives in regard to individual liberty and equality may change significantly over time. Within the Soviet Union, for example, the 1917–21 period of War Communism eliminated most property rights, with the seizure of agricultural produce from the masses as well as the expropriation of factories and homes of the wealthy. Yet, the New Economic Policy (NEP) in 1921–8 reestablished rights of ownership for small businesses and for farmers, creating a new era of personal material success. Stalin's imposition of Five Year Plans, beginning in 1928, once more retracted many of these individual economic rights, compelling farmers to enter collective farms and setting production quotas and planned procedures for most economic activities. In the mid–1960s, and again in the period since 1982, the decision-making rights of individual managers have been extended, with a new emphasis on financial rewards for successful decisions. One might regard each of these time periods as distinct economic systems, each having its own scope for individual rights and its own division between collective and individual rights.

Underlying the communist economic system has been a perception of freedom as an absence of exploitation. Therefore, freedom is seen as dependent upon the elimination of private property, and this has generally contrasted with the capitalist emphasis on the right of each individual to pursue his or her self-interest as he or she chooses. The communist view that abolition of private ownership eliminates exploitation, leaving individuals free to develop as they wish, has generally contrasted with the capitalist view that freedom and the development of one's individuality rest upon freedom to produce and exchange and, therefore, to own the means of production and exchange personally. Linked with these views, is the communist perception of democracy as a government that best represents the interests of the population as a whole, in contrast with the capitalist perception of democracy as a political process through which individuals and groups, having different interests, can decide together how best to achieve their own interests.

Philosophies of liberty and equality

In *Two Treatises of Government,* John Locke developed a notion of freedom which has formed a basis for libertarian theory and the capitalist system. Locke argued that "labour, in the beginning, gave a right of property wherever anyone was pleased to employ it."[1] Societies and governments were formed out of a response to the perils of existence in the state of nature. To protect the right of property, individuals came together in civil order. Freedom within this organization meant that the society would allow the individual to accumulate property and to use it, with the society providing the security which the state of nature lacked. If the government took away property and denied individual freedom, it acted unjustly, and an argument could be made for its overthrow. However, this view of property rights has been challenged by those who oppose the degree of inequality which can result from it. Even Locke acknowledged that "it was a foolish thing, as well as dishonest, to hoard up more than [one] could make use of"[2] and so the right to property was not without limit.

In the *Discourse on the Origin of Inequality*, Jean-Jacques Rousseau made several significant criticisms of Locke's liberal theory. First, Locke failed to recognize that one of the unique features of the individual was the ability of self-perfection. Nature made each individual a "free agent," able to escape the confines of restrictive rules of action that applied to other animals. Rousseau noted, for example, that "a pigeon would die of hunger near a bowl filled with choice meats"[3] because of its instinctive sense not to eat meat. Humans, however, have the ability to go against nature's rules and choose another course of endeavour. Over time, each individual encountered different circumstances and environments; consequently, as each reacted to these new surroundings, the human character changed. That human beings are creatures of evolution, was an idea most earlier philosophers had not emphasized. Rousseau perceived the significant impact a society could have on this evolution of human character.

In the *Discourse on the Origin of Inequality* and *On The Social Contract*, Rousseau argued that whereas liberals believed the individual in civil society had the capacity for free choice, in fact, "everywhere he is in chains."[4] By emphasizing the role of the individual in society, liberals did not consider the extent to which a society could reduce individual liberty. The relationship between the individual and the society was inextricable. On entering civil society, individuals could lose their freedom. They could become slaves to their own social institutions, whether feudal or capitalist. Individuals, though thinking in terms of self-interest and egocentrism, feel a need and desire to follow public opinion. In feudal society, for example, the individual was suppressed, with a commitment of service.

Rousseau discussed the individual's character while in prehistoric classless societies and concluded that it must "have been the happiest and most durable epoch."[5] In primitive societies, Rousseau identified a coincidence of interests that allowed individuals the experience of freedom known only in the state of nature. There was no internal conflict between the self and the community. Unfortunately, as the struggle with the environment became more difficult, and needs expanded, individuality became more pronounced. The balance between egocentrism and altruism, which Rousseau admired, was lost. In *On The Social Contract*, Rousseau attempted to devise a means by which the early classless society could be brought forward to a modern era. He believed that a society could develop a *general will* based upon common interests. Individuals would surrender their right to independent decisions as part of their membership in the social contract. Rousseau's theory can be seen as a precursor of the communist philosophy.

If therefore, one eliminates from the social compact whatever is not essential to it, one will find that it is reducible to the following terms. *Each of us places his person and all his power in common under the supreme direction of the general will; and as one we receive each member as an indivisible part of the whole.*

At once, in place of the individual person of each contracting party, this act of association produces a moral and colective body composed of as many members as there are voices in the assembly, which receives from this same act its unity, its common *self*, its life and its will.[6]

Like Rousseau, John Stuart Mill was frustrated by the state of man's character and could not accept it as permanent. The problem for Mill, as for Rousseau, was to discover how man might escape the pressures of capitalist society to experience a genuine freedom and happiness. John Stuart Mill, in *On Liberty*, recognized the extent to which society shaped the individual:

Society has had absolute power over them [the individuals] during all the early portion of their existence: it has had the whole period of childhood and nonage in which to try whether it could make them capable of rational conduct in life. The existing generation is master both of the training and the entire circumstances of the generation to come; it cannot indeed make them perfectly wise and good, because it is itself so lamentably deficient in goodness and wisdom.[7]

In *Utilitarianism*, Mill followed Rousseau and blamed the social institutions of the time.

The present wretched education, and wretched social arrangements, are the only real hinderance to its [happiness] being attainable by almost all.[8]

With different institutions, Mill imagined it might be possible to reach an ideal similar to that espoused by Rousseau, while still maintaining individual decision making.

[l]aws and social arrangements should place the happiness, or (as speaking practically it may be called) the interest, of every individual, as nearly as possible in harmony with the interest of the whole; and ... that education and opinion, which have so vast a power over human character, should so use that power as to establish in the mind of every individual an indissoluble association between his own happiness and the good of the whole.[9]

Mill agreed with Jeremy Bentham and James Mill, his father, that the ultimate measure of social value was the greatest happiness of the greatest number. His analysis, however, differed from theirs in that he believed capitalism did not allow individuals to be truly free and he believed that freedom necessitated changing both individual character and society. In addition, Mill submitted that "[i]t is quite compatible with the principle of utility to recognize the fact, that some kinds of pleasure are more desirable and more valuable than others."[10] He explained:

Few human creatures would consent to be changed into any of the lower animals, for a promise of the fullest allowance of a beast's pleasures; no intelligent human being would consent to be a fool, no instructed person would be an ignoramus, no person of feeling and conscience would be selfish and base, even though they should be persuaded that the fool, the dunce, or the rascal is better satisfied with his lot than they are with theirs.[11]

It was not sufficient to expect, as Bentham and James Mill had, that the greatest happiness would be associated with the greatest productivity. Utilitarianism required governments to seek the highest pleasures of existence for the society as a whole, but for John Stuart Mill this meant that individuals must be allowed the opportunity to develop themselves and for this end, each needed an educated and cultured mind. The protective state described by Locke now had the responsibility of ensuring that the nonmaterial measures of social success were realized. Even the labouring classes had to benefit from a more active state. As John Stuart Mill surmised, "It is better to be a human being dissatisfied than a pig satisfied; better to be Socrates dissatisfied than a fool satisfied."[12] Consequently, John Stuart Mill imagined that the experience of liberty required more than the protection of private property rights. Liberty involved, as well, sensitivity to a morality which other liberals and utilitarians had not emphasized.

To leave John Stuart Mill at this point, one might get the impression that an active state involved in the development of the individual could be justified; as a result it is necessary to consider the apprehension which Mill displayed in making such an implication. Mill did not have much faith in the ability of governments, or their bureaucracy, to lead society towards the higher moral experiences he valued. Instead, he believed that the key to the process by which the greatest happiness could be realized was to be found in the individual. In *On Liberty,* Mill explained that "The only part of the conduct of any one, for which he is amenable to society, is that which concerns others. In the part which merely concerns himself, his independence is, of right, absolute. Over himself, over his own body and mind, the individual is sovereign."[13] With this in mind, Mill accepted liberal capitalism as being fair, and the existence of a right to property as important; but for him, the implication of the liberty of the individual was human development and continued approximation to the ideal society.

Edmund Burke once wrote that "[t]he individual is foolish. The multitude, for the moment, is foolish, when they act without deliberation; but the species is wise, and when time is given to it, as a species, it almost always acts right."[14] Mill seemed to share a similar perception of the individual and social ability to reason. Mill believed individuals and societies were capable only of ascertaining partial truths; however, when opposing partial truths interacted the result was to direct individuals and society towards any absolute truth which might exist. The more individuals participated in constructive debate of this kind, the more the creative dynamic moved society towards a higher level of the greatest happiness for the greatest number. A danger of extensive state activity, or social pressure, was that new ideas and eccentricity might not be encouraged. Mill held that the status quo of liberal capitalism was unacceptable and hoped that the individual might provide the impetus for the moral improvement of the whole. For these reasons, Mill feared the repressive tendency of governments and bureaucracies. His inclination to approve popular education programs, for example, was therefore moderated. Government legislation should always be aimed at enhancing individuality and debate. Still, a redistribution of income to finance state education would be necessary to ensure that all children were educated for their own benefit, and hence, the benefit of the society as a whole. In Mill, one may see a philosophical defense of liberal egalitarianism and the development of the arguments in favour of a welfare state.

Some modern theorists, such as F. A. Hayek and Robert Nozick, have also examined various notions of freedom, and have condemned the socialist state. In *Law, Legislation, and Liberty,* Hayek promotes the spontaneous ordering of the market as the facilitator of freedom. The state must uphold private property and allow the individual the freedom to choose what to do with it so long as the use does not harm others. Happiness and liberty are experiences known only in a competitive market. When judges or legislators develop rules which are aimed at redistributing output, then they embark on a path of injustice. Hayek explains:

Socialism is indeed largely a revolt against the impartial justice which considers only the conformity of individual actions to end-independent rules and which is not concerned with the effects of their application in particular instances. Thus, a socialist judge would really be a contradiction in terms; for his persuasion must prevent him from applying only those general principles which underlie a spontaneous order of actions, and lead him to take into account considerations which have nothing to do with the justice of individual conduct.[15]

Robert Nozick makes the libertarian argument that given fair or just exchanges between individuals in the market, a society cannot be permitted to interfere with the outcomes that result. If people willingly offer money for some good or service, it is not for the society as a whole to intervene in the arrangement and assert that too much was paid. Nozick offers this example:

Now suppose that Wilt Chamberlain . . . signs the following sort of contract with a team: In each home game, twenty-five cents from the price of each ticket of admission goes to him. . . . The season starts, and people cheerfully attend his team's games; they buy their tickets, each time dropping a separate twenty-five cents of their admission price into a special box with Chamberlain's name on it. They are excited about seeing him play; it is worth the total admission price to them. Let us suppose that in one season one million persons attend his home games, and Wilt Chamberlain winds up with $250,000, a much larger sum than the average income and larger than anyone else has.[16]

Chamberlain, according to Nozick, has earned the $250,000 fairly. Justice requires that those who control the twenty-five cents individually decide on their own that they want to pay Chamberlain for the opportunity to watch him play basketball. In order for a society to decide that equality of income is to be sought, it must commission a government to be always involved in redistribution and always interfere with individual property rights. Nozick points out that no matter what distribution of output a society begins with, the tendency will always be to develop inequities since people will always seek to make exchanges that make them better off. The objective of liberty demands that people be able to do this and Nozick, therefore, summarizes the essence of libertarian justice:

1. A person who acquires a holding in accordance with the principle of justice in acquisition is entitled to that holding.
2. A person who acquires a holding in accordance with the principle of justice in transfer, from someone else entitled to the holding, is entitled to the holding.
3. No one is entitled to a holding except by (repeated) applications of 1 and 2.[17]

Milton Friedman, as an economist advocating free enterprise, has also written extensively on the concept of liberty. In a chapter entitled "The

Relation between Economic Freedom and Political Freedom," Friedman argues that

Economic arrangements play a dual role in the promotion of a free society. On the one hand, freedom in economic arrangements is itself a component of freedom broadly understood, so economic freedom is an end in itself. In the second place, economic freedom is also an indispensable means toward the achievement of political freedom. . . .

What the market does is to reduce greatly the range of issues that must be decided through political means, and thereby to minimize the extent to which government need participate directly in the game. The characteristic feature of action through political channels is that it tends to require or enforce substantial conformity. The great advantage of the market, on the other hand, is that it permits wide diversity.[18]

Robert Hale has questioned this sanguine view of free enterprise by emphasizing the issue of fairness in contractual exchanges. Hale believes that within every contract there are elements of coercion and competing bargaining power.[19] A substantial literature has developed which takes a line of enquiry similar to Hale's and questions the basis on which society accepts exchanges between individuals in the market as being just.[20] As an extreme example, it is generally accepted that exchanges induced by threat of gun point are not to be considered fair or reasonable; consequently, the state will not support them. At some point, however, the clear terms of fairness on which Nozick bases his argument of libertarian justice become ambiguous. The person who needs shoes or food to survive may pay too much because of a poor bargaining position and duress. Out of necessity, inequality may cause exchanges in the market to be tainted by characteristics of coercion which ought to be viewed as unacceptable. If this is the case, the libertarian notion of individual freedom in the market is significantly weakened. From this perspective, the economic system must be based on rules of exchange which are just. If Nozick is correct in his view that exchange will always lead to inequality, then the economic system must be designed so that outcomes or distributions of income and opportunity will facilitate just exchanges. From the libertarian perspective, liberty exists in a competitive market. From a liberal-egalitarian perspective, one must allow some encroachment on private property if liberty is to be experienced by all. From a communist perspective, liberty may require a rejection of private property, since liberty requires that everyone cooperate as equals within the society.

In *A Theory of Justice*, John Rawls uses the analytical device of the *original position* to discuss the issues of liberty and equality.[21] If individuals were stripped of their knowledge and placed behind a *veil of ignorance* they would not know what their fate would be in the future. They would not know whether they would be of a particular race, suffer some illness, inherit wealth, or benefit from being raised in an affluent class. These would all be factors behind the veil of ignorance, and the individual would not know how they would affect his or her future. Confronted with the tasks of imagining what kind of an economic system one would advocate, Rawls depicts people in this hypothetical original position when creating the just rules of a just society. Individuals would want the ability to acquire more than others. They would appreciate material incentives, and society could benefit from the existence of incentives. Nevertheless, there would also be the recognition that one might experience misfortune and live in the worst possible economic conditions. From the latter perspective, the economic system should be designed so that this very possible fate is manageable. From the original position, Rawls believes the following two principles of justice emerge, on which the economic system should be based:

1. Each person is to have an equal right to the most extensive total system of equal basic liberties compatible with a similar system of liberty for all.
2. Social and economic inequalities are to be arranged so that they are both:
    a. to the greatest benefit of the least advantaged; and
    b. attached to offices and positions open to all under conditions of fair equality of opportunity.[22]

The libertarian argument for liberty of the individual is altered so that the right of property is constrained by an economic system that offers an equality of liberty. In Rawls' view, the state will have to be regularly intervening to adjust the outcomes of exchange so that they are consistent with the second principle of justice. Only in this economic system, where differences in income are mitigated, will all individuals be capable of experiencing liberty.

From the perspective of Karl Marx's writings, however, the Rawlsian concept of justice suffers because it does not deal with an inevitable problem of capitalist society. If any individual is to experience liberty, it is imperative that the relationship between capital and labour be dramatically changed. So long as labour is hired to work for capital, there is an accumulation of surplus value or economic rent by capital owners. Employees produce goods, but in the process the employees are not paid the full value of their labour. Additionally, employees find themselves alienated from the product, lacking any direct connection or understanding of what they have produced. Capital owners have a similar experience in that they sell goods whose production they may not have even supervised. Both capital owners and employees focus on income and material possessions, losing sense of who they are as individuals and how they fit into the society as a whole. Marx expressed this view of history in the following way:

Hence, the historical movement which changes the producers into wage-workers, appears, on the one hand, as their emancipation from serfdom and from the fetters of the guilds, and this side alone exists for our bourgeois historians. But on the other hand, these new freemen become sellers of themselves only after they had been robbed of all their own means of production, and all of the guarantees of existence afforded by the old feudal arrangements.[23]

If liberty is to be experienced, labour must revolt against capitalism and acquire ownership of the means of production. If each individual shares in the ownership and in the production process, alienation and exploitation are overcome. In a sense, each individual begins to understand how he or she is defined by the economic environment and how each is in turn a part of that environment. There is no need for a state to control the actions of individuals; each is socialized to a morality that allows the state to wither away. In this society, individuals will experience the frame of mind of Rousseau's primitives in early classless society; they will understand Mill's higher morality; and they will achieve these without any exploitation or class conflict.

The nature of property

The right of ownership has been a central theme in the literature concerning economic systems. As the prior section has indicated, some philosophers focus on the concept of separate individuals in a state of nature attempting to negotiate a hypothetical social contract. Many postulate that the rationale for everyone accepting the constraints of a social contract can be found in the desire to protect private property. Others believe that the historical beginnings of political and social structures occurred, in fact, with the establishment of property rights. Still others analyze the implications of private property for income, wealth, and opportunity, and base normative philosophies upon these analyses, with implications for the choice of economic system.

Traditionally, the word *capitalist* has generally been applied to those economic systems where the government protects private property and sanctions the inequalities that accompany this right. The word *communist* has generally been applied to those economic systems in which individual ownership has been abolished. Today, however, ownership is not the clear-cut concept that it once was. In Part II of this book, we shall consider how alternative decision modes can impact ownership rights. Through a variety of decision modes, the society as a whole can constantly modify the terms and conditions of private ownership and of personal material gain. In most societies, the individual's freedom to use his or her property is severely limited, while incomes are taxed and subsidized in many ways. Even in communist systems, the custodianship of publicly owned property entails some personal responsibility for individual decisions about the use of that property, and it carries financial rewards for successful decisions.

In this context, it is important to see property as a much wider concept than physical plant and equipment or farm land. Recent years have witnessed an increasing emphasis on human capital as a form of property. Education and training have become substantial investments in human capital. Individuals own the future stream of income that will accrue to their special talents as a result of these investments. From this perspective, government policies and programs that alter people's income-earning opportunities can be seen as altering this human capital form of property.

With free enterprise, each individual owns the right to engage in any economic activity. Yet other decision modes limit this right for some people while expanding it for others. The regulation of occupational licensure, for example, excludes most people from the practice of certain professions. The granting of quotas to produce or to import a certain commodity similarly confers a special financial benefit on some people while reducing the right to produce or to import for other people. These government limitations on the rights to engage in certain economic activities clearly affect people's future stream of income and, from this wider concept of property, can be seen as altering property rights. In the extreme, the property rights conferred through government regulation can acquire a life of their own, being bought and sold just as other goods and services. Agricultural quotas, for example, are created solely through government intervention and yet they can become legal and marketable entitlements with a price determined by the present discounted value of the future income that they permit for their owners.

In considering the concept of liberty, it is useful to view property ownership as the ownership of a future stream of income. Ownership of a certain business can be seen as ownership of the profits that will accrue as a result of the operation of that business. The worth of a physical investment can be seen as the present discounted value of the future profits that will be generated by that investment. Consequently, when government policies and programs alter a future stream of income they alter property ownership. From this perspective, the entire range of government policies and programs alter property rights. Our analysis of alternative decision modes, in Part II of this book, will consider this issue.

Equality: Income redistribution – subsidies and taxation

Prior to the modern era, societies generally were based on an established hierarchy, which extended through all aspects of life – social and political, as well as economic. One's position in this hierarchy was often simply inherited. For hundreds of years, for example, feudalism dominated European societies. Periodically, armed revolution or war between societies altered the basic organizational structure or replaced particular individuals in the hierarchy with other people. Yet these revolutionary redistributions occurred only occasionally. Voluntary private contributions to charitable organizations often existed, but these were generally not under the operation or control of the state. Some governments did create orphanages or *poor houses,* but these provided a bare subsistence. Financial assistance to the poor – insofar as it existed – was seen as being necessary to prevent starvation. With the twentieth century, redistribution and the guarantee of a decent living standard seem to be considered rights of citizenship in most societies. Today, many societies have accepted a collective responsibility for the well-being of each member of that society.

To a major degree, nearly all of today's societies have created an economic system that redistributes income, wealth, and opportunities, and that gives some or all members a guaranteed minimum level of publicly provided goods and services. For example, it has been estimated that total expenditures on social and welfare programs by the U.S. government in the 1981 budget year were enough to give every person in the bottom 10 percent (in income) of the population $12,000, or $6,000 to every person in the bottom 20 percent of the population. This meant that a family of four in these two categories could have received transfers of $48,000 and $24,000, respectively, if all of these expenditures had been directed to the poor. However, since these payments included such transfers as education and health care, which were given to more people than just the poor, those in the bottom 10 and 20 percent of the population did not actually receive transfers equal to those levels. A more realistic estimate is that, in 1981, "according to Department of Health and Human Services' figures, a family of four on AFDC [Aid to Families with Dependent Children] with no source of support except government payments received $4,728 in cash and enough food stamps to bring the total up to $6,432 if food stamps are counted at their nominal value."[24]

An important question concerns the interpretation of equality for the purposes of income redistribution: Should welfare simply be a safety net to assist those experiencing economic misfortune? Should equality, from this perspective, be seen as the right of each person to an equal minimum level of goods and services? If this is the case, then the pursuit of equality involves the calculation of poverty levels and minimum living standards. Alternatively, should redistribution be a mechanism for achieving a certain measure of equality? Is a certain overall income distribution considered optimal, and, if so, is this an absolute equality in all time periods?

Considerable uncertainty and disagreement exist as to the actual beneficiaries of specific government programs. In most societies, a host of income maintenance programs seek to aid the poor. Each program has its own rules concerning qualification for receipt of benefits, and such rules are often subject to interpretation. Furthermore, applicants for assistance may rearrange their financial affairs for the specific purpose of meeting such rules. For example, suppose those under the poverty line were guaranteed an income equal to that level. Any family earning less than this amount would receive an income transfer payment to make up the difference and bring everybody up to the established minimum standard. However, strong incentives would exist for the persons just above the poverty line, in low-skill, low-paying jobs, to join the ranks of the unemployed. By quitting their jobs and declaring themselves below the established minimum income standard, thereby accepting a guaranteed income transfer payment, they would gain much more leisure time at minimal financial cost. Bradley Schiller, in taking note of the basic problems associated with income maintenance programs states, "we must recognize that the provision of income transfers may conflict with established work incentives, and consequently that both the observed size of the poverty population and the need for income transfers may be sensitive to the particular form our income transfers take."[25] Some observers even argue that such programs serve to perpetuate poverty by relegating recipients to *poverty traps*. Their program benefits may exceed the amount they could earn in gainful employment and so they give up looking for work. Children of such families may never learn an alternative lifestyle, and may be doomed to repeat their parents' dependence on this system.

The collective provision of particular goods and services to everyone can be of significant assistance to the poor. Public education, health care, pensions, and unemployment insurance can all increase the standard of living of poor people above the level they might otherwise attain. Yet it is not easy to assess the impact of these. The children of poor families may not be as inclined to take advantage of educational opportunities as are the children of the relatively wealthy. Even if health care is publicly provided, the rich may receive better treatment. To a major degree, the causes of bad health may be related to lifestyle, and the poor may generally lead a lifestyle that carries bad health with it. Pensions and unemployment insurance may be geared to income, and so the poor may not fare as well as others, even though the programs are provided to everyone.

In Part II of this book, we consider how societies use alternative decision modes to establish the desired pattern of income distribution. Government subsidies can take the form of cash, and some believe that utility is maximized when individuals are free to spend their cash as they think best. On the other hand, societies also use subsidies to reduce the cost of certain goods and services that are seen as necessities. Societies also control the prices of the goods and services that are considered necessities. By setting prices below free market levels, societies can try to ensure that everyone, including the poor, has access to these necessities, such as housing. Societies can regulate product standards to protect those who lack the information or wisdom to make purchases wisely. They can regulate the provisions of private pension funds to ensure fair treatment of participants, and they can regulate the activities of financial institutions to safeguard small depositors. Public ownership and operation of particular economic activities can be used to ensure that everyone is able to enjoy access to the goods and services produced, such as transportation facilities or communications systems. In a command economy with central planning, the direct allocation of goods and services would, in theory, enable a society to achieve the precise income distribution that it desires. Yet, in general, it is through taxation and subsidy expenditures that today's societies redistribute incomes and determine consumption patterns.

A substantial portion of income redistribution programs are tied to the age structure of the society's population. Education facilities have been expanded to accommodate the post–World War II "baby boom" in Europe and North America. As a population ages – with an increasing proportion entering the retirement stage – societies face steeply rising costs for health care, pensions, and special residential facilities such as nursing homes. Such shifts in the age profile can also have a major impact on the revenue-generating capacity of a government. An aging population can have a diminishing portion of the population in their working years, resulting in both higher social expenditures and lower revenues. This "fiscal crunch" is a prospect facing many societies as they enter the twenty-first century.

Linked with this fiscal crunch is the question of *intergenerational transfers*. Many societies have developed redistribution programs that will place a substantial burden on future generations. In contrast, many earlier societies consciously tried to leave their children better off financially than they themselves had been. Even today, the bulk of our educational expenditures enable young people to live richer lives. It is not yet clear how the changing age profile of a society will interact with its social programs in regard to intergenerational transfers. A central issue will be the rate of productivity improvement – largely determined by a society's collective investment in education and research. Another key issue – quite apart from social programs – will be the costs that must be borne by future generations to deal with the pollution and environmental problems that are being compounded by current generations.

It is not possible to predict with much precision what the human reactions will be to new programs of redistribution, or to changes in the qualification rules and benefit levels of existing programs. Some societies are now experimenting with new programs and modifications, choosing a sample group and examining their reactions. In the United States, such experiments have been conducted with programs that provide a guaranteed annual income. Other experiments deal with special financial support to assist single mothers on welfare as they attempt to move into the work force. Serious difficulties also arise in the evaluation of existing programs. Often the data necessary for such evaluations have simply not been collected. To a large degree, we do not know the impacts of current and proposed social programs. Theory is limited in what it can tell us, and adequate experimentation and evaluation lie ahead of us.

In discussing income redistribution, economic analysis by itself is quite limited. Poverty appears to be much more than an economic issue. In fact, definitions of poverty vary over time and among societies. Individual decisions concerning the work–leisure choice and concerning the personal development of one's abilities involve the disciplines of psychology and sociology. The factors underlying human motivation and creativity are complex. Some individuals seem to choose poverty as a way of life; and some families experience poverty generation after generation.

Equal rights to minimum consumption levels

In some societies, one might think of poverty in terms of starvation. But even starvation is a somewhat vague term. Death may come indirectly through disease, or starvation may mean that the average elderly person succumbs at a younger age. A major concern is not just the quantity of food or number of calories, but also the quality of food. Fruit, vegetables, fish, and meat are more expensive to produce than are grains or potatoes, yet they form essential ingredients in a healthy diet. How shall a society technically describe the diet that it considers to be part of a minimum living standard? Such ambiguities extend to other elements of consumption. The concept of "adequate housing" involves much more than a stipulated number of square feet of accommodation per person. Attempts to develop public housing projects, to subsidize residential rents, and to impose systems of rent controls have all encountered problems of defining quality standards and then ensuring that these are met.

The shift of health care from an individual responsibility to a collective responsibility has similarly raised questions about minimal acceptable features. How many demands should each citizen be permitted to make on a publicly funded system? Should any limits be placed on number or types of treatments? New technology has created a host of sophisticated and expensive medical treatments: Should the latest and most advanced of these be made available to everyone? For the elderly, what degree of public nursing home care should be provided?

A particular income level may have a varying degree of purchasing power from one geographical region to another. The ability to grow some of one's food differs between rural and urban areas. The cost of housing also differs. Such factors make interregional comparisons difficult. Comparisons between rich industrialized countries and underdeveloped agricultural societies confront similar problems. Even within a particular society, minimum acceptable living standards may differ between age groups and between families of varying size and composition. The elderly may not face as many financial demands as the young family. The single parent may confront special needs. For all families, a second or third child may not be as costly as the first child. Low-income people will not spend their income on the same goods or services as the rich. Consequently, different consumption patterns may mean that a specific dollar income gap is not as significant as it seems.

Recently, attempts have been made to calculate the size of the "underground economy," consisting of economic activities that are not counted in national income statistics. It seems that the underground economy is substantial. For some families, the official income reported for tax purposes may represent total earnings. For other families, hidden income may mean that their actual living expenditures exceed what appear to be their poverty incomes. The elderly, for example, may transfer assets to their children – perhaps receiving unreported interest payments from them. Such elderly people may then qualify for special government assistance to alleviate a poverty situation which may not actually exist.

The questions raised in this discussion indicate that any definition of poverty or of minimal acceptable living standards is a subjective definition which may change over time and which may vary from one society to another. For today's rich industrialized nations, programs of income redistribution aimed at reducing poverty are generally far more substantial than such programs in the much poorer underdeveloped societies. For today's rich industrialized nations, poverty may not entail the degree of human suffering that it did fifty years ago in these same nations. Yet, for these nations, the pursuit of the equality objective is far more significant than it was in the past.

A quantitative assessment of income inequality and the extent of income redistribution

Tables 3.1 and 3.2 indicate various types of government expenditures as a percentage of the particular nation's gross domestic product. Government expenditures are first divided into "traditional commitments" and "modern commitments." The former include debt interest and the "public wants" of defense and general government. Although Maddison labels these as traditional commitments, we should note that the level of debt interest may be the result of deficits arising from the huge expansion of the modern welfare commitments, and the level of general government expenditures may be the result of administration requirements for these modern commitments.[26]

In the second table, Maddison divides modern commitments into "merit wants" of education, health, and housing and "income maintenance" programs of pensions, sickness benefits, family allocations, and unemployment compensation. This dichotomy also is imprecise in that public pensions, for example, involve more than just the concept of

Table 3.1. *Structure of government expenditure as a percentage of GDP around 1980*

	France 1980	Germany 1980	Japan 1981	Netherlands 1978	U.K. 1979	U.S.A. 1978	Average
Total	46.9	48.5	34.1	57.8	43.4	33.8	44.1
	Traditional Commitments						
Debt interest	1.7	1.9	3.6	4.0	4.6	2.7	3.1
"Public wants" (Defense and general government)	7.4	8.5	4.2	10.3	8.7	8.5	7.9
	Modern Commitments						
Economic services	3.4	5.3	6.0	3.8	3.9	3.4	4.3
"Welfare state" (Merit wants and income maintenance)	34.4	32.8	20.3	39.7	26.2	19.2	28.8

Source: Maddison, "Origins and Impact of the Welfare State, 1883–1983," *Banca Nazionale del Lavoro Quarterly Review* 37 (1984), p. 69.

income maintenance that may underlie insurance for sickness or unemployment. Public pensions involve a belief that individuals are not capable of saving adequately for their retirement years.

Although Maddison's groupings of expenditures are not entirely satisfactory, nevertheless, these two tables do emphasize the major role played by collective redistribution and paternalism in a number of modern countries. Of interest is the fact that Japan and the United States have a somewhat lower level of both "merit wants" and "income maintenance" provided by their governments when this provision is expressed as a percentage of gross domestic product.

Maddison also examines the impact of the tax structure on income inequality. He concludes that taxes overall play a much smaller role in redistribution than do the expenditures presented above. Maddison uses Table 3.3 in which the numbers are the ratio of the top decile income group's average income to the bottom decile income group's average income. Column one shows the original distribution ratio. The distribution ratio after government expenditures – referred to here as "transfers" – is indicated in column two, and the difference between columns one and two is found in column four. Column three shows the distribution ratio after taxes, and column five indicates how taxes have af-

Table 3.2. *Detail of welfare state expenditure as percentage of GDP around 1980*

	France 1980	Germany 1980	Japan 1981	Netherlands 1981	U.K. 1979	U.S.A. 1978	Average
Merit wants	15.9	13.8	12.6	(18.7)	13.9	9.0	13.8
Education	5.7	5.1	5.0	7.1	5.4	5.7	5.7
Health	6.2	6.5	4.7	6.6	4.7	2.5	5.2
Housing	3.2	1.4	2.4 ⎫	(5.0)	3.3	0.4 ⎫	2.9
Other	0.8	0.8	0.5 ⎭		0.5	0.4 ⎭	

	France 1981	Germany 1981	Japan 1981	Netherlands 1981	U.K. 1981	U.S.A. 1981	Average
Income maintenance	18.4	16.8	7.7	19.3	10.5	9.0	13.6
Pensions	11.9	12.5	4.8	13.0	7.4	7.4	9.5
Sickness cash benefits	1.2	0.7	0.1	1.9	0.3	0.1	0.7
Family allocations	2.2	1.2	1.6	2.0	1.4	0.5	1.5
Unemployment compensation	1.9	1.4	0.4	1.0	1.4	0.5	1.1
Other	1.2	1.0	0.7	1.4	0.0	0.5	0.7

Source: Maddison, "Origins and Impact of the Welfare State, 1883–1983," *Banca Nazionale del Lavoro Quarterly Review* 37 (1984), p. 69.

fected the "post-transfer" ratios of column two. For the six countries being considered, the average decile ratio for "original" income is 49.1:1. Government transfers reduce this ratio to 15.3:1. The tax system reduces it further, to 13.2:1. Clearly the major redistribution impact occurs through expenditures.

A concept frequently used in computing income inequality is the "Gini coefficient." This concept is explained by Morley Gunderson through the use of Table 3.4 and Figure 3.1, based upon Canadian data for 1979.[27] In Table 3.4, families are divided into five equal groups, ranging from the 20 percent with the lowest incomes to the 20 percent with the highest incomes. In Figure 3.1, these data are plotted on a diagram whose horizontal axis represents the cumulative proportion of families and whose vertical axis represents the cumulative proportion of income received. In 1979, the bottom 20 percent of families received 6.1 percent of the total income. These numbers are plotted. The next 20 percent received 13.0 percent of the income. Together, the bottom 40 percent received 19.1 percent of the income – and these numbers are plotted. In this way, a "Lorenz curve" is drawn. Perfect equality would result

Table 3.3. *Ratio of top to bottom income decile*

	Original Income	Pre-tax post-transfer income	Post-tax income	Distributive impact of transfers	Distributive impact of direct taxes
France	33.7	20.7	21.7	13.0	−1.0
Germany	34.1	12.4	10.8	21.7	1.6
Japan	n.a.	9.9	9.1	n.a.	0.8
Netherlands	n.a.	13.5	10.7	n.a.	2.8
United Kingdom	66.8	11.8	9.4	55.0	2.4
United States	61.8	23.7	17.7	38.1	6.0
Average	49.1	15.3	13.2	32.0	2.1

Source: Maddison, "Origins and Impact of the Welfare State, 1883–1983," *Banca Nazionale del Lavoro Quarterly Review* 37 (1984), p. 73.

Table 3.4. *Percent of income possessed by each quintile of families, Canada, 1979*

Unit	Bottom 20%	Second quintile	Third quintile	Fourth quintile	Top 20%
Families	6.1	13.0	18.4	24.3	38.3

Source: Morley Gunderson, *Economics of Poverty and Income Distribution* (Toronto: Butterworths, 1983), p. 43.

in a straight line with a 45-degree angle, since 20 percent of the families would receive 20 percent of the income, 40 percent would receive 40 percent, and so on. As Gunderson explains,

This relationship between the Lorenz curve and the line of perfect equality enables the calculation of a single statistical measure that indicates the degree of inequality. Denoting the area between the Lorenz curve and the line of equality as A, and the area below the Lorenz curve and bounded by the axis as B, then the Gini coefficient is calculated as Gini = $A/(A + B)$; that is, it is the area between the Lorenz curve and the 45-degree line, divided by the area of the triangle below the 45-degree line. If the degree of inequality is small so the Lorenz curve is close to the line of equality, then the area A is small (approaching zero) and Gini = $A/(A + B)$ approaches $0/(0 + B)$ = 0. If the degree of inequality is large so the Lorenz curve is close to the axes and the area B is small (approaches zero), then the Gini = $A/(A + B)$ approaches $(A/(A + 0)$ = 1. Thus, the Gini coefficient lies between zero and one, with a smaller Gini (approaching zero) indicating greater equality.[28]

Gunderson is able to use the Gini coefficient to make comparisons across countries in regard to income inequality. In Table 3.5, he presents

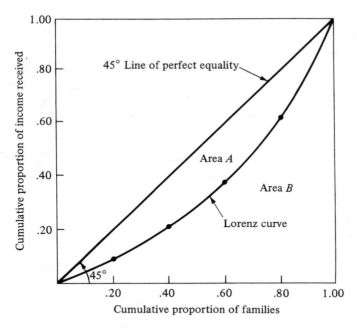

Figure 3.1. Lorenz Curve. *Source:* Morley Gunderson, *Economics of Poverty and Income Distribution* (Toronto: Butterworths, 1983), p. 46.

Table 3.5. *Income inequality in the United States, Canada, and the United Kingdom*

Country	U.K. Royal Commission Study			OECD Study		
	Gini	Share of poorest quintile	Share of richest quintile	Gini	Share of poorest quintile	Share of richest quintile
United States	.506	1.9	51.8	.381	4.5	42.9
Canada	.467	2.0	48.2	.354	5.0	41.0
United Kingdom	.462	2.6	47.7	.318	6.3	38.7

Source: Morley Gunderson, *Economics of Poverty and Income Distribution* (Toronto: Butterworths, 1983), p. 86.

pre-tax, pre-transfer data for the United Kingdom, the United States, and Canada. It is interesting to note that the income inequality calculations of the UK Royal Commission differ from those of the OECD Study.

Table 3.6. *Selected percentile ratios, distributions of wage earners and salaried workers by earnings, and GDP per capita, USSR and Western countries, specified years*

Country and year	Real GDP per capita (U.S. 1975 = 100)	P_{10}/P_{50}	P_{90}/P_{50}	P_{95}/P_{50}	$P_{90}/_{10}$
USSR: 1961	31	.50	2.0	2.4	4.0
1966	36	.55	1.8	2.2	3.3
1968	40	.56	1.8	2.1	2.8
1970	43	.58	1.7	2.0	
1972	45				3.1
1976	50				3.4
1981	55				3.0
Spain: 1964	27		2.0	2.4	
Austria: 1957	28		1.8	2.3	
Argentina: 1961	31		1.8	2.3	
Japan: 1968	47	.52	1.9	2.3	3.7
Canada: 1950–1	47		1.6	1.9	
1960–1	54		1.8	2.1	
France: 1963	49		2.0	2.7	
U.K.: 1964–5	49	.48	1.6		3.5
1976	66	.60	1.7	2.0	2.8
Belgium: 1964	53		1.6	2.0	
U.S.: 1949	58		1.7		
1959	72		1.8	2.2	
1972	99	.47	2.1	2.6	4.5
1975	100	.45	1.8		4.0

Source: Abram Bergson, "Income Inequality Under Soviet Socialism," *Journal of Economic Literature* 22 (September 1984), p. 1063.

Abram Bergson has compiled the two following tables to compare income distributions of the USSR with those of other countries.[29] In Table 3.6, he provides four different ratios: the bottom tenth percentile to the fiftieth percentile; the ninetieth percentile to the fiftieth percentile; the ninety-fifth percentile to the fiftieth percentile; and the ninetieth percentile to the tenth percentile. Perhaps the latter provides the clearest indication of income ranges. Most striking is the similarity between the USSR ratios, ranging from 4.0 in 1961 to 3.0 in 1981, and the ratios for Japan, the United Kingdom, and the United States which range from 2.8 in the United Kingdom in 1976 to 4.5 in the United States in 1972.

In Table 3.7, Bergson develops Gini coefficients for a number of countries. Once again, the degree of Soviet income inequality is striking.

Bergson does try to calculate the impact of taxes on income distribution. Some information is contained in Table 3.8. This supports the conclusion of Maddison that generally taxes have not significantly altered income distribution.

The USSR does not use taxes to alter the income distribution in the manner of the OECD countries, since the Soviet pretax income distribution is established by the central planners. Nevertheless, we should note that Soviet income inequality may be more extreme than indicated by Bergson's data. Many commodities are in short supply. The centrally determined prices are not set high enough to clear the market. In this

Table 3.7. *Income shares of selected percentile groups and Gini coefficients, distributions of households by per capita household income, and GDP per capita, USSR and Western countries, specified years*

Distribution, country and year	GDP per capita (U.S. = 100)	Income share (%) of				Gini coefficient
		Lowest 10%	Lowest 20%	Highest 20%	Highest 10%	
Nonfarm households, pre-tax						
USSR, 1967						
(McAuley)	38	4.4	10.4	33.8	19.9	.229
Urban households, post-tax						
USSR, 1972–4						
(Ofer-Vinokur)	48	3.4	8.7	38.5	24.1	.288
All households, pre-tax						
Australia, 1966–7	56	3.5	8.3	41.0	25.6	.317
Norway, 1970	64	3.5	8.2	39.0	23.5	.306
U.K., 1973	66	3.5	8.3	39.9	23.9	.308
France, 1970	68	2.0	5.8	47.2	31.8	.398
Canada, 1969	74	2.2	6.2	43.6	27.8	.363
U.S., 1972	99	1.8	5.5	44.4	28.6	.376
All households, post-tax						
Sweden, 1972	80	3.5	9.3	35.2	20.5	.254

Note: For comparability, all Gini coefficients computed from income shares of decile groups. Ofer-Vinokur coefficient in source, apparently calculated from frequently distribution, was .293.
Source: Abram Bergson, "Income Inequality Under Soviet Socialism," *Journal of Economic Literature* 22 (September 1984), p. 1070.

Table 3.8. *Income shares of selected percentile groups and Gini coefficients, distributions of households by total household income, pre- and post-tax, selected countries*

Country and distribution	Income share (%) of				
	Lowest 10%	Lowest 20%	Highest 20%	Highest 10%	Gini coefficient
Australia, 1966–7					
Pre-tax	2.1	6.6	38.9	23.8	.313
Post-tax	2.1	6.6	38.8	23.7	.312
Norway, 1970					
Pre-tax	1.7	4.9	40.9	24.5	.354
Post-tax	2.3	6.3	37.3	22.2	.307
U.K., 1973					
Pre-tax	2.1	5.4	40.3	24.7	.344
Post-tax	2.5	6.3	38.7	23.5	.318
France, 1970					
Pre-tax	1.5	4.3	47.0	31.0	.416
Post-tax	1.4	4.3	46.9	30.4	.414
Canada, 1969					
Pre-tax	1.2	4.3	43.3	27.1	.382
Post-tax	1.5	5.0	41.0	25.1	.354
U.S., 1972					
Pre-tax	1.2	3.8	44.8	28.4	.404
Post-tax	1.5	4.5	42.9	26.6	.381

Source: Abram Bergson, "Income Inequality Under Soviet Socialism," *Journal of Economic Literature* 22 (September 1984), p. 1072.

situation, the rich – who are the well-placed corporate and bureaucratic managers and government officials – can receive preferences in obtaining the commodities they desire. In real terms, their incomes have greater purchasing power per ruble than the incomes of the average worker.

The great expansion of redistribution has brought several major concerns to public policy discussion. The remainder of this chapter turns to these. Special attention is directed to the impact on work incentives, the fiscal problem of escalating costs, and the complexity and unfairness of many social programs.

Impact on work incentives

Some people claim that income redistribution discourages people from working. If part of one's material gain is to be taken through taxation, then the reward for work will be reduced, and people will work fewer hours or with less intensity. Similarly, if people can receive subsidies, then the need to work is reduced. When these benefits are provided to low-income people or to the physically or mentally handicapped, then an incentive may exist to remain poor or to exaggerate one's handicap in order to maintain the stream of benefits. Consequently, taxes and subsidies create incentives not to work. In the extreme, some individuals may receive a higher real income from social benefits based on need than they could earn by working in the marketplace. To shift from welfare to gainful employment could mean a reduction in real income.[30]

Many observers feel that the work disincentive of social programs is inappropriate: It is unfair to those who do work, it is self-perpetuating and even cumulative as increasing numbers are drawn into the welfare syndrome, and it has deleterious effects on the moral character and development potential of the recipients. Charles Murray argues in *Losing Ground: American Social Policy, 1950–1980* that poverty programs in the United States have hurt the poor.[31] Murray's arguments could be directed at the social policy of many other nations, and his indictment is not restricted to experiences in the United States. By institutionalizing welfare, we have made poverty an acceptable way of life. Masses of poor people simply have given up the search for work and have abandoned any attempts to improve their skills and education. This has left huge numbers of poor in a permanent poverty trap.

Murray believes that the United States should recognize the failure of its social policy and should eliminate many programs and reduce others.[32] People should be compelled to rely on their own initiative and work. In the long run, this harsh treatment will be best for the poor. A central feature of Murray's book – and his analysis of poverty in the United States – is the concentration of poverty in minority racial groups, particularly in the black population. Here the unemployment rates are higher, the average income levels are lower, the percentage of unwed mothers is greater, and the dependence on the welfare system is pervasive. In many societies, poverty is particularly acute in minority racial groups. Various aspects of discrimination combine to create barriers to economic and social mobility. Here one can see the need for general acceptance of new social attitudes in the war against poverty. Greater equality of opportunity is necessary if minority racial groups are to enter the mainstream of economic progress and material success.

Alternative decision modes for achieving liberty and equality

The above discussion has emphasized the subjective nature of equality standards, and the ambiguities and differences of opinion concerning appropriate subsidies and tax policies. We have seen that the degree of vertical inequality that would be optimal can be debated vigorously. Also of concern in an economic system is the issue of horizontal equity, with the question of whether people with the same wealth and income are treated the same by society's programs of redistribution.

Some observers believe that a large number of welfare programs are unfair in that access to them depends upon good luck or skills in application, or personal relationships. Studies of housing allowances, for example, have found that even in a wealthy and well-educated society only a portion of those who qualify for benefits actually apply for them. The remainder may be so poor and deprived that they are not aware of such programs or of how to apply. Furthermore, the timing of one's application may determine whether one is fortunate enough to gain access. When an elderly person wishes to enter a publicly funded nursing home, he or she may have to wait until a place opens. Personal relationships may speed the application process. Elected members of government may "pull strings" for their constituents if they are asked to do so by their political supporters. Family members or friends may be important in assisting those who otherwise might not apply. Of course, there is always a temptation to cheat in one's application. The elderly may transfer assets to their children in order to meet the wealth criteria for receipt of special help. Individuals may exaggerate their disabilities. Students applying for government grants may lie about their parent's income or the extent of family financial support.

These issues of fairness are intensified by the fact that often one's access is accepted or rejected rather than being a matter of degree. Either one gets into the nursing home or one does not. In such cases, a lack of fairness can be of major significance to one's well-being. Many tax exemptions and concessions can be criticized from this perspective, as can programs of business subsidies. Some individuals or firms may invest in particular activities that permit such assistance, whereas others may not be able to do so. The latter may have invested prior to the program being instituted, or their activities may be judged as not qualifying, or they may not be aware of application procedures. For the recipients, the programs may provide substantial income gains. Yet for others, the programs may be of negative value since one's competitors may achieve lower production costs, and so may reduce prices.

Fairness issues are linked with the complexity of taxes and subsidy programs. Faced with a large number of detailed application procedures, it becomes difficult for the individual or firm to be aware of all the criteria for assistance and to apply appropriately. Furthermore, complexity creates administrative costs. Civil servants must analyze the applications, must supervise the grant procedures, and in some cases must even operate particular facilities.

Not surprisingly, many societies are debating the advantages of replacing a host of welfare programs with straightforward cash assistance determined through one's tax return. It should be a simple matter to calculate the amount of cash transfer necessary to raise a person up to a specified level. Various ways have been proposed to attain a guaranteed annual income and to maintain some work incentive. Such a negative income tax offers hope for improving fairness and reducing complexity. Similarly, many societies are debating the advantages of reducing or eliminating tax exemptions and concessions. This would permit a lower overall tax rate. Again, fairness could be improved and complexity could be reduced.

Perhaps of greater importance as a factor shaping changes is the simple issue of total cost. The earlier discussion in this chapter presented data on the percentage of gross domestic product currently devoted to social programs. In recent years, the expansion of these programs – together with an increase in tax concessions – has led to a surge in fiscal deficits in many countries. Some now question whether our societies can maintain today's huge deficits, and many believe that the welfare state has grown to unmanageable proportions. Shifts in the population age structure have intensified these concerns. The attempt by current generations to transfer the fiscal burden of these programs to future generations may simply be unrealistic.

The remaining chapters consider these issues from several perspectives. Chapter 5 examines the implications of government price setting. By placing a ceiling on a particular price, the government can reduce the profitability of existing producers. By setting a price above the equilibrium level, the government provides extra income to suppliers, but it may result in surplus production. With the legal imposition of a minimum wage, some wage earners will receive a higher wage than they would otherwise. Yet some may not find employment since businesses will perceive their marginal productivity to be less than the legislated wage. Hence price setting may improve the economic position of some, yet at the same time it may diminish the economic position of others.

Chapter 6 discusses the subsidies that governments use today to change the free-market pattern of financial rewards. Technically, no individual is forcibly deprived of his or her property. Nevertheless, one may lose or gain property directly as a consequence of this type of government intervention. The institution of a new subsidy program can stimulate new investment by one's competitors, and their additional production can reduce the profitability and present discounted value of existing investments. Meanwhile, the recipient of subsidies will experience an increase in profitability and, therefore, an increase in the value of his or her property. These comments hold true for investment in human as well as physical capital. Today, governments direct many subsidies at education and training, with society paying for a substantial share of these investments. Tax provisions discussed in Chapter 7 alter the personal financial gain that individuals will enjoy as a result of their economic activities. A myriad of tax concessions can affect the profitability and hence the present discounted value of existing investments.

Non–price regulations by government directly limit or enhance income streams in ways that may be readily observed, and so the subject matter of Chapter 8 is intimately linked with law and property rights. By prohibiting or restricting certain business practices, such as predatory pricing or corporate mergers, government pursuit of a more competitive economy can reduce the profits of some firms while raising the profits of others. Regulation of foreign investment may prohibit some investment entirely, thereby depriving foreign shareholders of future income, and perhaps also reducing the value of the domestic property which was the object of the investment. Regulation of foreign investment may also entail undertakings, such as domestic sourcing commitments, that will reduce future profits below the levels attainable otherwise. Regulations concerning pollution emissions can directly affect corporate profitability through the expenses incurred in conforming to them. The requirement that licenses or quotas be obtained in order to pursue a particular economic activity can provide windfalls for some while depriving others of potential income. In the extreme, the benefits conferred by regulations – such as quotas to produce or to import – may themselves become property rights that are bought and sold independently of any physical assets.

Chapter 9 explores the reasons why societies have adopted government ownership and operation for certain economic activities at certain points in time. In these circumstances, the elimination of individual rights to ownership can be decisive and complete, even entailing the expropriation of private property. Chapter 9 considers the extension of government ownership and operation to the majority of economic activities such that detailed central planning becomes the predominant form of decision making. Such central planning makes government an active participant in determining most income streams and, consequently, most property rights. Government participation is thorough and continual. The division between the government and the economic enterprise is no longer clear-cut. Some private property rights may still exist, principally in the ownership of human capital and the income streams created by human capital. However, even the private property rights are so much under the control of government that one can see them as having been conferred by government rather than as having been determined in the marketplace.

The right of ownership assures individuals that their work, investment, and innovation will all be rewarded materially to the degree that they are successful in contributing to society's production of goods and services. Yet, as we shall see, the various decision modes that include collective decision making interfere with and modify the right of ownership that would develop in a free-enterprise system. The consequent impact on incentives to work, to invest, and to innovate forms an important feature of each economic system. As discussed in Chapter 10, individuals may feel that the economic system is failing to reward them appropriately, and they may consider a wide range of modifications in the economic system, including revolutionary activity to attain these modifications. Often a central focus of a revolution is the achievement of a dramatic and clear-cut change in the existing property rights.

Chapter 11 emphasizes that international trade and investment place limits on the degree to which each society can define its own economic system. Individuals can shift their capital – human, as well as corporate – in response to government intervention that they consider undesirable. The pattern and volume of trade flows can also be altered by the programs and policies that a government institutes for its domestic purposes. Hence, each society must consider the impact of its decisions concerning property rights on the mobility of capital and labour as well as goods and services. Meanwhile, each society's choices in regard to its economic system are affected, in turn, by the economic systems of other societies.

Essay and discussion topics

1. Compare and contrast capitalist and communist objectives in regard to liberty and equality.
2. Evaluate the degree to which subsidies and taxation have altered the distribution of income and wealth in alternative economic systems.
3. Discuss the concept of private property within alternative economic systems.

PART II

Decision modes

CHAPTER 4

Free enterprise

Introduction

Over two hundred years ago, Adam Smith presented a thorough and consistent defense of free enterprise in his book, *An Inquiry into the Nature and Causes of the Wealth of Nations.*[1] Smith wrote at the end of the mercantilist era with its collective decision making in many areas of economic life, particularly in the regulation of international trade and commerce, and he pointed to the inefficiencies of this collective decision making. His central theme was that a greater quantity of goods and services could be produced and consumed if decisions were made in response to market forces. These forces of demand and supply could best be analyzed by the millions of people reaching decisions individually; and the separate decisions based on these analyses would be more appropriate than decisions taken collectively. Smith described how the pursuit of self-interest could serve as an *invisible hand,* guiding each individual in this decision-making process.

Smith emphasized the concepts of specialization and economies of scale, and he discussed how these were linked to the concept of free enterprise. For example, his title for Chapter III in Book I was "That the Division of Labour is Limited by the Extent of the Market." Central to both specialization and trade was his belief that individuals pursue their own self-interest and in doing so make decisions that maximize the nation's wealth.

As every individual, therefore, endeavours as much as he can, both to employ his capital in the support of domestic industry and so to direct that industry that its produce may be of the greatest value; every individual necessarily labours to render the annual revenue of the society as great as he can. He generally, indeed, neither intends to promote the public interest, nor knows how much he is promoting it. By preferring the support of domestic to that of foreign industry, he intends only his own security; and by directing that industry in such a manner as its produce may be of the greatest value, he intends only his own gain; and he is in this, as in many other cases, led by an invisible hand to promote an end which was no part of his intention. Nor is it always the worse for the society that it was no part of it. By pursuing his own interest he frequently promotes that of the society more effectually than when he really intends to promote it.[2]

In examining free enterprise, this chapter demonstrates that under certain assumptions efficiency can be achieved automatically without government intervention. Greater efficiency means higher aggregate production. In Adam Smith's writings, we can also see a concern for the adoption of new technologies, and the importance of innovation for growth. With the free-enterprise model, individuals each face personal financial incentives to save, to invest, and to innovate. The market rewards people on the basis of their own achievement. These attributes are relevant not only for entrepreneurship, but also for the concepts of liberty and equality of opportunity. In fact, some authors have argued that the liberty inherent in free enterprise is important not only for itself, but also because it is essential for the attainment of political democracy.

Nevertheless, critics point to shortcomings. Unemployment can, at times, be substantial and serious, representing an inefficiency which entails severe personal hardships. Consumers may lack the ability and knowledge to allocate their incomes wisely. Producers may take advantage of *market failures* to make price and output decisions different from those that would be socially optimal. Hence, critics may argue that the prerequisites for much of conventional microeconomic theory concerning maximization of consumer utility and attainment of production efficiency are not valid in the modern economy. Karl Marx's writings can be seen as based upon a rejection of the classical perceptions in regard to the production process. Furthermore, the right to accumulate and inherit property may inevitably destroy equality of opportunity and may lead to undesirable exploitation of the less fortunate members of society.

In regard to the objective of growth, critics argue that the consumption–saving decisions of individuals can lead to a low savings rate and, consequently, a slow accumulation of capital. Modern innovation may require extensive research, education, and retraining. The public good and externality characteristics of these activities mean that the free-enterprise model will not provide them to a socially optimal degree. The market may also be seen as depriving many people of a real measure of economic liberty and equality of opportunity. The self-perpetuation of elites and the vicissitudes of fortune can block individual achievement.

From the perspective of these criticisms, one may advocate alternative decision modes. Hence the other chapters of Part II return to particular shortcomings of the free-enterprise model. In creating an economic system that incorporates various types of collective decision making, societies attempt to overcome some of these shortcomings. Throughout the world, the twentieth century has witnessed a substantial shift towards reliance upon these other models. Yet, actual experience has revealed shortcomings in these decision modes as well. Consequently, in recent years, a number of economists in many nations have supported an extension of free-enterprise competition to additional economic activities, pointing to the gains in efficiency and productivity that such a model may offer.[3] Some political leaders have, in fact, implemented this extension, including Margaret Thatcher in Great Britain, Ronald Reagan in the United States, Deng Xiaoping in China, and, most recently, Mikhail Gorbachev in the Soviet Union and leaders in Eastern European countries. These implementations have not covered all activities, and no economic system conforms to the free-enterprise model in all areas of its decision making. Furthermore, the adoption of this model can be concentrated on consumption and the individual choices concerning income allocation, rather than extended to industrial production. In this way, the focus can be on consumption efficiency rather than production efficiency. With Gorbachev's reforms, this possibility is likely, together with a reliance upon the price-control model rather than a complete shift to reliance upon the free market.

General equilibrium analyses

A century after Adam Smith's book was published, the economist Leon Walras developed a more theoretical analytical structure which he believed could help to explain the functioning of a free-enterprise economy.[4] Walras described each economic activity as an equation in which the dependent variable represents the product or output and the independent variables represent the many factors of production or inputs. The equation indicates the amount of each variable required in order to create a unit of the product represented by the dependent variable. Walras used this set of equations to describe the manner in which economic activities interrelate.

The thrust of Walras' work was to establish that the different markets in an economic system were interdependent. Equilibrium existed when demand and supply equalled each other in each market. How this equilibrium came to be is what interested Walras. Within his model, the price of each good or service adjusted as buyers and sellers "cried out" various bids or offers. A consumer who felt that a price was too high in one market could withdraw to another one; similarly, producers viewing low prices could alter their supply and consider investing in other markets. One good would serve as the standard of valuation and gradually the auctioning of offers would come to a stable equilibrium. Unless there was an external shock to the system, prices would eventually adjust to clear all markets at utility maximizing conditions with the price ratios equal to the ratios of marginal utility.

Since Walras, many economists have explored this mathematical structure seeking to clarify the nature and characteristics of general equilibrium.[5] Some have considered the significance of inelasticity of factor supplies and of fixity in coefficients. The introduction of elasticity in factor supplies and variability in coefficients makes this structure more compatible with the *neoclassical* perceptions. If factor supplies are elastic and if input coefficients are variable, then the movement towards equilibrium will lead to full employment. Some economists, such as von Neumann, have focused on the growth path of an economy that is portrayed by such a set of equations, describing and explaining dynamic equilibrium over time as well as static equilibrium.[6]

Since Walras developed his analytical method, economists have attempted to discern whether it is possible to describe an economic system in Walrasian terms. One of the difficulties is determining whether, with a series of equations and variables which link the various sectors of an economy, a unique solution or equilibrium may be generated. A. Wald first proved the existence of competitive equilibrium, in a Walras-type model of constant input–output coefficients and fixed factor supplies.[7] Although one may accept the basic argument that changes in one market will have effects on other markets, and hence the overall distribution of demand and supply, the extensive information required for a Walrasian analysis may be unattainable. Apart from theoretical analyses, some communist countries have attempted to develop central plans, often referred to as "material balances," that resemble this approach. Practical difficulties have repeatedly arisen in collecting and analyzing the requisite information.

In recent years, several economists have received Nobel Prizes for advancing the theory of general equilibrium analysis through equations that utilize sophisticated mathematical techniques.[8] Most of these mathematical analyses are based on the assumption of perfect competition in which individuals are not able to alter the market prices or total production by their own decisions, and they are not able to collude with their competitors. Each is assumed to have perfect knowledge of the relevant production techniques and of the demands of consumers and other producers. These mathematical analyses do not sweep away all concerns about the free-enterprise system. Rather they do provide insights into the overall functioning of a complex economy, and they demonstrate the manner in which individual maximization of self-interest can result in a general equilibrium which under certain specific conditions may be unique, stable, and efficient.

Partial equilibrium analyses

At the same time that Leon Walras was writing about general equilibrium analysis on the European continent, Alfred Marshall was beginning to conduct investigations into another form of analysis in Britain.[9] Marshall focused on each market separately; hence Marshall's work is often referred to as partial equilibrium analysis.

According to Marshall, one of the greatest obstacles to successful economic enquiries involves dealing with the element of time. He was aware of the dynamics among markets on which Walrasian economics based itself, but believed that it was important to segregate the analysis holding other things to be equal, so that more exact conclusions could be reached. The judicious application of *ceteris paribus* facilitates the analysis of how markets operate. For Marshall the demand for a product is a function of its price, the price of substitutes and complements, and consumer income and preferences. All other factors which might alter the market demand for the product are treated as constants. This view of demand and supply in a kind of quasi-isolation distinguishes Marshall from Walras. The examination of representative people, firms, and markets on a separate and individual basis can shed more light on the issues of equilibrium and optimality. Much of this analysis is based on demand and supply functions, which can be depicted on simple diagrams as a relationship between price and output.

In Figure 4.1, the demand curve DD represents the quantity of a good that will be purchased at alternative prices provided all other determinants of demand, such as preferences and income, are constant. Generally, it is drawn as sloping downwards to the right, reflecting the assumption that if the price declines then consumers will demand increasing quantities of the product. The supply curve SS slopes upwards to the right, reflecting the assumption that firms will make more of the product as the price is raised. These curves intersect at a point E which is a unique and stable equilibrium. If a price higher than P_E happened to occur in the market, say P_A, then firms would make Q_2, a larger quantity of output than Q_1, the amount that people would be prepared to buy at the price P_A. The excess supply $(Q_2 - Q_1)$ in the market would, through competition, drive the price downwards towards P_E. Similarly, if a price lower than P_E happened to occur in the market, say P_B, then firms would make only Q_1, a smaller quantity of output than

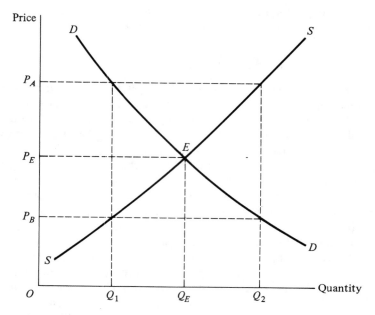

Figure 4.1. Demand, supply, and equilibrium.

Q_2, the amount that people would be prepared to buy at the price P_B. The excess demand $(Q_2 - Q_1)$ in the market would, through competition, drive the price upwards towards P_E.

This type of analysis suggests that competition guarantees a unique and stable equilibrium. Yet even here, the individual decisions may not, by themselves, attain this result. Introduction of discrete time periods, with planning based on the previous period's outcomes, can result in cycles rather than a direct and immediate convergence. Faced with the market price P_B, suppliers may reduce their production capacity to Q_1, only to find that the market price in the next period rises again to P_A. For each individual supplier, the expansion and subsequent contraction may seem rational at the time, but the concerted behaviour of all suppliers can result in perpetual market fluctuations. Consequently, an argument can be made for a shift to collective decision making by a government that sets the price at P_E, thereby establishing a stable equilibrium. Similarly, an argument can be made for a shift to the collective establishment of production quotas allocating to each supplier a right to produce a specified portion of the equilibrium quantity Q_E. The problems caused by such "cobweb cycles" vary from one activity to another, being most apparent in the agricultural sector where farmers tend to make each year's decisions concerning planting or number of livestock on the basis of the previous year's market prices.

Efficiency in consumption

Underlying the demand for each product is the conscious evaluation by each individual of the amount of the product that he or she should buy at each possible price, so as to maximize that individual's satisfaction or utility. Consumer theory has been elaborated to analyze these decisions.

In Figure 4.2, an individual consumer can spend his or her entire income on product X, in which case he or she can purchase the amount q_x. Alternatively, the individual can spend his or her entire income on product Y, in which case he or she can purchase the amount q_y. The straight line joining these points – the income line or budget line – indicates the various combinations of X and Y that can be purchased with one's income, and its slope is the market price ratio at which the consumer can exchange some of X for more of Y. This ratio of possible exchanges in the market is determined by the relative prices of the two commodities. The following identity summarizes these relationships.

$$\text{If } P_x q_x = \text{total income} = P_y q_y, \text{ then the slope } \frac{q_x}{q_y} = \frac{P_y}{P_x}.$$

In Figure 4.2, each indifference curve (U_1, U_2, U_3) indicates those combinations of X and Y which provide the consumer with the amount of satisfaction that it represents. The slope of the indifference curve at each point on it represents the amount of X that must be obtained to compensate for the surrender of a unit of Y, so as to leave the consumer as well-off as before the transaction. This slope is referred to as the marginal rate of substitution of X for Y. The assumption of diminishing marginal utility means that to surrender additional units of one product, the consumer must be compensated by ever increasing units of the other; that is, the indifference curves are convex to the origin. At point O, no X or Y is being consumed, and hence the individual receives no utility from these products. The indifference curves represent increasing levels of utility the farther they are from point O. The indifference curve U_3 represents a higher level of utility than the indifference curve U_2, which in turn represents a higher level of utility than the indifference curve U_1. To maximize satisfaction from a given income, the consumer will purchase that combination of X and Y represented by the point at which the line representing that income is tangent to an indifference curve, say at E. For any price, there is only one amount of X that is demanded

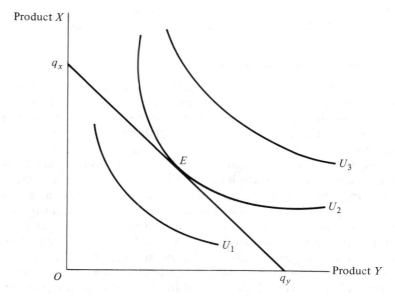

Figure 4.2. Consumer utility maximization.

by each consumer, and the point on the demand curve corresponding to this price is the sum of all of these individual amounts.

At E, the consumer's marginal rate of substitution (the slope of the indifference curve) is equal to the price ratio (the slope of the budget or income line). For our purposes, the important insight is that all consumers face the same price ratio in the market, and so the marginal rate of substitution of X for Y will be the same for all consumers. At equilibrium no alteration of consumption patterns could make consumers better off, except as a result of an income redistribution. A redistribution of income would make some better off only by making others worse off. For some consumers to shift to a higher indifference curve will mean that others must shift to a lower indifference curve. In a perfectly competitive market, each individual will decide upon his or her purchases in such a way that efficiency in the society as a whole is attained, given the income distribution. This concept of efficiency, given a certain income distribution, is often referred to as Pareto-optimality. The free-enterprise, market economy automatically leads to efficiency in consumption decisions, given the assumptions on which this analysis is based. Pareto-optimality is a very weak criterion for evaluating the well-being of a society, since it says nothing about distribution. For example, it is possible that an economy in which one person consumes everything, while the rest consume nothing, may be operating at a Pareto-optimal point. The conscious manipulation of market outcomes or the occurrence of errors could disrupt the precision of the relationships on which these analyses are based. The existence of *externalities* or *third-party effects* and of *public goods* could also add ambiguity to the uniqueness and optimality of the equilibrium, and hence could provide a rationale for collective decision making.

One could argue that a redistribution of income could enable some consumers to shift to higher indifference curves while requiring others to shift to lower indifference curves in a way that would in fact increase the consumer satisfaction or utility of society as a whole. However, theoretical analysis cannot shed much light on this issue even though it may be of great importance. Jeremy Bentham, for example, recognized that the satisfaction lost by taking away some income from those who are wealthy may be small compared to the gain in satisfaction achieved by giving the same income to those who are less prosperous.[10] Since Bentham's primary concern was to realize the "greatest good for the greatest number," one might see this as an argument for an active government redistribution of income. The utility analysis, however, had to be considered within certain constraints imposed by the market and society. Unless individuals could believe that their property was securely guaranteed, they would have little motive to attempt to acquire as much of it as possible. Economic growth, and hence a high standard of living for society as a whole, depended upon the self-interest of each individual. To pursue egalitarian distributions of income, a government would have to undermine the inspirational dynamic from which the society as a whole benefited. As a result, Bentham concluded that equality must yield to the need for the protection of the right of individuals to accumulate property.

Another argument against government redistribution emphasizes that comparisons among the indifference curves of different individuals cannot be made on the basis of theoretical assumptions. Such comparisons involve subjective judgements about how to measure the satisfaction of various individuals. To assert that the satisfaction derived from different activities is the same, or to believe some activities give more pleasure than others, one must make assumptions about individual preferences that lack objective support.

Efficiency in production

For each supplier of a product, the costs of production can be represented, as in Figure 4.3, by a relationship between units of output and

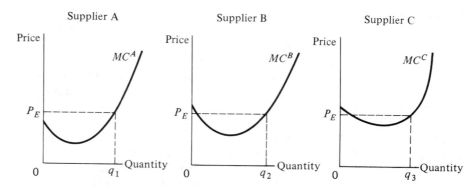

Figure 4.3. Efficiency with differences in production costs.

a unit of account, say dollars. Traditionally, such economic analysis has been based on the observation that, for each supplier, the cost of one additional unit falls for a certain range with economies of scale and then, at some point, it rises with diseconomies of scale. In order to maximize its profit, the supplier will expand production to the level at which marginal cost (MC) equals the market price (P_E). In the perfectly competitive model, there are many firms entering and exiting from the market. Each of them is a price taker in that the individual actions of one firm will not affect the market supply and hence, the market price. Consequently, each firm realizes that it will be able to sell as many units of a good as it desires at the given market price. In perfect competition, the marginal revenue function for every firm is perfectly price elastic at the market price. If the firm was producing at an output level where marginal cost was less than marginal revenue, it could increase profits by producing a greater amount. If the firm was producing at an output level where marginal cost was larger than marginal revenue and the market price, it could increase profits by producing a smaller amount. Different suppliers may face different cost configurations – as in Figure 4.3 – for many reasons. However, in the free-enterprise model, they all face the same price for the product. Consequently, in equilibrium, the marginal cost will be the same for every supplier. This means that society could not increase total output by shifting resources from one supplier to another. Each supplier makes decisions in its own self-interest, and yet society's overall production is maximized; that is, production efficiency is attained.

Implicit in Figure 4.3 is the assumption that suppliers will choose that combination of inputs which minimizes costs and so the marginal costs – which will be equal in equilibrium – cannot be reduced by altering the

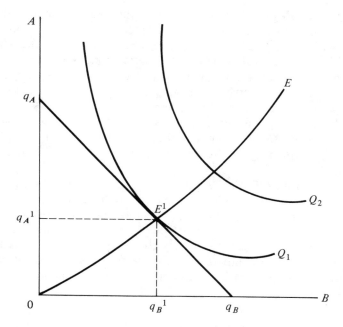

Figure 4.4. Inputs and production efficiency.

combination of inputs for any supplier. This can be demonstrated in a
manner analogous to consumer utility maximization. The ratio of prices
for inputs A and B can be portrayed by the slope of a line $q_A q_B$ in Figure
4.4. Instead of indifference curves representing points that provide equal
levels of utility, Figure 4.4 depicts isoquants (Q_1 and Q_2), representing
the various combinations of the inputs that enable the supplier to produce Q_1 and Q_2 levels of output, respectively. The farther the isoquant
is from the origin, the larger is the amount of output it represents. The
slope of the isoquant at each point on it represents the amount of A
that must be utilized to compensate for not utilizing a unit of B, so as
to leave the production level unchanged. This slope is referred to as the
marginal rate of technical substitution of A for B. The assumption of
diminishing marginal productivity means that to surrender additional
units of one input, the supplier must use ever-increasing units of the
other. That is, the isoquants are convex to the origin.

To maximize its production, the supplier must purchase inputs at a
point where their price ratio is equal to their marginal rate of technical
substitution; that is, at a point where a price-ratio line is tangent to an
isoquant. If not at such a point, the supplier could increase output at

no additional cost by simply altering the combination of inputs; that is, by moving along the price-ratio line to reach successively higher iso-quants. At the point of tangency no higher isoquant can be reached.

Unlike the consumer, however, the supplier does not face a fixed income and expenditure constraint. Rather, the supplier expands output by moving to successively higher isoquants – moving outward along OE – until the marginal cost of this movement equals the market price of the product. This equilibrium output, where price equals marginal cost, will be the level for each supplier that is depicted in Figure 4.3. For supplier A, isoquant Q_1 in Figure 4.4 represents the same output as q_1 in Figure 4.3.

At any point on OE, the supplier's marginal rate of technical substi-tution of one input for another is equal to the price ratio of the inputs. The important feature is that all suppliers face the same price ratio, and so all experience the same marginal rate of technical substitution. Given the input prices, total costs for society could not be reduced by altering the ratio of usage of the inputs by any supplier. The individual decisions of each supplier result in cost minimization and production efficiency for society as a whole.

Factor-price determination

In the free-enterprise model, the price – and consequently the income – of each factor of production is determined in the competitive market in a manner similar to that discussed in the section "Partial Equilibrium Analyses." The demand for each factor rests on the suppliers' production needs and the productivity of the factor. For any particular input, a relationship exists between the marginal product created by using more of the input and the total amount of the input that the suppliers use. In Figure 4.5, the marginal product of input A (MP_A) is assumed to de-crease as more of A is used. The supplier will increase its use of A to the point where the price of the input equals its marginal product. Since this is true for all suppliers and since they all face the same price, P_A, the marginal product of input A will be identical for all suppliers. Con-sequently, total output could not be increased by shifting amounts of A from one supplier to another; the decrease in product for the supplier losing A would exceed the increase in product for the supplier gaining more A. Again, this perspective demonstrates that individual supplier decisions will result in the maximization of society's production.

Figure 4.5 is also useful in that it provides an easily understood basis for the demand curve for an input. For any price of the input, P_A, the amount of A demanded is the sum of the individual suppliers' demands

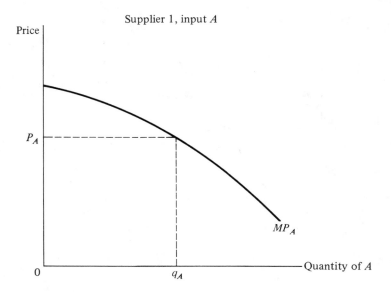

Figure 4.5. Production demand for an input.

at that price; that is, the sum of q_{A1}, q_{A2}, ..., q_{An} (say Q_A). For any other input price, the amount of A demanded can be calculated similarly. These points form the demand for the input.

For the various types of inputs, the supply curve, SS in Figure 4.6, can take many different shapes. For some inputs, supply may be unaffected by price, and so SS may be vertical. Some types of labour supply may even be backward bending. People may wish to work more when wages rise from a very low level; yet at some higher level, wage increases may result in the desire for more leisure time. Although many theoretical analyses discuss a general wage for a homogeneous labour supply, it is important and realistic to consider the elements which lead to wage differentials. Adam Smith pointed to five elements:

[F]irst, the agreeableness or disagreeableness of the employments themselves; secondly, the easiness and cheapness, or the difficulty and expense of learning them; thirdly, the constancy or inconstancy of employment in them; fourthly, the small or great trust which must be reposed in those who exercise them; and fifthly, the probability or improbability of success in them.[11]

Recent commentators generally emphasize Smith's second element, and they discuss the skills and education required in various kinds of employment, and the supply and demand for each of these levels of skills and education.

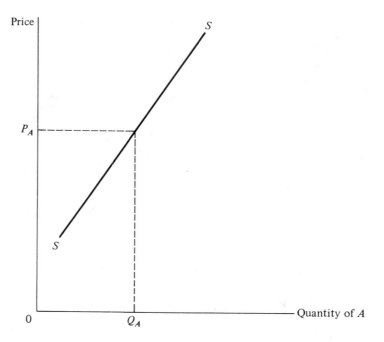

Figure 4.6. The supply of an input.

Maximizing utility over time

Individuals, as consumers, are concerned not only with utility maximization at the current moment, but rather with maximization over time. Consumers face not only a budget constraint for the current period, but rather a flow of future incomes. A variety of saving and investment techniques enable an individual to shift his or her income and consumption patterns over time. The manner in which individuals can rationally optimize their utility in this way has been analyzed by Franco Modigliani, whose *lifetime consumption hypothesis* added substantially to our understanding of how equilibrium can be attained over time by free enterprise with individual decision making.[12]

People wishing to shift current income and consumption potential towards the future create a supply of loanable funds, with the amount to be supplied dependent upon the rate of interest. Those wishing to shift their income and consumption potential to the present form a demand for loanable funds, with the amount to be demanded dependent as well on the rate of interest. A market rate of interest is determined by the intersection of the supply and demand schedules.

An important complication is that some of the demand for loanable funds comes from individuals who wish to invest the funds in business ventures. The amount that such people wish to borrow at any particular interest rate will depend upon the profitability they expect to gain from these ventures. This demand may shift dramatically over time as the business climate changes. Keynes believed, for example, that the business climate could become so hopeless that even at a negligible interest rate the investment demand for loanable funds would be insignificant.[13] Keynes concluded that this phenomenon would cause a "liquidity trap" such that monetary authorities might not be able to stimulate aggregate economic activity by expanding the money supply and lowering interest rates. In a severe depression such as the 1930s, monetary policy would therefore be of little help and governments would have to turn instead to an increase in their own expenditures in order to stimulate economic activity. Since the writing of Keynes, other economists such as Dale Jorgenson and Robert Lucas have developed sophisticated models using optimizing theory to analyze the investment decision.[14]

This demonstrates how the introduction of time to the perfectly competitive model serves to link micro theory and its analysis of individuals and firms, with macro theory and its analysis of the aggregate economy. Much debate among today's economists is concerned with the nature and implications of these linkages. Economists have devised scores of theoretically complex, mathematical models to describe these linkages and to develop conclusions about appropriate government policy based upon these models.

These models and analyses are made particularly complicated by the phenomenon of uncertainty. Uncertainty is closely related to time. Individuals as consumers cannot know for sure what their future income streams will be, or even what their future consumption preferences will be. Individuals as investors cannot know for sure what the financial outcome of their business ventures will be. Neither group can anticipate for sure what the future path of interest rates will be. Furthermore, the degree or intensity of these uncertainties may vary over time. How should one incorporate these uncertainties into an analysis of individual behaviour?

For our purposes, a very important point is that the answers to such questions about time and uncertainty lead to conclusions about the ability of free enterprise to achieve a unique and stable equilibrium on the basis of individual decision making without the intervention of government. Furthermore, they lead to important conclusions about the ability of a government to alter individual decisions through its macro policies. For example, a series of "rational expectations" analyses assumes that individuals act as if they are able to understand the impact of government macro policies. These analyses trace the manner in which individual decisions change as macro policies change. Often the conclusions are that individuals alter their behavior in ways that negate these government policies. For example, a current government deficit may be seen as requiring future tax increases, and so individuals may increase their savings to offset the deficit, with the result that the Keynesian prediction of deficits being stimulative may not hold.

Unemployment and the path towards equilibrium

Some recent work in macroeconomics, that of Robert Lucas and Thomas Sargent, for example, presents a new view of business cycle fluctuations.[15] For most of the twentieth century, business cycle fluctuations were seen as market failures. Fluctuations around the equilibrium path were viewed as representing disequilibrium. Price adjustments were related to the levels of excess demands in all markets. Since business cycle fluctuations were market failures by definition, there was clearly a role for government stabilization policy to move the economy towards equilibrium. For some of the macroeconomic theorists of the past two decades the business cycle is in fact part of the equilibrium path. Fluctuations are the result of optimal responses in competitive situations to random shocks. Thus in the absence of market failure there is no role for government policy since it is known that the competitive equilibrium is Pareto-optimal.

In his book, *The General Theory of Employment, Interest and Money*, Keynes presented the view that an economy could be in equilibrium at less than full employment. In particular, the labour market could experience forces that prevented the downward adjustment of wages. In Figure 4.7, an equilibrium wage, W_E, would exist at which the demand for labour would equal the supply of labour. In practice, wages might not fall to this equilibrium. Being stuck with wages at $\overline{W}$, the economy could experience unemployment of $L_2 - L_1$. Only active government intervention – through deficit financing – could shift the aggregate demand schedule from D_1D_1 to D_2D_2 to achieve full employment.

Many of today's economists have focused on labour-market adjustment problems, some seeing them as a rationale for government intervention. Writers such as Robert Hall have emphasized the tendency of contracts and other long-term economic arrangements to hinder the adjustment of wages and prices.[16] Others have concentrated on the difficulties of matching jobs and workers, particularly when an individ-

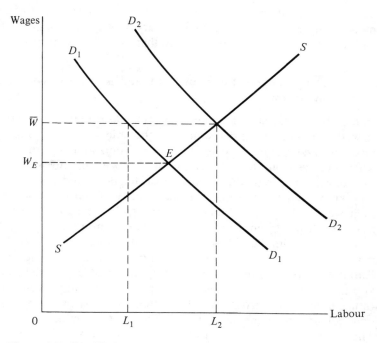

Figure 4.7. Equilibrium in the labour market.

ual's information is limited about future job availabilities and skill requirements, and is also limited about the educational process whereby
one can attain the requisite skills. Changes in methods of production –
resulting from technological progress or new trade patterns – can make
traditional skills obsolete, and unemployment may result for the workers
affected by such changes. Some see such situations as requiring government assistance for these workers to learn more appropriate skills
and, perhaps, to move from a depressed region to an area with more
job prospects. The importance of such migration in the adjustment
process has been emphasized by many authors. Some of these have
noted that government programs designed to assist those who have been
hurt by economic change may have the unintended effect of retarding
the migration that is a necessary part of the adjustment process.

The nature of the path towards equilibrium is an important characteristic of free enterprise. Some regard the difficulties encountered on
the path as so severe that they form significant shortcomings of this
model. As described already in the section on partial equilibrium analysis, the path may not even be a direct route, but rather may entail

oscillations of both price and output. Meanwhile, the alternative decision modes can be seen as attempting, in varying ways and degrees, to deal with these issues more appropriately than does free enterprise.

The achievement of growth: Incentives to work, innovate, and invest

In the above analysis, an underlying principle is that individuals (firms as well as people) make decisions with the objective of maximizing their incomes. The various aspects of utility maximization and the efficiency which derives from them depend upon this principle. Closely related is the concept that individuals work most diligently and effectively when they know that their income will be directly affected by the results of their work. Many observers of free enterprise emphasize this concept as one of its most important attributes. Furthermore, many suggest that innovation is stimulated when the innovator stands to gain or lose in a material sense from the introduction of a new process or a new product. Entrepreneurship is touted by the proponents of this model as being a key factor in economic growth and productivity improvements. The future success and prosperity of the economy is seen to be dependent on the degree to which innovation and entrepreneurship are stimulated. The amount and pattern of investment is also seen to be dependent on the material reward to private investors. Many technological innovations require new machinery and equipment. This need for innovations to be *embodied* in production facilities emphasizes the importance of private investment. Apart from this aspect, more investment may be necessary simply to provide additional jobs if the labour force is growing. Proponents of this model emphasize that individual decision making with the objective of income maximization will stimulate more work, innovation, and investment than could other decision modes.

From this perspective, it is important to minimize the role of collective decision making, and it is also important to minimize the taxation of individual success and the subsidization of individual failure. Many contemporary writers have developed this argument in the context of current public policies. On a popular level, George Gilder's books, *Wealth and Poverty* and *The Spirit of Enterprise,* provide anecdotal evidence concerning the experiences of a variety of countries.[17] Robert Bacon and Walter Eltis develop a more detailed and thorough examination in *Britain's Economic Problem: Too Few Producers.*[18] In this book, they stress unfortunate negative implications of the substantial growth of the British government's involvement in the economy, the rise of the British welfare system, and the consequent increase in British tax rates.

Arthur Laffer has gained fame through his presentation of what has come to be called "the Laffer curve."[19] A tax rate of zero will yield government revenue of zero, and so will a tax rate of 100 percent. In between – as the tax rate is increased – government revenue will first rise, reach a peak, and then fall. When governments are in the latter phase, a tax cut could actually increase total revenue. This concept underlay President Reagan's *supply-side* tax cuts of 1981, and some have pointed to the consequent U.S. economic recovery as evidence of the positive response of individuals to financial incentives.

Liberty and equality of opportunity

Hayek has warned that the twentieth-century shift away from free enterprise has necessarily meant a movement along *The Road to Serfdom.*[20] Other decision modes lead inevitably to a loss of personal freedom and also to political totalitarianism. With free enterprise, individuals enjoy a full range of freedom to choose among occupations and among acquisitions. With other decision modes, many of these choices are made by society's representatives, and individual liberty is thereby restricted. Hayek emphasizes that "the power conferred by the control of production and prices is almost unlimited."[21] In a chapter entitled "Why the Worst Get on Top," Hayek argues that this power will automatically fall into the hands of "the unscrupulous and uninhibited."[22]

In their book *Free to Choose,* Milton and Rose Friedman also focus on personal liberty.

An essential part of economic freedom is freedom to choose how to use our income: how much to spend on ourselves and on what items; how much to save and in what form; how much to give away and to whom.
Another essential part of economic freedom is freedom to use the resources we possess in accordance with our own values – freedom to enter any occupation, engage in any business enterprise, buy and sell to anyone else, so long as we do so on a strictly voluntary basis and do not resort to force in order to coerce others.[23]

In a chapter entitled "Created Equal," they claim that equality of opportunity is part of this economic freedom. However, the imposition of an equality of outcome strongly conflicts with the objective of liberty. The process of redistributing incomes to attain greater justice or fairness limits individual freedom, and it encourages people to alter their behaviour in undesirable ways.

Some argue that, with free enterprise, individuals do not enjoy real liberty because they can be exploited as consumers and as employees.

The Friedmans express confidence that individuals are protected as consumers by the existence of alternative products and by their freedom to choose. Individuals are also protected as employees by the existence of alternative employers; the competition among employers will ensure that each employee is paid the full value for work.

William Simon, in his book *A Time for Truth,* focuses on what he terms "the cancerous growth of government and its steady devouring of our citizens' productive energies."[24] Simon emphasizes that "political and economic freedom are inextricably related,"[25] and so the shift away from free enterprise inevitably reduces both political and economic freedom. He presents as a basic principle "that government planning and regulation of the economy will ultimately lead to shortages, crises, and if not reversed in time, some form of economic dictatorship."[26]

Consumption inefficiencies

Much of the theoretical analysis of free enterprise rests on the assumption that each individual is completely knowledgeable about the characteristics of each product and about the degree to which these characteristics can provide him or her with satisfaction or utility. The individual is able to compare this satisfaction among alternative prospective purchases. And the individual is able to do so for varying amounts of each; that is, he or she can make comparisons among marginal utilities that will be provided by varying the amounts of each. Furthermore, the individual is able to make wise judgements on the basis of this knowledge. These assumptions about the rationality of consumers are complicated by the nature of time and uncertainty. Consumers must compare these marginal utilities over future time periods which they cannot predict with certainty, and they must make wise judgements among alternative consumption patterns over time. Although different individuals may have different preferences among products and over time, the assumptions are that each individual arrives at his or her decisions concerning purchasing, and saving or borrowing, in a rational manner. Uncertainty may enter these decisions and expectations may not be precisely fulfilled, but the decisions are based on a conscious evaluation of some probability distribution of outcomes.

Some observers reject free enterprise because they are not satisfied with the concept of consumer rationality. Individuals do not, in general, possess much information about the vast array of potential purchases in a modern economy. The prices and qualities of alternative products from alternative suppliers are too numerous and complex for consumers to make their purchases in a rational manner. This difficulty is increased by advertising, through which consumers become the pawns of the media, responding blindly to the repetitious nonsense of continual commercials. Apart from this lack of accurate information, consumers are unable to make wise choices. They are concerned with their social status, and they strive to keep up with the material acquisitions of their friends and neighbours. In this mad pursuit of each other's social recognition, they stampede after particular designs that have momentarily caught the public's fancy. In deciding upon purchases that obviously affect one's health, many indulge in alcohol, drugs, and tobacco to a degree that demonstrates their irrationality.

John Kenneth Galbraith has written a classic commentary on the irrationality of consumers. In *The Affluent Society,* he casts doubts both on the adequacy of product information and also on the wisdom of individuals.[27] His solution is to shift a large portion of consumption decisions out of the hands of individuals and into the hands of government. Implicit in Galbraith's argument is the opinion that a wise elite can make better choices than can the mass of individuals. Apart from this consumer irrationality, Galbraith points to particular goods and services that, in his opinion, cannot readily be consumed individually. He believes that a significant portion of society's productive capacity should be shifted to such goods and services. Parks, education, and a cleaner environment should form a much larger share of society's consumption. For this to occur, the decisions about consumption must be shifted from individuals to society as a whole.

Some products cannot be easily consumed on an individual basis. Private arrangements can provide for joint consumption of some products. The family unit permits much joint consumption, and the free market can result in large groups coming together for entertainment and recreation. Nevertheless, some goods or services may have characteristics that make such private contractual arrangements unrealistic in practice. In such cases, free enterprise may fail to result in an optimal pattern of consumption. For such *public goods,* it is not enough for consumers to be rational in order for efficiency to be attained.

A host of writers have focused on particular types of consumption decisions and have advocated various modifications of free enterprise in order to improve these particular decisions. Many modifications will be discussed in the context of the alternative decision-making modes. Government price setting has been implemented for some products in order to alter the quantities that will be purchased by consumers. Subsidies and tax concessions have been provided to encourage suppliers to increase production. Regulations have sought to control product safety and quality and to ensure moderation in the consumption of some products. Regulations in the form of rationing and quotas can interfere directly in the consumption of certain products. Public enterprise can provide some products at market prices other than those that would evolve under free enterprise. Detailed central planning can enable the centralization of all consumption decisions and the allocation of all products by government directives. A society can deal with different products differently, in each case adhering to the decision mode which it believes is most appropriate for the particular product. It is even possible that the overall consumption–saving decision can be altered through the provision of subsidies and tax concessions for additional saving and investment, or through the imposition of consumption taxes. The rate of saving and investment may perhaps be raised, without adopting the Stalinist extreme of the command model.

Production inefficiencies

Economists point to several types of market failure that, in practice, interfere with the attainment of efficiency. The production conditions of some products may be such that the marginal cost declines over the relevant output range. In such cases, a single supplier will be able to produce at an average cost that will be lower than that of any potential new entrant. The creation of a new product or process can also be the cause of monopoly. Not threatened with competition, the solitary producer will be able to set prices above the marginal cost. Less than the socially optimal amount will be produced and consumed, and society would be better off if it could shift more resources into the production of such items. From society's perspective, this distortion of the production and consumption pattern creates an inefficiency. This distortion inefficiency is, in addition to the distortion of income distribution, caused by the monopoly profits which transfer income from consumers of the product to the monopolist.

Some commentators believe that these distortions are commonplace in today's world. In most sectors only one or, perhaps, a few producers supply the bulk of the product. John Kenneth Galbraith, in his book *The New Industrial State,* has presented this view forcefully.[28] Many others have attempted to calculate the percentage of each product supplied by the few largest firms. These *concentration ratios* do not by themselves indicate the degree of distortion actually created, but they do serve as warnings of potential distortion.

Other commentators feel that the threat of potential competition is enough to prevent distortions. The existing firms, although few in number, are aware that if they set prices above their marginal costs others will see this profit opportunity and enter the market. Consequently, the fact that a market is supplied by only a few firms does not negate the efficiency of the competitive model. This view is strengthened by the potential for international trade. Foreign firms are already operating and are able to export to any economy where monopolists or oligopolists are charging excessive prices. Furthermore, it can be argued that modern technology is able to create substitutes for most products and that excessively high prices will stimulate this. Monopoly or oligopoly situations are constrained in that the dominance of a few firms will only be temporary, with substitute products always a possibility. Faced with this, any small group of producers will be restrained in their price-setting decisions.

The impact of inadequate investment on growth

A society's growth and its future prospects for jobs and wealth depend upon its saving and investment. It may be seen as too risky to leave these determinants of the future in the hands of the individual members of the society. With free enterprise, wide fluctuations may develop in saving and investment, leading to unacceptable business cycles. For some societies, the greatest criticism is that individual decisions may not result in enough saving and investment to propel the economy fast enough. The pace of economic development may be unacceptably slow.

The rapid growth rate of the Soviet Union under Stalin's leadership was the result of an extremely high rate of saving and investment. In 1928, Stalin rejected the competitive framework of the New Economic Policy (NEP) and adopted a system of detailed central planning. This command structure of the 1928–53 period enabled Stalin to escalate the rate of saving and investment. His central concern was not efficiency in production and consumption, but rather the creation of new factories and equipment. Collectivization of agriculture resulted in a decrease in total agricultural output, but it permitted an increase in compulsory levies and in the amount of goods available in the cities. Hence a larger industrial labour force could be supported in the drive to industrialization. Leaders in other nations who have wanted to achieve similarly high rates of growth have also sometimes rejected free enterprise in favour of a system under which they could enforce a higher rate of saving and investment than that which would result from individual decisions. It is true that foreign investment may fill a gap caused by inadequate domestic saving. However, as we shall see in Chapter 11, foreign investment can bring with it certain undesirable features. Consequently, many societies wish to restrict their reliance on foreign capital in their growth process.

The need for collective intervention to stimulate innovation and adjustment

In the context of new technology and international competitiveness, the need to stimulate innovation and adjustment will acquire a new urgency. The ability of a society as a whole to attract desirable types of new technology and well-paying jobs will depend increasingly on the qualifications of the labour force. Rapid and significant changes in products and production technology mean that employee skills and education quickly become outmoded. Retraining will become increasingly necessary if employees are to shift into new occupations, with new products and processes. Otherwise, rising unemployment will place an ever greater burden on society as a whole. Yet, for the individual, the necessary education and retraining may cost more than one can afford. Furthermore, greater job mobility means that corporations will not invest in their employees' education as much as would be socially optimal because of the risk of losing the employees and the educational investment.

Although the empirical evidence about the relationships between research and growth is not extensive, it clearly indicates that external benefits do occur as a result of private research. Scherer investigated the annual rate of return in the United States from R&D expenditure occurring to downstream users of intermediate goods, and he found it to be about 100 percent.[29] Mansfield, Romeo, and Wagner surveyed seventeen "undramatic, run-of-the-mill" process and product innovations. They estimated the median private rate of return to the innovators to be 25 percent, whereas the median social rate of return was 56 percent. For 30 percent of the innovations studied, the private rate of return was too low to justify the investment effort even though the social rate of return was high.[30] With both education and research, the inability of the corporation or individual to capture these external benefits means that government funding may be necessary in order that the socially optimal levels will be provided.

Wonnacott has pointed out that natural resources are not typically an important factor in the development of new technology industries.[31] Moreover, the capital requirements are generally available because of the increasing international mobility of capital. Technology and a highly trained and skilled workforce have become the critical considerations. Government can engineer a comparative advantage in new technology products by providing an infrastructure conducive to its development and application through appropriate research and education policy. Wonnacott suggests that the advantages conferred on the first country to develop a product may overcome other disadvantages and permit the "first-in" country to enjoy the benefits of market power. Brander and Spencer show that this last point is significant for political entities considering the use of subsidies to optimize their interests vis-á-vis other political entities.[32] The decision to pursue the development of new technology industries by the Ministry of International Trade and Investment (MITI) in Japan is often cited as an example of a successful effort to engineer a comparative advantage.

Recent extensions of free enterprise

Each society has some activities where ownership and operation is left to individuals, as well as other activities where concerns about individual decision making have led to collective decision modes. In recent years, the opinions of many have been changing in regard to the relative advantages and shortcomings of these alternative modes for economic decision making. Throughout the world, some political leaders won electoral victory in the 1980s on a platform advocating an extension of free enterprise to cover activities that had previously been subject to various forms of collective decision making. Here it is sufficient to refer to some broad movements, each of which includes a new emphasis on the attributes of free enterprise.

In 1979, Margaret Thatcher led the British Conservatives to form a new government based upon this philosophy. Early Thatcher programs included the privatization of government-owned industries, the sale of government-owned "council" housing to the tenants, and the reduction of subsidies to businesses. Martin Holmes, in his book, *The First Thatcher Government, 1979–1983*, describes Thatcher's position in the following words:

A central and important tenet of Mrs. Thatcher's conservatism was the emphasis put on the use of markets and free enterprise to produce and distribute goods and services wanted by consumers. Furthermore, the rolling back of the state and the ending of the socialist ratchet effect decreed not only an encouragement of the existing private sector but its expansion.[33]

In the United States, the term *Reagan Revolution* is frequently used to refer to a set of policies aimed at reducing the role of government and extending the areas of individual decision making. President Reagan advocated a reduction in the amount of government regulation as well as cuts in nondefense spending, especially social programs. He sought to stimulate individual effort and entrepreneurship by decreasing marginal tax rates and thereby ensuring greater material incentives. "Reaganomics," as it came to be known, was based on the "supply-side" view that full employment and maximum growth would be achieved through this reliance on free enterprise. To the degree that government intervention was necessary, it should be determined at the state and local levels as much as possible. These levels are more sensitive to citizens' wishes than is the federal government, and these wishes may be different in the various areas of the country. In implementing these policies, differences arose between campaign rhetoric, Presidential proposals, and actual legislation. Considerable disagreement exists today over the degree to which the Reagan objectives were actually achieved, and whether the Reagan era really was a "revolution." Nevertheless, the Reagan advocacy of the free-enterprise, competitive model did represent an important point in public debate over the appropriate role for collective *versus* individual decision making.[34]

The 1980s have also seen a major shift in the dominant economic philosophy within China. Rural reforms have included the dismantling of the commune system, the expansion of private plots, and the proliferation of free markets for agricultural produce. Decisions in regard to what to produce and how to produce it have been transferred from the planning apparatus to those actually involved at the farm level. Within industry as well, the reforms have emphasized a greater reliance on the market instead of administrative planning, a decentralization of decision making to the individual enterprises, and an expansion of material incentives.[35]

In the Soviet Union, Mikhail Gorbachev has led a similar movement. Direct negotiations between economic enterprises give greater scope to the market concept, and result in individual contracts rather than the traditional central planning. Decentralized responsibility is encouraged through requirements for self-financing rather than reliance on government allocations. Gorbachev has stated that production should be more closely geared to consumer preferences, and wages should depend upon economic performance.

It is especially important to give enterprises and organizations greater autonomy in the sphere of consumer goods, manufacture and services. Their task is to react quickly to consumer demand. It is along these lines that we are reshaping the economic mechanism of light industry. The range of targets approved from above is being sharply limited for enterprises in this sphere; their plans will be drawn chiefly on the basis of contracts with trade organizations, which, in turn, must see to it that their orders conform to the actual consumer demand.[36]

These features of Gorbachev's reform movement will result in an increasing reliance on the market rather than on central planners. Nevertheless, it is quite likely that this movement will be relevant for only certain sectors. In particular, individual preferences may impact the allocation of consumption goods and services more directly, while other industries may be much less affected. Consequently, although consumption efficiency may be improved, production efficiency may not be altered significantly. Furthermore, it is likely that Gorbachev's reforms will leave the setting of most prices as a responsibility of planners. This limitation of the market's role, and the likely impact on efficiency of the price-control model, is the subject to which we turn in Chapter 5.

Appendix

Marx's critique of free enterprise

In his writings, Karl Marx discussed many reasons why the equilibrium and optimality predicted for free enterprise would not be achieved. In order to appreciate Marx's criticisms, it may be helpful to place his comments in the context of other economic literature.

Some economists, such as Leontief and Chenery, have suggested that a production function with fixed input coefficients may present a useful approximation of reality.[37] Samuelson and Hicks have emphasized that a fixed capital–output ratio results in an accelerator which can lead to business cycles when combined with the Keynesian multiplier.[38] Many writers have stressed that technological progress is intimately connected with investment. These concepts conflict at many points with ideas underlying much classical and neoclassical writing. They conflict because they present an alternative view of the production process. Many implications of this alternative view were first seen by Marx. In fact, Marx's writings can best be understood in the context of this alternative view of the production process.

In such a Leontief system, with given technology there is one preferred set of input ratios which will continue to be preferred no matter what the desired bill of final consumption happens to be.... Remember that everything is congealed labour in a Leontief system. Hence, when you raise wages you are raising the cost of machines by the same proportion. Even if technical substitutability is possible, there will be no actual substitution because there will be no change in the relative prices of any factors.[39]

A two-input isoquant emphasizes the difference between the fixed coefficient case (Figure 4.8) and the classical case (Figure 4.9). To un-

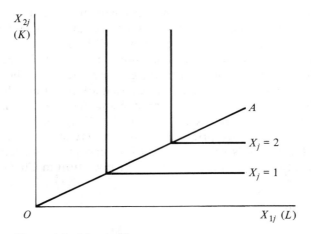

Figure 4.8. Marxian isoquants.

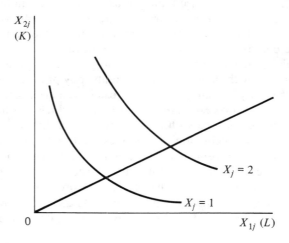

Figure 4.9. Classical isoquants.

derstand Marx's analysis, it may be helpful to assume that input X_{1j} is labour (L) and X_{2j} is capital (K).

Marx's predictions concerning income distribution can be understood in the context of Leontief production functions. In such a system, "Relative prices of commodities will depend only on their direct and indirect labour content."[40] In Figure 4.10, we see the marginal physical product of labour MPP_L, so long as all economic activities require a fixed capital–labour ratio, there are no scale economies, and there is a fixed supply

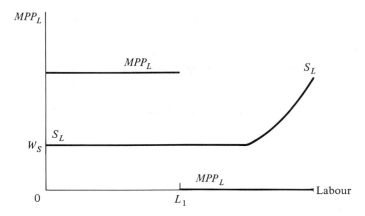

Figure 4.10. The Marxian marginal product of labour.

of capital. The supply of labour is represented by $S_L S_L$ and wages are expressed in units of output. We should note that Marx rejected the Malthusian belief that $S_L S_L$ is infinitely elastic at the subsistence wage because of population growth. Given the Leontief production function, the Malthusian prediction of population growth is not necessary in order for wages to rest continually at the subsistence level W_S.

Suppose that when capital is fully utilized, L_1 of labour is employed. The marginal physical product of labour is indeterminate, and this opens the possibility of conflict in wage determination rather than the classical competitive solution. Moreover, it is quite likely that $S_L S_L$ is of such a shape that extra workers desire, but cannot find employment. The reserve army of the unemployed can exist.

Prior to the industrial revolution, the amount of capital required to open an economic enterprise was relatively small. Many employees did manage to accumulate capital and open their own businesses. Given this possibility of self-employment, the wage conflict and the reserve army of unemployed might not be significant. The Leontief production function may offer this possibility, if capital is seen to be infinitely divisible. For Marx's predictions to hold, we must add the requirement that technological change continually increases the minimum necessary amount of capital for each type of production activity.

Recently, many economists have emphasized that a particular technology may be built into each piece of capital equipment; and, for improvements to occur in the production process, investment in new equipment may be necessary. The isoquants in Figure 4.8 may shift up or down, but in general their cost-minimizing points must be above

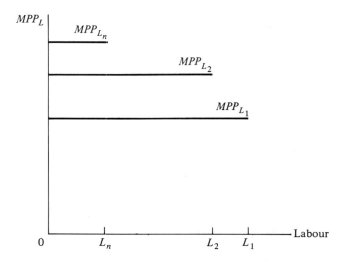

Figure 4.11. Marxian marginal product of labour with technological progress.

the ever-rising ray OA, where OA is the ray joining the current cost-minimizing points on the isoquants. The marginal physical product of labour in Figure 4.11 continually shifts from MPP_{L1} towards MPP_{Ln}. Given the indivisibility of capital and the nature of technological change, the natural evolution of capitalism can affect the income and employment implications of a Leontief production function in the manner Marx predicted. The reserve army of unemployed can steadily increase in size; the plight of employees can steadily worsen; and the conflict over wage determination can become increasingly bitter. At any point in time, constant returns to scale may exist; yet the minimum size, in terms of capital requirement, of each type of economic enterprise will steadily increase. Economies of scale in this dynamic sense can cause an increasing tendency towards big business and monopoly.

This Marxian analysis begins with a pure labour theory of value where prices depend only on their direct and indirect labour content. With capital-embodied technological change, however, actual prices may deviate from such a value pattern. Consider two pieces of equipment with the same direct and indirect labour content but produced on different dates. One is necessary for an improved production process, whereas the other is geared towards an older technique. Clearly, they will not exchange at the same price. Dynamic economies of scale and monopolistic situations based on them present another reason why relative prices in the real world might not depend upon the labour embodied.

If all output other than wages is referred to as profit, then it would appear that additional investment without technological progress would not necessarily alter the profit rate. As long as $S_L S_L$ is parallel to the labour axis, investment will increase aggregate capital, wages, and profit by the same percent. This will be true, however, only if the extra output so produced can be sold at the previous price. This possibility deserves further examination. In the light of Keynesian theory, it may be reasonable to assume that the marginal propensity to consume is a decreasing function of income and that the multiplier is a relevant concept. With the Leontief production function, the capital–output ratio is constant except for the influence of technological change; and a constant capital–output ratio makes the accelerator a relevant concept. The possibility of business cycles is now apparent.

From the perspective of Marx's writings, an argument could be made that with the evolution of free enterprise, the marginal propensity to consume will fall. With technological change, the same quantity of output is produced using more capital and less labour than previously used. The wage bill for this output may fall, and total profit may increase. A larger percentage of society's output tends to go to the owners of capital and a smaller percentage tends to go to the employees. If owners of capital have a smaller marginal propensity to consume than workers because of their higher income, then society's propensity to consume, and hence the multiplier, will tend to fall as time passes.

Let us assume that the capital–output ratio will continually increase; that is, technological change shifts the isoquants of Figure 4.8 upwards or up and to the left. The capital goods sector will have to increase at a more rapid pace than the consumer goods sector.

Suppose $I_t = v(Y_{t-1} - Y_{t-2})$ and $C_t = c_1 (Y_{t-1}) + c_2 (Y_{t-2})$, where I is investment, Y is income, C is consumption, c is the marginal propensity to consume, v is the marginal capital–output ratio, and subscripts refer to time.

R. G. D. Allen's diagram, Figure 4.12, illustrates the relationship between the marginal propensity to save, S, and the *reduced investment coefficient w*, where $w = v - c_2$.[41]

A continually rising S and a continually rising w make the economic system increasingly explosive. An increasing w with a constant S would reduce the oscillatory tendencies. The fact that both increase suggests that business cycles will continue and may increase in intensity. Private enterprises will spend an increasing proportion of their time operating with equipment that is not fully utilized because of the marketing problem of an economic depression. Here we see a tendency for the rate of profit to fall.

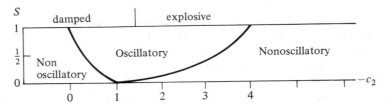

Figure 4.12. Business cycles under alternative assumptions.

Kaldor has emphasized that an essential difference between Ricardian and Marxian theory is that "Marx paid no attention to (and did not believe in) the Law of Diminishing Returns."[42] For Marx, the marginal product of an input does not decline steadily as more of it is combined with a constant amount of other inputs. Marx did not believe in the classical or neoclassical production function. What did he believe about the production function? Joan Robinson has commented, "This assumption is not stated explicitly, but it is taken for granted that, in a given state of technique, there is only one amount of labour that a given amount of capital will employ."[43] Given this assumption, the isoquants are shaped like those in Figure 4.8 rather than those in Figure 4.9 and the marginal physical product of labour can be represented by MPP_L in Figure 4.10.

In Marx's opinion, will technological change raise the capital–labour ratio? Robinson has commented, "Marx takes the view that there is on balance a strong tendency for capital per man to increase as time goes by."[44] She also states, "In Marx's view, technical knowledge is not an independent factor, and when accumulation is rapid a strong stimulus is applied to labour-saving invention."[45] Fred Gottheil has claimed,

Marx defines the state of technology by the "organic composition of capital," a ratio measuring the proportion of total capital expenditures on production that is fixed in machinery, physical plants, and raw materials. Marx's formulation of labour displacement due to the application of higher forms of technology, or increasing competition of capital, under conditions of constant capital outlay, can be expressed by:

$$IRA = K_1 [(c/K)_2 - (c/K)_1] \, w,^{46}$$

where K_1 is total capital outlay, $(c/K)_1$ and $(c/K)_2$ are the organic compositions of capital before and after technological change, w is the prevailing wage rate, and IRA gives the change in the industrial reserve army. Marx believed, then, that the capital–labour ratio is fixed in the short run but that technological progress tends to raise it. Marx also felt that because of modern technology a minimum amount of capital is necessary to open an economic enterprise and the necessary minimum is increasing as technology advances. This feeling is illustrated in quotations such as the following:

The lower strata of the middle class – the small tradespeople, shopkeepers, and retired tradesmen generally, the handicraftsmen and peasants – all these sink gradually into the proletariat, partly because their diminutive capital does not suffice for the scale on which Modern Industry is carried on, and is swamped in the competition with the large capitalists, partly because their specialised skill is rendered worthless by new methods of production.[47]

As Robinson's chapter on "Effective Demand" demonstrates, Marx did appreciate the importance of aggregate demand in affecting the business cycle. As indicated above, Marx believed that the marginal propensity to save would increase over time. In addition, the fixed capital–output ratio was part of his fixed input-coefficient assumption. As Figure 4.12 indicates, the only way we can support Marx's prediction of an ever-increasing severity in the cycle is to assume that the capital–output ratio increases over time. This assumption is consistent with Marx's emphasis that the capital goods sector must expand more rapidly than the consumer goods sector. In the 1940s, Schumpeter wrote, "The fact is that he had no simple theory of business cycles. And none can be made to follow logically from his laws of the capitalist process."[48] Yet an essential part of Marx's analysis was the belief in the continuance and increasing severity of the business cycle. An advantage of the above analysis of Marx's writings is that the basis for his theory of the business cycle becomes more apparent.

Marx's prediction of a continually falling rate of profit does not fit into this analysis except through the increasing severity of business cycles. We are forced to agree with Joan Robinson that "however we interpret it, Marx's argument fails to establish a presumption that the rate of profit tends to fall, when the problem of effective demand is left out of account."[49] In theory, capital accumulation without technological progress could increase employment, from L_1 to L_2 to L_n, as Figure 4.13 illustrates. It may even raise wages above the range between the horizontal S_L and MPP_L. For Marx's dire predictions to hold, this employment created by capital accumulation without labour-saving technological progress must be less than the unemployment created by capital accumulation with labour-saving technological progress. Marx predicted,

The unceasing improvement of machinery, ever more rapidly developing, makes their [the workers'] livelihood more and more precarious; the collisions between

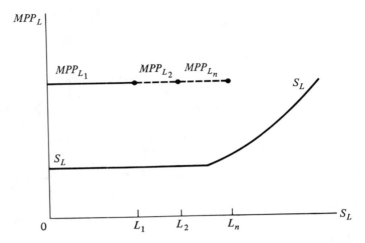

Figure 4.13. The impact of capital accumulation without technological progress.

individual workmen and individual bourgeois take more and more the character of collisions between two classes.[50]

In the immiserization process, technological change is the motivating force, and it is "ever more rapidly developing."[51]

Writing in 1941, Robinson saw that Marx envisaged a world with Leontief-type production functions. "He assumes that, with given technical knowledge, there is only one possible combination of labour with capital in each industry." She commented, "This makes his analysis appear somewhat primitive."[52] Since Robinson wrote this, however, a substantial body of economic analysis has been based upon versions of this assumption. In 1941, Robinson pointed to similarities between Kalecki's trade-cycle theory and that of Marx. Today, the Leontief production function and the Samuelson–Hicks multiplier–accelerator approach have become embedded in countless journal articles.

The field is less clear when we turn to technological change. Phelps has commented that "[i]nvestment has been married to technology. . . . Now investment is prized as the carrier of technological progress."[53] The precise form of the marriage between investment and technology is open to dispute, however. Marx's key assumptions in this regard must remain as unsubstantiated perceptions. In 1962, Abramovitz commented, "we are indeed, just at the beginning of serious work on the subject of economic growth in the United States."[54] In spite of substantial analysis of this subject since Abramovitz's comments, these issues remain unclear.

No doubt some industries in the nineteenth century operated along the type of production function envisaged in the above assumptions, and Marx based his thinking upon them. Bitter labour disputes occurred in such industries. Wages could be increased without any decrease in employment; that is, a conflict could raise real wages. Wages were not kept down by features of the production process alone, but also by the process of wage negotiation. In a real sense, a class struggle was involved; one that involved more than the free-enterprise features of the marketplace. The depression of wages to W_s in Figure 4.10, instead of their establishment at a higher level, could be regarded as a type of ruthless exploitation, rather than the receipt by workers of their marginal product. Marx expected industry to move increasingly towards production functions of this type.

In considering free enterprise, Marx's writings are a useful focus. They suggest many reasons why a full-employment, optimal equilibrium may not automatically be attained, and some of these hypotheses or perceptions have also been expressed by modern-day economists. From this Marxian perspective, collective decision making may be necessary in order to improve upon the outcomes of free enterprise.

Essay and discussion topics

1. Compare the extent of free enterprise within two or more economic systems. For each system, indicate the relationship between the reliance on free enterprise and the attainment of the society's objectives.
2. For two or more economic systems, compare a particular economic activity where free enterprise is a prominent organizational model. Indicate the advantages and shortcomings of free enterprise as illustrated by this economic activity.
3. Discuss the role of free enterprise within Gorbachev's reform program.
4. Evaluate Marx's critique of free enterprise.

CHAPTER 5

Price controls

Introduction

With free enterprise, prices are determined in the market through negotiations between buyers and sellers. Many have criticized this process and have advocated a decision mode in which prices are determined collectively, while production and consumption decisions remain decentralized. Arguments in favour of price controls can rest upon one or more of the society's objectives discussed in Chapters 2 and 3, and can be supported by the various criticisms of free enterprise presented in Chapter 4.

A market structure with only a few participants can result in prices that are not socially optimal from the perspective of efficiency. Most frequently, perhaps, this argument for price controls is directed towards monopolies. This efficiency argument can also underlie the rationale for wage controls in cases where unions may be exerting monopoly pressure, or it can underlie the rationale for a general wage and price control program.

Certain market prices may be subject to pressure from imported goods and services. International trade can result in domestic price ratios that retard the growth of certain sectors. Throughout modern history, many societies have wished to ensure prosperous industrial and agricultural sectors. Tariffs have frequently been imposed to raise domestic prices above the level they would otherwise attain, as a means of stimulating the growth of these sectors. Often this has rested upon an "infant industry" argument, that, after a time, the protected activity can grow to a size where it can be competitive internationally, and then tariffs may no longer be needed.

The concept of liberty as freedom from exploitation can lead to concerns about people paying excessive prices as consumers, and also to concerns about people receiving inadequate wages as employees. From this perspective, the efficiency arguments in regard to market structure may be joined by arguments in terms of social justice and fairness. In particular, many communist societies have rejected a general reliance on market prices, including interest rates and rents, because of a conviction that most, or all, such prices entail exploitation. The equality objective has often led to a belief that everyone should have equal access to certain goods, and that for these goods, prices should be kept at a lower level than a free market would establish. Some argue, for example, that the poor should have equal access to housing, and that this should be achieved through rent controls. Also, inflation may be seen as disrupting production and consumption plans in a manner that is arbitrary and unfair.

Any one of these arguments may be considered sufficient to justify the adoption of the price-control model. The degree to which each argument is believed to be correct or significant may vary from one observer to another, and from one product to another. Changes in production technology, demand conditions, or income levels may alter the perceived significance of each of these arguments. Consequently, it is not surprising that each society has adopted this model for different groups of products. For each society, the extent to which this model has been considered appropriate has varied over time. In practice, the objectives underlying the adoption of price controls have often not been achieved to the degree that was expected. Furthermore, price controls can lead to a number of significant problems. Distortions may develop, and inefficiencies may become severe. Quality may deteriorate. Innovation may be retarded. Referring to price controls in capitalist societies, Gary Becker has commented that "[p]rice controls are almost always rationalized, at least in part, as a desire to help the poor, yet it is remarkable how frequently they harm the poor."[1] This chapter examines the arguments that support adoption of this model, and it also analyzes some of the difficulties that can accompany it.

Oskar Lange and Fred Taylor in their book, *On the Economic Theory of Socialism,* argue that government planners can easily set prices so as to achieve efficiency.[2] The key, in their opinion, is for the planners simply to observe whether surpluses or shortages exist, and then to lower prices in the former cases and raise them in the latter cases. With firms instructed to maximize their profits, the neoclassical efficiency conditions discussed in Chapter 4 would be attained. This chapter emphasizes that the process described by Lange and Taylor may not operate as smoothly as they predict. Central planners may not be able to discern shortages or surpluses easily. Once a society has abandoned market prices, shortages may be particularly difficult to perceive. Not all products would be associated with readily observable queues. If tuition fees for educational institutions are set centrally, for example, and if they are set below market prices, then how can one predict the number of students who really want to attend at that price? The rationing process – requiring higher grades in this example – may blur the existence of a shortage of educational facilities.

Central planners also have little guidance as to demand and supply conditions at other possible price levels. Hence it is not clear how much they should alter their established prices if they discern a shortage or surplus. If tuition fees are set centrally, what process could reveal how many students would have wanted to attend at a higher or lower tuition level? If government sets ceilings on residential rents, then new construction will be reduced. How many new units would have been built at other rent levels? The details concerning demand and supply for a wide price range involve substantial information which planners cannot easily obtain. To predict the appropriate direction for price changes is not enough if distortions caused by inappropriate prices are serious or if considerable time must elapse between the changes in prices.

An important issue ignored by Lange and Taylor is the ability of producers to modify the quality of their products in the face of centrally determined prices. Quality deterioration may frustrate planners' wishes and prevent the attainment of production and consumption optimality. Another significant issue ignored by the authors is the impact of prices on innovation. Public servants responsible for setting prices cannot readily provide for, or encourage, innovations that could improve quality or reduce costs.

Lange believes that producers can be instructed to expand production to the point at which their marginal costs equal the product price. That is, he believes that producers in a situation of centrally determined prices can make production decisions in the same fashion as capitalist profit-maximizing firms. However, concern about the results of profit maximization has led some countries to supplement it or replace it with sales maximization. For government-owned enterprises, this choice of success criteria is important, whether in communist or noncommunist nations.

The rationale for centrally determined prices is relevant for all societies, as are the difficulties and shortcomings that accompany centrally determined prices. Even in those nations most closely associated with free enterprise, many prices are set by government or require government approval. Frequently, for example, societies have imposed rent controls when the prices of rental accommodation have been escalating. Although such collective price setting seems to have increased in the period since the Second World War, the use of tariffs to raise import prices and modify the free-market ratios has been widespread for hundreds of years. A more recent phenomenon has been the imposition

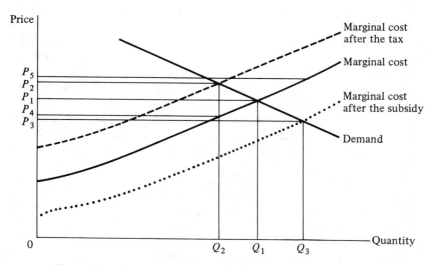

Figure 5.1. Use of price controls to affect the quantity produced and consumed.

of economywide price controls to restrain inflation. With all these situations, the theory of collective price setting is of significant relevance.

Suppose, as in Figure 5.1, that the amount demanded by customers is a function of the price charged, that the cost of producing an additional unit of the commodity is a function of the total amount produced, and that enterprises are seeking to maximize their profits. The only price that will clear the market – without leaving customers or producers desirous of changing the amount they consume or produce – is the price P_1. This price is the competitive equilibrium price that will tend to be established if central planners do not intervene. The amount that will be produced and sold at this price, during a specified time period, is represented by Q_1. The price P_1 will be optimal from the point of view of customer welfare as seen through the eyes of individual customers. Customers will not be willing to pay the extra cost entailed in producing more than Q_1. If less than Q_1 is produced, customers will be willing to pay the cost of expanding output to Q_1.

Political leaders may disagree with this evaluation of the relative desirability of the commodity. They may feel that use of the relevant commodity should be restricted to the amount Q_2 and simply declare that P_2 should be the market price. If producers are seeking to maximize their profits, however, they will be willing to expand their production and accept prices less than P_2 on a black-market basis. Detailed supervision will then be necessary to prevent such behaviour.

The society might wish to set prices below the level that would be established in the market. If the price is set at P_4, for example, suppliers will restrict production to Q_2. However, the excess customer demand will require some rationing process. This rationing process can be random, in which there can be no assurance that the customers most desirous of the commodity will actually receive it. Alternatively, the society can implement a detailed allocation of the commodity to each customer, along the lines of the centralized decision making discussed in Chapter 9.

If they wish to expand production of the commodity to Q_3, central planners might set the market price at P_5. Customers, however, will not purchase all that is produced at this price, and surplus inventories will accumulate. If the price is set at P_3, customers will demand Q_3, but suppliers will be reluctant to expand production to the desired level, unless a government subsidy is provided of $P_5 - P_3$. Imposition of a legal requirement to sell to all customers who wish to buy at the price P_3 will not solve this problem if the average cost of production is higher than P_3 or if suppliers can shift their enterprises into the production of more profitable commodities. As this analysis suggests, central planners may supplement their price-setting policies with subsidies and taxation where rates vary from one industry to another. These issues are discussed further in Chapters 6 and 7.

Government price controls may be desired for ideological reasons. Political leaders may feel that the citizens underrate the harmful effects of some commodities, such as alcoholic beverages, and so they may implement policies to restrict consumption of such items. On the other hand, the political leaders may feel that citizens underrate the beneficial effects of some things, such as education, and so they may desire to expand such activities beyond the level that free choice by the citizens would maintain. Hence, the desirability of this decision mode partly depends upon the degree to which the wishes of political leaders diverge from those of the citizens.

Price controls are often advocated for reasons relating to *market failures* and *externalities*. The marginal costs on the basis of which enterprises make their decisions relate to private costs rather than social costs. Political leaders may wish to restrict an industry that has a detrimental effect on other industries or on human beings – that is, an industry whose social costs exceed its private costs. This may be the case with industries that pollute the environment, for example. On the other hand, political leaders may wish to expand an industry whose production results in social benefits beyond those that the firm can capture in the market.

Private profitability is the enterprises' guide in decision making. From the society's point of view, it could be argued that an evaluation of consumers' surplus should be included in production and investment decisions. The relevant measure of benefits should not be the market price of the product but rather the integral under the demand curve. It is the demand curve that reflects the productivity or benefit of different amounts of the commodity for potential customers. From the perspective of society as a whole, the difference between the integral under the demand curve and the production costs should be the guide in decision making, rather than the difference between the integral under the market price and the production costs.

Some industries may stimulate the economic development of other industries to an extent not reflected in the market price or even in the demand curve for the former's products. This is an additional reason why decisions made on the basis of current profitability as seen through the eyes of the individual enterprise may not result in a satisfactory rate of expansion from the perspective of the economy as a whole. A more rapid growth of transportation and communication networks or of basic industries such as steel or chemicals may increase the profitability of other economic activities. The size of such a catalytic impact varies from one industry to another, and so central planners may decide to give special encouragement to specific industries.

The government may wish to stimulate certain regions of the nation that have persistently high unemployment rates and relatively low income levels. On the basis of the profitability criterion of individual enterprises, expansion in such regions may not be undertaken. Yet, because of externalities like those just mentioned, the government may believe that investment should be encouraged. Hence the government may offer special assistance to all enterprises that locate there – through the guarantee of higher prices than those that exist elsewhere.

Prediction or forecasting acquires a new significance when prices are set centrally, and when enterprise personnel, local government officials, and individual citizens have freedom to make decisions. The government must predict what the decentralized decisions will be. This prediction need not deal with each decision maker separately; rather it is concerned with the total result of each type of decision. When central planners wish to affect the amount of a commodity that is produced and consumed, they must alter the current set of market prices. In considering how much the prices should be changed, they do not need to know how much of the commodity will be supplied by each individual producer, given a possible set of prices, but they must predict the total amount that all producers will supply. They do not need to know how much each individual customer will purchase, given each possible set of prices, but they must predict the total amount that all customers will purchase. That is, for each commodity, central planners must predict the industry's marginal cost or supply function and the customers' demand function. Such prediction requires that central planners obtain and analyze information concerning each industry or commodity. When considering policies for regional development, they must obtain and analyze information concerning the different regions in the nation. In such situations, the necessary information concerns an industry, a commodity, or a region rather than the individual enterprise and citizen.

An additional element of uncertainty enters in that the decentralized decision makers are under no legal obligation to behave in precisely the way that central planners have predicted. Central planners may survey intentions of decentralized decision makers, but the planners must guess the extent to which actual behaviour will resemble the surveyed intentions. To deal with the problems involved in forecasting or prediction, government planners may develop sophisticated analytical techniques. It is possible that the development of economic theory can also assist in dealing with such problems. Relatively little has been written concerning behaviour patterns of decentralized decision makers operating with centrally determined prices. In recent decades, interest in this subject has increased, and a number of economists have turned their attention to an analysis of the implications of certain aspects of this planning framework.

For each commodity, it is likely that both the marginal cost or supply function of a producing industry and the demand function of its customers will change as time passes. The market prices that government planners should set to achieve their goals will shift as such changes occur, and some lag will occur before the planners ascertain what the new set of relevant prices should be. Government planners may find it quite difficult to acquire detailed information concerning the impact on cost and quality of potential innovations, and hence the implications of price adjustment lags are particularly germane in the realm of technological change. Will potential cost and quality innovations actually be implemented if central planners fail to adjust prices appropriately? Incentive schemes in communist nations have based managerial bonuses on both the profit and the sales of an enterprise. Hence, it is necessary to consider the implications of price lags in two different situations: when managers behave so as to maximize their enterprises' profits and when they behave so as to maximize their enterprises' sales.

The manager of a small firm may be doing a better job than the manager of a large firm even though the latter has a greater total profit. If the enterprise is publicly owned, should bonuses and promotions be based upon total profits or should they be based upon some other success criterion? The Soviet Union has, from time to time, changed its emphasis on alternative success criteria. The manner in which each of these criteria can lead to distortions in the enterprise's production processes may also deserve consideration. In particular, the appendix to this chapter explores the implications of sales maximization as well as profit maximization under a model of price controls.

When governments set prices, the individual decisions concerning product quality may acquire several significant new characteristics. Monopolistic or oligopolistic behaviour may appear, for example. Separate firms may reduce their costs by colluding to reduce product quality in a manner that resembles the price collusion with market failure in the free-enterprise model. Government planners face a set of problems (and require techniques to solve them) that they do not encounter in the free-enterprise framework.

An important conclusion of the analysis in the appendix to this chapter is that, with either profit or sales maximization, any time delays in price adjustment may deter the adoption of innovations. The deleterious impact of time delays depends upon the type of innovation being considered; and with profit maximization it also depends upon the precise shapes of the demand and cost curves. Even if innovations are adopted, production may not occur at the optimal level. In several cases, it is impossible to predict whether misallocation of resources will be greater with profit maximization or with sales maximization. The sales maximization criterion seems especially unsatisfactory in regard to the adoption of cost-reducing innovations and with respect to its tendency to result in excess supply of the commodity. The profit maximization criterion seems particularly unsatisfactory in regard to the adoption of quality-improving innovations and with respect to its tendency to result in excess demand for the commodity. The relative disadvantages of the sales-maximization criterion may be more obvious to the populace than the relative disadvantages of the profit-maximization criterion. Everyone may notice the production of excess supplies of a commodity, whereas few may notice the underproduction that can occur with the profit criterion. This underproduction may not always result in unsatisfied demand at the given product price; queues, for example, would not be formed to obtain the commodity. Here we may see a political reason for leaders to choose profit rather than sales maximization as a central criterion for purchase and production decisions at public enterprises.

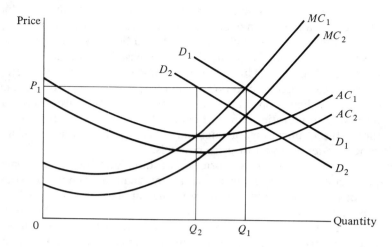

Figure 5.2. Monopoly and the determination of quality with central price setting.

Price controls and efficiency

Monopoly

Suppose a monopolist is producing a commodity for which central planners have set the price P_1 in Figure 5.2. To produce this commodity, the monopolist experiences marginal and average costs indicated by the curves MC_1 and AC_1, respectively. The demand for this product is indicated by D_1D_1. It may be expected that the monopolist will produce the quantity Q_1 and earn a profit equal to P_1 minus AC_1 (at the output Q_1) times Q_1. However, the monopolist may be able to earn a greater profit by reducing the quality of its commodity, even though such a reduction will curtail the demand for its product.

Suppose, for example, that the monopolist can reduce costs from AC_1 to AC_2 and from MC_1 to MC_2, while the demand for the inferior product shifts from D_1D_1 to D_2D_2. The monopolist's profit is now equal to P_1 minus AC_2 (at the output Q_2) times Q_2. It may be that this profit from the inferior product exceeds the profit the monopolist could earn on the original quality of the commodity.

The monopolist may have no way of ascertaining the precise extent to which the demand for this product will shift with a reduction in quality. The monopolist may have to experiment with such quality variations. It should be noted that even if the product is subject to gradual reduc-

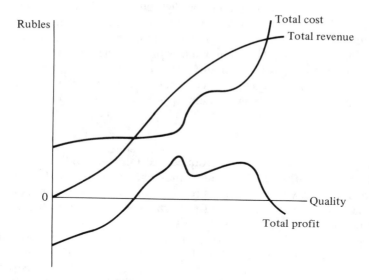

Figure 5.3. The effect of quality variations on a monopolist's profit.

tions in quality, nevertheless, it is not clear that quality reductions will affect the monopolist's profit in a consistent manner. As the monopolist decreases the product quality, alternating stretches of increasing and decreasing profit might be encountered.

Suppose that quality can be measured in an ordinal fashion. As indicated in Figure 5.3, the monopolist may earn a different total revenue for each type of product quality. The higher the quality of the product, the more total revenue the monopolist will earn. Since the price of the product has been set by central planners, there may be some quality level at which no customers are willing to pay the required price for the product. Let this quality level be represented by the intersection of the quality axis with the axis on which currency units are measured. At this quality level, total revenue will be zero. As the quality of the product is improved, the monopolist's total costs rise. Even to produce a quality of product that no customers are willing to buy may require a monetary outlay, and so the total cost curve may intersect the currency unit axis at a positive amount. As quality is improved, both total revenue and total cost increase, but the slope of each may change repeatedly. As a result, the monopolist's total profit may reach a number of local maxima such that a movement from any one of them would reduce total profit. It is not clear, therefore, that a monopolist would arrive at the greatest possible profit.

We should note that if a monopolist sells its commodity in more than one market or if it can divide its customers into a number of separate groups, then the quality of product that maximizes profit in one market may not be the quality that maximizes profit in the other markets. Hence the monopolist may produce different qualities of the same commodity, and may engage in quality discrimination similar to the price discrimination by monopolists in free enterprise.

Duopoly

Suppose that only two firms produce a certain commodity. If either firm alters the quality of its product, then the customer demand for each firm's product will shift. Let us refer to the two firms as firm A and firm B, and let us suppose that firm A changes the quality of its product while firm B keeps its quality constant. If firm A raises the quality of its product, it will be able to sell more than it could previously, firm B will not be able to sell as much as it could previously, and the total amount sold will increase. If firm A reduces the quality of its product, it will not be able to sell as much as it could previously, firm B will be able to sell more than it could previously, and the total amount sold will decrease.

In this situation, a type of warfare could develop in which each firm would seek to produce a better quality product than its competitor. With the price having been set by the central planners, however, such warfare would result in a decrease in the total profit of each duopolist. In view of this, the duopolists might decide to collude concerning the quality of their products. Such collusion could occur as the result of face-to-face negotiations or it could develop tacitly as each observed the other's behaviour. In either case, the collusion could result in the same type of behaviour as that of the monopolist already described, or it could be interrupted by periods of warfare as each decided to fight for a larger share of the market. In the process of determining market shares, one firm could become dominant and acquire a greater total profit solely because of its negotiating ability or willingness to fight vis-à-vis the other firm.

Oligopoly

If several firms compete in a certain product market, then the quality decisions of any one firm affect the sales volume of each of the others. If one oligopolist raises the quality of its product all the other firms may be forced to copy this example or lose the bulk of their customers.

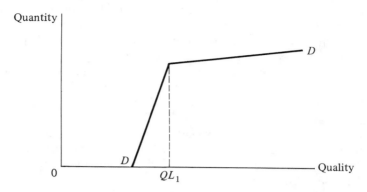

Figure 5.4. The oligopolist's demand curve with centrally set prices.

Hence if an oligopolist raises the quality of its product, the amount it can sell may not change much. If it lowers the quality of its product, on the other hand, most of its customers may desert to its competitors. Therefore, the situation depicted in Figure 5.4 may be relevant for the oligopolist, where the quantity the oligopolist can sell is a function of the quality of its product.

A quality leader may emerge in such a situation. The leader may set quality standards that the other firms tend to follow. If another firm should raise the quality of its product above these standards – thereby violating the tacit collusion under which they all operate – the leader could respond by raising the quality of its product. As a result, the profit of each firm would be below its original level. Each of the nonleaders would realize, due to this experience, that it could maximize its profit only by producing a commodity of the same quality as the leader's commodity. Hence the demand curve may have a kinked shape with a tendency to produce a commodity of the quality QL_1, where QL_1 is determined by the dominant firm.

Monopolistic competition

Suppose that a firm must obtain permission from the central planners in order to shift into the production of commodities other than those it has traditionally produced. Suppose that the central planners are reluctant to permit such diversification, preferring instead to restrict each market to a given number of suppliers. Let us consider such a market where the number of suppliers is large, and consequently no one firm can dominate the market as in the oligopoly case. No new entry is permitted, and so the total number of producers is fixed. If the central planners set a certain price P_1, so as to clear the market for the commodity, any one of the producers, say, firm A, can act as if it controls a segment of the market. If the greatest amount that all producers, behaving as competitors, are willing to supply is Q_1, and if the greatest amount that all firms other than A are willing to supply is Q_x, then firm A controls the market for $Q_1 - Q_x$.

Firm A can now reduce the quality of its commodity in the knowledge that a demand will exist for its debased product. True, customers will first seek to obtain the commodity from firm A's competitors. If the latter keep to the government price, however, the competitors will have to turn away some of the customers. The shape of the demand curve for the debased product will depend upon the intensity of demand of those particular customers who have been rejected. Hence it may vary from one time period to another. Any one of the producers, such as firm A, may act as a monopolist toward these rejected customers in deciding upon the degree of quality debasement that will maximize its profit. In this decision process, the monopolistic competitor, like the monopolist discussed above, may experience the difficulty that a number of local profit maxima exist and the movement towards the greatest possible profit may not increase its total profit at every point in this adjustment.

Each of the monopolistic competitors may find that it is in its interest to reduce product quality. The result may be that customers receive commodities significantly inferior to the commodity whose price central planners originally established, while each supplier may receive a total profit in excess of the amount it would have received initially.

Quality standards

This analysis indicates that if in a nation there exists monopoly, duopoly, oligopoly, or monopolistic competition, it is not enough for central planners to set prices. Planners may also have to set specific and detailed quality standards. In the above discussion, only in the case of monopolistic competition did an excess demand exist for a commodity, and in no case did any of the firms produce an excess supply. Hence central planners could not use the existence of excess demand or excess supply as an indication that quality had been debased. For central planners to respond to quality debasement by lowering the market price is not a reasonable solution if central planners desire production of a better quality product.

Implementation of quality standards may be a difficult task. Enterprise personnel may be involved in discussions concerning quality standards and, if so, they may advocate those types of standards that they believe can be violated without such violations being detected readily. Faced with such conduct, central planners might not be able to obtain adequate information on which to base their standards. To be completely effective, standards would have to deal with every aspect that could be debased. A comprehensive inspection system would have to be capable of detecting infractions of the established standards.

An alternative solution might be for central planners to permit free entry into each industry. If any enterprise could produce any commodity it wished or if any group of individuals could create a new firm whenever it wished, then a monopolist, duopolist, oligopolist, or monopolistic competitor might not behave in the manner described in the preceding sections for fear that a higher-than-normal profit would attract new competitors. It is not clear what specific institutional regulations could best provide for such free entry. Necessary modifications in the nation's legal, financial, and planning structure might be opposed because of their effect on other aspects of the economy. The optimal criterion for entry is also not clear. A higher-than-normal profit would not necessarily indicate the existence of a market imperfection. Such profit might be the result of exceptional initiative, exertion, skill, or care; and this possibility further complicates the solution of relying on the entry of additional suppliers. Potential competitors might be barred by cost considerations alone. Economies of large-scale production, for example, might effectively limit the market to one firm.

The comments in this chapter concerning the possible behaviour of monopolists, duopolists, oligopolists, and monopolistic competitors resemble analyses of these kinds of market imperfections in free enterprise. A fundamental difference, of course, is that within the framework of central price setting each enterprise may increase its profit by debasing quality rather than by increasing its prices. With this difference in mind, insights that are meaningful in this second planning framework can be found in several works.[3] The possibility of such market imperfections complicates the task of setting prices centrally and so may detract significantly from the desirability of this second decision mode.

Differential pricing

At various times, the Soviet leadership has decided that differential pricing should be followed in the Soviet Union. Low-cost producers, such as firm A in Figure 5.5, will be paid a lower-than-customary price for their output while high-cost producers, such as firm C, will receive a price that is higher than customary.

From a short-run point of view, it seems that differential pricing will result in inefficient production. If each firm seeks to maximize its profit, it will expand production to the point where the price it receives equals its marginal cost. Hence firms A, B, and C, being paid P_A, P_B, and P_C, respectively, will produce Q_A, Q_B, and Q_C, respectively. If firm A's output is increased by one unit while firm C's output is decreased by one unit, total output will remain unchanged while total costs will fall, since A's marginal cost at Q_A is below C's marginal cost at Q_C. Hence differential pricing seems to lead to inefficient production.

From a long-run point of view, however, differential pricing may be a reasonable means of encouraging the economic development of a nation's low-income regions. Production costs may be affected over time by the level of economic activity in the individual firms or in the region as a whole. The individual firms may benefit through the production of larger volumes. This may occur, for example, if some learning-by-doing is involved in the production process. As high-cost producers increase the volume of their output, they may experience a decrease in their average and marginal costs over time. Both the average cost curve and the marginal cost curve of firm C may fall as time passes. Economic development may be viewed as a cumulative advance in which the initial steps are the most difficult and least profitable. Hence, it can be argued that the initial steps should be assisted in this manner. Existence of external economies may mean that an expansion of one firm, say, firm C, may have a stimulating impact on other economic activities of the depressed region. From this point of view, differential pricing may be a reasonable policy to pursue. It may be applied to the purchase prices firms pay for their inputs as well as to the prices they receive for their output. Central planners may charge firms in a depressed region a lower-than-prevalent interest rate for the capital they use. Firms in advanced regions may be charged a higher interest rate.

Differential pricing may be considered a necessary and powerful weapon in the nation's struggle to stimulate its economically depressed regions. It may also be used as a means of achieving a greater equality of incomes among regions. In fact, it is this pursuit of greater income equality that has usually been mentioned in the Soviet press in support of differential pricing. What is clear in either case is that, in using differential pricing, central planners must forecast the impact of alternative sets of prices on current production volumes and on future production costs. Such forecasting of the effects of differential pricing add to the difficulty and complexity of the tasks facing central planners.

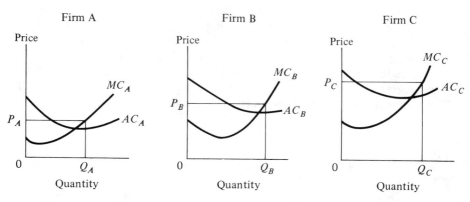

Figure 5.5. Determination of output with differential pricing.

Using tariffs to control relative prices

Throughout history, tariffs have been used as a means of modifying production and consumption decisions. Tariffs have been imposed on certain goods in order to raise the prices of imports, and thereby to stimulate their domestic production. Used in this way, tariffs have often been a central element of an economic development strategy, creating higher prices for "infant industries." Certain activities may be considered essential for economic growth, serving as a purchaser of inputs in a manner that can encourage expansion of many other firms. Over time, these protected firms are expected to grow and become strong enough to compete against foreign producers, without the need for such a tariff. At other times, tariffs have been imposed to protect existing jobs from increasingly intense foreign competition. In recent years, agricultural producers in many countries have lobbied for tariffs to ensure the viability of their activities. In times of economic depression and high unemployment, this argument has strong political appeal. Tariffs have also been regarded as appropriate means of guaranteeing some minimum level of domestic production of a commodity. Concern over national defense and the military need for particular items has often supported this concept.

Regardless of the purpose for their imposition, tariffs do retain individual decision making on the part of both the producer and also the consumer. Consequently, many of the advantages of free enterprise are retained. However, the shortcomings of central price setting can be severe. In addition to the price control problems discussed above, a tariff can lead to short production runs if domestic firms serve only the local market. Economies of scale and specialization may be lost in this process, and, consequently, costs may be raised unnecessarily.

The General Agreement on Tariffs and Trade (GATT) came into effect in 1948, and since then has formed the framework for international trade negotiations for noncommunist nations. Most countries are members of GATT, and even many nonmembers adhere to some of its agreements. There have been eight rounds of tariff negotiations:

1947	Geneva;
1949	Annecy, France;
1950–1	Torquay, England;
1955–6	Geneva;
1961–2	The "Dillon Round" in Geneva;
1964–7	The "Kennedy Round" in Geneva;
1973–9	The "Tokyo Round" in Geneva;
1987	The "Uruguay Round" in Geneva.

In the first seven rounds, most of the negotiating agenda concerned the reduction of tariff rates, and the Tokyo Round did establish a timetable for future tariff cuts. Recent years, however, have seen a growth of other barriers or interferences with trade, including subsidies, countervailing duties, product standards, customs valuation, government procurement, and import-licensing procedures. In view of this, later negotiations also attempted to create fair and uniform rules for these nontariff barriers.

The Tokyo Round tariff reductions were phased in gradually over the 1979–87 period with the depth of cut varying from one country to another, depending on the height of the 1979 tariff levels. The average tariff cuts ranged from 28 percent for Sweden to 49 percent for Japan.[4] These cuts still leave some differences in tariff rates among the signatories, but overall international tariff barriers have been lowered. Table 5.1 indicates that significant tariffs will still remain for many products even after the Tokyo Round tariff cuts are fully implemented. In particular, tariffs for semimanufactured and finished manufactured products will be substantial on average.

For some products, tariffs will be much higher than the average levels presented in Table 5.1. It is important to realize that the tariff rates in Table 5.1 are all average rates for groups of products. Within many product groups, tariff rates vary widely. From the perspective of each enterprise, the important point is the tariff level for the specific products that the particular enterprise produces or imports.

Table 5.1. *Post-MTN average tariffs on industrial products*

Country	Depth of cut[a]	Raw materials	Semi manufacturers	Finished manufacturers
USA	31	0.2	3.0	5.7
Canada	38	0.5	8.3	8.3
Japan	49	0.5	4.6	6.0
EEC	29	0.2	4.2	6.9
Sweden	28	0.0	3.3	4.9

[a]Depth of cut is for all industrial products; depth of cut and average post-MTN rates are weighted on the basis of actual customs collections.
Source: Frank Stone, *Canada, The GATT, and the International Trade System* (Montreal: The Institute for Research on Public Policy, 1984), p. 182.

Rent control

Many societies have concluded that residential rents should be determined collectively through government, rather than set by market forces. It is argued that without government intervention, low-income people will have to devote too large a portion of their income to paying for rent. Furthermore, the price of residential accommodation can rise as a result of factors that have nothing to do with greater consumer satisfaction. A general increase in population or a shift to urban centres can cause rent increases not based on any improvements in residential accommodations. Such rent increases are seen by some as unfair.

Among the many difficulties experienced in the collective setting of rents, quality deterioration has often been prominent. Consequently, it is not surprising that the economics of quality have been analyzed in this context. For example, Richard Arnott has developed diagrams that explicitly introduce housing quality and maintenance expenditure as important variables in the residential market.[5] Arnott focuses on the profit-maximizing maintenance expenditures under various kinds of rent-control programs. He also emphasizes that if rent increases are permitted each year, then landlords will tend to apply exactly the guideline rent increase. This tendency for government guidelines on rent increases to become a floor rather than a ceiling can mean that some rents may actually be higher with a control program than without one.

Another prominent feature of some rent-control programs is the ability of a landlord to raise rents when new tenants take over an apartment. Meanwhile, tenants of long duration are protected against these sporadic increases. A substantial gap can develop between the rents for identical units solely because of differences in tenant turnover. Some see this as a serious inequity.

With most rent-control programs, the difficulties of the theoretical analysis become increasingly apparent with the passage of time. Price anomalies develop and distortions occur. A wide variety of exemptions and concessions have been introduced to redress some of these. Most significantly, new units built after a certain date may be exempted in order to encourage the construction of new units. Without this exemption, rents that are set below market prices may severely retard new construction. Another concession often permitted is to control only those rents below a specified level. Here the rationale is that the poor need special assistance whereas the wealthy do not. In practice, such exemptions and concessions lead to further distortions and anomalies with the passage of time. Due to quality deterioration caused by low maintenance expenditures, it is not clear whether rent controls in the long run provide better housing value for renters than a free market would provide.

Many studies have investigated the impact of particular rent-control programs. Milton Friedman and George Stigler, for example, have compared the housing market in San Francisco after the 1906 earthquake, when there were no controls, with the period following World War II, when there were controls.[6] In 1906 one might have expected a housing shortage given the extent of the destruction of the earthquake. However, the free market provided a rationing of space which was efficient and adequate. Friedman and Stigler emphasize several advantages to the establishment of rents in a free-enterprise market:

> In a free market, there is always some housing immediately available for rent – at all rent levels.
> The bidding up of rents forces some people to economize on space. *Until there is sufficient new construction, this doubling up is the only solution.*
> The high rents act as a strong stimulus to new construction.
> No complex, expensive, and expansive machinery is necessary. The rationing is conducted quietly and impersonally through the price system.[7]

As a result, San Francisco's housing market did not experience any kind of crisis at the time. In contrast, Friedman and Stigler found that the post–1945 period of rent controls resulted in severe shortages of rental units.

In 1906, when both rents and selling prices were free to rise, the San Francisco Chronicle listed 3 "houses for sale" for every 10 "houses or apartments for rent." In 1946, under rent control, about 730 "houses for sale" were listed for every 10 "houses or apartments for rent."[8]

With the imposition of controls, shortages in rental housing develop. People building new units, as well as landlords owning existing apartments, decide to sell rather than rent, thereby avoiding the rent controls. What compounds the problem of a reduction in the supply of rental accommodation space is an increase in the demand for rental units. Incomes increase but at a faster rate than rents, and so there is an increasing demand for what becomes a smaller supply. As evidence, Friedman and Stigler note,

In 1906, after the earthquake, when rents were free to rise, there was 1 "wanted to rent" for every 10 "houses or apartments for rent;" in 1946, there were 375 "wanted to rent" for every 10 "for rent."[9]

Finally, Friedman and Stigler emphasize that such a situation misleads observers to support the continuation of rent controls when these controls have been the cause of the problem.

As long as the shortage created by rent ceilings remains, there will be a clamour for continued rent controls. This is perhaps the strongest indictment of ceilings on rents. They, and the accompanying shortage of dwellings to rent, perpetuate themselves, and the progeny are even less attractive than the parents.[10]

In analyzing Sweden's very long experiences with rent control, Sven Rydenfelt has calculated the percentage increase in rents permitted over the period 1939–75, and he has compared these with the percentage increase in average wages. While rents were permitted to rise on average by only 4.2 percent annually, wages rose by 8.7 percent annually. This inevitably resulted in shortages of rental accommodation. Rents, since they could not be increased, lost the ability to restrain demand.

The cause of the housing shortage is to be found entirely on the demand side. As a consequence of rent control and the relative reduction of the rent – the manipulated low price – demand has increased to such an extent that an ever-widening gap between supply and demand has developed in spite of the high level of construction activity. . . . The housing shortage will be our companion forever, unless we prevent demand from running ahead of production.[11]

In a survey of economic analyses of rent controls, Peter Navarro has concluded:

On the subject of rent control, the economics profession has reached a rare consensus: Rent control creates many more problems than it solves. The primary effects of rent control, it is commonly agreed, are a reduction in the supply of rental housing, the deterioration of existing housing stock, and the erosion of a community's property tax base.[12]

Price controls as an inflation restraint program

Throughout history, periods of rapid inflation have often occurred. From time to time, rulers have expanded the money supply rapidly with a consequent fall in the value of money vis-à-vis goods and services. In earlier centuries, rulers could do this by "debasing the coinage," adding base metals to the coinage of gold or silver, thus increasing the number of coins. In modern times, many governments have engaged in monetary expansion, in a similar attempt to pay for expenditures without relying on tax increases.

Though some observers focus entirely on monetary expansion as the cause of inflation, others also emphasize a tendency for workers and firms to raise wages and prices in anticipation of future inflation. Inflationary expectations can intensify the process whose origins may lie in the rate of monetary expansion. Price controls can be seen as a way of restraining these inflationary expectations, often in conjunction with a new conviction to pursue monetary restraint.

In practice, general price controls as an inflation restraint program have encountered the difficulties already discussed in this chapter. The extent of distortions has depended on such things as the length of time that the program has been in effect, the gap between permissible price increases and those that would have occurred in a free market, and provisions for exemptions. In general, critics have emphasized the distortions and have suggested that any inflation reduction has been only temporary. The pressures have been merely bottled up, to be released in a higher inflation when controls are eliminated than would otherwise have occurred. Nevertheless, many countries have adopted some form of price-control program at one time or another as a way of restraining inflation. Politically, such programs may be seen as government action at a time when reliance solely on free-market forces could be interpreted as a callous disregard for the plight of citizens attempting to cope with rapid price increases.

In evaluating particular wage- and price-control programs, many analysts have been critical. Robert Lanzillotti and Blaine Roberts, for example, have referred to several analyses and have concluded that "European evidence indicates that controls soon become unmanageable and are discarded."[13] Jerry Pohlman has also concluded that post–1945 income policies in European countries "have, for the most part, been characterized by very limited degrees of success."[14] Nevertheless, Pohlman sees them as

> an inevitable response to stagflation and the unemployment–inflation dilemma. . . . With the traditional tools of macroeconomic monetary and fiscal policy becoming increasingly unable to deal effectively with this situation, interest has grown in other policies. As in the United States, the imposition of wage and price controls looks attractive only in comparison with the alternative.[15]

In his book, *In Pursuit of Price Stability: The Wage-Price Freeze of 1971*, Arnold Weber has examined President Nixon's program and, although criticizing certain impacts, has also predicted that wage and price controls will reappear from time to time:

> Direct controls over wages and prices now have joined monetary and fiscal policies as officially acknowledged remedies for dealing with the problems of inflation, employment, and growth. In the future, economic policy makers in the United States will be able to consider controls as one of the precedents in responding to political and economic pressures to maintain growth with price stability.[16]

Hugh Rockoff began the research for his book, *Drastic Measures: A History of Wage and Price Controls in the United States*, with an initial conviction "that controls were always harmful. . . . I did not reverse my attitude toward controls 180 degrees; but I did come to the conclusion that there is a role for controls in certain inflationary emergencies."[17] In particular, Rockoff's analyses of World Wars I and II, the Korean War, and the Vietnam War suggest that in times of rapid military growth and the accompanying redeployment of resources, wage and price controls may offer significant advantages over a sole reliance on monetary and fiscal policies.

The 1960s price-control reforms in the Soviet Union

Under the Stalinist central planning system, the Soviet government awarded bonuses to enterprises for fulfilment of their production plans. Even with centralized decision making, government officials realized that the local personnel of the individual firm could affect the volume of their firm's output. Although they worked for a stipulated number of hours, the personnel could vary production in accordance with the effort, initiative, and thought they applied to their tasks. Measurement of output and development of success criteria often required the use of prices. Because many enterprises produced more than one commodity, government officials required some method of weighting the different commodities to arrive at an index of a firm's total output. Without such weights or prices, a change in the ratio of these different products to each other, in quantity terms, would preclude comparison of total output. It would be difficult, without prices, to compare one firm's production levels over time, to compare production volumes among firms, or to compare an enterprise's actual output with its total planned output. Furthermore, prices were adjusted from time to time in accordance with alterations in demand and supply conditions. Although the underlying principle of the Stalinist system was the centralization of decision making, nevertheless, it was generally recognized that decentralized initiative could occur and that prices could serve as a guide for these.

In the past, Soviet government officials have also used cost reductions as one of the success criteria on which to base bonuses and promotions. The government officials realized that the local personnel of the individual firm could affect the firm's production costs. Although the firm received specified amounts of each input, the local personnel could waste the supplies they received. On the other hand, the personnel could exercise diligent caution in making the fullest possible use of the firm's supplies. If the firm used more than one input, the relative value to society of these different inputs would have to be clearly stated. Otherwise, neither the personnel nor the government officials could ascertain the extent to which cost had truly been reduced when the input mix per unit of output had changed.

Under the Stalinist central planning system, the role and importance of price setting were restricted in that a firm could not change its mix of inputs or outputs significantly without the prior approval of the nation's central planners. The firm's personnel could alter the initiative, effort, and care that they applied to their jobs, but this variability of productivity was the only legally recognized sphere within which prices could influence enterprise decisions. In practice, failures of supervision did extend this decision-making role of the firm. An enterprise might act contrary to the clearly expressed wishes of central planners, in the expectation that its infractions would not be detected. A firm, for example, might refuse to implement quality-improving innovations if such innovations would raise its costs and, consequently, would reduce its production volume. Centrally issued declarations concerning the need for quality improvements might be ignored. To the extent that their wishes were being violated without punishment, central planners could use prices to assist in eliciting the production responses they sought. When they could not enforce their commands for quality improvements, central planners could raise the prices of more advanced models of a commodity.

Both the variability of productivity and the undetected infractions of centrally issued decrees affected the Soviet Union's economic activities to such an extent that the nation's leaders often expressed dissatisfaction. Even without any expansion in the rights and responsibilities of the individual firm, a revitalized approach to price setting could have been a reasonable reform. With the post-Stalinist experiments in decentralized decision making, the urgent need for a more adequate price structure became widely accepted.

In 1961, Khrushchev indicated that significant decentralization reforms might be adopted in an effort to overcome the problems that had been experienced in central planning. "We must elevate the importance of profit and profitability. In order to have enterprises fulfil their plans better, they should be given more opportunity to dispose of their profits, to use them more extensively to encourage good work of their personnel, and to extend production."[18] Prior to the 1960s, prices had been set by central planners. In shifting decision-making authority from central planners to the individual enterprises and consumers, a key issue was whether prices should be set in the market, or whether price controls should be continued for the purpose of guiding individual decisions. If firms were to make decisions so as to maximize their profits, then prices would acquire a new role. In this period of reform discussions and experiments, the difficulties of the price-control model with decentralized decision making became significant.

Early in the national discussion of decentralization reforms, it was generally recognized that the relative prices for different goods and services would become much more important than they had been previously. If each individual enterprise was to be granted freedom to alter its inputs, outputs, or production technology solely on its own initiative, and if in such alteration it was being urged by national leaders and its own self-interest to maximize profits, then the pattern of prices that it faced at present and the pattern it estimated for the future would affect its decisions. Hence, a series of questions concerning prices attained new significance. Could prices and profit maximization by themselves result in optimal resource allocation, or did successful operation of the economy require other indices for planning and evaluation as well? Should the individual enterprise be restricted in the scope of its decisions, and should certain areas, such as investment decisions, be reserved for determination by central authorities? What should a price represent? What factors should enter its determination? In particular, should land rent and interest on capital be included in price; or should prices, for example, be differentiated so that in any industry those enterprises having poorer management, land, or equipment would receive higher prices to compensate them for their higher costs? Should prices be changed frequently to reflect changes in production conditions such as cost-reduction innovations or quality improvements? Most important, could any central planning organization, in practice, formulate and revise prices rapidly enough to prevent incorrect prices from causing incorrect decisions at the enterprise level?

In a 1962 article, Gatovsky stressed the division between the current operation of an enterprise on the one hand and investment decisions on the other. Although appropriate for the former, profit maximization was inappropriate, he believed, for the latter. Under free enterprise, investment funds move towards those sectors of the economy enjoying higher than average profits. In the Soviet Union however, investment funds should, according to Gatovsky, be allocated through direct intervention by central planners. In addition to this restriction on the role of profit, Gatovsky also felt that restrictions should be placed on the importance of profit maximization in a firm's decision concerning current operations. "Life confirms at every turn that for us the level of profitability can by no means serve as a single absolute criterion of an enterprise's success and replace the other value indicators of production, not to mention the physical ones."[19] He referred to the volume of output, the mix of products, and the quality of the product as indicators still useful in planning and evaluation. Why should the role of profit be restricted even at the enterprise level? Gatovsky suggested that price formation was a considerable part of the answer.

One of the prerequisites for heightening the role and significance of profits is further price adjustment. . . . Evidence indicates that it is not only periodic general revisions of prices that are needed but also systematic current measures to adjust prices. . . . If prices are not revised for a long time, then great lack of coordination inevitably arises in profits. . . . The existing price-setting methods often do not create an incentive for an enterprise to produce new machines or machines with improved qualities. . . . An incorrect price structure not only neutralizes the stimulating role of profits but even creates a situation in which profits have a negative influence on production.[20]

Thus as early as 1962, doubts were voiced as to the ability of central-planning agencies to formulate and revise prices accurately enough to justify reliance on profit maximization. On December 13, 1963, at the Plenary Session of the CPSU Central Committee, Khrushchev again stressed, "We must display the highest exactitude towards the quality of manufactured goods in general. Evidently we should introduce a system whereby factories and firms are directly responsible to the consumer for the quality of their output."[21] On July 1, 1964, a new system was introduced on an experimental basis at the Bolshevichka and Mayak garment firms located, respectively, in the cities of Moscow and Gorky.

M. Kuznetsova, the chief economist and assistant general director of the Bolshevichka enterprise, has described this system.

The right has been granted to us to compose plans on the basis of orders from the trade organizations and to determine for ourselves the volume of production, the volume of output sales, the necessary materials, and the wage fund. The only report indices are now the volume of output sold on orders and the percentage of profit. Now it is not the economic council that imposes the assortment on us, but we who inform the economic council of what we are going to be making in our shops.[22]

In October 1964, the presidium of the USSR Council of Ministers charged the USSR Council of the National Economy with preparing a draft resolution on spreading the experiences of Bolshevichka and Mayak to other light-industry enterprises. On October 19 and 20, 1964, a special session of the Council of the National Economy was convened to discuss the four-month-old experiment. "Those who spoke in the subsequent discussion stressed the need for increasing the number of enterprises in light industry that work according to direct contracts with trade organizations and stores."[23] The experiment was judged, by this Council, to have been a success. It is important to note that in this experiment, the firms were allowed to set their own retail prices on the basis of their own individual and independent evaluation of the market.

On July 1, 1965, one year after the initial experiment was begun, all the garment and footwear factories of Moscow and several other cities started to operate according to direct contracts with their purchasers and also with their suppliers. This new experiment embraced some 400 enterprises. In several respects, the new experiment seemed to offer considerable improvement over traditional methods. According to an article by O. Lacis, each firm now planned its assortment of goods in such a way as to correspond more fully to the desires of those who would receive them. The firm accepted orders for goods on a contract basis and the direct contacts between supplier and purchaser enabled information concerning the capabilities of suppliers and the wishes of purchasers to flow in more accurate detail than when communication channels ran through the central-planning bureaucracy. Fines for failure to meet delivery dates were considerable and reduced profits, which now meant a reduction in the enterprise fund and bonuses.

However, several major shortcomings existed in the July 1, 1965 experiment. Lacis noted that although garment factories could make the same demands for appropriate goods from textile factories, the latter could not carry on the chain of direct contacts and responsibilities. Those who supplied spun fiber, cotton, wool, artificial fiber, dyes, and equipment were free from the local responsibility of the new system. Hence, textile suppliers were limited in their responses to garment firms and the whole system could not achieve its maximum impact.

Of more importance, Lacis criticized the retreat to the formation of prices by governmental agencies rather than by individual firms.

The experiment disclosed more clearly than ever before the imperfect condition of prices. In particular, scarce output exists not per se, but only at the given price. . . . It is no accident that the management of Bolshevichka, which has the most experience in operating in the new way, is demanding that the enterprises' participation in the establishment of prices be expanded. . . . In the second resolution of the USSR Council of the National Economy – the one that expanded the experiment – this right was no longer provided for. Bolshevichka was deprived of it, along with the newcomers. After that what was the point of the experiment? After all, there had been no instances to cast doubt on the usefulness of this step. On the other hand, there are countless examples to confirm the imperfectness of the present system of price formation.[24]

For many advocates of a new system, profit maximization was not the obvious alternative to maximization of the traditional index of gross output. Instead, some advocated the "normative value of processing" or NVP. These writers criticized the gross-output criterion most severely. "Above all, with identical labour outlays at enterprises, the volume of their gross output may increase or decrease depending on the cost of the initial materials they are using and the planned rate of profit. . . . Calculating the enterprise's output by using the gross output indicator does not stimulate fulfilment of the plan for product assortment because the enterprise has an interest in producing the items with the largest material inputs."[25] They felt that an index of value added could solve the basic shortcomings of the traditional system. The NVP would be equal to gross output minus profit and minus those basic materials and purchased semimanufacturers that do not lose their consumable properties, yet are included with little alteration in the finished product. Those inputs that do lose their consumable properties, such as fuel and power, would be included in NVP. "The distorted incentive for enterprises to produce items that consume much material and are highly profitable is thereby removed."[26] Implicit in this argument was the belief that the size of an enterprise's profits was without economic meaning – because profit depended upon wholesale prices and these prices were determined arbitrarily by central planners. Wholesale prices, and therefore profits, did not systematically reflect usefulness, production costs, or scarcity. Some believed that prices should have definite meaning in order that the profit margins that prices affect would have definite meaning. Individual enterprises should have a role in price formation. "A more flexible and improved procedure for planning prices would make it possible to eliminate completely any contradictions between price and plan. Only in this event will prices be able to perform their basic role as an economic regulator."[27]

The 1960s decentralization reforms failed, and the detailed central-planning framework was reinstated. A key element in this retreat was widespread concern about the price system. It is likely that Gorbachev's current decentralization reforms will also encounter price problems. If it is decided to rely upon price controls, will central planners be able to adjust prices continually so as to lead producers to supply that amount of each good that is demanded in the market at the particular price? Will shortages and rationing develop, and will overproduction, with undesired inventory accumulations, destroy the increased efficiency that is being sought? Can central planners revise prices accurately enough to foster the technological progress that the nation's leaders desire? The bureaucratic framework for price formation may prove unsatisfactory in the future as it has in the past.[28] In November, 1966, the Chairman of the USSR State Planning Committee acknowledged that "the perfecting of wholesale prices is a decisive prerequisite for a large-scale transfer of branches of industry to the new work conditions."[29] The Chairman and the Vice-Chairman of the USSR State Price Committee both described publicly the difficult nature of their task. They realized that prices must be adjusted continually in accordance with changes in quality. The price reform, completed in 1967, required several years of detailed discussions and calculations. The last overall review of prices, prior to this reform, had been finished in 1955.

The success of a decentralized framework with price controls will be influenced by the rapidity with which central planners can, in fact, adjust prices and the accuracy with which they can forecast the results of different sets of prices. The costs incurred in the process of revising prices may also affect the desirability of this framework. Soviet experience provides no assurance that central planners can revise prices rapidly enough and appropriately enough to elicit the enterprise behavior that Gorbachev is expecting.

To what extent will market imperfections frustrate the efforts of central planners? With monopoly, duopoly, oligopoly, or monopolistic competition, central planners may not be able to achieve their goals by relying solely on price setting. Detailed quality standards and inspections may also be necessary. Legal and financial regulations may have to be imposed, together with market mechanisms that permit the entry of additional enterprises into an imperfectly competitive market. Hence, price controls as a decision mode can be criticized for a number of reasons, and they may have to be accompanied by the additional decision modes to which we now turn.

Appendix

A theoretical analysis of price controls

Throughout this analysis it is assumed that, for any commodity, marginal and average costs rise as the total amount produced increases within the range of quantities being considered. This assumption rests on the belief that different firms experience different production costs and that low-cost suppliers either are limited in their expansion possibilities by physical or financial constraints or else encounter rising expenses as they do expand their production. In Figure 5.6, the industry's marginal and average costs are depicted as being convex, the form traditionally assumed in Western economic analysis, although the only aspect of these curves necessary for the following arguments is that they rise as the amount produced increases in the range of quantities being considered. Individual enterprises may produce several commodities. Our examination considers each commodity separately, concentrating on the minimum additional cost the industry must incur to produce more of the commodity, the average cost it experiences in producing different amounts of the commodity, and the prices that customers are willing to pay to obtain various amounts of the commodity. It is assumed in this appendix that the demand schedules are the optimal or socially approved schedules. It may be that the commodity being considered is a consumption good and that the demand schedules reflect the market demands of individual consumers. In this case, it is assumed that consumers have been subsidized or taxed to achieve the income distribution that central authorities desire. Whether the commodity is a consumption good or an item necessary in another industry's production process, it is assumed that the demand and cost curves are the schedules that exist after government planners have imposed a tax on the commodity or have provided a subsidy. The original market price, in each case, is the price that central planners consider socially optimal prior to any shifts or potential shifts in these schedules.

An autonomous shift in demand

In Figure 5.6, suppose that average and marginal costs for the industry are represented by MC_1 and AC_1, respectively, and that demand for the product is responsive to price in the manner represented by D_1D_1. Price

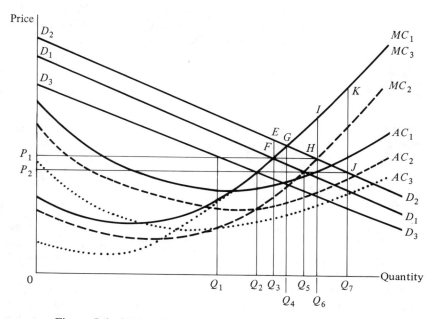

Figure 5.6. The implications of changes in an industry's cost and demand functions.

and output are at the optimal levels P_1 and Q_3, respectively. Suppose that an autonomous shift in demand occurs from D_1D_1 to D_2D_2. If producers are maximizing sales they will expand output to Q_6; if they are maximizing profits they will continue to produce Q_3, as long as a black market is prevented. Neither output level is equal to the optimal amount Q_4.

Under the sales-maximization criterion, the cost to society of producing excess amount $Q_6 - Q_4$ is represented in Figure 5.6 by

$$\int_{Q_4}^{Q_6} MC_1 \, dQ.$$

The amount that customers are willing to pay for the extra $Q_6 - Q_4$ is represented by

$$\int_{Q_4}^{Q_6} D_2D_2 \, dQ.$$

Clearly, the former exceeds the latter and the difference, the area *GHI,* represents the loss to society from producing Q_6 instead of Q_4. Under profit maximization, the customers would be willing to pay

$$\int_{Q_3}^{Q_4} D_2 D_2 \, dQ$$

for the amount $Q_4 - Q_3$. The cost to the economy producing $Q_4 - Q_3$ would be

$$\int_{Q_3}^{Q_4} MC_1 \, dQ$$

and the loss to society due to underproduction can be represented by the area *EFG.* It is not clear which of *GHI* or *EFG* is greater, and hence it is not clear which criterion will result in the greater misallocation of resources.

Suppose that an autonomous shift in demand from $D_1 D_1$ to $D_3 D_3$ occurs. Both profit-maximizing and sales-maximizing firms will tend to reduce output to Q_1 if they must continue to sell their product at the price P_1. Excess supply can exist in the market until they reach Q_1. Excess supply can exist even though total output of the particular product is less than the optimal amount Q_2.

Innovation that reduces both average and marginal costs without affecting the demand for the product

Suppose that a suggested change in technology can reduce both average and marginal costs for an industry from AC_1 to AC_2 and from MC_1 to MC_2, respectively, in Figure 5.6. The demand for the product is represented by $D_1 D_1$. Maximization of social welfare will require expansion of production from Q_3 to Q_5.

Under profit maximization, if no collusion exists each firm will adopt the innovation and will expand its production. Total production will tend towards Q_6, exceeding Q_5; and excess supply of the product will exist. This tendency towards overproduction will continue until government planners lower the product price to P_2. The sales-maximizing industry, on the other hand, will not be interested in the innovation since its ability to expand output and sales would not be improved. Hence, it might tend to produce less than the optimal amount Q_5 and its average cost might be higher than that in a profit-maximizing industry.

Innovation that reduces average cost but raises marginal cost in the relevant output range without affecting the demand for the product

Suppose that the demand for a product is represented by D_2D_2 in Figure 5.6; average and marginal cost are represented by AC_2 and MC_2, respectively. Price has been set at P_1 and output equals Q_6. It is at least theoretically possible that an innovation could reduce average cost from AC_2 to AC_3 and at the same time shift marginal cost from MC_2 to MC_3, where MC_3 is equal to MC_1 for large quantities of the commodity but lies below both MC_1 and MC_2 for small quantities.

For maximization of social welfare, the industry should adopt the new technology if the reduction in total costs exceeds the reduction in aggregate customer satisfaction, that is, if AC_2Q_6 minus AC_3Q_4 (where AC_2 is calculated at output Q_6 and AC_3 at output Q_4) exceeds

$$\int_{Q_4}^{Q_6} D_2D_2 \, dQ.$$

Whether or not the new technology should be adopted depends on the precise nature of the demand and cost curves. The sales-maximizing industry will disregard such an innovation regardless of the precise nature of demand and cost curves. The profit-maximizing industry will adopt it if AC_2Q_6 minus AC_3Q_3 (where AC_2 is calculated at output Q_6 and AC_3 at output Q_3) exceeds $P_1 \, (Q_3 - Q_6)$. This decision-making rule is not the rule for maximization of social welfare, and it is possible that the innovation will be adopted when it should be ignored. Even if the profit-maximizing industry should innovate and does so, nevertheless, its output of Q_3 will be less than the socially optimal amount Q_4, and excess demand will exist for this product.

Innovation that improves the quality of the product, increasing demand but raising both average and marginal costs

Suppose that demand is represented by D_1D_1 and average and marginal costs are represented by AC_2 and MC_2, respectively. The product price is set at P_2 and output equals Q_5. Suppose that a quality improvement can shift the demand for the product from D_1D_1 to D_2D_2 but that this quality improvement will raise both average and marginal costs from AC_2 to AC_1 and MC_2 to MC_1, respectively.

It is clear that the profit-maximizing industry will not be interested in adopting the innovation unless the product's price is increased. That is, any such innovation definitely requires prior consultation with the central planners. Sales-maximizing firms will be quick to adopt the innovation since it will permit them to expand sales from Q_5 to Q_7. However, this expansion is too great from the view of maximizing social welfare. In order to determine which position is worse, it is necessary to compare these amounts:

$$\int_0^{Q_4} D_2D_2 \, dQ - \int_0^{Q_4} MC_1 \, dQ - \int_0^{Q_5} D_1D_1 \, dQ + \int_0^{Q_5} MC_2 \, dQ$$

and

$$\int_0^{Q_4} D_2D_2 \, dQ - \int_0^{Q_4} MC_1 \, dQ - \int_0^{Q_7} D_2D_2 \, dQ + \int_0^{Q_7} MC_1 \, dQ.$$

It is possible that the innovation can not improve social welfare even if the optimal amount Q_4 is produced; that is,

$$\int_0^{Q_4} D_2D_2 \, dQ - \int_{Q_5}^{Q_4} MC_1 \, dQ \text{ may be less than } \int_0^{Q_5} D_1D_1 \, dQ$$
$$- \int_0^{Q_5} MC_2 \, dQ.$$

Innovation that improves the quality of the product, increasing demand, raising average cost, and reducing marginal cost in the relevant output range

Suppose that demand is represented by D_1D_1; average and marginal costs are represented by AC_3 and MC_3, respectively. Price is set at P_1 and output is Q_3. Suppose that an innovation can shift demand from D_1D_1 to D_2D_2, but it raises average cost from AC_3 to AC_2 and shifts marginal cost from MC_3 to MC_2.

In this case, the profit-maximizing industry might adopt the new technology. It would do so if $(P_1 - AC_2) Q_6$ exceeds $(P_1 - AC_3) Q_3$, where AC_2 is calculated at Q_6 and AC_3 at Q_3. It is impossible to predict whether its output Q_6 would be greater or less than the optimal output should it adopt the innovation since MC_2 might intersect D_2D_2 to the left or right of H. It is clear that this decision-making rule varies from the socially optimal rule that such an innovation should be implemented if

$$\int_0^{Q_6} D_2 D_2 \, dQ - AC_2 Q_6 \text{ exceeds } \int_0^{Q_3} D_1 D_1 \, dQ - AC_3 Q_3.$$

Sales-maximizing firms would be quick to adopt the new technology, whether or not the latter criterion was met.

Essay and discussion topics

1. Compare the extent of price controls within two or more economic systems. For each system, indicate the relationship between the reliance on price controls and the attainment of the society's objectives.
2. For two or more economic systems, compare a particular economic activity where price controls are a prominent organizational model. Indicate the advantages and shortcomings of price controls as illustrated by this economic activity.
3. Discuss the advantages and disadvantages of the temporary use, by two or more societies, of a general wage- and price-control program.

CHAPTER 6

Subsidies

Introduction

Subsidies have become an important decision mode within most economic systems. Subsidies may assist certain economic activities by reducing their production costs. Subsidies may assist individuals by reducing the price they pay for particular goods and services, and some cash subsidies are designed to raise the income levels of the poor. The objectives of production subsidies are generally to improve efficiency and to stimulate growth, whereas consumption and income subsidies generally pursue some aspect of equality. Nevertheless, some production subsidies are directed specifically at regions with higher than average unemployment, and these may be seen as an attempt to achieve a more equal distribution of opportunities and incomes geographically within the society. Some consumption and income subsidies, such as those to support education, may be seen as fostering efficient labour adjustment and growth. Hence, many subsidies may be advocated on the basis of each broad social objective.

Subsidies alter the price ratios that would result in a free, competitive marketplace. Consumption subsidies encourage people to purchase those goods and services whose prices are being subsidized. The business recipients of subsidies will likely offer their goods and services for sale at lower prices than would exist in the absence of subsidies, and so business subsidies may also alter consumption patterns. Foreign-based corporations may regard these lower prices as unfair competition. Hence international trade negotiations have come to focus on many of these subsidy programs as a trade distortion that should be limited by formal international agreements. The GATT Tokyo round of negotiations resulted in subsidy codes for particular types of subsidies. Meanwhile, some countries impose special countervail duties if their corporations are being hurt by foreign subsidies. Hence the role of subsidies must be considered in the context of international trade negotiations. With current and projected reductions in tariff barriers, subsidies will become relatively more important as a trade-determining process. Hence, international trade negotiations will likely devote more attention to these government subsidies. In particular, discussions about freer trade will have to confront this issue, since the elimination of tariffs increases the vulnerability of a nation to the subsidies provided by its trading partners. Nevertheless, subsidies are implemented to pursue certain social objectives, and so an intergovernmental pact that limits subsidies may diminish, rather than improve, the well-being of signatories.

For production subsidies, the objectives of efficiency and growth are particularly important. High levels of unemployment and low rates of productivity growth underlie much of the argument in favour of business subsidies. If all political entities were to experience rapid growth and full employment, the economic rationale for business subsidies would lose some of its significance. Nevertheless, in many cases investment by a private firm provides benefits which cannot be appropriated by the firm but which are significant for others within the political entity where the investment is located. Such benefits, which are external to the firms, may include the following:

> Government cost savings. Government may decrease expenditures, particularly payments to the unemployed, if firms hire workers who would otherwise be unemployed.
>
> On-the-job training. Many of the unemployed will need to learn new skills in order to work, and these skills may best be learned in an apprentice-type of training within a firm. Without such retraining, many of the unemployed may remain jobless indefinitely.
>
> Sharing of costs. New investment is often seen as a means of spreading these high government costs over new taxpayers. Recession and diminished productivity growth can strengthen this view.
>
> The advancement of productivity growth. The general level of scientific knowledge and skill through investment in high-tech industries can assist other firms and individuals in their adoption of new technology. Consequently, many point to certain high-tech activities as deserving production subsidies.

Underlying these, and forming the focus for much of the public concern and political debate, is the perception that a society's international competitiveness will be strengthened by the use of subsidies. Many advocates of financial incentives believe that a society can, in fact, engineer a comparative advantage in its international trade relations.[1]

A useful analytical structure is based on the view that externalities are offered by potential investors for sale to governments. An international market exists for these externalities, as many governments compete to attract business investment and production. It is not clear whether a government will focus only on externalities as they affect government revenue and expenditures, or whether the government will also consider the impact of externalities on other individuals within the political entity. Recently, a substantial literature has developed concerning the ability of individuals to influence a government's decisions so as to benefit themselves, and this will be discussed further in Chapter 10. The extent to which a government includes considerations of externalities will depend, to some degree, upon the society's political structure. For example, private costs of unemployment caused by plant closings may or may not be included in a government's calculations. Some would argue that at least some private costs should be included, such as loss of income due to job search and retraining, if the political entity's overall welfare is to be maximized. Negative externalities are also relevant. If an investment or production decision results in negative as well as positive externalities, political entities seeking to maximize their welfare may tend to offer a subsidy equal to net externalities.

Also of importance is the impact of subsidized investment on existing manufacturers. Subsidized investment will expand the supply of a product, and existing manufacturers of that product may consequently suffer reductions in output, employment, and profits. For a government, the calculation of net externalities and appropriate subsidies may also include estimates of these negative results.

The previous discussion has dealt with *production subsidies.* Also of importance are *consumption* and *income subsidies,* which are based upon the equality objective of assisting low income groups. Since consumption and income subsidies differ from production subsidies so markedly, in objectives as well as mechanics, this chapter deals with them separately. Usually, consumption subsidies are directed at certain goods and services that are considered to be necessities in the modern economy. Often, these are subsidized for all consumers. Yet, receipt of these subsidies is sometimes dependent upon one's income, with a central objective being assistance to low-income people. The bulk of consumption subsidies are provided for health, education, and housing. Furthermore, most societies have developed a set of income subsidies aimed at certain low-income groups. Terms and conditions are related, in many programs, to specific characteristics of prospective recipients, such as marital status, age, or types of infirmities. Consumption and income subsidies are discussed later in this chapter.

I. Production subsidies

Introduction

The use of production subsidies has varied significantly among countries and over time. Tables 6.1 and 6.2 present OECD subsidy data for eighteen countries for the years 1960, 1965, 1970, 1975, and 1980. These data have been compiled on the basis of the following definition:

Public subsidies are transfers to firms, rather than to individuals; formally, they are grants on current accounts made by government to private industries and public corporations; and grants made by the public authorities to government enterprises in compensation for operating losses when these losses are clearly the consequence of the policy of the government to maintain prices at a level below costs of production.[2]

Table 6.1 presents subsidies as a percentage of GDP for each of these years. These figures range from 0.24 percent in the United States in 1960 to 8.38 percent in Ireland in 1980. The unweighted average has increased from 1.46 percent to 3.02 percent over the twenty-year period, reflecting a substantial increase in the use of production subsidies. Table 6.2 presents subsidies as a percentage of current government outlays. These figures range from 0.96 percent in the United States in 1960 to 17.34 percent in Ireland in 1980. Table 6.2 indicates that subsidies are a major component of total government expenditures. The unweighted average has increased slightly, from 5.68 percent in 1960 to 6.88 percent in 1980, indicating that the use of subsidies has grown slightly faster than other government expenditures.

To illustrate the diversity in types of production subsidies, the next two sections of this chapter discuss some types of subsidy programs. These discussions do not seek to cover the entire range of production subsidies, but rather attempt to convey examples of alternative terms and conditions for providing subsidies. We then turn to brief discussions of agricultural subsidies, bailout subsidies, wage subsidies, regional subsidies, and R&D subsidies. Finally, we consider international agreements that seek to limit production subsidies. As we consider these various subsidies, we encounter a number of programs that have probably not been included in Tables 6.1 and 6.2, indicating that the OECD data may significantly underestimate the role of production subsidies.

In many countries, government agencies and programs provide loans, investments, and loan guarantees.[3] Such programs do not involve outright grants, but rather the provision of capital on terms more favourable than the recipients could obtain in the market. It is not possible to

Table 6.1. *Public subsidies as a percentage of GDP in advanced capitalist democracies*

	1960	1965	1970	1975	1980
Australia	0.52	0.71	0.92	0.49	0.77
Austria	1.58[a]	2.25	1.73	2.89	3.01
Belgium	1.93	2.28	2.88	3.88	4.06
Canada	0.81	0.82	0.87	2.31	2.38
Denmark	0.31[a]	0.83[a]	2.69	2.78	3.18
Finland	2.87	3.22	3.01	4.06	4.07
France	1.62	2.17	1.97	2.44	2.51
Germany	0.83	1.25	1.74	1.99	2.02
Ireland	3.28	3.95	4.88	6.88	8.38
Italy	1.36	1.28	1.49	2.66	3.01
Japan	0.34[a]	0.71	1.10	1.49	1.47
Netherlands	1.21	0.70	1.26	1.78	2.68
New Zealand	1.14	0.97	1.01	3.40	1.43
Norway	4.45	4.50	5.15	6.23	6.88
Sweden	0.97	1.43	1.67	3.07	4.35
Switzerland	0.98[a]	0.93[a]	0.84[a]	1.20[a]	1.32[a]
United Kingdom	1.93	1.61	1.74	3.53	2.35
United States	0.24	0.45	0.50	0.32	0.41
Unweighted average	1.46	1.67	1.97	2.83	3.02

[a]Former SNA.

Source: J. J. Blais, "The Political Economy of Public Subsidies," *Comparative Political Studies* 19 (July 1986), p. 203.

estimate precisely the extent of the subsidy involved in such programs, since one could not be sure of the terms the recipient would in fact have to accept in the market if these programs did not exist. Hence, programs such as these suggest the difficulties in comparing the significance of production subsidies among societies. It is also important to recognize the large and growing role of subnational governments in the provision of subsidies in some societies.[4] Many countries have created programs to encourage research and development (R&D) innovation and the adoption of new technology. These programs, to the extent that they provide financial assistance, could also be regarded as subsidies. Furthermore, as discussed in Chapter 7, it could be argued that tax concessions aimed at providing financial incentives for R&D and particular investments also represent a form of subsidy. Export development corporations are particularly important in international negotiations because of the direct impact they can have on trade patterns.

Private corporations in other countries may feel that certain firms

Table 6.2. *Public subsidies as a percentage of current government
outlays in advanced capitalist countries*

	1960	1965	1970	1975	1980
Australia	2.72	3.36	3.91	1.58	2.53
Austria	6.29[a]	7.16	5.26	7.50	7.04
Belgium	4.49[a]	3.88[a]	4.01[a]	2.89[a]	3.14[a]
Canada	3.19	3.26	2.71	6.29	6.32
Denmark	1.41[a]	3.19[a]	—	6.39	6.08
Finland	12.65	12.46	10.03	12.63	11.87
France	4.97[a]	6.43	5.68	6.23	5.83
Germany	2.93	4.07	5.35	4.57	4.71
Ireland	13.43[a]	14.50	14.23	16.40	17.34
Italy	5.21	4.17	4.95	6.96	7.27
Japan	2.51[a]	5.00	7.84	7.14	5.77
Netherlands	4.50	2.21[a]	3.30	3.68	4.95
New Zealand	—	—	—	—	—
Norway	15.50[a]	14.86	14.12	14.90	15.26
Sweden	3.60	4.73	4.49	6.85	7.62
Switzerland	5.69[a]	4.72[a]	3.94[a]	4.17[a]	4.51[a]
United Kingdom	6.47	5.19	5.23	8.61	5.57
United States	0.96	1.77	1.64	0.99	1.23
Unweighted average	5.68	5.94	6.04	6.93	6.88

[a]Former SNA.
Source: J. J. Blais, "The Political Economy of Public Subsidies," *Comparative Political
Studies* 19 (July 1986), p. 204.

enjoy an unfair competitive advantage to the degree that they receive
subsidized export loans at interest rates below market levels, together
with government guarantees of commercial bank loans and insurance
to cover the risk that foreign buyers will default on their payments.
Public enterprises produce and sell significant quantities of goods in
competition with private firms in other countries. Generally, such government operations do not base their prices on the same market criteria
followed by private firms, nor do they always pay the same levels of
corporate income taxes as private firms. A market rate of return on
capital invested is usually not of the same concern in government as in
private business operations. Government provision of capital to such
firms at less than market rates, and government payments to cover
operating losses, can provide significant subsidies for the products concerned, and these subsidies may also distort trade patterns.

Government agricultural marketing agencies may also subsidize private domestic producers in a manner that affects international trade.

The EEC's common agricultural policy (CAP) has had serious effects on world trade in recent years, for example, involving disputes with the United States over exports to Egypt and China. For its own part, of course, the U.S. government's price-support programs have a major effect on the prices and quantities of traded agricultural products. This subject of agricultural production subsidies will be discussed further in a later section.

U.S. production subsidies for high-tech firms

Substantial U.S. production subsidies have been directed to "high-tech" activities. Much of these have been developed at the state rather than the federal level, and the purpose of this section is to provide some examples. An Office of Technology Assessment Study in 1983 indicated that there were 153 state government programs with at least some emphasis on high-technology development and that of these, thirty-eight were specifically dedicated to high-tech firms. Most of these 153 initiatives were launched between 1980 and 1983, with the vast majority (85 percent) having had no form of evaluation.[5] The study also revealed the range of diversified industries which states were attempting to foster. The two most sought after industries were those pertaining to computer software and biomedical activities.[6]

By the end of 1985, about twenty states had invested a total of $200 million in venture-capital pools.[7] The reasons for state involvement may stem from two factors. First, as emphasized by a U.S. Small Business Administration study, the initial seed capital phase of high-tech business development is the stage at which a private venture capitalist is least likely to take part.[8] Second, most venture-capital firms are found in either California or New York, and the few venture-capital firms located towards the interior of the nation are reluctant to deal with local high-tech firms; for example, midwest venture capitalists account for only 11 percent of the nation's total venture capital and the majority of those funds go to firms located on either the East or West coast.[9]

States participate in venture-capital programs in various ways. A state government may invest directly in firms, utilizing funds from tax revenues, general-obligation bond financing, or Federal agency programs, such as the Economic Development Administration (EDA) of the U.S. Department of Commerce. An example of direct state investment can be found in the Connecticut Product Development Corporation (CPDC). Created in 1975, the corporation provides risk capital for new products and procedures and typically receives royalty payments of 5 percent of product sales.[10] The CPDC also runs two other financial programs for firms producing new products: A program provides funding for firms in the start-up phase of development, and the Connecticut Innovation Development Loan Fund provides low interest loans to companies with innovative new products.[11]

Illinois offers grants to universities, research groups, and small businesses for projects which lead to new product development. Both products and services are eligible for the program, but they must be marketed by in-state firms. Furthermore, these funds can be utilized towards any aspect of the "commercialization of the product or service, including R&D, marketing, location of additional funding, or establishing or upgrading technology transfer networks."[12]

The New York Corporation for Innovation Development (CID) was established in 1981 by the New York State Science and Technology Foundation. CID provides assistance to technologically based new business ventures or new product/process development in existing business in federal EDA eligible areas.[13] Assistance is granted to small, locally controlled businesses which demonstrate substantial benefits to the state, usually through employment and infrastructure improvements. The projects must be ready to be marketed and the entrepreneur must obtain a three-to-one match in additional funds from other sources. Some state direct-financing programs also involve conventional debt and equity financing, for example, those in Louisiana and Maryland.[14]

State participation in venture-capital initiatives can also be indirect. Often, the private sector is encouraged to undertake economic development on behalf of the state. Such a corporation can be a profit or nonprofit organization. Tax reductions or tax credits which are equal to a predetermined percentage of the investment are often used to entice private investors to invest in such a corporation.[15] The Massachusetts Technology Development Corporation (MTDC), for example, was created as an independent nonprofit public venture-capital firm in 1979 to provide technical assistance and start-up capital to small, innovative technology-based businesses. The only restrictions were that 50 percent of MTDC investments must be in designated low-income areas and that participating firms must have been unable to secure conventional financing.[16]

Indiana and Utah are among the states that facilitate venture-capital availability through tax breaks. Indiana's Corporation for Innovation is a private, for-profit corporation created to "stimulate the growth of venture capital for investment in innovative small business enterprises."[17] The Corporation has been given the power to grant tax credits for private investment in its venture-capital fund.[18]

Some states, such as Utah, have approved a credit against the state income tax for investments in R&D Limited Partnerships (RDLPs). Such a partnership allows companies to work together to develop a product without violating federal antitrust regulations.

Subsidy programs such as these attempt to stimulate high-tech activities in order to create jobs for the unemployed and to increase growth. Other nations have also focused on high-tech activities. At this point in time, it may be too early to evaluate the effectiveness of many such programs. Consequently, we can expect to see considerable experimentation, together with changes in terms and conditions for receipt of production subsidies.

Agricultural subsidies

A 1987 OECD study, *National Policies and Agricultural Trade,* discussed a trend in many countries towards increasing amounts of government assistance to farm producers.

In the United States, expenditures by the Department of Agriculture in 1985 were, in nominal terms, more than double those in the reference period (1979–1981) and were almost 70 per cent higher in constant price terms. In Canada, in the course of the same period, budgetary expenditure on agriculture rose more than 60 per cent in nominal terms and 15 per cent in real terms. In the EEC, FEOGA expenditures almost doubled in nominal terms and rose by just under a quarter in real terms over the same period. However, for a number of EEC member countries for which the data is available there was a real decline in budget expenditures on national agricultural measures over the same period. The fastest rate of increase had occurred in New Zealand up to 1983 but subsequently public expenditures showed a considerable decline. . . . Australian expenditure more than doubled in nominal terms over the same period and increased about 40 per cent in real terms. More modest although significant increases have occurred in Austria, while Japan succeeded in maintaining more or less constant expenditures in nominal terms, i.e. a reduction in real terms. It is striking that these increases in expenditure have occurred during a difficult economic period in which economic policy in many countries was focused on the need to reduce budget deficits whilst meeting increasing claims from other sectors or groups in the economy. This reflects a number of factors including the open-endedness of most price support policies, the deterioration in world market prices and the political strength of the farming sector.[19]

Policies that protect domestic agriculture have encouraged the production of more food than can be consumed at prices prevailing in the market. Agricultural subsidies are often accompanied by government controls over marketing, so that prices are prevented from falling to a level at which markets would clear. The OECD report emphasized "it must be recognized that world markets can no longer absorb the over-capacity of OECD agricultural sectors."[20] As evidence, the report noted that value of stocks in major commodities reached 22.5 billion U.S. dollars or 17.5 billion ECUs in 1983. For a breakdown of the stock piles which had accrued by product and country see Table 6.3.

These figures illustrate that government efforts to support farm incomes and maintain a domestic agricultural sector can cause resources to be wasted. The World Bank in 1986 reported a number of studies, each of which revealed that the costs borne by the consumers and tax-payers exceeded the size of the transfers made to farmers.[21] "World Bank and OECD sources estimate that total costs to consumers and taxpayers of agricultural support in OECD countries range from $100 billion to $150 billion annually. . . . A recent analysis by the United States Department of Agriculture estimates that for every dollar producers may lose through trade liberalization, consumers and taxpayers gain more than a dollar ($1.40 in the United States)."[22] In addition, programs can not only cause overproduction, they can also cause the costs of production to rise. Transfers are generally capitalized into assets such as land and this raises future production costs. Furthermore, the benefits of agricultural subsidies are often directed towards wealthier farmers who own the land and who can afford the capitalized costs as opposed to those who are in the most need of assistance.[23]

The extent to which agriculture is subsidized may be best understood through a measure known as the producer subsidy equivalent (PSE) which is the amount that would have to be paid to farmers as compensation for the loss of income resulting from a cancellation of the various subsidies. Table 6.4 shows that for each country, dairy farmers receive the most assistance as a percentage of income, and among countries the size of the assistance varies. Generally, Australia and New Zealand appear to have the smallest involvement in subsidies, whereas Japan and European countries seem to rely most on these subsidies. Canadian support exceeds that of America and approaches a leading position in terms of the producer subsidy equivalent. As these studies indicate, the cost may exceed the benefits of subsidization. Often, governments have willingly supported agriculture because of the strength of a farmers' lobby and the belief that self-sufficiency is desirable. The 1987 OECD study calculated that with a cut in assistance of 10 percent, existing stocks of dairy products could be reduced to near zero in four to five years, without major adjustments to the world price level.[24] From the perspective of the consumer and the taxpayer, there is a compelling argument for a reduction in agricultural subsidies. A key element however, must be the realization that one or two countries cannot implement

Table 6.3. *Stocks of selected agricultural products (1000 tons)*

	1972	1973	1974	1975	1976	1977	1978	1979	1980	1981	1982	1983	1984	1985	1986[a]
Butter															
EEC	303	201	148	164	255	194	418	372	240	147	306	553	949	1,124	1,324
United States	89	68	53	45	37	90	128	114	134	230	246	268	234	130	132
Australia	17	9	12	29	11	18	22	13	6	11	15	24	32	29	19
New Zealand	25	13	28	38	31	24	23	32	29	20	27	21	80	90	112
Skimmed milk powder															
EEC	220	116	365	1,012	1,135	965	674	227	230	279	576	983	617	520	757
United States	20	34	89	200	219	278	318	244	249	333	514	636	645	493	449
Australia	17	9	5	57	38	7	6	10	9	18	10	17	24	12	9
New Zealand	114	92	41	183	214	129	64	90	76	80	114	77	75	60	34
Wheat															
EEC	7,600	6,200	7,600	10,600	8,500	8,700	7,700	10,100	8,800	9,300	7,600	10,800	7,500	16,200	18,200
United States	26,800	16,200	9,300	11,800	18,100	30,300	32,000	25,100	24,500	26,900	31,700	41,200	38,100	38,800	51,900
Australia	1,400	500	1,900	1,700	2,700	2,100	800	4,600	4,300	2,000	2,600	2,300	7,500	8,500	5,700
Canada	15,900	9,900	10,100	8,000	8,000	13,300	12,100	14,900	10,700	8,600	9,800	10,000	9,200	7,600	8,500
Beef and veal															
EEC	0	34	225	221	356	292	191	272	310	180	204	368	606	646	481
Australia	85	103	113	106	107	137	136	82	69	67	49	42	36	45	45

Closing stocks

Notes:

Butter

EEC	Public intervention stocks plus privately aided stocks	31.12
US	CCC plus private stocks	01.07
Australia	Private stocks in cold stores	01.07
New Zealand	Export stocks	01.07

Skimmed milk powder

EEC	Public intervention stocks	31.12
US	CCC plus private stocks	01.07
Australia	Private stocks in cold stores	01.07
New Zealand	Export stocks	01.07

Beef

EEC	Public intervention stocks (product weight)	31.12
Australia	Stocks of frozen beef (carcass weight)	31.12

Wheat

EEC	August/July
US	June/May
Australia	December/November; from 1983: October/September
Canada	August/July

^aForecast for 1986.

Source: OECD, *Structural Adjustment and Economic Performance* (Paris: OECD, 1987), p. 195.

Table 6.4. *Producer subsidy equivalents by commodity and country, average 1979–81 (percentages)*

	USA	Canada	EEC[a]	Australia	Japan	N. Zealand	Nordic[b]	Mediterr.[c]	Austria	OECD[d]
Dairy	48.2	66.5	68.8	20.8	83.3	18.0	70.8	68.4	77.9	63.5
Wheat	17.2	17.6	28.1[e]	3.4	95.8	−8.2	56.6	10.7	21.1[f]	21.5
Coarse grains	13.1	13.3	27.9	2.9	107.1	5.3	54.7	14.8	19.5	19.0
Beef and veal	9.5	13.1	52.7	4.0	54.9	12.5	61.6	17.6	42.9	30.0
Pig meat	6.2	14.5	21.7	2.7	14.0	7.4	23.5	16.7	32.2	16.5
Poultry meat	6.3	25.7	16.4	2.5	20.5	4.7	43.4	19.4	28.4	14.0
Sugar	17.1	12.5	25.0	−5.0	48.4	··	··	39.7	39.4	26.6
Rice	5.4	··	13.6	14.4	68.8	··	··	41.9	··	61.0
Sheep meat	··	··	45.0	3.1	··	18.2	63.5	14.8	··	28.5
Wool	··	··	··	3.9	··	16.3	0.0	26.9	··	9.4
Soybeans	6.9	··	36.2	··	108.1	··	··	21.9	··	9.0
Average, all above commodities	16.0	23.9	42.8	4.7	59.4	15.5	56.1	26.1	42.8	32.1

Notes: ·· not calculated. Minus sign indicates a tax on producers. Different combinations of commodities are included under the headings coarse grains and dairy for different countries.
[a]EEC-10.
[b]Finland, Iceland, Norway, Sweden, Switzerland.
[c]Portugal, Spain, Turkey.
[d]Based on national currencies converted to U.S. dollars at prevailing exchange rates.
[e]Common and durum wheat.
[f]Wheat and rye.
Source: OECD, *National Policies and Agricultural Trade* (Paris: OECD, 1987), p. 117.

the change alone. Cooperation is crucial in the negotiation of an inter-governmental agreement.

Finally, it is worth noting the summary made by William Miner and Dan Hathaway in their book, *World Agricultural Trade: Building a Consensus.*

There is growing recognition that these policies of support and protection to agriculture are responsible for excess production and are adding to the market and income instability that farm policies are designed to overcome. These policies create conflicts among producers who use the higher-priced farm inputs in their own production. The policies also increase the costs to the food processing industries and to the consuming public, thus adding to overall cost structures. ... Substantial public expenditures on agriculture add to the fiscal burdens and to budget deficits in some industrial countries, giving rise to further domestic policy conflicts.[25]

Bailout subsidies

In recent years, a widely used form of subsidy has been the government bailout of firms that are approaching bankruptcy and closure. The bailout is usually advocated as a means of restructuring the organization so as to make it more efficient and hence to enable a continuation of the firm. When many employees are involved, the local community and the society as a whole have a strong interest in ensuring that operations continue. If the firm shuts down a plant or lays off workers, society must suffer from the strains of increased unemployment. In their book, *New Deals: The Chrysler Revival and the American System,* Robert Reich and John Donahue present the following three examples of bailouts.[26]

Hyster Company makes forklifts which are produced and sold worldwide. In 1982, Hyster's management believed that plant closures were inevitable. In 1979, the firm had earned a net profit of $63 million but by 1982 sales had fallen by some 40 percent. Hyster informed the governments in the respective areas where operations existed that plant closures could be avoided if adequate financing were made available. Hyster thus managed to raise $72.5 million in direct aid by seeking government bids. In the end, "[the] biggest winner was Danville, Illinois. With an unemployment rate of 16 per cent at the time, Danville agreed to provide roughly $10 million in operating subsidies and training grants."[27] Perhaps the biggest winner, however, was Hyster itself. The firm had recognized that by threatening to close plants it could encourage competition among governments for the social benefits accruing from continued production. The result was the bidding up of subsidies.

A second case raises the issue of whether a government should offer assistance to a corporation which appears to lack the ability to make a requisite turnaround to profitable status. British Leyland's (BL) financial situation became precarious for the first time in 1974. BL's market share in Britain fell from 45 to 33 percent and on the Continent from 10 to 7 percent. Initially, the losses incurred over 1973–4 were managed through $1.2 billion worth of new loans secured from Britain's major banking institutions. Unfortunately, this could not alleviate the ills of BL. The 1975 Ryder Report blamed the losses on "inadequate investment, poor labour relations, and an awkward organization"[28] but recommended that the government offer assistance since "vehicle production is the kind of industry which ought to remain an essential part of the United Kingdom's economic base."[29] Consequently, Prime Minister Harold Wilson began the bailout with $425 million of new capital and an offer of more, provided performance standards were met. The British government was now a senior partner in British Leyland.

By 1979, BL's market share had fallen below 20 percent and production was down almost 50 percent from its level in 1973. Losses reached $242 million dollars for the year. Reich and Donahue note, "This sorry performance, to be sure, was by no means exclusively the fault of British Leyland's management. Revenue from North Sea oil sales had strengthened the pound, making all British exports less attractive and drawing in competitive foreign products, including cars."[30] The new Thatcher government had committed itself to continued support, but repeated subsidies were required in the early 1980s, totalling the equivalent of several billion U.S. dollars. By 1983 British Leyland's operations were almost at a financial break-even point. The costs of recovery had been extensive, and in the end 100,000 jobs were lost and plants throughout the Midlands were closed, aggravating regional disparities.

In contrast to the British Leyland bailout, Reich and Donahue present the case of a Japanese car manufacturer, Toyo Kogyo. In 1951 Toyo Kogyo began producing a successful line of trucks under the brandname of Mazda. By 1973, Toyo Kogyo was Japan's third largest auto manufacturer employing 37,000 people. The 1973 oil shock was disastrous for Toyo Kogyo, however, since its rotary engine proved to be an inefficient source of power.

Toyo Kogyo's president Kohei Matsuda responded to the developing crisis by introducing a redesigned rotary engine which would be 40 percent more efficient. Rather than cutting back current production until the new models were ready for sale, Matsuda insisted on continuing to produce the less efficient cars, ignoring the declining demand. As a result, Toyo Kogyo found itself with 126,000 cars unsold and with huge operating losses. Unable to accept Matsuda's business decisions, Toyo Kogyo's bankers replaced key officials and took over management of the firm in the fall of 1974 and implemented an austerity program. Part of the austerity program aimed at innovation, and between 1977 and 1980, ten new cars were introduced, some with the remade rotary engine and others with the conventional piston engine. When other creditors, accounting in total for 84 percent of Toyo Kogyo's $9.6 billion debt, threatened to demand payment, the Sumitomo Bank stepped in as the largest creditor, accounting for 14 percent of the debt, and promised it would stand behind Toyo Kogyo. The move reestablished faith in the firm and bought the time for the benefits of the austerity program to be realized. The government assisted indirectly by announcing its support of the survival of Toyo Kogyo. The pledge strengthened the resolve of the Sumitomo Bank and further helped Toyo Kogyo's dealings with other creditors. Reich and Donahue explain that "[by] 1980 Toyo Koygo was making money; it sold more than 1 million vehicles, slipping past Chrysler to become the world's ninth-largest carmaker and reclaiming its number three spot in Japan."[31] Success had finally come to Toyo Koygo but not without difficulty. Government support had been important but it had not been the kind given by the British Government. The key appears to have been the early recognition that restructuring was necessary and the belief that with it, the firm could eventually be competitive. By changing the models and production process, Toyo Koygo avoided closures and minimized its layoffs.

These three examples illustrate the use by various societies of bailout subsidies in order to assist the adjustment process. They emphasize the need to consider each case on its own merits, and they suggest the considerable uncertainty involved in predicting the ultimate viability of the enterprise. Even after the bailout is completed, calculation of costs and benefits of the subsidy may be quite imprecise.

Wage subsidies

Recognizing that subsidies may be used to replace employees with new equipment, Metcalf has suggested that aid should be given to "sectors where the elasticity of substitution between capital and labour is low, if the aim is to minimize adverse employment consequences of industrial assistance."[32] A more direct approach is to subsidize wages directly. The British Temporary Employment Subsidy (TES) offered firms a certain amount per week for a maximum of fifty-two weeks for each employee they refrained from terminating. A study of the TES found that of the jobs protected by the program for a year, 40 percent were continued after assistance ended.[33] Labour subsidies may be particularly useful in minimizing unemployment at times of recession, with a temporary reduction in demand.

Some have argued for wage subsidies directed at on-the-job training as a way of assisting the apprenticeship process. Davies and MacDonald have examined the use of public funds for on-the-job training,[34] and they have emphasized the needs of young people. Initially, all young people require substantial on-the-job training, and this makes corporations reluctant to hire them. Subsidies to corporations are justified in the interests of achieving this practical education. Administrative costs and bureaucratic red tape could be minimized by simply giving all corporations a uniform wage subsidy geared to the employee's age. According to Davies,

One universal and administratively cheap proposal would be to offer wage subsidies inversely related to age for all young workers – for example, $1.50 per hour for those aged 16 to 18 and $1.00 per hour for those 19 to 20. It will be argued by some that this would just lead to an expansion in dead-end jobs for the young, because of the lack of a required training component in the jobs subsidized. Some of the subsidy would no doubt go to support such jobs, but this has to be weighed against the benefits of the scheme, including reduced youth unemployment as well as greater OJT [on-the-job training] and the considerable cost of enforcing standards. If the minimum wage is severely reducing OJT for workers in the target age brackets, then the subsidy creates critical room for the intensity of training to increase.[35]

Regional subsidies

Many nations have implemented large-scale regional development programs to provide special investment subsidies to firms locating in depressed regions. In France, the Regional Policy Grant (PAT) is a project-related grant made to manufacturing, research, and service-sector activities in areas suffering from high levels of structural unemployment. PAT awards have often been scaled to the number of jobs created with a maximum rate per job available. Ceilings limit the size of grants, and these are expressed in terms of a percentage of eligible project investment for manufacturing investments, usually 17 to 25 percent. Another French program involves the Regional Employment Grant (PRE) which offers a certain amount per job created in towns with populations of over 100,000 and a larger amount per job created in outlying areas. The PRE applies only to the first thirty jobs created, and consequently, aims at fostering an expansion of small-business enterprises. A third form of assistance exists in tax concessions which may be granted by local authorities for a period of up to five years.[36]

In 1984, the French government departed from its emphasis on employment subsidies by denoting some fifteen regions as *conversion poles.* Within these less prosperous areas, the government offered aid to firms in a variety of ways. It could make direct grants irrespective of employment, subsidize wages, sponsor technical training, or improve the basic social infrastructure of the community.

In West Germany the constitution provides that "all regions of the country should enjoy the same standard of living."[37] As a result, West Berlin and the territory which connects it with the rest of West Germany qualify for extensive assistance as areas which lack the basis for a strong indigenous economic development. Since 1969, regional policy has been facilitated by a constitutional amendment which directs Lander or state governments to coordinate policy with the national government. Most assistance takes the form of tax allowances or basic investment grants with limits according to the location and size of the project. In addition European Recovery Program soft loans are available to small and medium-size firms. Udis has claimed,

As German industrial policy has evolved, the main actors have become the Ministry of Economics, which has demonstrated an aversion to providing large subsidies to traditional industries in structural decline (steel, coal, textiles, shipbuilding) and has forced rationalization (mergers and capacity reductions) upon them; and the Ministry of Research and Technology ... [, which was] formed in 1972 to administer support for high technology industry.[38]

The extensive array of policies described above seem to have evolved to meet particular problems as they arose rather than to form the components of a coherent industrial policy. Indeed, recent government responses to questions raised in the Parliament (Bundestag) by Social Democratic spokesmen concerning regional economic development and the creation of new jobs through "an active industrial policy" stress that the necessary innovation, risk taking, and investment require a reduction in state intervention and reliance on a market-oriented policy.[39]

In 1984, David Metcalf noted that "by far the largest measure of industrial assistance in Britain over the last decade has been the Regional Development Grant (RDG). . . . Gross spending on RDG in 1972–82 was some \$6 billion (in 1981 prices)."[40] The RDG is a form of assistance directed towards improving capital development and not solely towards enhancing employment opportunities. The central objective is to make Britain's industry efficient and competitive. Rather than providing capital grants to firms anywhere, the government uses the assistance to entice firms to locate projects in depressed areas. Studies indicate that the effect of the RDG may be to decrease aggregate employment, since firms are offered incentives to substitute capital for labour. Metcalf has stated that "it seems clear that the industrial distribution of the subsidy has harmed employment."[41] As a result, this program may redistribute employment and also increase the aggregate level of unemployment.

R&D subsidies

Ronald Wonnacott has pointed out that natural resources are not typically an important factor in the development of high-technology industries. Moreover, the capital requirements may often be available through the increasing international mobility of capital.[42] Technology and a highly trained and skilled work force have become the critical considerations. Government can engineer a comparative advantage in high-technology products by providing an infrastructure conducive to its development and through appropriate research and education policy. Wonnacott suggests that the advantages conferred on the first country to develop a product may overcome other disadvantages and permit the first-in country to enjoy the benefits of market power. The early decision to pursue the development of high-technology industries by the Ministry of International Trade and Investment (MITI) in Japan is often cited as an example of a successful effort to engineer a comparative advantage.[43]

Brander and Spencer show that this last point is significant for political entities considering the use of subsidies to optimize their interests vis-á-vis other political entities.[44] Whether a comparative advantage can be engineered or not, education and research will require attention if countries are to attract investment in high-technology industries. A nation's position as a society endowed with highly trained professionals and technicians cannot be taken for granted. Rather, these perspectives emphasize the importance of R&D subsidies, particularly those that link university research and education with commercial applicability. Table 6.5 indicates the widely differing roles played by governments in the United States, the United Kingdom, France, Germany, and Japan.

Subsidy pacts

Certain private-sector investments may provide the society as a whole with externalities or public benefits such as new job opportunities, a larger tax base, and a market for the products of existing firms. Those countries for whom a certain private-sector investment would provide the greatest externalities or public benefits may be expected to offer the

the

Table 6.5. *Government R&D funding of manufacturing industry*

	United States	United Kingdom	France	Germany	Japan
Government funding as percentage of total R&D expenditure (1983)	31.6	31.8[b]	23.6	13.6	1.5
Government funding as percentage of total R&D expenditure in high R&D-intensive sectors[a] (1983)	42.7	44.0[b]	36.2	19.0[b]	0.9
Share of high R&D-intensive sectors[a] in total government funding (1983)	94.8	96.3[b]	91.3	67.0[b]	25.7
Defense R&D expenditure as percentage of total government funding (1983)	64.3	49.6	32.7	9.6	2.4
Share of government-funded R&D performed in the public sector (1983)	26.0	39.0	47.0	32.0	—

[a] Aerospace, computers, electronics (including telecommunications), pharmaceuticals, scientific instruments, and electrical engineering.
[b] 1981.
Source: OECD, *Structural Adjustment and Economic Performance* (Paris: OECD, 1987), p. 218.

highest subsidies to attract that investment. Suppose that an international agreement imposes limits on subsidies to a stipulated level. With such a subsidy pact, investments and production will not be located in the country where they may provide the greatest public benefits. The lower the maximum permissible subsidy level the greater will be this effect. Generally, externalities or public benefits will be of most value to those countries or regions with the highest rates of unemployment, and so these may be the territories most hurt by such a noncompetition pact.

In recognition of these problems, the EEC established four different subsidy levels to reduce distortions caused by its noncompetition subsidy pact. In the first, and poorest, area, the ceiling on aid was set at 75 percent net grant equivalent of initial investment. In the second group, the ceiling was set at 30 percent net grant equivalent. In the third group, the ceiling was set at 25 percent net grant equivalent. For the final group, which comprises the major part of the EEC, the ceiling was set at 20 percent net grant equivalent.[45]

In each noncompetition pact, regulators, such as those who set the EEC subsidy levels, need to retain the right to alter those levels; that is, a noncompetition pact of this type should provide for changes to be made over time, whenever the regulators see that the ratios are, indeed, causing distortions. The process of establishing such ratios may well involve political trade-offs and noneconomic elements, and the procedures for establishing these ratios may affect the ratios themselves. In many countries, considerable discussion has focused on the impact of tariffs and tariff reductions on different regions of the country. With current and projected tariff reductions, such discussion will probably shift its focus to subsidies, and regional political forces will advocate their respective interest in any subsidy pact negotiations.

A pact of this type also exposes all of its participants to the risk that nonsignatories will gain benefits from the pact. Firms with externalities having a market value higher than the permissible subsidy levels will consider locating where they are not subject to the pact. The participants in the pact will have deprived themselves of a set of potential investments. The post–1945 expansion of international investment suggests that such a pact will become less useful since firms are increasingly able to shift production facilities to other countries, particularly with recent and projected decreases in tariff barriers.

A subsidy pact that deals only with new investment may shift the competitive bidding towards bailout subsidies, as pact members strive more vigorously to retain investment they already have. The extent to which such bailout competition will intensify will depend upon the degree to which the subsidy pact forces new investment to other countries. Hence, a subsidy pact which firms can avoid through international investment will cause particularly severe difficulties in terms of bailout competition among the signatories.

A subsidy pact may also focus on one particular type of subsidy, such as government export financing, and OECD countries have agreed to minimum government interest rates for export financing. The comments just made are also applicable for such agreements. In particular, the volatility of interest rates and exchange rates has emphasized the need for flexibility in the provisions of such a pact. Recent amendments to this OECD understanding provide a formula for automatic adjustments in permissible interest rates for export financing.

A 1985 Government of Canada publication provides an overview of this issue.

Official export financing among OECD countries is subject to OECD Consensus guidelines on maximum maturity limits in a range of 8½ to 10 years, minimum cash payments (down payments) of 15 percent, and minimum interest rates for the three categories of countries classified by degree of development, with higher rates for "rich" countries.

These rates are subject to adjustment semi-annually to reflect changes in market interest rates. The last changes took effect July 15, 1984 when minimum rates were increased by 1.2 percent. They now stand at 10.7 percent for "poor," 11.9 percent for "intermediate" and 13.6 percent for "rich" countries. On January 15, 1985 these rates were to decline in line with recent lower market interest rates. For currencies where market interest rates are below OECD Consensus rates, a system of commercial reference interest rates apply (e.g. for the Deutsche mark, Swiss franc, Japanese yen, Dutch guilder).

The Consensus does not cover all sectors. There is a separate agreement for nuclear power plants. Ships, other than off-shore "rigs," are covered under another OECD understanding. Aircraft are not yet covered by the Consensus but it is hoped that negotiations on an agreement will be concluded in 1985. Export credits for agricultural and military products are not subject to the Consensus. Negotiations on export credits of agricultural products are underway but progress is expected to be slow.

The OECD Consensus also sets ground rules for the use of mixed credits aimed at reducing their disruptive effect on regular commercial transactions. These specify that mixed credit transactions must have a minimum subsidy element of 20 percent and be subject to prior notification. The Development Assistance Committee (DAC) of the OECD has established guidelines for the use and reporting of "associated financing," which is any financing involving both export credits and ODA or other concessional loans. The DAC guidelines are aimed at ensuring that associated financing meets genuine developmental objectives.[46]

The problem of defining subsidies

Negotiation of a subsidy pact also has to deal with the difficult question of defining subsidies, as illustrated by the following examples:

i. Since all levels of government provide goods and services at less than market prices in a manner that subsidizes the costs of private firms, a subsidy pact will be different from those aimed at tariff reductions. In many countries, it is difficult to imagine effective national government commitments which control the actions of subnational governments within their borders. The mechanics for including provincial and state governments in negotiations would be new for many participants, and the process somewhat unclear. A pact that includes subnational governments will likely have to focus initially on a narrow and precise definition of subsidies, with gradual extensions in future agreements to include additional types of government assistance.

ii. As we shall see in Chapter 7, special tax concessions can also reduce a private firm's costs and provide a competitive advantage to much the same extent as direct subsidies. Consequently, it is likely that governments negotiating a subsidy pact will wish to include special tax concessions in such discussions. On a general level, some countries have relied on a value-added tax which is not payable on exports. In countries that impose corporate income taxes instead of value-added taxes, the argument can be made that foreign competitors' firms are being subsidized by the VAT export-rebate programs.

iii. Many governments have developed significant subsidy programs to stimulate the growth and refinement of a distinctive culture.[47] No doubt some recognition must be given to a nation's desire to strengthen its cultural identity, and some level of subsidy must be permitted for this purpose. What level of such activity and what types of programs exceed reasonable behaviour and so should become the subject for international subsidy negotiations?

Preferential treatment for domestic investors

The exclusion of foreign investors from some of the subsidies offered to domestic investors has created another area of potential conflict that could be the subject of international negotiations. In Canada, for example, special assistance to the exploration activities of oil companies through the Petroleum Incentives Program (PIP) established "a system of incentive payments for exploration and development on a scale reflecting the degree of Canadian ownership and control."[48] This left foreign-owned firms at a competitive disadvantage even if their performance within Canada was no different from that of Canadian firms. "The objection to the PIP is that it violates the principle of national treatment by making the incentive payments conditional on the degree of Canadian nationality and control of firms."[49] To qualify as having Canadian content, film productions must fulfil an arbitrary set of nationality requirements in terms of the individuals in such productions. Within any subsidy pact, an important question will be the right of access by foreigners to the subsidies being offered, and the conditions that should govern that access.

Adjustment subsidies

Increases in exports create jobs; increases in imports often threaten jobs and require costly adjustment on the part of domestic producers competing against the imports. For the population as a whole, an increase in imports that are less expensive or of better quality and more variety than domestic goods may be of great importance. But individual citizens do not stand to gain sufficiently to justify active lobbying for new trade agreements to increase imports. In addition, the beneficiaries of the new business opportunities created by such agreements may be future corporations and future employees, who have no voice in today's debate. On the other hand, increased imports would hurt a relatively small group of producers and employees, who may see their potential losses as so great as to warrant powerful political lobbying. In such a situation, a government may choose not to focus on the growth objective, but rather to cater to the vocal segment that fears possible injury.

The political strength of these vested interests is likely to be greater if they are clustered in a specific region. Furthermore, their cries of hardship may be more justified to the extent that regional concentration makes readjustment to new trade conditions more difficult. That is, entire communities could be compelled to transform their industrial structures, a process that is more difficult than if the adjustments were evenly dispersed across the country.

New trade agreements will always threaten to hurt some individuals, some corporations, some economic sectors, and some geographical regions. Those who fear they will be hurt not only object to such changes; quite naturally, they also often lobby for special government assistance to compensate for their losses.[50] Many countries may have reached a crossroads at which any significant shift in direction will have to involve adjustment subsidies. Without it, political agreement on the pursuit of a new direction will not be possible. Thus, new trade agreements may have to include adjustment subsidies as part of the arrangements.

Enforcement mechanisms with subsidy pacts

A discussion of enforcement of subsidy pact provisions crystallizes the ambiguities and complexities of this subject. State, provincial, and local governments cannot be prosecuted before international judicial bodies, and their place in international agreements and enforcement bodies has been unclear. Definitions of subsidies are necessary for compliance and essential for enforcement. Yet such definitions will not be developed easily. A wide array of government activities can act as substitutes within the subsidy field, and the prohibition of a few specific types of subsidies may lead to a shift to the use of other types of financial incentives. Furthermore, many programs such as those assisting R&D can be tailored so that, in practice, they benefit only one, or a few, firms.

An injured nation may have difficulty in retaliating directly against a violator of the pact without at the same time punishing all the signatories. An illustration of this type of problem was the 1983 U.S. restriction of specialty steel imports in retaliation against EEC subsidies. As noted by Robert Stern, "U.S. actions to restrict imports of specialty steel during 1983 were aimed primarily against government steel subsidies in certain member countries of the European Economic Community (EEC). Yet Canada may be affected adversely even though its exports are not subsidized. Thus, Canada may find its economic interests damaged by U.S. policy actions in cases when it is, so to speak, an innocent bystander."[51] This "innocent bystander" problem is likely to occur regularly in the enforcement of subsidy pacts. In addition,

Canada's exports of selected steel products to the U.S. may have been adversely affected by relief granted to U.S. producers under the Trade [Agreements] Act [of 1979]. In this case, countries other than Canada represented the source of the alleged difficulties, but the policy of restraint made no distinction among supplying countries.[52]

In this process of enforcement and regulation, interesting questions will arise concerning the effectiveness of each country's ability to retaliate if injured. Important to this will be the nature and extent of one's relations with the violating government. Small signatories may have to rely on joint retaliation or upon the goodwill of larger members.

Political elements will no doubt enter the enforcement and dispute-resolution mechanism. This has been illustrated in the U.S.–EEC 1982 steel subsidies conflict.

The Reagan Administration had repeatedly voiced its resolve to stay out of the conflict and not to interfere with the steel industry's efforts to seek relief under the laws of the land from alleged unfair competition. This resolve did not endure, however. What had begun as private legal action turned into a bitter international dispute and, also, as on previous occasions, high-level government officials soon found themselves engaged in "shuttle diplomacy."[53]

A series of observations can be made in regard to intergovernmental negotiations concerning subsidies:

These negotiations will be extremely complex, more so than traditional tariff negotiations. In particular, they will have to deal with problems of definition and with the ability of signatories to switch their subsidies to forms that have not been prohibited, and they will have to cope with new enforcement problems.

Simple agreements to reduce the level of subsidies may reduce the welfare of the signatories.

Sharing information in regard to the subsidy–investment–externality process may reduce errors in estimation and, consequently, may improve the well-being of all participants.

An optimal subsidy pact will likely involve a set of pacts, some dealing with specific types of subsidies, and some dealing with specific firms. In particular, subsidies to firms possessing market power and considering large investment or production decisions may require special intergovernmental negotiations on a case-by-case basis. This will likely be true for aircraft, automobiles, energy, petrochemicals, and defense equipment.

An optimal set of pacts will have to provide for review and adjustments to its provisions on a frequent or continual basis. A permanent structure for such review may deserve consideration.

In negotiations, all levels of government will have to be involved. This contrasts in fundamental ways with traditional tariff negotiations, which usually have involved only national governments.

Negotiations will have to consider the impact of a subsidy pact on trade with nonsignatories. Pursuant to tariff negotiations, concessions can be extended to other governments whenever the latter choose to participate in the agreements. With a subsidy pact, nonsignatories may automatically benefit from signatories' reductions of subsidies without themselves providing any concessions. This factor alone is a sufficient condition to necessitate review and flexibility with a subsidy pact, as experience accumulates and as circumstances change.

Externalities may spill over into other jurisdictions. In this case, a pact to pool subsidies and rationalize subsidy offers could make all participants better off than if the investments went elsewhere.

Analysis of the externality–subsidy market and the process of negotiating subsidy pacts will rely heavily on studies of specific firms, production processes, groups of unemployed workers, and regional disparities. This industrial organization approach will involve elements not central to traditional trade theory – elements that seek, through cost–benefit calculations, to place estimates on the various aspects of the externality–subsidy relationships. Consequently, analyzing and negotiating on a sector-by-sector basis may be most appropriate, together with the recognition that this must be an ongoing process.

II. Consumption subsidies

Introduction

Most societies provide consumption subsidies to reduce the price of certain goods and services below the price that would prevail in a free, competitive market. The objective is not to create and maintain jobs or stimulate investment and R&D; rather the objective is to assist low-income consumers. The production of these goods and services is often left to the marketplace, rather than being undertaken directly by the government. However, the amounts that are produced and their distribution among individuals are affected by the terms and conditions of the subsidy programs. In most cases, the subsidy programs are designed so that the producer receives financial assistance in return for fulfilling certain requirements. For health care, subsidies may be geared to the number of patients treated and to the nature of each treatment. For education, subsidies may be based upon the number of students and the completion of a specified curriculum. For housing, subsidies may depend upon renting to people whose incomes are below a stipulated level. With programs such as these, the producer is usually required to adhere to prices set by the government in order to receive the subsidy. Hence the analysis of price controls in Chapter 5 is relevant for these programs; and the shortcomings and limitations of price controls often appear in subsidy programs.

As an alternative or a supplement to consumption subsidies, most societies also provide income subsidies through a variety of social security and welfare programs. The relative advantages and shortcomings of income subsidies will be examined in a later section. With consumption subsidies, governments often impose regulations that require consumers to deal with specified suppliers. Freedom to choose the supplier is often limited in order to facilitate program administration or to restrain production costs. Each person may be assigned to a certain medical doctor; each student may be assigned to a certain school; each renter may have to complete a formal application and be assigned to a certain building. In this respect, consumption subsidies may require the continual and direct involvement of a public service, and so may encounter administrative problems that limit the cost-effectiveness of the program. Such administrative problems are dealt with more fully in Chapter 9.

As a way of avoiding direct public-service involvement, enhancing freedom of choice, and fostering competition among suppliers, some commentators support the concept of consumption vouchers. Each person to be assisted would receive a voucher from the government entitling the holder to acquire the particular good or service at a certain price. In the United States, for example, subsidy programs have provided food vouchers to the poor. Some commentators have advocated that educational vouchers should be given to students, permitting greater choice among schools. On the other hand, society may believe that consumers lack the knowledge and ability to make wise choices, and so a society may prefer the direct government involvement in the distribution process. Conceivably, consumption vouchers might even be bought and sold in such a way that the original recipients do not receive the consumption pattern that society believes they should have.[54]

Regardless of the program design, consumption subsidies usually rest upon a philosophy of paternalism. A society concerned solely about the consumption levels of low-income people could provide cash transfers or income subsidies to the poor. A guaranteed annual income or a negative income tax could provide each person with a level of purchasing power adequate to maintain a certain standard of living. A poverty level could be defined in monetary terms, and everyone could be assisted so as to reach or exceed that level. The next chapter will deal with this concept more fully, but here it is important to note the arguments in favour of the paternalism underlying consumption subsidies.

Paternalism in consumption subsidies rests on several related arguments. First, it stems from concerns about the nature of poverty. A society may agree upon minimum acceptable standards for particular kinds of expenditures. That is, poverty may be defined not in terms of a cash income, but rather in terms of levels of schooling, housing, food, and health care. To alleviate poverty means to raise the amount of such specified expenditures enjoyed by each member of society. One way of ensuring that these minimum standards are attained is through government programs that assist these specific expenditures directly. A society may target a host of product characteristics and consumer characteristics for special programs. For example, housing needs may be differentiated according to people's age, physical inabilities, and size of family. Various special programs may be developed for each such group. The elderly may receive general public housing assistance if they are in good health, as well as a range of subsidies for nursing home facilities if they encounter chronic illness.

Second, paternalism can rest on the belief that individuals generally will not make wise expenditure decisions, and that, consequently, the political and governmental elite should make such decisions for everyone. From this perspective, consumption may be divided into necessities and luxuries, with the necessities being subsidized to ensure that everyone does fulfil their appropriate needs. In a modern society, education, housing, and health care may be seen as necessities. A wise elite will make better decisions about these expenditures than would many individuals. An important component of this second perspective is the concern that a family unit may not provide fairly and adequately for all its members. Cash transfers might not be divided appropriately among all family members. In particular, the needs of a wife and children require the paternalistic intervention of society – and so do the needs of elderly family members. There may be some connection between the deterioration of family responsibility and the acceptance by society as a whole of a collective responsibility.

A third perspective sees paternalism as necessary to impose a greater measure of equality. Equality in particular types of consumption may be a basic social goal – even a moral or religious goal. For some people, inequality in health care is simply an unacceptable concept. Some regard equal access to education as an essential component of the equal opportunity which should underlie their society. Consumption subsidies may achieve greater equality in the consumption of such goods and services.

Some people have particular handicaps or special needs and this may be a reason for subsidies for certain goods and services. A society may wish to provide for each such category. A universal system of cash redistribution would not suffice. Some people need transportation in vehicles designed for wheel chairs; some need day care for their children; and some need particular kinds of assistance from social workers in order to deal with their problems of alcohol, drugs, family discord, or psychiatric rehabilitation. Mothers who want to work may need day care centres in particular locations.

Paternalism may be much more than the decision to subsidize particular goods and services. Paternalism may involve a myriad of decisions about the terms and conditions under which they will be provided. These decisions are more difficult and more paternalistic to the degree that they are taken out of the marketplace. Within the marketplace, individual purchasers calculate the benefit they will gain from a purchase and weigh this against the market cost. When the market has been discarded, the government must calculate these benefits and also must calculate the costs of providing various levels and qualities of service. What might be done by millions of purchasers and suppliers must now be done in government offices. Even if the government elite are capable of making wiser decisions, the information which they need may be difficult to obtain.

With publicly provided schooling, how many years of attendance should be compulsory? Beyond this compulsory level, should higher education be provided to all who want it? When money and prices have been discarded as rationing devices, what alternative rationing devices should be imposed? Are grades an adequate rationing device? If public housing and nursing homes are to be built, what level of quality is in the best interests of society? If demand exceeds supply – as may well be the case if the service is free – what rules should govern accessibility? The ambiguities and uncertainties that underlie such collective decisions are explored more fully in Chapter 9.

Before examining these subsidies individually, it is important to recognize that in many countries subsidies may be provided by more than one level of government. Unfortunately, most of the data referred to in the following comments are based solely on central-government expenditures, and so they underestimate the role of subsidies, and this underestimation varies among countries.

Health care subsidies

Table 6.6 indicates that health care subsidies are one of the largest categories of consumption subsidies. Over the 1970–83 period, they formed an average of 9–10 percent of central-government expenditures throughout the world. These percentages are highest in the industrial countries, reaching an average of 11.34 percent of central-government expenditures in 1983. Health care expenditures in developing countries reached only 4.14 percent of total government expenditures in 1983, in spite of the much lower level of total government expenditures per capita.

The mechanisms for providing health care subsidies vary significantly among countries, as do the terms and conditions for recipient qualification, and the percentage of costs covered by subsidies. A comparison of Canada, the United Kingdom, and the United States indicates the variety of differences. Canada has universal medical-hospital subsidies, which pay 100 percent of most expenditures. Drugs and dental care are the principle remaining exclusions. Physicians in Canada operate on a

Table 6.6. Central government expenditures on health (as a percentage of total expenditures)

	1970	1971	1972	1973	1974	1975	1976	1977	1978	1979	1980	1981	1982	1983	1984
World	...	...	**9.45**	**9.44**	**9.59**	**10.03**	**10.06**	**9.64**	**9.61**	**9.81**	**9.82**	**9.78**	**9.72**	**9.67**	...
Industrial Countries															
United States E%	...	...	8.56	8.29	8.85	9.34	9.70	◆ 10.02	10.19	10.51	10.43	10.70	10.81	10.65	11.04
Canada G#	...	9.73	...	...	7.63	7.73	8.33	6.94	7.62	7.57	6.70	6.22	5.17	6.27	...
Australia D*	...	...	...	7.92	8.05	7.87	13.04	10.96	10.39	10.18	10.02	10.11	7.12	7.12	7.83
Japan	...	...	...	...	...	...	...	...	...	...	...	...	...	...	...
New Zealand B#	51.21	15.54	14.79	14.84	15.35	15.03	15.72	14.98	15.04	15.21	15.17	14.24	13.52	12.65	...
Austria D	10.22	10.29	10.08	9.93	10.79	12.28	12.60	13.16	12.83	12.87	12.97	12.88	12.23	1'48	...
Belgium A	1.49	1.39	1.47	1.67	1.48	1.64	1.53	1.78	1.79	1.86	1.65	1.70	1.65	...	...
Denmark D	9.76	9.78	9.98	6.94	7.02	3.55	◆ 2.89	1.94	1.74	1.62	1.72	1.41	...	...	...
Finland D	...	...	10.63	11.20	10.88	10.68	10.81	11.48	11.15	10.48	10.46	11.19	10.87	10.55	...
France B	...	...	...	...	...	14.99	14.81	14.59	14.83	14.99	15.01	14.72	14.60	...	...
Germany D	16.72	16.90	17.47	18.73	19.49	19.81	19.75	19.28	19.33	18.99	19.04	19.23	19.32	18.64	...
Iceland D	...	...	16.62	15.13	16.48	17.94	17.96	19.99	19.72	19.49	20.58	21.19	21.02	...	...
Ireland A	...	...	...	...	...	...	...	...	...	...	...	...	...	...	...
Italy A	...	...	...	13.54	11.62	16.76	...	...	◆ 7.55	10.47	12.55	10.70	10.64	11.52	11.49
Luxembourg B	2.22	2.23	2.16	2.21	2.39	2.23	2.06	2.07	2.27	2.02	2.15	2.37	2.23	2.21	...
Netherlands A	...	...	...	...	12.08	11.70	11.61	11.79	11.87	11.71	11.68	11.63	11.62	11.29	10.97
Norway C	...	...	12.31	12.84	12.79	13.45	13.25	11.23	...	...	...	10.28	10.59	10.55	...
Spain C	1.12	.87	.94	.85	.88	.92	.78	.75	.72	.84	.67	.62	.58	.60	...
Sweden E*	4.17	4.09	3.57	4.13	3.18	3.14	3.11	2.64	2.56	2.51	2.18	1.98	2.06	1.50	1.35
Switzerland E	10.33	10.57	10.00	9.43	9.71	10.39	10.07	10.62	10.90	11.37	11.67	12.66	12.92	13.44	...
United Kingdom C	...	...	12.19	12.11	12.90	12.90	12.90	12.63	12.54	12.43	...	...	...	...	...

Region														
Developing Countries	⋯	⋯	5.29	5.27	5.09	5.17	5.27	4.31	4.38	4.36	4.18	4.08	4.10	4.14
Africa	⋯	⋯	⋯	4.57	4.53	4.04	4.34	4.29	4.43	⋯	⋯	⋯	⋯	⋯
Asia	⋯	⋯	⋯	2.39	2.67	2.96	3.04	3.11	3.00	2.84	2.67	2.86	3.01	3.18
Europe	10.02	9.68	9.74	9.41	9.11	9.69	9.40	2.73	2.98	3.27	3.48	3.12	⋯	⋯
Middle East	⋯	⋯	3.86	4.08	3.78	4.17	3.70	4.21	4.52	4.99	5.29	4.62	4.93	⋯
Western Hemisphere	⋯	⋯	6.27	6.34	5.91	5.78	6.13	5.55	5.58	5.54	5.00	4.96	4.85	4.71

Notes: Letters A–G following country name indicate percent of general government tax revenue accounted for by central government, where data are available, as follows: A, 95 and over; B, 90–4.9; C, 80–9.9; D, 70–9.9; E, 60–9.9; F, 50–9.9; and G, 20–49.9.

Symbol ◆ indicates break in continuity of time series as described in country notes on coverage of data.

Most recent fiscal years, other than those ending Dec. 31, are indicated as: #, beginning April 1; *, ending June 30; %, ending September 30; and +, other.

Source: International Monetary Fund, *International Financial Statistics: Supplement on Government Finance*, Supplement Series No. 11 (Washington, DC: International Monetary Fund, 1986), pp. 36–7.

specified fee schedule, with government reimbursing them on the basis of that schedule. Because physicians in Canada operate on a fee-for-service basis, there is an incentive for abuse, which may lead to more care than is necessary and a consequent misallocation of resources.

The United Kingdom also has universal comprehensive coverage, but it is quite different from that of Canada in that it is a more centralized system. Both health insurance and health care provisions are provided directly through the National Health Service. Some advocates of this system believe that health care subsidies can be more easily monitored with less misallocation of resources. Physicians work under a capitation system, where they are paid by the number of patients registered as their own, multiplied by a set capitation fee per patient. Here, the physician has the incentive to register as many patients as possible, while providing the least amount of care possible. Some people are so dissatisfied with the system that they buy private insurance even though there is alternative health care provided at zero cost. The British system, therefore, may become a two-class system where the rich receive a higher quality of care than the poor. One of the primary purposes of health care subsidies is to eliminate financial barriers to health care, and the British system may be criticized from this perspective.

The United States combines a system of public subsidies for low-income people and the aged with a system of private insurance. A for-profit insurance sector in the United States competes as any other business, with the profits going to shareholders. This type of insurance usually involves cost sharing through deductible amounts and copayments. There is also a not-for-profit government system present in the United States, including Medicare, which provides for the elderly, and Medicaid, which provides for the poor.

In recent years, several changes have been creating new difficulties for health care subsidies. Medical technology has advanced rapidly in its ability to provide increasingly sophisticated treatments that are increasingly expensive. For society as a whole, this has complicated the decisions about how much of these costs should be subsidized, and whether everyone should have equal access to government subsidies. For many societies, health care costs are rising because of the aging of the population, and the special needs of the elderly may involve new types of health care facilities. Even with a system designed to provide equal access to subsidies, some individuals and groups are able to benefit more than others. In particular, people living in cities may obtain better care than those in remote areas. These developments mean that subsidy programs are constantly being altered in hope of improving the overall outcomes.[55]

Housing subsidies

Table 6.7 indicates that housing subsidies formed a relatively uniform share of central-government expenditures over the 1970–83 period, ranging from a world average of 1.99 percent in 1972 to 2.12 percent in 1983. In the industrial countries, housing subsidies formed an average of 2.20 percent of total government expenditures in 1983. The average in developing countries was relatively close to this, at 1.84 percent.

However, these figures have varied significantly among countries, reflecting different collective decisions concerning the appropriate role of public versus private responsibilities, and concerning the appropriate instrument for public assistance. Societies have relied on subsidies for new construction, and on special tax concessions geared to housing, as well as on direct rental assistance. It is likely that the data in Table 6.7 do not accurately include the subsidies involved in the programs for new construction and in the special tax concessions. Furthermore, the kinds and amounts of "community amenities" are varied, and many may not be included in each country's data on a comparable basis.

Most societies in the post–1945 period have concluded that they should provide housing programs. To some degree, the post–1945 increase in the birth rate may have supported this view, as well as the hiatus in housing construction during the Second World War. Furthermore, for some countries, the war had destroyed a portion of the existing housing stock. Consequently, the public attitude was a response to the low vacancy rates, and the obvious inability of many families to find accommodation. Yet to some degree, the intervention by government reflects a public attitude towards the appropriate role for collective decision making. This right of access to adequate housing has become a politically acceptable tenet in many countries. From this perspective, housing subsidies are a component of a society's redistribution policies and are a means of assisting those with low incomes. In some countries the political parties have espoused different positions in this regard. The Labour and Conservative parties in the United Kingdom, for example, have altered the scope and nature of housing subsidies when they have exchanged power, and the percentage of total government expenditures devoted to housing has shifted dramatically, from a low of 1.75 percent in 1972 to a high of 4.80 percent in 1977.

Construction subsidies have been based on the view that the stock of housing should be expanded more rapidly than would occur if left solely to free enterprise. In some cases, construction subsidies have been directed to low-income housing, and landlords receiving these subsidies have had to comply with certain conditions, such as those concerning

Table 6.7. *Central government expenditures on housing and community amenities (as a percentage of total expenditures)*

	1970	1971	1972	1973	1974	1975	1976	1977	1978	1979	1980	1981	1982	1983	1984
World	···	···	**1.99**	**2.12**	**2.28**	**2.28**	**2.23**	**2.18**	**2.27**	**2.22**	**2.31**	**2.30**	**2.20**	**2.12**	···
Industrial Countries			**2.07**	**2.16**	**2.36**	**2.35**	**2.23**	**2.26**	**2.37**	**2.33**	**2.37**	**2.29**	**2.27**	**2.20**	···
United States E%	···	···	2.61	2.66	2.97	2.88	2.44	◆2.40	2.92	2.72	2.82	2.62	2.60	2.34	2.58
Canada G#	···	1.04	···	···	1.42	1.99	1.65	2.04	2.50	2.99	2.35	2.38	2.31	2.07	···
Australia D*	1.45	1.49	1.53	1.00	1.43	1.74	1.66	1.17	.78	.47	.79	.66	.70	.99	1.37
Japan	···	···	···	···	···	···	···	···	···	···	···	···	···	···	···
New Zealand B#	1.40	1.26	1.26	1.53	3.57	1.11	1.87	1.82	1.75	1.35	1.25	1.17	1.00	.94	···
Austria D	3.29	3.47	3.81	3.61	3.85	3.32	3.14	3.24	3.14	3.17	3.21	3.27	3.21	3.05	···
Belgium A	1.28	1.38	1.45	1.56	1.57	1.61	1.64	1.60	1.64	1.77	2.50	1.64	1.76	···	···
Denmark D	1.45	1.49	1.50	1.71	1.72	2.01	◆1.92	1.81	1.65	1.91	1.90	2.03	···	···	···
Finland D			1.16	1.22	1.26	1.38	1.41	2.21	2.48	2.46	2.66	2.75	2.69	1.77	···
France B						3.17	3.08	2.90	2.79	2.90	3.10	3.16	3.40	···	···
Germany D	.17	.15	.26	.23	.22	.25	.43	.42	.36	.44	.40	.40	.33	.31	···
Iceland D	···	···	3.49	2.90	3.48	4.11	4.90	5.00	4.09	3.57	2.88	2.65	2.34	···	···
Ireland A	···	···	···	···	···	···	···	···	···	···	···	···	···	···	···
Italy A					2.39	2.05			◆.96	1.04	1.01	1.02	.61	1.22	.80
Luxembourg B	1.39	1.68	1.66	1.99	1.99	2.56	2.30	2.08	1.95	2.59	1.97	1.72	1.62	1.30	···
Netherlands A	···	···	···	···	1.96	2.19	2.45	2.71	2.77	2.78	2.75	2.90	2.90	3.47	3.63
Norway C	···	···	7.41	6.49	6.45	5.79	6.16	6.51	···	···	···	1.79	1.45	1.16	···
Spain C	2.33	2.06	2.02	1.74	1.61	1.70	1.84	2.01	1.23	1.41	1.33	1.36	1.30	1.27	···
Sweden E*	1.16	1.20	1.51	1.53	1.54	1.31	2.93	2.81	2.83	2.83	2.95	3.12	3.52	3.34	3.38

Switzerland E	.41	.59	.54	.86	1.08	1.33	1.55	1.20	1.15	1.11	.98	.81	.74	.71
United Kingdom C	…	…	1.75	2.73	3.32	3.49	3.98	4.80	4.29	4.14	…	…	…	…
Developing Countries	…	…	1.72	1.96	2.01	2.04	2.23	1.90	1.89	1.82	2.09	2.36	1.94	1.84
Africa			1.23				2.71	1.99	2.72					
Asia	…	…	…	1.51	1.48	1.71	1.70	2.04	1.81	2.50	2.44	2.59	2.18	2.00
Middle East	…	…	3.54	4.15	4.32	4.47	4.12	3.84	3.10	3.15	2.85	2.63	2.81	2.79
Europe	1.30	1.26	1.23	1.36	1.25	1.37	1.32	1.56	1.41	2.00	2.02	3.40	…	…
Western Hemisphere	…	…	1.64	1.84	1.59	1.54	1.98	1.34	1.45	.96	1.54	1.80	1.39	1.39

Notes: Letters A–G following country name indicate percent of general government tax revenue accounted for by central government, where data are available, as follows: A, 95 and over; B, 90–4.9; C, 80–9.9; D, 70–9.9; E, 60–9.9; F, 50–9.9; and G, 20–49.9.

Symbol ◆ indicates break in continuity of time series as described in country notes on coverage of data.

Most recent fiscal years, other than those ending Dec. 31, are indicated as: #, beginning April 1; *, ending June 30; %, ending September 30; and +, other.

Source: International Monetary Fund, *International Financial Statistics: Supplement on Government Finance*, Supplement Series No. 11 (Washington, DC: International Monetary Fund, 1986), pp. 38–9.

income of rental applicants and level of rents. In other cases, subsidies
have been available for middle- and upper-income groups as well. Construction subsidies have been provided in a variety of ways. The government may pay for the infrastructure costs of roads, water, and sewage
facilities, rather than require that they be paid for by the developer. In
addition, the government may provide cash grants, or loans at interest
rates below those prevailing in the market. With subsidized loans, it
may be particularly difficult to calculate the extent of the subsidy being
provided, since it is not always clear – particularly after the fact – what
interest rate the developer would otherwise have paid. In his book
Private Rented Housing in the United States and Europe, Michael Harloe
has documented the experiences of many countries:

[O]nly in Britain was no attempt made after the war to stimulate the production
of private rental housing with subsidies. In contrast the Netherlands, the USA,
France and Denmark have all, at one time or another, subsidised construction
by methods which, in effect, made low cost loans available. Indirect (tax) subsidies have been the main source of support in West Germany, they have also
been important in the USA. It has been normal to have some controls on rent
levels, the levels of incomes of those accommodated, and the cost and quality
of construction.[56]

Harloe has documented a shift in the 1970s away from construction
subsidies and towards rental allowances. Rental allowances do not directly increase the supply of housing, although they may indirectly encourage an expansion of private construction in response to the increased
housing demand which they support. The size of rental allowances is
usually based on family income levels, and allowances are generally
provided specifically to low-income people. Their impact on income
distribution is, therefore, more obvious. Harloe sees this as an "ideological shift" where the new position includes a greater reliance on free
enterprise for both construction and rent setting. Harloe warns that this
shift may cause a relative decline in the private rental sector, and he
points to two problems that can develop:

First, the limited usefulness of demand side subsidies when there is an urgent
need to increase lower income housing supply. Second, the failure of such
subsidies to bring about more than minimal improvements in housing quality.[57]

In their review of housing policies, George Sternlieb and David Listokin document this shift in the United States. New subsidized units
increased as a percentage of total new units from 2.2 percent in 1950
to 29.3 percent in 1970, and then fell to 4.0 percent by 1985.[58] The U.S.
Housing Act of 1983 instituted a housing allowance program as an alternative which was advocated by President Reagan and which has now

become a central feature of the U.S. housing policy. Sternlieb and Listokin predict that "the debate over the proper format for housing subsidies will continue."[59]

John English examines various policy changes in the United Kingdom. Of special significance was the Housing Finance Act of 1972. The Conservative government's intention "was the eventual phasing out of all general assistance by a progression toward fair rents to be approved for all houses by independent rent-scrutiny committees. Tenants unable to afford these rents would be eligible for rent rebates while better-off council tenants would be encouraged to become owner occupiers."[60] English concludes that this philosophy will lead to "a residual public sector, serving only the disadvantaged and those accepted as having special needs."[61]

Tax exemptions and deductions have also been used extensively, to reduce the private costs of both home ownership and rental accommodation. Various formulas have been devised, for example, to permit the deductibility of mortgage interest or of rents that exceed a certain percentage of income. Harloe presents estimates of the monetary value of tax subsidies, divided between home owners and renters, for each of the United Kingdom, the Netherlands, Germany, and the United States. In each case, the tax subsidies to homeowners have greatly exceeded the tax subsidies to renters. Most extreme has been the United States, where "the estimated cost in 1975 of the main federal tax reliefs for owner occupiers was about $8.3 billion dollars compared with $0.65 billion dollars for rented housing."[62]

Rigorous statistical analyses of the actual impacts of housing policies have only been possible in recent years, with the gradual accumulation of necessary data. Claire Hammond, for example, has developed an intertemporal general equilibrium model to analyze the impact of certain housing programs on household consumption patterns. Examining U.S. data, Hammond is able to estimate the effects on consumption of housing as opposed to consumption of other goods. She also calculates the cash grant that would provide equivalent consumer satisfaction.

The system of rental housing subsidy programs that has been analyzed was designed primarily to induce low- and moderate-income families to occupy better housing than they would without the subsidies. The results confirm that the present system of in-kind subsidies does increase housing consumption of participating families. I find that, in the aggregate, subsidized families consumed 40 percent more housing in 1977 than they would have in the absence of the programs. In addition, I find that consumption on nonhousing goods also increased as a result of the housing subsidies, but by less than 2 percent in 1977.
. . .

However, I also find that there is a substantial difference (over $400) between the mean annual benefit and the mean annual subsidy provided by the programs. This difference stems from the subsidies' in-kind nature. Thus, if we are concerned solely with helping low-income families and if we consider them to be the best judges of what is best for themselves, we should replace the in-kind subsidies with unrestricted cash grants. We could increase the perceived benefit to subsidized families by 66 percent at the same taxpayer cost. Or, we could decrease taxpayer cost by 39 percent while maintaining the perceived welfare of participating families at the levels resulting from participation in the in-kind subsidy programs.

The goal of the housing programs, however, is not just to increase the welfare of the subsidized families but also to increase their consumption of housing beyond what would result from unrestricted cash grants.[63]

Hammond concludes by advocating housing allowances, since these can be directed at specific objectives such as housing that meets certain standards, for people who have certain incomes and family size.

Education subsidies

As Table 6.8 indicates, most societies have accepted responsibility for providing certain levels of education to each young person. The United Nations Declaration of Universal Rights includes the right of every child to primary education, and the right of those who could benefit to attend secondary schools and institutions of higher learning. Acceptance of this collective responsibility rests, at least partially, on the desire for some measure of equality of opportunity. Lack of a basic education would bar a young person from many jobs. This desire for equality of opportunity has led to public funding and universal access. However, this position has frequently conflicted with the rights of individual families to choose a particular type of education, such as one presented in a religious format, and to choose a particular institution, such as one with a superior reputation. Brian Holmes in his book, *Equality and Freedom in Education,* explores "the difficulties of increasing equality of access, provision, and indeed outcomes in education, while retaining the freedom of individual parents to have their children educated in accordance with their wishes."[64] In his examination of the U.S. educational system, David Turner has emphasized that "while the educational system of the USA has been developing, there has been a continual conflict between the ideal of liberty in development to meet state, local, or individual needs and the ideal of equality, either between individuals or between larger groupings."[65]

R. Murray Thomas has pointed to five social dichotomies where this conflict has frequently occurred.

Table 6.8. *Public expenditure on education (in percent of GDP in current prices)*

	1970	1980	1981	1982	1983
Australia	4.3	5.7	5.7	. .	. .
Austria	4.6	5.5	5.7	5.9	5.9
Canada	8.8	7.2	7.2	7.6	7.5
Denmark	6.7	6.6	. .	. .	. .
Finland	5.9	5.4	5.5	5.5	. .
France	. .	5.1	5.2	. .	. .
Germany	3.7	4.7	4.7	4.6	4.4
Greece	2.1	2.2[b]	. .	. .	. .
Ireland	5.0	6.3	6.7	6.2	. .
Italy	4.6[a]	5.0	5.5	5.5	. .
Japan	3.1	5.5	5.5	5.4	. .
Luxembourg	4.6	7.4	7.6	8.3	. .
Netherlands	6.8	7.6	7.4	7.3	. .
New Zealand	4.8[c]	5.7	5.4	5.3	5.0
Norway	6.0	5.9	6.2	6.3	6.3
Portugal	. .	4.1	4.4	4.2	. .
Sweden	7.2	9.0	8.4	8.2	7.6
Switzerland	4.1	5.2	5.1	5.2	. .
Turkey	2.5	. .	. .	2.8	3.3
United Kingdom	5.3	5.5	5.4	5.4	5.3
United States	6.4	5.6	. .	. .	. .

[a] 1971.
[b] 1979.
[c] 1972.
Source: OECD, *Structural Adjustment and Economic Performance* (Paris: OECD, 1987), p. 83.

In all countries, but perhaps most noticeably in developing nations today, five social dichotomies are prime sources of dissent over the support of, and access to, education. The five are rich people versus poor people (usually meaning the upper class versus the lower class), urban versus rural, ethnic majorities versus ethnic minorities, the religious majority versus the religious minority, and politically-favored regions against politically-disadvantaged regions. . . . Usually in the struggles over educational support and access, the favoured member of the pair is seeking to maintain its present superior position while the disadvantaged member of the pair is striving for at least equal treatment. Finally, it seems safe to conclude that the greatest sound and fury witnessed in the arena of politics and education is produced by dissent among political groups over what types of education are supported and over who has access to those types.[66]

In their book, *Comparative Education,* Altbach, Arnove, and Kelly discuss a sixth social dichotomy: male versus female.[67] They indicate the relatively low percentage of educational enrolments that are female, as well as the noticeable increase in these percentages since 1950, except for Africa. Eastern European countries have consistently had the highest percentages of female enrolments, while less developed countries have had the lowest percentages.

As a way of reconciling equality and freedom, some have advocated that public funding take the form of vouchers. The government would issue a voucher to each student who would then take the voucher to the school preferred by the student. The school would return the voucher to the government and would receive a cheque from the government. Milton Friedman has advocated a scheme in which schools could charge supplementary fees. This would allow private schools to offer a variety of programs at different prices. In this process, the educational system would benefit from the free-enterprise market and its attributes. Christopher Jencks has advocated an alternative voucher process in which schools could not accept supplementary payments, and in which low-income students would receive a voucher of greater value than those received by high-income students. Jencks' solution would provide extra assistance to the poor, and this might offset, to some degree, the educational advantages often enjoyed by children of higher-income families.[68] Atkinson has suggested that with alternative voucher proposals

[T]he main questions of difference are (a) is the scheme open to private schools? (b) can the schools ask for additional money? (c) do poor or otherwise disadvantaged groups receive vouchers of higher value? Differences such as these mean that the effects of the schemes would vary substantially.[69]

Philip Coombs has emphasized the disparities and inequalities that persist in spite of education subsidies. In particular, children of low-income families often lack the motivation to take advantage of free education. Coombs discusses "the stubborn fact, often overlooked earlier, that all educational systems have a built-in bias favouring children whose parents attach high value to education and who instill in their offspring a strong motivation for education."[70] T. N. Postlewaite has referred to studies "showing the fairly strong relationship between measures of the differences in home backgrounds and differences in achievement."[71] This perspective has frequently led to special programs, publicly funded for target groups. Disadvantaged children, for example, may receive larger education subsidies in these programs than the average level.

Equality has been a particular concern in the Soviet Union. In the 1930s, a national objective was established to provide a ten-year general education for all children. Although this objective has been achieved,

Table 6.9. *Students in higher education in East European countries, 1960 and 1973 (per 10,000 population)*

	1960	1973
Bulgaria	70	125
Czechoslovakia	69	93
German Democratic Republic	59	86
Hungary	45	94
Poland	68	144
Rumania	39	69
Yugoslavia	76	145
USSR	111	186

Source: Glowny Urzad Statystyczny [Main Statistical Bureau], *Maly Rocznik Statystyczny* [Small statistical yearbook], (Warsaw, 1975), p. 351.

the question of uniform curricula has been persistently difficult. Vocational training schools and specialized institutions offer alternatives to the general schools, and this variety may provide differences in opportunities. Some have pointed to the scholarships, stipends, and early testing as evidence that the Soviet system fosters the maximum development of each individual.[72] Others acknowledge the differences that inevitably persist:

[I]n its present, mature form, the educational system for under 18's must cater for a very differentiated demand, and a complex society. There is nothing surprising in that; but it does place a question mark over the official concept of increasing social homogeneity. By and large, the senior classes of the full-time general school, in any given locality, offer better educational service and potential prospects than the "general" PTUs or specialised secondary educational institutions; all these types give a better deal than on-the-job training. Of course, within each system there are hierarchies of quality and desirability. The degree to which this differentiation may be compared with that of bourgeois educational systems is a matter of considerable interest.[73]

Table 6.9 indicates that differences exist among communist nations as well as within each of them. In 1973, the number of students in higher education per 10,000 population varied from 186 in the Soviet Union to only sixty-nine in Rumania.

Finally, it should be noted that the educational system can be used to strengthen the society's acceptance of a particular philosophy. Roberta Marine, for example, in her article, "The Socialization of Children in China and in Taiwan: An Analysis of Elementary School Textbooks," has emphasized the differences in basic values presented to students in the school curricula. "They are being socialized to be citizens of two divergent societies."[74] Other authors have also discussed this feature of the educational system. In introducing their book, *Education and Socialist Modernization: A Documentary History of Education in the People's Republic of China, 1977–1986,* Shi Ming Au and Eli Seifman quote Bernard Baelyb who, writing about education in the United States, suggested that "education not only reflects and adjusts to society; once formed, it turns back upon it and acts upon it."[75]

Income subsidies

When a society provides subsidies for certain goods and services, such as education, health care, and housing, low-income people must actually use the subsidized item in order to benefit. For each person or family, the amount of benefit depends upon the extent to which they use the subsidized good or service. Hence, benefits may not be allocated in a manner considered to be purposeful, consistent, and fair. Income subsidies, on the other hand, enable the recipients to choose any consumption pattern that they wish, and income subsidies provide a level of benefits that is not affected by that choice. Hence, the impact of income subsidies on the well-being of low-income people may be predicted more clearly, and there may be a greater assurance that a certain minimum living standard will be provided equally to everyone. As indicated in Chapter 4, microeconomic theory concerning consumption efficiency and utility maximization can be used to justify income subsidies. To the degree that recipients are able to calculate accurately the relative utility they could receive from alternative purchases, recipients can choose the particular consumption pattern that will maximize their well-being.

Nevertheless, many feel that recipients of income subsidies often do not choose appropriately. A recipient may not be adequately concerned about the well-being of other family members, and this is seen as especially important in regard to the well-being of children. Low-income people may not be in a position to choose wisely, because of ignorance or possibly because of alcoholism and drug abuse. Consequently, a society may be reluctant to rely entirely on income subsidies, but rather may opt for a combination of the various alternatives. Although all types of consumption subsidies can be used to provide welfare assistance to the poor, it is customary to refer solely to income subsidies as *social security* and *welfare*. The data presented in Table 6.10 indicate that income subsidies have been used extensively in all societies, both developed and undeveloped. However, the degree of reliance on this mechanism has varied significantly among countries.

Table 6.10 indicates that central government expenditures on social security and welfare as a percent of total expenditure have been far higher in the industrial countries than in the developing countries. The 1982 average for the former group was 37.84 percent, whereas it was only 15.68 percent for the latter. Even among the industrial countries, this varied, in 1982, within a range of 27.90 percent to 62.62 percent. To some degree, these differences may result from variations in statistical practices. Furthermore, the division of fiscal responsibility among the central government and other government levels does differ considerably. Also, the composition of welfare may explain some differences, particularly the demographic profile and the role of public pensions. Nevertheless, it is clear that societies have made different choices in regard to their use of income subsidies.

Each society's choice of the terms and conditions for receipt of income subsidies has depended upon a mixture of the desire to ensure a minimum level of consumption for all, and the desire to attain a greater or lesser degree of equality among society's members. These choices have also depended upon the society's preferences for alternative decision modes that can be used for achieving these purposes. Price controls on goods and services purchased by the poor, the use of alternative types of taxes and rates of taxation, regulations in regard to various aspects of the lives of the poor, and the centralization of all decisions can each be chosen as alternatives to income subsidies. These choices have been influenced by many factors. Improvements in the productive capacity of the society have often provided the financial means for increasing income subsidies. The desired amount of assistance may be so high that a single decision mode cannot readily provide the total amount. Yet, the general political philosophy of the society has also been important, quite apart from these factors. Chapter 10 deals with the processes through which a society reaches its choices in regard to alternative decision modes. Among these choices, the terms and conditions for receipt of income subsidies are particularly important. Many commentators have advocated various reforms of consumption and income subsidies, and it is to some of these possible reforms that we now turn.

Reforms of consumption and income subsidies

In his book, *The Economics of Poverty and Discrimination*, Bradley Schiller has emphasized that reliance solely on income subsidies would not solve the causes of poverty for many of the poor. In fact,

exclusive reliance on income transfers as a solution to poverty serves to perpetuate the poverty problem. . . . Simply transferring income to the needy does little to improve their opportunities for employment and upward mobility.[76]

Table 6.10. *Central government expenditures on social security and welfare (as a percentage of total expenditures)*

	1970	**1971**	**1972**	**1973**	**1974**	**1975**	**1976**	**1977**	**1978**	**1979**	**1980**	**1981**	**1982**	**1983**	**1984**
World	…	…	**32.47**	**32.14**	**32.69**	**33.84**	**33.71**	**33.28**	**33.39**	**33.25**	**33.17**	**33.43**	**33.43**	…	…
Industrial Countries															
United States E%	…	…	**36.34**	**35.72**	**36.71**	**37.93**	**37.97**	**37.72**	**37.72**	**37.42**	**37.47**	**37.70**	**37.84**	**38.14**	…
Canada G#	…	33.94	32.70	31.64	33.91	36.60	36.18	◆34.19	34.19	33.72	34.10	34.24	33.54	33.99	32.07
Australia D*	…	…	22.35	…	22.24	23.78	24.84	27.61	28.47	28.26	27.71	27.37	27.90	28.98	28.91
Japan	…	…	…	…	…	…	…	…	…	…	…	…	…	…	…
New Zealand B#	24.44	22.84	24.38	25.17	24.11	24.06	27.41	29.91	29.36	29.80	29.83	27.92	29.37	29.25	…
Austria D	50.13	50.55	49.93	46.34	46.72	45.73	46.26	46.13	47.03	46.64	45.51	45.10	45.45	45.55	…
Belgium A	39.53	38.97	39.54	40.70	41.86	43.75	44.57	44.25	42.98	42.86	42.25	41.81	41.00	…	…
Denmark D	38.39	38.80	39.88	40.20	41.43	43.81	◆40.61	40.57	41.90	41.62	41.36	40.19	…	…	…
Finland D	…	…	27.28	27.32	27.03	26.02	27.61	27.77	28.38	27.08	25.56	25.98	27.98	30.19	…
France B	…	…	…	…	…	40.83	41.40	43.25	43.99	44.14	44.39	43.89	44.19	…	…
Germany D	46.75	46.84	46.62	44.70	45.61	49.43	49.15	50.46	49.90	49.58	49.22	49.54	49.66	49.97	…
Iceland D	…	…	19.06	16.88	14.53	13.06	14.53	14.79	15.36	14.48	15.22	15.89	16.26	…	…
Ireland A	…	…	…	…	…	…	…	…	…	…	…	…	…	…	…
Italy A	…	…	…	42.30	41.10	33.48	…	…	◆29.14	28.91	28.39	31.08	33.02	33.07	31.17
Luxembourg B	46.14	46.30	46.75	45.46	44.94	46.92	48.45	49.08	49.77	50.16	48.37	51.73	49.08	48.33	…
Netherlands A	…	…	…	…	36.12	35.74	36.70	36.38	37.01	36.66	36.43	36.63	37.44	37.73	37.42
Norway C	…	…	32.52	33.24	32.83	32.78	31.36	30.57	…	…	…	33.51	34.27	35.05	…
Spain C	44.01	45.19	47.77	49.15	50.35	51.60	51.63	53.13	55.95	57.32	57.19	60.98	62.62	62.89	…
Sweden E*	39.10	40.39	42.75	42.80	45.83	45.50	46.43	47.78	49.26	48.29	48.53	46.43	46.96	46.07	46.67
Switzerland E	40.80	40.93	38.96	46.32	45.79	48.15	46.66	49.18	49.16	48.18	48.31	48.30	49.27	48.95	…
United Kingdom C	…	…	24.76	23.58	22.59	21.68	23.17	24.66	25.49	25.47	…	…	…	…	…

Developing Countries											
Africa	16.89	17.77	16.53	17.41	16.58	15.41	15.96	16.51	15.88	16.27	15.68
Asia	⋯	⋯	⋯	⋯	⋯	⋯	⋯	⋯	⋯	⋯	⋯
Middle East	⋯	⋯	⋯	⋯	⋯	⋯	⋯	⋯	⋯	⋯	⋯
Europe	4.09	4.77	5.38	6.68	6.15	6.11	7.77	7.57	7.84	9.99	9.61
Western Hemisphere	⋯	⋯	⋯	26.28	⋯	⋯	⋯	⋯	⋯	⋯	⋯
	26.88	28.16	25.58	27.46	26.05	25.94	26.15	27.67	25.93	25.93	24.24	25.14

Notes: Letters A–G following country name indicate percent of general government tax revenue accounted for by central government, where data are available, as follows: A, 95 and over; B, 90–4.9; C, 80–9.9; D, 70–9.9; E, 60–9.9; F, 50–9.9; and G, 20–49.9. Symbol ◆ indicates break in continuity of time series as described in country notes on coverage of data.

Most recent fiscal years, other than those ending Dec. 31, are indicated as: #, beginning April 1; *, ending June 30; %, ending September 30; and +, other.

Source: International Monetary Fund, *International Financial Statistics: Supplement on Government Finance*, Supplement Series No. 11 (Washington, DC: International Monetary Fund, 1986), pp. 32–3.

Many other authors have agreed with this conclusion, and therefore have advocated particular types of subsidies to deal with particular causes of poverty. As Robert Lampman has explained, the result has been that welfare reform has often meant "separating out groups of the poor for special consideration. Criminals, mentally ill persons, orphans, widows, veterans, the aged, and the disabled were among those singled out for study, concern, and legislation."[77] Consequently, William Albrecht has concluded,

The multibillion-dollar welfare system in the United States is hardly a system at all. It is a mélange of uncoordinated programs that have been created by a variety of federal, state, and local agencies. As a result, welfare benefits vary widely from person to person and from state to state.[78]

Robert Friedman notes that this will likely mean "heightened conflict among these groups"[79] as a basic element of future reforms. This competition will require a "shift in the function of the welfare state . . . to provide a mediating mechanism among competing interests."[80] Sherer also suggests that three additional factors will likely shape the future of the welfare state. First, societies will need less manpower, and so unemployment and leisure time will become increasingly important issues. Second, the role of the family will be changing as well as the demographic profile. In particular, the elderly will pose an ever-greater problem for societies due to these demographic shifts and due to the disintegration of family responsibility.[81] Third, most societies will decentralize their programs to local and private agencies as a means of directing aid more accurately and more efficiently.[82]

These perspectives emphasize the permanent nature of reform. Research and program evaluation will remain important. The following statement about the writings of Gunnar Myrdal will remain valid:

The welfare state . . . is nowhere, as yet, an accomplishment, it is continually in the process of coming into being. Even where the process was furthest advanced he saw its architects continually labouring with the tasks of simplification, co-ordination, rationalization and achievement of efficiency. Indeed this planning becomes pressing as the edifice of the welfare state rises.[83]

Gordon Tulloch has emphasized the importance of research in this process of change. Yet he has warned that "research in this area is difficult because the details of programs for aid to the poor are not only radically different from time to time and place to place, but are continuously shifting."[84]

Bradshaw and Deacon have discussed the importance of gradual changes with continual evaluation of these changes.

Change needs to proceed not by sweeping away what we have and replacing it with untried schemes, but by carefully planned incremental reform which builds on the real achievements of the present arrangements.[85]

Essay and discussion topics

1. Compare the use of subsidies within two or more economic systems. For each system, indicate the relationship between the reliance on subsidies and the attainment of the society's objectives.

2. For two or more economic systems, compare a particular type of subsidy. Indicate the advantages and shortcomings of subsidies as illustrated by this study.

3. Discuss the relationships between subsidy programs and international trade agreements. Choose one or more specific international trade agreements to illustrate these relationships.

CHAPTER 7

Taxation

Introduction

Taxation is another decision mode through which society as a whole can alter incentives and outcomes. Rather than relying on a single kind of tax, most societies impose a wide variety of taxes. Each type of tax has its own impact in regard to efficiency, growth, liberty, and equality, and this chapter examines several taxes individually. A number of reasons underlie the use of a mix of taxes, and for each society an important question is the choice of tax mix. Taxes may be imposed on many bases, including factors of production, goods and services, individuals, and businesses. The well-being, or ability to pay, of individuals cannot be adequately reflected by one single indicator, and so to rely on a single tax base could be seen by many as unfair. Circumstances such as health and marital and family status can vary among individuals, and can directly affect the benefits they receive from the tax revenue that is collected. Similarly, circumstances vary among the producers of alternative goods and services. These differences may justify the imposition of taxes on a range of activities, often geared to the benefits each receives from public expenditures. Individuals also vary in terms of their preferences for work, leisure, consumption, and saving. To levy all required revenues through a single tax would compound the inequities and distortionary effects of this particular tax. Furthermore, to rely on only a single tax or a small number of taxes would mean that the tax rate would have to be high, and this could lead to severe compliance problems. Reliance on a large variety of taxes enables a society to minimize the tax rate of each and so to minimize tax evasion. Atkinson and Stiglitz have explained the need for a variety of taxes in the following terms:

[T]he necessity for any form of taxation other than a uniform lump-sum tax arises from the fact that individuals have differing characteristics (endowments or tastes). If we could observe all relevant characteristics costlessly and perfectly, we should be able to achieve a first-best solution. However, in practice, we have to make use of surrogate characteristics, which are related systematically to the characteristics on which we would like to differentiate individuals, but which are not perfectly correlated and which are, to some extent, under the control of the individual. Certain ethical principles, notably those which fall under the rubric of horizontal equity, limit further the set of surrogates which may be used. Having established an admissible class of characteristics, the problem then becomes one of determining which are to be employed (the choice of tax base) and the structure of the tax schedule.[1]

In many circumstances, those who are legally obliged to pay a certain tax are able to shift the burden of this tax forward to purchasers of their products, or backwards to suppliers of their inputs. Consequently, the legal incidence of a tax is different from its economic incidence. Often, it is impossible to predict the degree of tax shifting that will occur with a particular tax. Even after the tax has been paid, it is often impossible to state how the tax burden was shared. Hence, the possibility of tax shifting greatly complicates the use of taxes to pursue society's objectives. Inflation can also alter the impact that a certain combination of taxes is expected to achieve. In particular, inflation can alter the flow of investment income to such a degree that the real value of the original investment may actually fall over time, even if there is a positive return in nominal terms. Furthermore, inflation can intensify variations across sectors in the after-tax costs of borrowing. The rules concerning deductibility of interest payments for tax purposes can add to these distortions.

The choice of tax base will also be influenced by certain economic characteristics of the jurisdiction involved. The mobility of labour and capital may result in the shifting of taxes, and so may result in a tax burden that may be unintended. For example, the burden of factor taxes may be shifted onto the less mobile elements of the economy, such as land and unskilled labour. Revenue stability may also be a concern for governments. To the extent that incomes fluctuate more than consumption over time, the latter will be a more stable source of tax revenues. The relative importance of household production that results in imputed incomes could also be an issue in determining the proportion of revenue to be derived from income taxes versus other sources of income, such as property taxes. Finally, in a political federation, the choice of tax base is also related to the legal and constitutional division of taxing powers among political jurisdictions.

Chapter 4 has indicated that, under free enterprise, prices reflect both marginal demand and marginal cost. The imposition of taxes alters prices, and so taxes can lead consumers and producers to make decisions that are not optimal. By changing the utility maximization and cost minimization decisions described in Chapter 4, taxes can create inefficiencies and distortions. Yet, in the pursuit of the growth objective, some people argue that certain price distortions can stimulate economic activities, and so are desirable. Tax deductions or exemptions may be designed with the hope of increasing saving and investment, expanding research and development (R&D), providing labour retraining, and fostering entrepreneurship. Furthermore, in order to encourage a socially approved consumption pattern, some people argue that supplementary taxes are necessary to restrain the purchase of dangerous or hazardous products. Special excise taxes on alcohol or cigarettes, for example, may impinge on individual consumption decisions in a manner society as a whole finds desirable. Taxes can also be designed to change the income distribution. The rich may be taxed more heavily than the poor, and so the progressiveness of the tax structure may be a means of furthering equality. Society's choice of the aggregate level of taxation may impact the rate of inflation and the rate of unemployment, and it may affect the intergenerational transfer of wealth. Hence, taxation involves issues that are relevant for each of society's objectives.

Government expenditures form an addition to the aggregate demand of the nongovernment sectors. If a government expands the money supply to pay for its expenditures, then shortages and inflation could result. Taxation is a means of reducing nongovernment aggregate demand, so that government expenditures replace private expenditures rather than supplement them. However, taxation is not the sole means of reducing the aggregate demand of nongovernment sectors. Governments can also issue bonds, offering an interest payment to encourage private saving. The relationships among deficits, money supply, and inflation have been analyzed on the basis of alternative theoretical models, resulting in disparate conclusions. As Chapter 9 indicates, the direct allocation of goods and services through centralized decision making offers another method of reducing consumption. Taxation may not be necessary if prices and incomes can be set centrally rather than in the market. If firms are not owned privately, then profits do not form a component of aggregate demand. Nevertheless, to the extent that incomes are altered in unforeseen ways, even a centrally planned economy may utilize taxes as a way of limiting shortages and inflationary pressures.

Efficiency

Chapter 4 has demonstrated the efficiency conditions of a free enterprise economy. Most taxes alter prices. If the pre-tax prices reflect relative demand and supply and lead to efficiency, then this alteration of prices may introduce distortions and inefficiencies. For a good or service that is taxed, purchasers must pay a higher price than suppliers receive. Consequently, in equilibrium the production of an additional amount would result in an additional value to consumers that exceeds production cost. Efficiency would require that the additional amount be produced. Yet, because the tax is added to the production cost, the supplier has no incentive to expand production.

The only tax that would not disturb the conditions described in chapter 4 is a lump-sum, or a poll, tax. Because such a tax does not distort relative prices, it would not affect the taxpayer's pattern of activity or consumption. Otherwise,

the imposition of a tax on the market drives a wedge between the amount the demanders are willing to pay and the amount required to compensate suppliers to produce additional amounts. The value the economy places on having another unit produced exceeds the cost to society to produce it, but because of the tax, no more will be produced. The result is that society's resources are not being used efficiently. In general, too little of the taxed commodity (or factor) will ultimately be produced and sold.[2]

Overall, efficiency is disturbed by the tax system when differences in tax rates occur across goods and services and create a wedge between their marginal cost and their price. As a result, the marginal benefits are not proportional to the marginal costs, and resources are likely to be misallocated. Variations in sales-tax rates among commodities, or in tax burdens (whether corporate, property, or social security taxes), among industries, can be the source of such distortions.

As is the case with tax shifting, the distortionary impact of a tax will depend on the market circumstances.

Generally speaking, the inefficiency associated with a tax will be greater as the reduction in market output induced by the tax distortion is greater. The more elastic are demand and supply, the greater the change in output will be and the more inefficient the tax. Therefore, from an elasticity point of view, it is best to impose taxes on markets that do not respond much to price changes.[3]

Each type of tax can impose inefficiencies through distortions of one sort or another, as the following list suggests:

> The Personal Income Tax (PIT)
> taxes capital income from different sources differently (for example, capital gains exemptions, dividend tax credits, non-taxation of imputed rents);
> distorts the labour market by driving a wedge between wages paid and wages received; the importance of this distortion

increases as income rises, due to the progressiveness in the rates;

distorts the savings and investment market by driving a wedge between the net return on savings and the price paid by borrowers; also by taxing savings, the PIT favours current, rather than future, consumption;

favours activities yielding imputed (nontaxable) income.

The Corporate Income Tax (CIT)

may distort the capital market by misallocating resources away from the corporate sector and into the unincorporated sector and by reducing the net rate of return to capital and, hence, reducing the overall amount of capital investment;

may distort the allocation of resources within the corporate sector by taxing various industries at various rates due to special tax provisions (for example, depreciation allowances and investment tax credits) and differential rates (for example, manufacturing, small business);

by taxing part of the return for risk taking, the CIT may discriminate against entrepreneurship and innovation;

by allowing firms to deduct the interest on debt but not the cost of equity finance, the tax may influence the financial structure of firms.

The Retail-Sales Tax (RST) and the Value-Added Tax (VAT)

the RST and VAT favour tax-exempt or zero-rated purchases because they usually do not apply across the board to all goods and services;

to the extent that the tax results in lower demand for the taxed items, there will be a reallocation of resources;

because these taxes decrease the real wage rate, they may result in work disincentives.

The Excise Tax

discriminates against the use of the goods which are taxed. Excise taxes on products such as tobacco and alcohol may be justified as user fees because the consumption of these products is believed to generate costs for society as a whole, such as the loss of productivity, higher health care costs, and crime prevention expenditures. These taxes are also viewed as good sources of revenue because the demand for the taxed items tends to be inelastic.

The Property Tax

discourages the accumulation of property if the supply of the latter is elastic;

creates incentives to reallocate property from high-tax to low-tax jurisdictions to the extent that tax differentials do not reflect differentials in levels of services received;

creates distortions by taxing at different effective rates, different types of property (for example, residential, nonresidential, single-family dwellings, multi-family dwellings, etc.).

There has been an increased interest, in recent years, in the distortions caused by tax measures, and several studies have attempted to estimate the costs to society of tax induced misallocation of resources. The terms "excess burden," or "deadweight loss," are used in referring to such costs. These studies suggest that the resource allocation costs of distortions caused by the tax system may be much larger than has often been supposed in the past. The corporate income tax may cause significant misallocation of capital among industries. The personal income tax may favour current consumption over saving and future consumption. The costs of these distortions appear to be much greater than those associated with the disincentive effects of taxes on labour supply.

Growth

As mentioned above, the concept of efficiency is based on the premise that resources in competitive markets will be allocated to their most productive use. In this context, taxes are seen as introducing a distortion in the efficient operation of the market. Through their impact on the rates of return involved, taxes can affect the supply of labour, the rate of saving, and the rate of investment. Because taxes affect the supply of labour and capital, which are major determinants of growth, governments often attempt to design taxes that will foster the accumulation of these factors of production. Another target of tax policy is the rate of technical progress; that is, the productivity with which resources are used. By providing R&D tax incentives, preferential tax treatment of small businesses, and investment tax credits, governments hope to foster innovation and entrepreneurship in such a way as to increase factor productivity and economic growth. From a policy point of view, the dilemma is whether the economic benefits achieved by using the tax system to influence the workings of economic activity will outweigh the costs associated with the potential misallocation of resources.

Taxes levied against labour income may alter the choice of leisure versus work for the individual. Higher tax rates reduce the material reward for work. Consequently, we might expect that higher tax rates will reduce the number of hours worked – people will opt for more leisure and less work. This leads to several important implications for the design of the tax structure.

First, in order to minimize this reduction in hours worked, a government may decide to limit its reliance on labour income taxes. A government may feel obliged to impose other types of taxes, in spite of their distortions, and it may rely on a mix of taxes. Second, a government may decide to limit its marginal tax rates for high-income people even if it might prefer greater tax progressiveness for equity reasons. Third, a government may decide to tax different kinds of labour at different tax rates if it believes that the labour–leisure choice varies across occupations.

Recent years have seen an increased interest concerning the impact of income taxes on hours worked. Popularization of the *Laffer curve* has been an element of this. Arthur Laffer has claimed that when tax rates are raised, the total revenue of the government may actually fall because of this impact. A relationship – the Laffer curve – can be drawn between tax rates and total revenue. With tax rates at zero, revenue will be zero, and when tax rates are 100 percent, revenue will also be zero. Hence, total tax revenues must reach some maximum when the tax rate is between zero and 100 percent. In the early 1980s, Laffer suggested that tax rates in the United States were so high that a reduction in rates would actually increase government revenue. Laffer's position was part of the *supply-side economics* that underlay President Reagan's initial tax cuts in 1980–2.

Closely related to this view is the concern about nonmarket activities. If tax rates reach a certain level, then people will devise schemes to exchange their labour without any formal records that would attract tax. Some observers believe that tax rates have been so high that this non-market sector has grown rapidly in size. For example, Ethier estimated that the *underground* sector in Canada generated output equal to 6 percent of measured GNP in 1981.[4] Moreover, though many people may not try to evade taxes, they may spend a great deal of effort discovering and utilizing legal tax loopholes. Even though these activities are legal, they are a waste of society's resources.

Hausman provides an extensive discussion of the results of a large number of empirical studies on the effects of taxes on labour supply. An important conclusion is that there are substantial differences in the labour supply behaviour of different categories of workers. For example, tax cuts seem to have a relatively insignificant impact on the labour supply of males, whereas the labour supply of wives is very responsive to tax cuts.[5] As Rae points out, this information could affect a government's choice of tax structure: "This would imply a policy of lower tax rates for secondary workers in the family and higher tax rates for primary workers."[6] Overall, the issue of the impact of taxes on labour supply is still unresolved. However, indications are that the effect is probably much less than some used to assume. A Canadian study by Hartle found that the elimination of the entire personal income tax on wages would have very little effect on the supply side of labour.[7] The issue of non-market activities is probably more important, particularly for societies where primary production (farming, fishing, logging, for example) is relatively important.

It is generally agreed that the main influence of the tax system on economic growth occurs through its effect on saving and capital formation. A larger capital stock, combined with labour, renders the latter more productive. Taxation may reduce the demand for investments or reduce the supply of savings used to finance investment, by taxing capital income (interest, dividends, and capital gains) and by reducing the marginal rate of return to corporations from investing (corporate income tax). The impact of tax policy on private-sector savings is important because it affects the division of resource use between current and future consumption (saving implies a delay in present consumption to provide for future consumption), and between current consumption and capital formation.

The tax system affects household savings in two ways. The progressive income tax is seen as a deterrent to savings because household saving, as a percentage of income, rises with income. However, the difference in impact on the consumption–saving decisions of low-income and high-income households depends not on the difference in their average rates of savings but on the difference in their marginal rates of savings, which do not vary as much as the former. From this perspective, feasible changes in the tax structure are unlikely to have a major effect on the savings rate of the economy. However, the savings rate may be altered by taxation, not only because the income of the taxpayer is reduced, but also because the income tax reduces the net rate of return on saving by taxing interest income. The issue here is to what extent the savings rate is influenced by changes in the rate of interest.

For the most part, corporate savings are in the form of depreciation charges. These charges are not affected by the profits tax (although their timing may be) because the profits tax is imposed after the deduction of depreciation. The remaining portion of corporate savings are more likely to be affected by taxes. To the extent that profit taxes are not shifted, after-tax profits will be reduced by the tax and this may reduce corporate savings by lowering retained earnings.

Taxes not only affect the saving activity, but also the investment activity necessary for capital formation. A combination of tax effects will impact on investment behavior. Three relationships can be identified: (a) The profits tax reduces the expected net rate of return on investment; (b) by affecting the level of corporate sales, the tax system influences the need for increased capacity and the investment behaviour of the firm; and (c) by affecting the form of depreciation reserves or retained earnings, the profits tax influences the availability of internal funds, which is a variable in the investment decision.[8] In this context, investment may be stimulated by reducing the rate of tax, speeding up depreciation, or granting investment credits.

A number of tax measures can be implemented to reduce the taxation of interest income. These can perhaps best be understood as following either of two approaches. First, taxes can be levied on those types of income that do not include a return for saving and investing, and specific exemptions and deductions can be allowed for income that is related to saving and investment. This would shift the taxation of income to a labour-income base. This approach is reflected in the taxation of corporate dividends at a lower rate than other income, the exemption of capital gains from taxation, the delayed taxation of some types of interest income until that income is actually realized, and the special tax treatment of owner-occupied housing where the imputed rent and the capital gains on such property are usually both exempt from taxation.

The second approach is to permit deductions of various kinds of savings in the calculation of taxable income. This would shift the focus of personal taxation from an income base to a consumption (expenditure) base. If savings are deducted from income in calculating taxes payable, then only actual expenditures are taxed. In many countries, contributions to pension plans are treated in this manner. Such tax measures have resulted in wide variations in effective tax rates on capital among sectors and activities. Yet, at this point in time, the net impact on saving remains unclear. After reviewing a number of Canadian studies designed to measure the responsiveness of saving to various tax incentives, Boadway and Bruce conclude,

at the moment, "not proven" is the best verdict one can base on the empirical evidence of the effects of tax incentives on saving, although it remains plausible that they have elevated Canadian savings rates relative to U.S. rates.[9]

There are many reasons why these tax incentives may not have the desired effect. Many theoretical studies note that if individuals save to achieve a particular level of retirement income, then any increase in after-tax rates of return would mean they could actually lower their savings rate and still reach their targeted level. With regard to the incentives actually introduced in Canada, for example, some authors argue that many of them were essentially lump-sum transfers to households which had no effect on marginal savings.[10] Their effect on aggregate savings, moreover, depends on how the government responds to the loss of tax revenue. Either the government budget deficit is permitted to rise or extra revenue is collected by raising the general level of taxes. A higher deficit means that the government sector's dissaving is rising and thus offsetting the higher saving by the household sector. Higher taxes, on the other hand, while preventing a rise in government dissaving, reduce the ability of households to save.

Whether tax incentives have much of an impact on aggregate investment is also an unsettled question.[11] Early work by Hall and Jorgenson showed that U.S. investment tax incentives had very large effects on the investment expenditures of the U.S. manufacturing sector.[12] In Canada, studies by McFetridge and May and Harman and Johnson confirmed that investment by the Canadian manufacturing sector was sensitive to changes in tax incentives.[13] However, it appears that the tax revenue forgone was almost equal to the extra investment generated.

In addition to examining the effects of taxes, economists have also been interested in the effects of overall government budget policy on savings and investment behaviour, and on the welfare of current and future generations. The framework used in much of this research builds on the theory of economic growth developed by Solow and Uzawa with an emphasis on the steady state of the economy under different government policies.[14] The evidence indicates that, compared with equal-yield consumption taxes, income taxes depress saving, and hence investment (at least in a closed economy), resulting in a long-run welfare loss. Investment and capital formation may also be depressed by the use of debt financing, as will be discussed later in this chapter. A pay-as-you-go or unfunded public pension system may have a similar impact: Public pensions can replace private saving and hence, the private capital stock is reduced. Although there is no agreement on the exact size of these effects, there is a consensus that they are quite large.[15]

Overall, the impact of fiscal incentives on saving and investment is constrained by the relative openness of most economies. Because of the mobility of capital, the rate of return to savings has to be in line with that determined by the world market. It also means that the volume of domestic investment is not exclusively dependent on the level of domestic savings. The tax concessions designed to increase savings could mean less reliance on savings from foreign sources, but not necessarily an increase in the total supply of savings. If foreign investors can deduct the taxes that they pay against taxes payable in their homeland, then their total tax burden is unchanged by the incentive measures and tax concessions which simply raise the foreign government's revenue by an equivalent amount. For example, under current tax provisions in the United States, some foreign taxes can be deducted by investors in the United States when they calculate their taxes payable in that country. If a foreign government were to reduce these taxes, then U.S. investors would pay the same total tax bill, however, a larger share would accrue to the U.S. government. Since a substantial proportion of industry in many societies is owned by firms based in the United States, many people regard the corporate income tax from this perspective. Reduction of corporate income taxes would, to some extent, be a transfer of tax revenue to the government of the United States. For example, Deutsch and Jenkins calculated that a decrease in the corporate income tax rate on Canada's manufacturing sector from 46 percent to 40 percent would result in a revenue loss of $72 million. Of this total, $56 million (or 78 percent) "would end up in the coffers of the United States government in the form of additional taxes collected."[16] For these reasons, we see that a certain tax, that may be desirable as a way of increasing savings and investment in a closed economy, may not be desirable in a small, open economy.

Two additional types of tax policies are important in the context of the economic growth objective. First, R&D tax incentives aim to encourage firms to undertake this form of activity in the hope that it will lead to innovation and increased productivity. Second, tax incentives may encourage the development of new small business. Many people believe that new small businesses provide society with special economic benefits. Evidence exists that job creation occurs to a greater degree in new small businesses rather than in the expansion of older, larger firms in traditional industries, and that innovation occurs to a greater degree in small businesses. It is often argued that shortcomings or "failures" in capital markets make it difficult for small businesses to acquire financing on the terms and conditions that would be socially optimal. Tax concessions to increase the availability of new-small-business capital and decrease its costs may consequently be desirable.[17]

It must be emphasized that the issue of the impact of taxes on economic growth is really a question of whether the benefits to be reaped from providing special tax measures to encourage saving and investment outweigh the costs from the misallocation of resources resulting from the interference in the capital market. It may be that minimizing the tax-induced distortions is a preferable policy approach. A major concern is that special tax measures inevitably result in a narrower tax base that compounds the distortionary effects of the taxes in a number of ways. This was one of the major issues raised early in the U.S. tax reform discussions in the 1980s, and the U.S. Treasury I report presented it in the following manner:

The lack of a comprehensive income tax base has two obvious and important adverse effects on the ability of the marketplace to allocate capital and labour to their most productive uses. First, the smaller the tax base, the higher tax rates must be to raise a given amount of revenue. High tax rates discourage saving and investment, stifle work effort, retard invention and innovation, encourage unproductive investment in tax shelters, and needlessly reduce the nation's standard of living and growth rate.

Second, tax preferred activities are favored relative to others, and tax law, rather than the market, becomes the primary force in determining how economic resources are used. Over the years, the tax system has come to exert a pervasive influence on the behavior of private decision-makers. The resulting tax-induced distortions in the use of labour and capital and in consumer choices have severe costs in terms of lower productivity, lost production, and reduced consumer satisfaction.[18]

Furthermore, it is not clear whether the tax incentives introduced in the tax system have had the desired effects. The widely held view in the United States presently is that they have not, and there is even concern that the net impact might have been negative. Studies in Canada indicate that provisions such as the accelerated depreciation allowances and the investment tax credit are largely responsible for the wide dispersion in effective marginal corporate tax rates across industry groups.[19] On the other hand, it has also been demonstrated that investment is sensitive to tax changes, although it appears that the revenue loss due to the measures may be of the same order of magnitude as the amount of investment induced. Numerous studies have also analyzed the effect of the corporate tax on savings and risk taking, but the evidence so far is inconclusive.

In view of these considerations, it is likely that the concern for economic growth will shift from ways to encourage economic growth through special tax incentives to a desire to design tax systems that interfere as little as possible with free-enterprise decisions. Certainly, a concern underlying both the 1986 U.S. Tax Reform Act and the 1987 Canadian White Paper on Tax Reform was minimization of distortions instead of creating new ones. These taxation reform proposals both sought to increase the scope for private decision making, to reduce the role of collectively determined incentives, and to minimize differences in tax treatment among individuals and corporations.

Equity

Equity involves a comparison of how a specific tax affects the well-being of one individual versus another. There are two aspects of equity which should be identified. *Horizontal equity* deals with whether taxpayers with equal ability to pay bear the same tax burden. *Vertical equity,* on the other hand, concerns the relative tax treatment that should be given to taxpayers with different levels of ability to pay. Both these concepts of equity require the use of some universally accepted measure of "well-being" or ability to pay in order to make comparisons among taxpayers. It is usually assumed that a general notion of broad income is adequate for this purpose. The concept of *comprehensive income,* often described as Haig–Simons income, is commonly used as an indicator of well-being and therefore as the appropriate background against which to evaluate equity.

However, as Boadway and Kitchen indicate, there are several conceptual problems to consider if comprehensive income is to be used as the sole indicator of equity. First, the fact that leisure is not taxed could lead to inequities. For instance, two individuals with equivalent income-tax burdens could spend very different amounts of time earning this income. The individual who worked less, perhaps by choice, has more leisure time, and leisure can be considered a form of imputed income. Another problem arises from the fluctuations of income over time.

A person's income can fluctuate over time so that the income, as measured at any one time, may not represent the average income level or standard of living achieved over the lifetime.[20]

A tax or tax system is termed progressive if those with higher incomes pay a higher percentage of their income in taxes than do those with lower incomes. Under a progressive tax system, two individuals can have the same average level of income over their lifetime, but if the income of one fluctuates more than the other, there will be a discrepancy in tax liability. The individual whose income fluctuates more will end up paying more taxes. There are two ways to deal with these problems. One is to use some notion of permanent income as the tax base. The other way is to allow a system of income averaging for tax purposes. Again, this involves a judgement concerning the adequate indicator of ability to pay, and one's opinion as to the equity of the tax system is largely influenced by this judgement.

As Kaldor has pointed out, it appears that over time, the notion of income has become synonymous with taxable capacity.[21] The Haig–Simons concept of comprehensive income is probably the most widely accepted measure. It is defined in terms of *use* as the sum of current consumption plus additions to net worth or saving, and in terms of *source* as the sum of all real current additions to purchasing power. Ideally, the comprehensive income tax base should include labour income, real and imputed housing rents, dividends, interest, transfers, accrued capital gains, gifts and inheritances, and the value of household services. It should exclude the value of expenditures that do not increase consumption of wealth, such as maintenance and repair costs, or business operating costs. Today, this is the yardstick generally used to evaluate tax systems.

However, there are several conceptual and practical difficulties encountered in trying to implement a comprehensive income base. The equal treatment of all sources of income is certainly desirable in theory. In practice, however, this would involve the inclusion of all sources of imputed income including leisure income and the imputed rental income from owner-occupied housing. Not only are there technical and practical problems in measuring these various forms of income, but also the taxation of such intangibles is likely to be perceived as unfair. Capital gains taxation is another problem area where taxation on an accrual basis is generally considered impractical. This approach would involve imputing changes in asset values and tax liabilities for taxpayers on gains not yet realized. The usual procedure has been to tax capital gains upon realization, which can be seen as impeding the efficiency of capital markets due to the incentive to postpone realization in order to defer tax payment. It effectively provides the taxpayer with a tax-averaging device which creates inequities if annual income is viewed as the proper tax base. Other difficulties associated with the implementation of a comprehensive income base include the need to account properly for inflation in measurements of capital income, deductions, and tax brackets. There is also the need, in the presence of both a corporate and personal income tax, to integrate the two systems to avoid double taxation of some sources of capital income and to prevent certain types of income from escaping taxation altogether.

The concept that people should pay taxes on what they consume or take out of the social pot, rather than on what they earn or contribute, can be traced back to the writings of Hobbes in the seventeenth century. However, there has been renewed interest in this approach in recent years, particularly following the Meade Committee Report in the United Kingdom, and the U.S. Treasury's Blueprints for Tax Reform in the United States.[22] There are several factors contributing to this interest. First, it can be argued that a consumption base is more equitable. Boadway and Kitchen state that "consumption expenditures represent a better indicator of a taxpayer's well-being than does income since it is consumption that ultimately yields satisfaction, not income."[23] Second, a consumption tax eliminates one of the major negative effects of the income tax, namely, the disincentive effect on savings resulting from the taxation of interest, dividends, and capital gains which reduce the return to savings. Finally, the most severe difficulties in implementing an ideal comprehensive income base are eliminated under a consumption tax. The tax base is equivalent to the difference between current income and net savings and, therefore, there is no need to include accrued capital gains or to index the base for inflation.

There are several different ways to define a consumption tax base. In its pure form, the consumption tax would be levied on realized income less the net accumulation of financial and real wealth (including consumer durables), plus the current services of consumer durables. However, as is the case with imputed rent, measuring the flow of services from durables is difficult. A second way of treating durables is on a cash-flow basis where the expenditures on durables are included in the tax base as opposed to the value of their services. A third variation on the consumption tax theme is the wage tax. This is essentially an income tax with all capital income exempt. Under this approach, there is no deduction for savings or investment in assets, but neither is the income from those investments taxed. Each of these three tax bases is equivalent in present value terms. However, the pure consumption tax base would involve considerable tax liabilities in the earlier years of life when consumption is relatively high and sometimes greater than income. On the other hand, the cash flow approach, because of the inclusion of durables, would tend to be lumpy, and tax liabilities would probably occur even earlier in time than under a pure consumption tax base. As for the wage tax approach, the exemption of capital income eliminates some liquidity problems from the former two, and the tax liabilities are more easily financed since they are closely related to income.

Another area of choice in tax design – although mainly in the context of the personal income tax – is that of the rate structure. The issue in this case is to achieve, through the structure of marginal tax rates, a certain degree of vertical equity or progressiveness which would result in a higher tax burden for those with higher ability to pay. The degree of progressiveness in the PIT is also seen as a means of compensating for the regressive nature of other taxes such as commodity taxes. However, there are a number of elements which make the choice of tax structure not as straightforward as might appear.

For one thing, the degree of progressiveness, to a great extent, is related to the choice of indicator of ability to pay. Statutory rates are such that tax payments will undoubtedly increase more rapidly than taxable income. However, because of all the exemptions, deductions, and exclusions from the tax base, the progressiveness of the tax will be severely reduced if one uses annual comprehensive income as a basis for comparison. One of the basic points of the U.S. Treasury I tax reform proposals was that by eliminating many of the exemptions and deductions which erode the tax base, it is possible to move from fourteen to three substantially lower tax rates without dramatically decreasing tax progressiveness.[24] The perceived degree of progressiveness of a specific tax structure would also be substantially different if an annual lifetime consumption base were used to assess equity. Other elements to consider are the disincentive effects of progressive taxation on work, saving, and investment, the added incentive to escape or avoid tax, the relation of tax payments to benefits received, and the potential of the tax as an automatic stabilizer via the rate progression.

From the perspective of equity, an important issue for some societies is whether inheritances and gifts should be taxed. Some argue that this would represent double taxation, since the donor has already paid an income tax. Others argue that the gift or inheritance represents income to the recipient, and so it should be taxed in the same way as any other income. Some are concerned about intergenerational accumulation of assets and the power attached to them, and so they advocate taxation on the grounds that otherwise people will not face equality of opportunity. Societies have adopted a wide variety of practices in regard to taxation of gifts and inheritances.

Incidence

The legal incidence of taxes indicates who is legally liable to pay the various taxes. However, this does not necessarily correspond with the effective incidence which indicates who actually bears the burden of taxes once all market adjustments have taken place. The difference between legal and effective incidence is directly related to the tax shifting that has taken place. For instance, corporate income tax might be collected directly from corporations but if the tax is passed on through higher prices for the corporation's products, then the effective burden of the tax is either partially or totally shifted forwards to consumers.

Conversely, if the tax results in lower wages for the employees of the corporation, then the tax burden is shifted backwards onto labour. The extent of tax shifting will depend on the elasticities of supply and demand involved.

There is little doubt that tax shifting does occur and that legal tax incidence is therefore a poor indicator of effective tax incidence. Unfortunately, there is no clear consensus as to the actual patterns of tax shifting. Tax incidence has been the subject of numerous studies over time. However, these studies must be evaluated with the clear understanding that the results are directly related to underlying assumptions. These assumptions, in turn, depend on the analyst's perception of the size of the elasticities involved and of the significance of other economic elements such as factor mobility.

The income concepts used in incidence studies vary considerably. Comprehensive income, which is commonly used, includes not only conventionally defined money income, but also other elements not included in basic income data, such as capital gains, imputed rent from owner-occupied housing, and retained earnings. These series must be constructed from aggregate estimates allocated by income range on the basis of specific assumptions as to their distribution. Further adjustments can be made to measure income in the absence of the public sector (by subtracting subsidies) or in the presence of the public sector (by including subsidies and the value of government services and subtracting taxes). Each of these variations in the income concept substantially affects the estimates of income by income range used to calculate effective tax rates and this can affect the pattern of incidence which is obtained.[25]

A further issue in incidence analysis concerns the choice of time frame within which to evaluate tax incidence. If lifetime rather than annual tax incidence is considered more relevant, then one's perception of effective incidence is likely to be quite different. The distributions of earnings, subsidies, and consumption by income range in the lifetime context tend to be substantially less skewed than the annual distributions. Because of this, the incidence results are much less sensitive to the choice of alternative incidence assumptions. Using standard shifting assumptions, it has been found that progressive taxes, such as income taxes, are less progressive in the lifetime context. Furthermore, regressive taxes, such as sales and excise taxes, are less regressive, with the overall pattern indicating mild progression.[26]

In view of the above issues, one's perception of tax incidence must be based upon what is essentially an educated guess concerning the most realistic set of assumptions. The following is a brief description of the standard incidence assumptions associated with various taxes.

Personal income tax (PIT): Usually it is assumed that the PIT is un-shifted and that the burden is distributed according to tax payments in a progressive pattern.

Corporate income tax (CIT): The incidence of the CIT has probably been the subject of more controversy than any other tax. A full range of shifting assumptions have received support in various studies over time from those that assume no shifting (the tax is entirely borne by shareholders), to those that assume the tax is entirely shifted either backwards onto labour and/or forwards onto consumers. However, the more widely accepted view is that the CIT is borne almost entirely by capital owners in the economy as a whole.

Property taxes: Until recently, it was commonly accepted that property taxes were regressive taxes. The portion of the tax that falls on land was assumed to be borne by landowners, but the tax on structures was assumed to be entirely shifted onto the consumers of the services provided by the structures. This view of property tax is now being challenged by a new view that sees the property tax as a tax on capital income which results in a reduction of the rate of return to capital.

Sales and excise taxes: Sales taxes can be applied to a wide variety of tax bases. When a sales tax is applied to a narrow range of goods, such as alcohol, tobacco, or gasoline, then the sales tax is referred to as an excise tax. Taxes on consumption are generally assumed to be borne entirely by the user, and allocated on the basis of consumption of each good and service that is taxed.

Social security taxes: The standard incidence assumption for payroll taxes is that they are entirely borne by labour. In competitive labour markets, the employer is able to shift its portion of the tax by lowering the wage rate correspondingly.

Simplicity

Whereas equity and efficiency have long been considered important objectives to achieve in tax design, it is only in the past decade or so that simplicity has become a prominent issue. In fact, the current tax reform trend in the United States can be said to be motivated, to a considerable extent, by the desire to simplify a tax system so riddled with exemptions, deductions, loopholes, and special concessions that it has alienated the majority of taxpayers. The need to simplify the tax system is also a concern in many other societies although the situations there may not be perceived to be as serious.

The current state of complexity of the tax system can be seen to be the result of two factors. The first is inherent in the tax reform process itself.[27] Tax reform is not a continuous process. Attempts to evaluate and modify tax systems on a comprehensive or broad basis are, in general, few and far between. When they do occur they usually result in the implementation of a wide range of proposals following a series of compromises, adjustments, and deletions to initial recommendations, which may or may not have been adequately conceived. What follows between reform episodes is what could be called the *band-aid* approach, whereby series after series of special provisions are implemented to (a) remedy specific problems, (b) bring relief to specific entities judged to be unduly affected by the tax system, and (c) promote specific economic activities considered desirable. Essentially, the problem stems from the noncompatibility of basic tax objectives. Efforts to achieve greater equity or more rapid economic growth will necessarily generate more intricacies. This approach inevitably leads to a system of ever-increasing complexity which eventually calls for a broad simplification.

The second factor contributing to the tax system's complexity is a consequence of the choice of tax base. For example, many tax systems are based on the notion of comprehensive income as a measure of ability to pay. The problem with this tax base is that it is practically impossible to implement in its ideal form. Theoretically, all sources of revenue should be included in the tax base on an accrual basis and in real terms. Also, individual sources of income should be taxed only once. A large number of complexities found in the personal and corporate income tax system stem from attempts to either approximate this ideal tax base despite practical constraints or to minimize the related problem of tax avoidance.

The current concern over the complexity of the tax system is the result of an increased awareness of the direct and indirect costs of this complexity. "Complexity is seen as undermining general confidence in the fairness of the tax system, fuelling the growth in the underground economy, and reducing compliance."[28] Some of these costs are tangible; others are not. The more complex the system is, the more costly it is to administer and enforce. This, in turn, results in the need to increase statutory tax rates to collect the necessary revenues which compound any negative impact of tax rates on incidence. On the other hand, from the taxpayer's point of view, tax compliance requires more time and resources, and this in itself is incentive to both avoid and evade taxes.

These concerns over complexity have led to the creation of the *flat-*

tax movement, which supports the idea of implementing a single flat tax imposed at the same low rate on everyone's income regardless of the source. The idea is that by eliminating most exemptions and deductions it would be possible to collect the same amount of revenue while drastically cutting tax rates to one basic low rate. The resulting system would be far superior in terms of horizontal equity, and it also would eliminate the problem of income fluctuations and would reduce the disincentive effects of the income tax. However, many would criticize the flat tax from the perspective of vertical equity.

The appropriate mix of taxes

It is clear that a society's objectives are to a great extent incompatible, and that to subscribe to any one or more of these objectives immediately involves trade-offs. For instance, enhancing the progressiveness of the income tax may improve the equity of the tax system, but the higher tax rates may cause inefficiencies through the distortionary effects of the tax. Special tax provisions to encourage R&D activities or entrepreneurship may stimulate growth, but they also might create a more complex tax system and generate additional distortionary effects in the economy. The dilemma reflected in the current tax-reform debate in both Canada and the United States is whether the tax system should be used as a policy tool to stimulate economic growth, or whether it should be designed to interfere as little as possible with free enterprise. On balance, the latter approach seems to prevail at the present time.

Current economic analysis is not able to develop accurate measurements of the various trade-offs involved in tax design. Consequently, the relative importance attached to various objectives and trade-offs at any point in time will involve subjective judgement on the part of governments. As indicated in the following quotation concerning Canadian tax reform commissions, these judgements can vary significantly.

[W]e must balance the relative importance of the criteria, making compromises and trade-offs among them. Each of us will have personal preferences about the proper ranking of the criteria. . . . The Belanger Commission [on taxation in Quebec] felt that adequacy was the primary purpose of taxes. The highly influential Carter Commission gave primacy of place to equity. The Smith Committee [on taxation in Ontario] also felt that equity "rises above all the rest, both because the majority of the remaining characteristics flow from it and because it goes to the core of constitutional democracy." The Meade Committee [on direct taxation in the United Kingdom] declined to address the question considering it to be a matter for the political process to determine. The Asprey Committee felt that the three dominant tests were equity, practicality, and neutrality. Among contemporary policy analysts, neutrality is growing and equity is declining in importance. Our choice depends upon what we consider to be the most serious economic, social, and political problems.[29]

This issue is further complicated by the fact that the assessment of the economic, social, and political problems is likely to be quite different depending on the perspective adopted. A federal government, for example, can be expected to view these problems in a very different light than may a provincial or state government. For provinces or states concerned about relatively high unemployment rates and lower than average per capita incomes, it very much matters whether the federal government approaches tax reform with the view to improve the redistributive impact of the tax system. On the other hand, economically prosperous provinces or states are more likely to benefit from capital gains exemptions, increased limits on deductible pension contributions, or the accelerated depreciation allowances available to manufacturing industries. The point is that the national interest may not always coincide with regional interests. The federal government, having chosen a particular combination of taxation objectives, may very well find that the effects of the tax measures vary substantially among provinces or states. For most state or provincial governments, it is also important to recognize that there is limited room to manoeuvre in pursuing various tax objectives.

The definition of *direct* and *indirect* taxes is that of John Stuart Mill. A direct tax is "one which is demanded from the very person who it is intended or desired to pay it."[30] Indirect taxes, on the other hand, are "those which are demanded from one person in the expectation and intention that he shall indemnify himself at the expense of another."[31] Typical examples of indirect taxes are import tariffs, export tariffs, and excise taxes. Examples of direct taxes include property taxes and income taxes. We now turn to a discussion of the choices by societies of an appropriate mix of various direct and indirect taxes. Not surprisingly, these choices have varied significantly among societies.

Tax systems are usually designed to incorporate a tax mix in which revenues will originate from both direct and indirect taxation. The distinction between direct and indirect taxes can be related to the circular flow of income and expenditures. Direct taxes are ones levied directly on the source side; that is, on income before it is used. Indirect taxes are levied on the use side on the basis of this use. However, some conceptual uncertainty remains when trying to distinguish between direct and indirect taxes. For instance, authors such as Atkinson and Stiglitz, Kesselman, and Thirsk[32] characterize direct taxes as those that can be adjusted to reflect the circumstances of the taxpayer, whereas indirect taxes are those levied at rates independent of taxpayers' attributes. According to Thirsk, identifying the effect of a tax on relative, rather than absolute, prices may be a more reliable procedure to distinguish how one tax differs from another. "Taxes will diminish the welfare of households either through a reduction in their money incomes, through an increase in the price of their purchases, or through a combination of both."[33] The impact of a direct tax tends to be observed on money income, whereas that of an indirect tax is reflected by increases in the price level. Although the price-level manifestations are quite different for the two types of tax, it is possible for a direct tax (a single-rate expenditure tax) and an indirect tax (a broad, uniform value-added tax) to have an equivalent impact on the structure of relative prices. In such a case, the distribution of income and the allocation of resources would be the same under either tax. This is clearly significant given certain reform trends. Carlson and McLure point out that the flat-rate personal income tax, which was proposed in the United States on several occasions in the early 1980s, was practically equivalent to a broad-based, uniform-rate value-added tax (VAT) that allowed personal exemptions.[34]

If we ignore questions of administration, it can be argued that direct taxes are superior under both equity and efficiency criteria since these taxes have the built-in capacity to take account of taxpayers' circumstances. They are more likely to be compatible with equity objectives and may, if broadly based, be less distortionary than indirect taxes. An alternative point of view is that direct taxes should be used to achieve the equity objective, leaving indirect taxes to address the issue of efficiency. As Thirsk notes,

For a given revenue requirement, marginal tax rates would be higher with exclusive reliance on a single direct tax base. Introducing an indirect tax base, even though it might detract from the equity objective, would permit lower marginal tax rates on the direct tax base and since efficiency is a function of the square of the marginal rates, the combination of direct and indirect tax bases would impose a lower efficiency cost on the economy than would the use of the direct tax base itself.[35]

However, Thirsk further indicates that these propositions, derived from the optimal-tax literature, do not rest on very solid theoretical ground, and the results of studies in this area are as of yet inconclusive.

Wealth can also be used as a direct tax base. However, difficulties associated with achieving a proper market-value assessment of the various forms of wealth, including human wealth, and the problems of enforcing a tax on such a base, make a true wealth tax disadvantageous.

The property tax levied on real property is essentially the only form of wealth tax commonly used in most societies even though the paid-up capital taxes levied in some countries can be seen as another form of wealth tax.

According to Buchanan and Flowers, the personal income tax meets the criterion of directness more than any other tax that can be used as a major source of revenue in modern fiscal systems.[36] Boadway and Kitchen's review of the tax indicates that

the personal income tax is the fairest form of taxation available. Its potential effect on the behavior and on the supply of labour is far from obvious. There is little, if any, support for the contention that the personal income tax has retarded economic growth.[37]

The major criticisms directed at the PIT are most likely related to the following.

1. An ideal income-based PIT is impractical due to the difficulties in measuring and including accrued capital gains in the tax base, and due to the issues of proper treatment of inflation and full integration with the corporate income tax.
2. Because of these and other difficulties, various sources of income are taxed at different effective rates, causing distortions and inefficiencies, as well as inequities.
3. The resulting exclusions, deductions, and special provisions involve considerable administrative and compliance costs. Consequently, higher marginal rates are required which further compound the distortionary effects of the tax.
4. The personal income tax, because of the way it is designed and enforced, is susceptible to tax evasion and avoidance.

The position that the personal income tax has a detrimental impact on savings and investment has, until recently, received some credibility in spite of a lack of evidence.

Although the personal income tax remains, on average, the most important source of revenue, governments also rely upon a variety of indirect taxes to help finance their expenditures. Thirsk notes that the structure of these taxes can vary widely as can their characteristics.

The transaction to which the tax applies may be either an act of production by firms in the economy or an act of consumption by households. Except in an open economy, it does not matter in principle on which side of the market, supply or demand, an indirect tax is assessed. Indirect taxes may apply to a large number of transactions, in which case they are described as sales taxes, or to only a few transactions. With such a limited scope, indirect taxes are referred to as excise taxes. The base for an indirect tax is either the price of the transactions (ad valorem taxation), as in the case of sales taxation, or the quantity transacted. The rates of indirect tax may be either uniform or variable across different kinds of transactions.[38]

The rationale for excise taxes is unrelated to the choice of direct tax. For instance, these taxes can be used to serve the equity objective by exploiting the differing income elasticities of demand for various commodities. Taxes levied on the consumption of luxury items have traditionally been used for this purpose. Similarly, by exploiting the differing price elasticities of demand for various commodities, excise taxes can be used to collect revenues while minimizing efficiency costs. Also, to the extent that a tax can be targeted on consumption directly related to benefits received from certain public expenditures, the benefit principle of taxation may apply. Taxes on gasoline consumption, which is complementary to public highway usage, may be categorized as such. Finally, excise taxes on products such as tobacco and alcohol may be justified because the consumption of these products is believed to generate negative externalities for society as a whole, which are costly in terms of loss of productivity and higher health care and crime prevention expenditures.

On the other hand, the case for a general sales tax is related to the type of direct tax in place. As is emphasized throughout taxation literature, perhaps the most serious distortion attributable to the broad-based income tax is the fact that it favours the inefficient, intertemporal allocation of resources by giving preferential treatment to current consumption over future consumption. Restricting the use of the PIT by relying on a general sales tax, such as a broad-based VAT, has the advantage of limiting the severity of this distortion. As for the work–leisure distortion associated with the PIT, the use of a general sales tax could be advantageous in this case as well. However, this would require that a tax illusion take place, meaning that the taxpayer not perceive that the reduced tax burden on the income side is matched by the increased tax burden on the expenditure side. There is no evidence that such an illusion does operate.

Another argument on the role of indirect taxes concerns the fact that in present value terms, a single-rate general indirect tax is equivalent to an equal-rate payroll tax on labour incomes. Relying more on a general sales tax would therefore lighten the burden on income from capital under the PIT, thereby moderating saving inefficiencies. The fact that the PIT reform proposals in many countries indicate a move away from consumption-tax measures adds weight to these arguments.

Perhaps the most important argument in favour of using sales taxes relates to the fact that the PIT is subject to more evasion and avoidance than the sales tax and the fact that broad-based indirect taxes are an effective revenue raiser. This practical element would also be a factor in the presence of an expenditure tax where the latter could be applied mainly for equity reasons at a multiple rate on high-level consumers. Other less significant benefits in such a case would be that the flat sales tax could act as a cushion against the imperfect averaging and the labour–leisure choice distortions that would occur if only a progressive expenditure tax were in place. Thirsk concludes that

a mixture of direct and indirect taxes may be better able to achieve the goals of equity, efficiency and administrative simplicity under either a pure income tax system or a pure expenditure tax design. Much depends on the form of indirect taxation.[39]

To obtain the benefits from indirect taxation, it is important that such taxes adhere as closely as possible to the basic principles of sales taxation. As Cnossen notes, these include production and consumption neutrality.

Production neutrality is achieved if a sales tax does not induce firms to change the forms and methods by which they carry out business. . . . A sales tax should also be neutral in its effects on consumer choice; that is, the actual tax incorporated in a consumer price, expressed as a percentage thereof, should equal the nominal or statutory rate of sales tax.[40]

Furthermore, in light of the criteria of interjurisdictional equity, locational neutrality, and administrative feasibility, the destination principle emerges as the preferred basis; that is, the commodity is taxed in the jurisdiction where it is consumed. According to Cnossen, only the retail-sales tax and the value-added tax (VAT) come close to meeting the neutrality requirements. These taxes are also the only ones suitable in terms of implementing the destination principle. Increasing attention is being given to the concept of a value-added tax (VAT) in North America while many European countries have considerable experience with a VAT.

The retail-sales tax is collected only on the final sale to consumers, whereas the VAT is collected at each stage as goods and services pass through the sequential stages of the production–distribution process. That is, the VAT is applied on all transactions, including those between suppliers. In most countries that have implemented a VAT, goods and services are taxed at several different rates. In Europe, a reduced rate, or an exemption, commonly applies to items that might reasonably be considered necessities, that is, food, housing, transportation, utilities, and social and medical services. Conversely, differentially higher rates apply primarily to luxuries and some of those goods and services where countries such as Canada and the United States have levied excise taxes.

The value added by a firm can be calculated in two different ways. Either it is obtained by taking the differences between the revenue from the sale of the firm's product and the total cost of all purchases of material inputs used in the production of this good, or it is equal to the sum of all factor payments including wages, salaries, rent, interest, and profits incurred in the production of the same product.[41] Boadway and Kitchen provide a simple example to illustrate the equivalence of the two approaches.

Assume an entrepreneur spends $1,000 for all material inputs used in the production of a particular good that he subsequently sells for $1,500. This differential of $500 reflects the value that has been added to the product and includes wages, salaries, interest, rent and profit to the owners. Equivalently, the $500 is the difference between the selling price and the costs of material inputs purchased.[42]

In calculating the tax, either of the two approaches mentioned above can be used. The authors note that a firm may apply a tax to the total value of all factor payments, or as is customarily the case, the firm may simply pay a tax on the difference between its selling price and the cost of materials purchased. In theory, the latter approach is simple to operate. Based upon the above example,

the firm merely calculates the tax on its final selling price and deducts the tax that was imposed on its purchases. With a 10 percent rate, sales of $1,500 and purchases of taxable inputs of $1,000, the tax liability would be $150 on the selling price less $100 previously paid on the purchased items for a net liability of $50 on the second firm. This effect is the same as if the firm summed the value-added and applied the 10 percent rate.[43]

To summarize, there is a case to be made for using a general form of indirect taxation in combination with a direct tax, even if an ideal form of direct taxation were possible, but particularly because it is not. Indirect taxation does not lend itself easily to pursuing equity objectives because it does not recognize taxpayer attributes. Credits against the PIT might be a way to counteract the regressivity of sales taxes.

The choice between a broad-based or specifically designed tax base

Of all the taxes currently levied, there are few that could be described as truly broadly-based taxes. For most societies, the personal income tax is significantly narrowed by numerous exemptions, deductions, and exclusions from the tax base, which means that it is in fact a combination consumption–income tax base. The corporate income tax (CIT) often provides accelerated depreciation allowances and investment tax credits, as well as various deductions and diverse rates related to specific types of economic activity. The sales tax is also frequently subject to numerous exemptions such as food, clothing, and certain types of services.

In general, any tax provision that introduces nonneutralities will result in efficiency loss. Boadway and Kitchen state that "for complete neutrality, the imposition of a tax must affect all forms of economic behaviour in exactly the same way."[44] The exemptions from the sales tax effectively distort consumption behaviour between taxed and untaxed goods.[45] The rationale for these tax provisions varies in each case. For instance, the exemptions from the sales tax have a number of purposes. Food, prescription drugs, and sometimes clothing are exempt in order to remove some of the tax burden on low-income taxpayers associated with the purchase of items considered as necessities. Other exemptions are provided to encourage the consumption of these goods according to specific economic goals or to eliminate multiple taxation, as in the case of goods used in the production process. The latter example would be seen as improving efficiency. As already mentioned, the impact of the distortions caused by these exemptions is directly related to the elasticities of supply and demand involved and to the level of the tax rate.

The special provisions under the corporate income tax in many societies occur mostly in the context of the economic growth objective. For the most part, they operate to provide an incentive (or disincentive) for the purchase of assets for particular uses or by particular industries. Such is the case with the accelerated depreciation allowances and investment tax credits available to manufacturing, processing, and mining industries in many societies.

The reasons for the numerous exemptions and deductions from the personal income tax base in many societies can be categorized broadly in terms of two objectives: (1) those aimed at achieving certain social goals, including improving horizontal and vertical equity, and (2) those aimed at stimulating growth through encouraging saving and investment. Personal exemptions and deductions for medical expenses, charitable donations, education costs, social insurance, and child care expenses qualify under the first category of objectives, whereas exemptions for interest, dividends, and capital gains involve the second objective.

An important fact to consider in this discussion is that special tax provisions can significantly narrow the tax base. This process involves direct costs in terms of tax revenues foregone, and indirect costs in terms of the losses incurred from the misallocation of resources in the economy.[46] In addition, tax exemptions and deductions usually result in the need for higher statutory rates which further exacerbate the distortionary effects of taxes. These costs must be weighed not only against the benefits to be gained from tax provisions, but also in the context of whether these benefits might not be obtained more efficiently through other means. For instance, it has been argued that sales-tax exemptions on items such as clothing do not reduce the regressiveness of the sales tax, and that perhaps a sales-tax credit against the PIT would be a more efficient way to reduce the tax burden on low-income individuals.[47] Tax credits have also been contemplated as a replacement for personal tax exemptions and deductions, because the value of the latter effectively increases as the marginal tax rate rises.

Finally, tax incentives have come under criticism for creating wide margins in effective tax rates among industries, and more important, for becoming a determining factor in the business decision process while not necessarily providing the desired impact. It has also been argued that the equality and growth objectives may be better served on the expenditure side of the budget equation in the form of the subsidies discussed in Chapter 6.

The tax revenue structure: international perspectives

The choice of tax bases and the resulting tax mix adopted by governments vary considerably among countries. Table 7.1 reports the total tax revenue (of all levels of government) as a percentage of GDP for twenty-three OECD member countries. In 1987, the three main sources of tax revenue in all twenty-three countries were taxes on income and profit, taxes on goods and services, and social security contributions (see Table 7.2). However, the relative importance of each of these categories varied among countries. In Canada, taxes on income and profits were the most important (47.3 percent), followed by taxes on goods and services (28.9 percent), and social security taxes (13.3 percent). By contrast, in France, the largest single source of tax revenue was social security contributions (43.0 percent of total tax revenue), followed by taxes on goods and services (29.3 percent), and taxes on income and profits (18.0 percent). In the United States, taxes on income and profits ranked first (44.3 percent of total tax revenue), followed by social security taxes (28.8 percent), and taxes on goods and services (16.7 percent). Most OECD member countries relied heavily on social security taxes, with an OECD (unweighted) average of 24.3 percent.

Table 7.1. *Total tax revenue as percentage of GDP*

	1965	1966	1967	1968	1969	1970	1971	1972	1973	1974
Australia	23.2	22.6	23.4	23.2	24.0	24.2	24.7	23.7	25.3	27.1
Austria	34.7	35.4	35.3	35.3	35.8	35.7	36.4	36.9	37.1	38.1
Belgium	30.8	32.8	33.5	34.3	34.5	35.2	36.2	36.5	37.4	38.3
Canada	25.4	27.0	28.2	29.0	31.2	31.3	30.7	31.2	30.8	33.2
Denmark	29.9	32.5	33.1	36.0	35.7	40.4	43.5	42.9	42.4	44.2
Finland	29.5	30.7	31.6	32.0	30.5	31.4	32.8	32.9	33.5	32.7
France	34.5	34.3	34.7	34.9	35.8	35.1	34.5	34.9	35.0	35.5
Germany	31.6	32.2	32.2	32.2	33.9	32.9	33.4	34.7	36.3	36.5
Greece	20.6	22.2	23.3	24.3	24.3	24.3	24.3	24.4	24.6	23.2	24.0
Ireland	26.0	28.1	28.7	29.1	29.8	31.2	32.3	31.0	31.2	31.6
Italy	25.5	25.3	26.2	27.0	26.4	26.1	26.9	26.9	24.4	25.7
Japan	18.3	17.8	18.3	18.5	18.8	19.7	20.0	20.7	22.5	23.0
Luxembourg	30.4	30.1	30.8	29.7	29.6	30.2	32.9	32.7	33.1	33.9
Netherlands	33.2	34.7	35.7	36.4	36.7	37.6	39.4	40.3	41.8	42.3
New Zealand	24.7	25.6	25.4	25.2	25.2	27.4	27.5	27.3	28.6	31.4
Norway	33.3	34.6	36.6	37.7	39.1	39.3	42.4	44.9	45.3	44.8
Portugal	18.4	19.0	19.7	19.8	20.6	23.1	22.7	22.4	21.9	22.5
Spain	14.5	13.4	16.8	16.1	16.6	16.9	17.2	18.1	18.8	18.1
Sweden	35.4	36.2	37.1	39.3	40.3	40.2	41.1	42.5	41.6	42.8
Switzerland	20.7	21.5	21.6	22.6	23.7	23.8	23.5	23.9	26.3	27.3
Turkey	15.0	15.1	16.2	16.0	17.3	17.7	19.5	19.1	19.6	17.9
United Kingdom	30.4	31.6	32.9	34.5	36.1	37.0	34.8	33.3	31.4	35.0
United States	25.9	26.2	27.3	26.8	29.3	29.2	27.8	28.7	28.7	29.2
Unweighted average:										
OECD Total	26.6	27.3	28.2	28.7	29.4	30.0	30.6	30.9	31.1	32.0
OECD Europe	27.5	28.3	29.2	29.8	30.4	31.0	31.9	32.1	32.2	32.8
EEC	27.2	28.0	29.0	29.5	30.0	30.8	31.5	31.5	31.4	32.3

Figure 7.1 indicates the composition of central government tax receipts for 1987. The composition of state and local tax receipts is shown
in Figure 7.2. There is a great deal of variety in the way governments
raise tax revenues. The balance between income and profits taxes and
goods and services taxes – the two major taxes – differs significantly
among central governments. In Canada, as in the United States and
Japan, state and local governments raise most of their tax revenue using
income, sales and excise, and property taxes. By contrast, in some
countries there is complete (or almost complete) reliance on a single
source of tax revenue, such as property taxes in the United Kingdom,
New Zealand, the Netherlands, and Ireland; and income and profits
taxes in Switzerland, Sweden, Luxembourg, Finland, and Belgium.

1975	1976	1977	1978	1979	1980	1981	1982	1983	1984	1985	1986	1987
27.6	28.2	28.2	27.1	27.9	29.0	29.9	29.9	29.2	30.7	30.4	31.0	31.3
38.6	38.5	39.1	41.4	41.0	41.2	42.5	41.2	41.1	42.4	43.1	42.9	42.3
41.1	41.4	42.8	44.0	44.5	43.5	44.0	45.4	45.3	46.3	46.5	45.8	46.1
32.4	31.8	31.1	30.8	30.6	31.6	33.7	33.5	33.0	32.9	32.9	33.2	34.5
41.4	41.6	41.9	43.4	44.5	45.5	45.3	44.5	46.5	47.6	49.0	51.0	52.0
35.1	38.6	38.2	35.1	33.3	33.0	34.6	34.0	34.0	35.5	36.8	38.1	35.9
36.9	38.7	38.7	38.6	40.2	41.7	41.9	42.8	43.6	44.6	44.5	44.1	44.8
35.7	36.8	38.1	37.9	37.7	38.0	37.6	37.4	37.3	37.5	38.0	37.6	37.6
24.6	27.3	27.6	27.9	30.1	29.4	29.6	33.4	33.3	34.9	35.2	36.8	37.4
31.5	35.0	33.3	31.5	31.2	34.0	35.2	36.8	38.3	39.0	38.4	39.5	39.9
26.2	27.1	27.4	27.4	26.6	30.2	31.4	33.7	35.8	34.8	34.4	36.1	36.2
20.9	21.8	22.3	24.0	24.4	25.5	26.2	26.7	27.2	27.4	28.0	28.9	30.2
39.2	39.2	42.5	43.5	40.2	40.9	40.7	40.9	44.9	43.2	43.6	42.8	43.8
43.7	43.4	44.0	44.6	45.0	45.8	45.2	45.4	46.7	45.0	44.9	45.9	48.0
31.3	31.0	33.4	32.0	32.9	33.1	34.1	35.0	32.8	32.9	33.9	34.9	38.6
44.9	46.2	47.3	46.6	45.7	47.1	48.7	47.9	46.6	45.8	47.6	49.9	48.3
24.7	26.8	27.4	26.4	26.0	28.7	30.4	31.1	32.9	32.2	31.6	33.4	31.4
19.6	19.6	21.5	22.8	23.4	24.1	25.5	25.8	27.9	29.2	29.1	31.0	33.0
43.9	48.2	50.5	50.9	49.5	49.4	51.1	49.9	50.6	50.3	50.6	53.7	56.7
29.6	31.3	31.6	31.6	31.1	30.8	30.6	31.0	31.6	32.3	32.0	32.5	32.0
20.7	21.1	21.7	21.3	20.8	21.7	23.4	22.4	20.7	17.3	19.7	22.8	24.1
35.7	35.5	34.8	33.2	32.8	35.3	36.7	39.1	37.6	37.8	37.8	38.5	37.5
29.0	28.3	29.1	29.0	29.0	29.5	30.0	29.9	28.4	28.4	29.2	28.9	30.0
32.8	33.8	34.5	34.4	34.3	35.2	36.0	36.4	36.7	36.9	37.3	38.2	38.8
34.1	35.3	36.0	36.0	35.8	36.7	37.5	37.9	38.6	38.7	39.0	40.1	40.4
33.4	34.4	35.0	35.1	35.2	36.4	37.0	38.0	39.2	39.3	39.4	40.2	40.6

Source: OECD, *Revenue Statistics of OECD Member Countries 1965–1988* (Paris: OECD, 1989), p. 83.

Deficits, money supply, and inflation

Deficits and money supply may shape a society's economic system in several important ways, having significant implications for the society's growth, and for the allocation of financial burdens between current and future generations. Of particular interest at the present time is the ability of a communist society, which has relied upon public enterprise and central planning, to shift towards decentralized decision making without rampant inflation. Many see the danger of inflation as a serious threat to the success of such decentralization reforms. Clearly, the adoption

Table 7.2. *Tax revenue of main headings as percentage of total taxation (1987)*

	1000 Income & profits	2000 Social Security	3000 Payroll	4000 Property	5000 Goods & Services	6000 Other
Australia	55.7	—	5.4	9.2	29.8	—
Austria	26.0	32.3	5.9	2.3	32.3	1.3
Belgium	39.3	33.9	—	2.1	24.7	—
Canada	47.3	13.3	—	9.2	28.9	1.3
Denmark	56.5	3.7	0.7	5.1	33.9	0.2
Finland	49.5	9.0	—	3.2	38.2	0.2
France	18.0	43.0	1.9	4.7	29.3	3.1
Germany	34.0	37.3	—	3.2	25.4	—
Greece	17.0	32.6	1.1	2.5	46.6	—
Ireland	37.9	14.0	1.3	4.4	42.5	—
Italy	36.1	34.3	0.5	2.6	26.4	—
Japan	47.0	28.6	—	11.2	12.9	0.3
Luxembourg	42.4	26.4	—	6.8	24.4	—
Netherlands	27.4	42.7	—	3.6	26.0	0.3
New Zealand	59.4	—	0.9	7.0	32.6	—
Norway	33.1	23.7	—	2.5	40.1	0.7
Portugal	19.4	28.2	—	2.0	49.3	1.0
Spain	29.6	36.2	—	3.7	30.4	0.2
Sweden	41.3	24.2	4.5	5.7	24.1	0.2
Switzerland	40.3	32.1	—	8.5	19.1	—
Turkey	35.6	15.9	—	3.2	32.0	13.3
United Kingdom	37.2	18.1	—	13.2	31.4	—
United States	44.3	28.8	—	10.2	16.7	—

Unweighted average:						
OECD Total	38.0	24.3	1.0	5.5	30.3	1.0
OECD Europe	34.5	27.1	0.9	4.4	32.0	1.1
EEC	32.9	29.2	0.5	4.5	32.5	0.4

Source: OECD, *Revenue Statistics of OECD Member Countries 1965–1988* (Paris: OECD, 1989), p. 85.

243

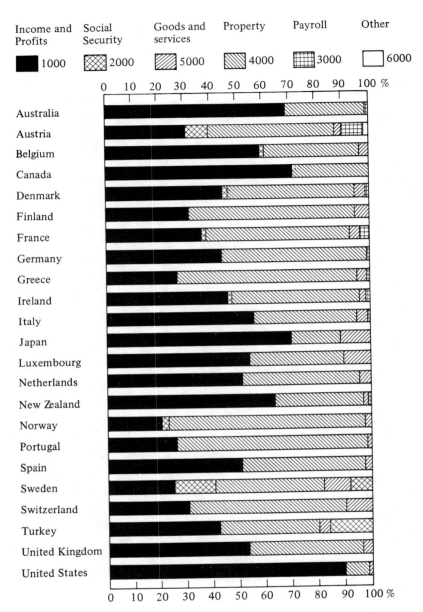

Figure 7.1. The composition of central government tax receipts, 1987. This refers to only those taxes which are classified as central government taxes. Social Security contributions paid to social security funds are excluded. *Source:* OECD, *Revenue Statistics of OECD Member Countries 1965–1988* (Paris: OECD, 1989), p. 202.

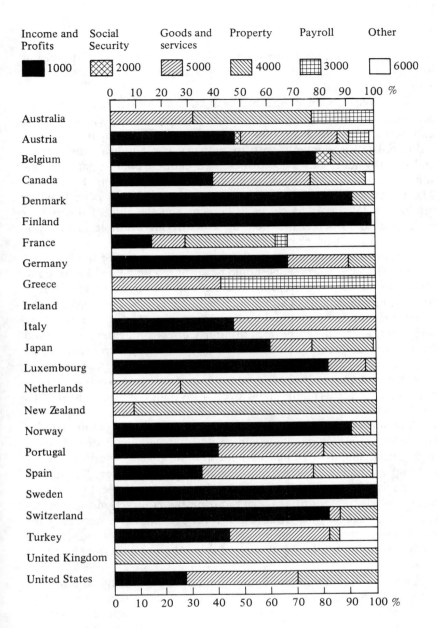

Income and Profits ▓ 1000   Social Security ▒ 2000   Goods and services ▒ 5000   Property ▒ 4000   Payroll ▒ 3000   Other □ 6000

Australia
Austria
Belgium
Canada
Denmark
Finland
France
Germany
Greece
Ireland
Italy
Japan
Luxembourg
Netherlands
New Zealand
Norway
Portugal
Spain
Sweden
Switzerland
Turkey
United Kingdom
United States

Figure 7.2. The composition of state and local government tax receipts, 1987. This refers to only those taxes which are classified as state and local government taxes and excludes transfers from central governments. *Source:* OECD, *Revenue Statistics of OECD Member Countries 1965–1988* (Paris: OECD, 1989), p. 203.

245

of an economic system that relies more heavily on decentralized decision making must be accompanied by a new concern for deficits, money supply, and inflation.

The simple version of the National Income Model taught in most first-year economics courses explains changes in aggregate income and employment as being due to fluctuations in aggregate demand. An initial fall in demand, with its negative consequences for income and employment, can lead to increased caution on the part of consumers and investors, which generates further reductions in demand. The behaviour of most economies during the 1929–33 period, when production fell by as much as 30 percent and the rate of unemployment rose to 25 percent, is held up as a striking example of the consequences of this process.

According to Keynes, whose theories form the basis of the National Income Model, governments should have shored up demand during the Great Depression by increasing their deficits. Government deficits represent direct injections of additional spending into the economy. To the extent that income generated by a government deficit is then spent by recipients, a deficit can have a multiplier effect on aggregate demand far greater than the size of the deficit itself. Although government deficits did rise during the 1930s, this was not due to a deliberate policy of stimulating demand. In fact, governments strove to contain deficits at what were viewed as manageable levels. This policy of restricting deficits has been blamed for prolonging the depression.

More sophisticated modern versions of Keynes's original model also conclude that deficit spending can be an effective means of stabilizing aggregate demand. It should be kept in mind that Keynesianism does not imply a policy of permanent deficit spending. Rather, Keynesians assign a useful role to government deficits only when the level of private spending falls temporarily. By minimizing the contraction in total demand, a deficit helps to restore the level of confidence necessary for an eventual upturn in private expenditure. As income and employment return to their normal levels, the need for a government deficit disappears.

However, Keynesian economics has never commanded universal acceptance and has come under increasing attack in recent years. Opponents of Keynes reject his view that the economy can become stuck at an underemployment equilibrium. Non-Keynesians tend to have greater faith in the ability of the economy to bounce back from a cyclical downturn. This conflict is essentially over the flexibility of market prices.[48] Keynesians believe that market rigidities may permit involuntary unemployment of productive resources to persist over long periods of time. Therefore, government action may be the only means by which the economy can be returned to full employment. Non-Keynesians argue that temporary fluctuations in the levels of production and employment are corrected by the automatic adjustment of market prices in a free-enterprise economy. According to this view of the world, fiscal stabilization is unnecessary and may even be counterproductive.

Crowding-out

Opposition to government deficits is often based on fears that a higher deficit will drive up interest rates, thereby depressing interest-sensitive private expenditures. One of the components of private spending that is widely believed to be most negatively related to the rate of interest is investment. Investment in productive capital is a necessary ingredient for future economic growth. If a higher government deficit forces interest rates up, the resulting decline in investment will reduce growth potential over the longer run as well as offset any positive impact of the deficit on demand in the short run. It is the possible consequences of government deficits for future economic growth that many of their opponents find most disturbing.

This crowding-out argument can be demonstrated in the simple *IS-LM* model of the closed economy (Figure 7.3). The closed-economy model, which ignores imports, exports, and capital flows, is especially applicable to a country such as the United States, whose foreign-trade sector is small relative to the domestic sector. Consequently, American economists have tended to debate the merits of deficit spending within the closed-economy framework. Since this American debate has influenced attitudes in other countries towards deficits, it is worthwhile setting out the case against fiscal activism in a closed economy. The open-economy case will be discussed in the next subsection.

The simplest textbook version of the Keynesian model assumes a constant rate of interest. A fixed interest rate implies that the *LM* curve depicting points of money market equilibrium is horizontal. Given a horizontal *LM* curve, an increase in the government deficit, which shifts the goods market *IS* curve outwards, moves the economy to a new equilibrium at a higher level of national income.

An early criticism of deficit spending was that the *LM* curve, far from being horizontal, is, in reality, vertical (or nearly so), because the demand for money is independent (or nearly so) of the rate of interest. A vertical *LM* curve means that an increased deficit merely pushes the

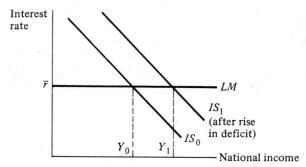

Zero crowding-out and fully effective fiscal policy
(horizontal *LM* curve at constant *r*)

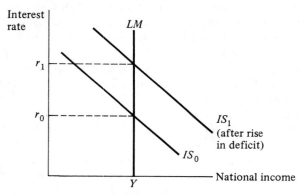

Full crowding-out and completely ineffective fiscal
policy (vertical *LM* curve)

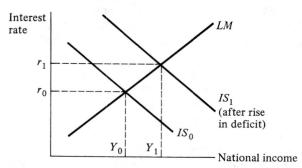

Partial crowding-out and partially effective fiscal policy
(positively-sloped *LM* curve)

Figure 7.3. Crowding-out in a simple *IS-LM* framework. *Source:* David
Conklin and Adil Sayeed, "Overview of the Deficit Debate," in David
W. Conklin and Thomas J. Courchene, eds., *Deficits: How Big and How
Bad?* (Toronto: Ontario Economic Council, 1983), pp. 33–4.

economy to a new *IS-LM* intersection at a higher rate of interest, while having no effect on national income.[49] In other words, private spending in the form of interest-sensitive investment expenditures falls to offset exactly the increase in the deficit.

Though the slope of the *LM* curve was a controversial topic during the 1960s, substantial evidence indicating that money demand is interest-sensitive has effectively put an end to this debate. In any event, the crowding-out argument does not rest solely on the possibility of a vertical *LM* curve.

An increase in the deficit financed by the sale of government bonds to the public increases the stock of privately held wealth under the assumption that government debt is not treated as a liability by taxpayers. Empirical evidence indicates that the demand for money is positively related to net wealth. Eventually, a deficit-induced rise in wealth causes the *LM* curve to shift upwards. One contention is that the end result of shifts in both the *IS* and *LM* curves is a new long-run equilibrium at a higher interest rate and the same level of national income.[50] Once again, the effect of an increased deficit on aggregate demand is neutralized by a fall in interest-sensitive private expenditures, as indicated in Figure 7.4.

Whether or not long-run wealth effects ultimately neutralize the initial stimulative impact of a higher deficit is an empirical question. During the late 1960s, economists at the Federal Reserve Bank of St. Louis sought to test the impact of fiscal changes on U.S. national income. Econometric results derived from the St. Louis equations indicated that fiscal changes had no effect on income beyond the very short run. However, the statistical methodology underlying the St. Louis equations has been called into question. From the econometric point of view, the jury is still out on the crowding-out issue in the United States.[51] Nevertheless, many do believe that crowding-out does reduce the aggregate capital stock, and so future generations are required to pay for current consumption. Franco Modigliani has presented this view in the following terms:

Whenever the government runs a deficit, it finances that deficit by tapping current saving that would otherwise have gone into investment. Therefore, investment is reduced. Investment is a source of income for the future, and that income has been lost. The disposable income argument is false, for while it is true that when we have a deficit one hand pays the other, if we did not have the deficit one hand would receive not from the other but from the capital that produces income. Therefore we have lost the income that the capital would have produced.[52]

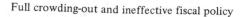

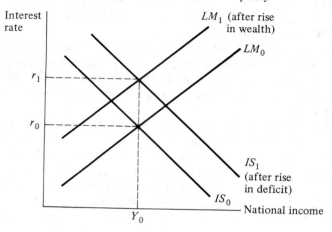

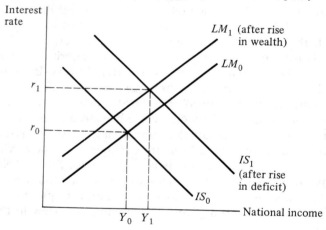

Figure 7.4. Long-run crowding-out in the *IS-LM* framework. *Source:*
David Conklin and Adil Sayeed, "Overview of the Deficit Debate,"
in David W. Conklin and Thomas J. Courchene, eds., *Deficits: How
Big and How Bad?* (Toronto: Ontario Economic Council, 1983), p. 35.

International capital flows: Implications for crowding-out

The previous subsection considered the crowding-out argument exclusively within the framework of a closed economy. For many economies,
aggregate demand is heavily influenced by foreign demand for exports

and by the division of domestic demand between domestic products and foreign imports. Even if it could be proven conclusively that fiscal policy is effective in an economy closed to foreign trade, many economists would still be faced with the task of gauging the impact of fiscal policy in an open economy.

If the result derived in the widely taught Mundell–Fleming model is to be believed, fiscal policy is impotent in a small, open economy under a flexible exchange rate system.[53] The key to the model lies in the definitions of the terms "small" and "open." An open economy is simply one in which domestic residents are free to purchase foreign goods and assets, while foreigners are able to buy domestic goods and assets. Smallness refers to the fact that the economy is too insignificant a demander or supplier of internationally traded goods and assets to be able to affect their prices.

In other words, exports from a small, open economy must compete with products from other countries and cannot be priced arbitrarily without regard to world market conditions. Similarly, consumers must accept import prices determined on the world market. In addition, interest rates cannot deviate from interest rates prevailing in the rest of the world. If bonds are priced too high, both domestic and foreign holders will exchange their domestic bonds for cheaper foreign assets. This will drive prices of domestic bonds down to prevailing world levels. Conversely, if bond prices fall below world levels, increased demand for cheap domestic bonds will push prices back to world levels. As long as no restrictions are placed on capital flows across international boundaries, interest rates in each country are determined, not by domestic supply of and demand for bonds, but by world supply and demand. Of course, world market conditions are beyond the control of the domestic authorities.

The ramifications of smallness and openness can be illustrated in the *IS-LM* framework of Figure 7.5. Assume the economy is initially in equilibrium, with the *IS* and *LM* curves intersecting at the world rate of interest, r^*. An increase in the government deficit tends to shift the *IS* curve outwards to *IS'*, thereby putting upward pressure on the domestic interest rate. However, any upward movement in the domestic rate induces asset holders to switch out of foreign bonds into domestic bonds. The resulting capital inflow places upward pressure on the exchange value of the domestic currency in terms of foreign currencies. As the domestic currency appreciates, foreign demand for exports falls and domestic demand shifts towards imports at the expense of home goods. This shifts the *IS* curve back towards the initial equilibrium position.

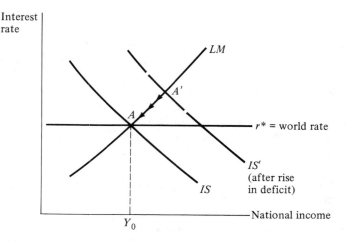

Figure 7.5. Crowding-out in a small, open economy. *Source:* David Conklin and Adil Sayeed, "Overview of the Deficit Debate," in David W. Conklin and Thomas J. Courchene, eds., *Deficits: How Big and How Bad?* (Toronto: Ontario Economic Council, 1983), p. 37.

The end result of the rise in the deficit is currency appreciation and deterioration of the trade balance, with no change in the level of national income. The speed at which all this takes place depends on how quickly bondholders react to deviations in interest rates. If capital is highly mobile, currency appreciation follows almost immediately after a rise in the deficit, with not even a temporary rise in income. Crowding-out occurs with the interest rate unchanged. In this model, a deficit affects the exchange rate, rather than the interest rate, and crowds out spending that is affected by changes in the exchange rate. The obvious question is the extent to which the Mundell–Fleming model is applicable to each economy.

Finally, open-economy macroeconomics has changed considerably since the Mundell–Fleming model was introduced in the early 1960s. The importance of expectations in the determination of exchange rates has been repeatedly emphasized in recent work. The simple version of the Mundell–Fleming model outlined above contains the implicit assumption that asset holders do not expect the fully flexible exchange rate to change over time. A more realistic view of exchange-rate expectations could alter the conclusion that fiscal policy is ineffective under flexible rates. These considerations should not obscure the main lesson of the Mundell–Fleming analysis. What can be learned from the Mundell–Fleming model is that, in a flexible exchange-ra` ` system, fiscal policy is likely to have much less effect on income and employment the smaller the size and the greater the openness of the economy.

Bond financing versus tax financing

Robert Barro has put forwards yet another argument against fiscal activism. Barro's case against deficit spending rests on the assumed ability of taxpayers to forecast their expected lifetime tax liabilities.[54] It has long been recognized that the stimulative impact of deficit spending depends upon the extent to which taxpayers realize that government debt issued to finance today's deficit must be serviced with higher taxes tomorrow. If taxpayers expect that their future tax liabilities will be increased as a result of bond financing of a current deficit, they will tend to increase current saving in order to prepare for higher taxes in the future. Thus, the stimulative impact on aggregate demand of a higher deficit will be offset by a shift towards saving and away from consumption expenditure.

At one time, the general consensus was that, while some public awareness of the link between future taxes and current deficits must be allowed for, full discounting of the future tax liability attendant upon bond financing is highly improbable. It was held to be unrealistic to assume that all taxpayers act on the basis of a fully worked-out lifetime plan. Furthermore, even if full rationality could be assumed, governments can postpone repayment by rolling debt over. Consequently, taxpayers may not expect to be liable for debt that will be retired long after their deaths.

Barro argued that economic behaviour is affected by considerations of events beyond the expected lifetime of the individual, so long as concern exists for the welfare of descendants. If this is the case, rational individuals may be expected to set aside savings to pass on as bequests in order that their beneficiaries might meet tax liabilities resulting from past deficit financing.[55] If the Barro model is a close approximation of reality, the effects of bond financing of government spending do not differ from those of tax financing. By levying taxes, governments force a reduction in private expenditures. With full discounting of future taxes, a substitution of bond financing for taxation reduces private spending by an equivalent amount, as income is set aside to cover future tax obligations. Consequently, a change in the government budget position has no effect on aggregate demand. This proposition was dubbed the *Ricardian equivalence theorem* because of its similarity to comments on the same subject made by David Ricardo, the great classical economist of the nineteenth century.[56]

Barro's achievement lies in his derivation of theoretical conditions under which full discounting is possible. Critics have not found flaws in the analytical structure of Barro's model. Rather, they have cast doubt on the practical relevance of the Ricardian equivalence theorem. The uncertainties facing individuals in the real world, however interested they may be in the well-being of their descendants, are said to be so great as to ensure that planning for future taxes is of only minor importance.[57]

Since criticism of Barro's work has focused on its practical plausibility, empirical testing would seem to offer the only basis for resolving this issue. Much of the statistical analysis of the Ricardian equivalence theorem has involved estimation of the aggregate consumption function. Unfortunately, a clear-cut answer has not yet emerged from the econometric literature. Results of some studies indicate that consumer spending does fall on approximately a one-to-one basis as government debt issue rises. This is the expected result if Barro's proposition holds in the real world. In other work, however, no consistent relationship between aggregate consumption and government borrowing is found.

Before moving on, it might be instructive to examine within the *IS-LM* framework the Ricardian argument that deficit financing is equivalent to tax financing. Supporters of the Ricardian equivalence theorem believe that a rise in the deficit will not affect national income. However, their argument is that any increase in the deficit is immediately offset by an equivalent rise in private saving, and so the position of the *IS* curve never changes. Full discounting of future taxes implies that government bonds are not treated as net wealth by the private sector, so a change in the deficit does not affect the position of the *LM* curve either. The level of national income, the rate of interest, and the exchange rate are unaffected by a change in the deficit. Crowding-out occurs, not through the effect of a higher deficit on the interest rate or exchange rate, but via the direct impact of deficit financing on the consumption–savings decisions of rational individuals.

To this point, the possible effects of fiscal policy on income and employment alone have been discussed. Macroeconomic policy can be set with another target in mind – the rate of inflation. Some critics of fiscal activism have taken the position that deficit spending, in addition to being an ineffective means of stabilizing aggregate demand, can do real harm by adding to inflationary pressures. The most direct link between fiscal policy and the rate of inflation runs through the effect deficit spending can have on the rate of growth of the money supply. Up to now, analysis has been restricted to the effects of a government deficit financed by bond sales to the private sector. However, central government bonds can also be purchased by the central bank. The end result of a series of transactions arising from government spending financed by bond sales to the central bank is an increase in the reserve holdings of the private banks. Increased bank reserves can be used to back an expanded volume of demand deposits, which are a principal component of the money stock. A greater supply of money, all other things being equal, puts upward pressure on the general level of prices.

It is important to recognize that there is no necessary connection between government deficits and monetary policy. Central banks in most countries, not being under a legal obligation to purchase bonds from the federal government, enjoy some degree of independence. Moreover, when a central bank does buy bonds, it remains free to take steps that neutralize the effect of its purchases on the money supply. Nevertheless, many observers attribute the upsurge in inflation rates during the 1970s to accommodation by the central banks of large government deficits. It is argued that the nominal freedom granted to central banks is, in actual practice, a façade. Government officials, motivated by political concerns, are said to exert considerable pressure on central banks to finance budget deficits.[58]

Since the alleged link between deficits and inflation is not a theoretical necessity, but rather an alleged probability, empirical evidence of such a relationship would seem to be required. Attention has been focused on the early 1970s, when double-digit inflation made its first appearance. For most countries, this period was also marked by a drift towards larger federal deficits, large purchases of government bonds, and high annual rates of money growth.

Another theoretical basis for linking deficits and inflation has emerged. Thomas Sargent and Neil Wallace have developed a model in which continued deficits eventually force an inflationary expansion of the money supply. Their result hinges on the assumption that there exists "an upper limit on the stock of bonds relative to the size of the economy."[59] If large deficits continue for so long that this limit is reached, the government has no recourse but to finance continued deficits by money creation. Furthermore, if expectations of future inflation play an important role in current price formation, inflation may remain high, despite an anti-inflationary monetary policy, because current high deficits lead rational agents to believe that an inflationary policy will be adopted in the future.

These analyses suggest that the aggregate level of taxation may be important as a means of allocating payment for government expenditures between current and future generations. A society may be able to shift the payment burden onto future generations by imposing aggregate taxes less than aggregate government expenditures and having a deficit. The deficit may then be covered, at least in part, through expansion of the money supply, and such situations can stimulate inflation. Consequently, a society's choices in regard to taxation can impact that society's growth. Furthermore, to the degree that inflation causes inefficiencies and alters income distributions, taxation can also affect society's efficiency and equality objectives through these linkages with inflation.

Essay and discussion topics

1. Discuss the distortions and inefficiencies caused by each of the alternative types of taxes that a society may impose.
2. Discuss how the choice of taxes and tax rates involves trade-offs among the objectives of a society.
3. Compare the use in two or more economic systems of special tax treatment, such as R&D incentives and accelerated depreciation, as a means of stimulating growth.
4. For two or more societies, compare the role of taxation as a component of the economic system. Can the use of alternative forms of taxation result in significant differences among economic systems? Can a society's decisions concerning taxes and deficits be a means for increasing current consumption and shifting financial obligations onto future generations?

CHAPTER 8

Non–price regulations

Introduction

A production or consumption decision, even if it is optimal from the perspective of the direct participants, may result in externalities that make the decision inappropriate from the perspective of society as a whole. A decision that is optimal for the direct participants may create inefficiencies, retard the society's rate of growth, or create inequities that the society refuses to tolerate. Economic decisions may be directed at a myriad of features and attributes of a product and its production process. Societies can choose any of these elements as the focus for non–price regulation, including, for example, the working conditions of employees; the impact of production facilities and waste materials on the purity of air and water, or on the aesthetic appearance of the community; the appropriateness and accuracy of advertising and marketing programs; the health and safety of customers who use the product; and the financial obligations of the producer to its suppliers, employees, customers, and government. For any aspect of any economic activity, a society may conclude that private decision making could be contrary to the best interests of the society as a whole. Through non–price regulations, a society is able to withdraw any particular economic decision from the direct participants and make that decision collectively. Furthermore, for many of those decisions that it leaves to individuals and firms, society is able to restrict the freedom of choice. In this process, non–price regulation involves balancing the liberty of individuals against the rights of society as a whole.

In designing such regulations, a society can institute many kinds and degrees of legal standards, and can enforce its regulations in a variety of ways. Because of the wide diversity of non–price regulations, this chapter examines five examples individually, seeking to explain the rationale for their imposition, and the advantages and shortcomings of each. These examples illustrate general themes. Non–price regulations frequently take the form of laws, and so the relationships between law and economics are particularly significant in this model. Interpretation

257

and enforcement are often delegated to public servants, and this raises issues of the appropriate role of legislators and of the judicial system. Some critics argue that these administrative procedures enable those being regulated to "capture" the regulatory process and to use it to enhance their own positions. The processes for evaluating costs and benefits of a regulation are not clear-cut or straightforward, and they often involve difficulties in quantifying certain attributes such as cultural sovereignty, clean air, and public safety. Recently, some countries have adopted deregulation programs on the grounds that efficiency and growth are reduced by the compliance costs and distortions caused by regulations. Throughout these examples, another central theme is the tendency for changing circumstances to render some regulations obsolete. A regulation that appears to be appropriate at a certain time may later be seen to encounter practical difficulties that limit its usefulness. Long-term impacts may turn out to be less desirable than short-term impacts. Of particular concern today are those regulations that interfere with international trade and investment, and international agreements are increasingly focusing on these regulations and are seeking to restrict them. In view of these themes, this model for collective decision making is complex, and it is subject to considerable uncertainty and frequent change.

It may be instructive, at the outset, to consider how this model differs from price controls, subsidies, and taxation. As discussed in Chapter 5, Oskar Lange's writing suggests that the price-setting model requires little bureaucratic sophistication, since the economic planners can simply observe the development of shortages or surpluses and can alter prices accordingly.[1] Our analysis suggests that the work of economic planners would be considerably more difficult than Lange believes because of the nature of quality, the desirability of innovation, the likelihood of changing tastes, and the possibilities for perverse behaviour on the part of the decentralized decision makers. Nevertheless, an important attribute of the price-control model is that substantial scope is still left for the decisions of individuals and firms. Faced with the centrally determined prices, the decentralized decision makers are free to purchase any combination of inputs, use any production technology, and choose any output levels. Relations between producers and consumers are left to the marketplace, and hence these relations are subject to the disciplines and rewards of the market.

In Chapters 6 and 7, we considered the situations in which societies collectively alter private decisions concerning investment, production, and consumption by providing subsidies, or by levying taxes. The private decision makers have freedom within the incentive programs and the tax structure. Clearly, individuals realize that their decision making is altered by subsidies and taxation, and they know that this is true as well for their customers and competitors. Nevertheless, central planners are not involved, on a continuing basis, in the decision process of individuals and firms. Planners can establish a set of incentive programs and taxes, and then observe the total production and total consumption. Based on the general results, planners can modify the subsidy programs and taxes, and so can fine-tune the system. If firms are not producing adequate quantities of a particular commodity, for example, an investment or production subsidy, or a tax concession, can be increased. If a depressed region needs more investment to create more jobs, regionally targeted subsidies or tax concessions can be increased. These guidelines can be developed from the perspective of a society's needs and interests, taking into consideration any externalities or contract failures, as well as the distribution of income and wealth. A major advantage of these decision modes lies in the wide scope that they leave for decentralized decision making. A subsidy program, or tax incentives, may cover a range of investments or products. Any one program may be applied to many items. Hence, private decision making faces looser guidelines than under the ensuing models.

In this chapter, we turn to a more complex set of tasks for central planners. Society believes that some specific aspects of production and consumption are not in the society's best interests. Individuals must be told explicitly to modify those aspects of their decisions to conform to centrally determined regulations. In some cases, these regulations may be directed at everyone. In some cases, they may be directed at particular types of activities or groups of individuals. In some case, there may be special rules for each individual.

This decision mode requires that central planners monitor the behaviour of each individual to ensure that non–price regulations are being obeyed. That is, even the regulations that are applied most broadly require that supervision and enforcement be conducted in regard to each of the individuals and firms that is involved in the regulated activity. Consequently, the central planners must obtain detailed information about the economic activities of each individual and firm. They must coordinate or synthesize this information in order to evaluate the overall impact of their regulations and in order to decide whether their regulations should be altered. They must be able to isolate particular offenders and develop methods for coping with violations.

This decision mode introduces a new complexity for the individual and the firm. Each must learn about a compendium of regulations, must think about their meaning for the possible alternatives one faces, and must calculate how best to order one's activities so as to minimize compliance costs. These calculations may also include the possibilities of conscious violation of some regulations. This decision mode introduces a new type of face-to-face continuing relationship between central planners and individuals. The latter have much to gain by influencing the former in the establishment of regulations and in their enforcement. In fact, this decision mode may provide the greatest possibility for individuals to capture the regulators and to develop regulations that serve their own interests rather than the interests of society. A substantial literature has developed in this context concerning the *capture theory* of regulation.[2]

Law and regulation

With this model of direct regulation, law and economics are inextricably interwoven.[3] In many cases, the regulations are imposed through formal legislation such that the regulations become part of the laws of the land. Anyone who violates the regulations may be subject to arrest by the law enforcement authorities and may be subject to prosecution in the courts. In recent decades, legislatures have frequently delegated the making of particular kinds of regulations to specialized agencies. For most societies, this proliferation of agencies has resulted in the development of extensive bodies of administrative laws. The agencies have often been granted the power to enforce their regulations, and so administrative bodies have adopted judicial powers and processes. Often, such bodies can examine evidence and impose penalties for violations. Relationships between regulatory agencies and the court system have sometimes been unclear, with some uncertainty as to the rights of the individual to appeal the decisions of the agencies.

Societies differ in the relationships and reporting practices between regulatory agencies and their legislatures. They differ in the relationships between the administrative law of regulatory agencies and that central body of law that has been approved explicitly by the legislature. They differ in procedures for appealing the decisions of regulatory agencies. Within each society, significant differences exist among the various types of agencies with regard to each of these issues.

Albert Dicey is the author of a classic work on the nature of British constitutional law. Dicey's comments indicate the traditional British view of these relationships. The nineteenth-century British rule of law focused on the rights of the individual, with the principles of equality for everyone before the law and the supremacy of the law over the wishes of particular authorities. Dicey viewed these elements as being worthy of greater respect – perhaps being essential for the preservation of democracy.

No man is punishable or can be lawfully made to suffer in body or goods except for a distinct breach of law established in the ordinary legal manner before the ordinary courts of the land. In this sense, the rule of law is contrasted with every system of government based on the exercise by persons in authority of wide, arbitrary, or discretionary powers of constraint.[4]

Dicey wrote more explicitly that it

means in the first place, the absolute supremacy or predominance of regular law as oppose to the influence of arbitrary power, and excludes the existence of arbitrariness, or prerogative, or even of wide discretionary authority on the part of the government.

It means, again, equality before the law, or the equal subjection of all classes to the ordinary law of the land administered by the ordinary law courts; the *rule of law* in this sense excludes the idea of any exemption of officials or others from the duty of obedience to the law which governs other citizens or from the jurisdiction of the ordinary tribunals; there can be with us nothing really corresponding to the administrative law (*droit administratif*) or the administrative tribunals (*tribunaux administratifs*) of France. The notion which lies at the bottom of the administrative law known to foreign countries is that affairs or disputes in which the government, or its servants, are concerned, are beyond the sphere of the civil courts and must be dealt with by special and more or less official bodies. This idea is utterly unknown to the law of England, and indeed is fundamentally inconsistent with our traditions and customs.[5]

Today, even Britain has instituted semi-independent agencies with substantial powers of interpreting legislative intent. Dicey's analysis presents a set of principles against which to gauge the actual practices of the regulatory agencies in any nation, and his concerns still deserve attention. Does a clear and established body of regulatory interpretations and precedents exist, so that individuals can refer to it and know which actions are deemed acceptable and which actions will be punished? Are all individuals treated equally in the enforcement of regulations? Are individuals protected from arbitrary or unusual decisions of particular regulators at particular times? Does a clear and appropriate appeal procedure exist?

Throughout this text, the word individual is meant to be interpreted broadly to include various types of corporate structures as well as private persons. In the nexus of law and economics, this distinction between individuals and corporations has interesting aspects. There are many regulations which are aimed at the behaviour of persons, but many – such as environmental or antitrust regulations – are directed at corporations. In the latter case, who should bear the responsibility for adherence to the regulation? When fines for violations are levied, it is customary for the corporation to pay. Yet, in recent years, there has been a tendency to look to individual executives and members of boards of directors, as well as to the corporate entity. Although the violation of regulations usually entails only a fine, there are instances where prison terms have also been imposed on executives and/or board members.

Which laws can be said to be economic regulations and which can not? This division cannot be drawn with precision, and every law may have some economic impact. In this sense, one might bring a society's entire body of law into the subject matter of this chapter, and regulation can be seen as an immense subject area. It is simply not possible to cover all types of regulations in one chapter. Rather, we shall discuss some of the principles and issues encountered in this subject, and then we shall turn to a few regulatory areas to illustrate these.

Evaluating the benefits and costs of regulations

Individuals make decisions which they believe to be optimal from their own perspectives. Yet, it is usually the case that others are also affected by these decisions. Regulations attempt to limit the undesirable side effects – in some situations by prohibiting certain actions entirely and in other situations by circumscribing acceptable behaviour. Attempts are made to calculate the costs to others of a particular kind of action and the effectiveness of various possible regulations in reducing these third-party costs. Yet regulations raise the costs to the initial actor. How do the benefits of a possible regulation compare with these latter costs? Such analyses are a key element in the sphere of direct regulation.

Over the past thirty years, there has been a widespread and rapid adoption of a host of regulations. From a society's point of view, and prior to the accumulation of actual experience, proposed regulations often appear to have substantial advantages over other decision modes. Explicit fiscal commitments may be relatively small compared with subsidies or government ownership. The regulatory model promises more detailed involvement by society as a whole in determining specific aspects or characteristics of economic activities. It seems to offer more thorough control over the processes of production and consumption and a greater certainty of outcomes.

Shortcomings of regulations may become apparent only a considerable time after implementation. Benefits may be fewer than expected. Distortions, side effects, and compliance costs may appear in ways and to degrees that were not anticipated. Evaluation of the benefits and costs of regulations as they have actually developed in practice has been difficult and complicated for a number of other reasons. The choice of timing for evaluation of regulation is important. One might argue that the recent and rapid imposition of new regulations has meant that for many regulations, it is not yet clear what the benefits and costs will be. Over the long run, some side effects may become more significant than they initially appeared to be. For example, a negative impact on private decisions to invest or to innovate may become apparent only after many years. One might also argue that shortcomings can be dealt with through minor modifications of the regulation in question. Defendants of a regulation can urge that a definitive evaluation must be delayed until such modifications have been given a chance.

For most societies, there now exist tens of thousands of regulations, affecting a substantial proportion of aggregate output. Since each regulation must be evaluated on its own merits, one must choose an appropriate priority for their consideration. The impacts of a regulation can be extremely far-reaching and complex. How thorough an evaluation is appropriate? Many benefits and costs cannot be quantified with precision; a range of estimates may be all that one can provide. Subjective interpretation and judgement enter into these evaluations, and so differences of opinion may remain.

Often, scientific information is necessary as part of these analyses, and the relevant information may change as time passes. The calculation of damages caused by particular agricultural chemicals or industrial wastes has altered significantly in recent years. Only recently have statistical studies begun to reveal the cause–effect relationships between the release of toxic elements, the impact on the environment, and the state of human health. Only recently have statistical studies demonstrated without doubt that a clear link exists between cigarette smoking and the development of cancers. Ambiguities persist about the benefits and costs of most regulations. Not surprisingly then, the nature and content of regulations vary significantly from one society to another, and also over time within any particular society.

Many regulations – either directly or as a side effect – act to redistribute income and wealth among different groups. Agricultural marketing boards, for example, have become powerful mechanisms for redistributing income, and, consequently, we can expect considerable debate over the way in which they function. In the communications sector, we may expect conflict among the proponents of systems based upon the different technologies: television, cable, satellites, microwave, and telephone. Many regulations involve the conferring of special rights, or entitlements, such as quotas or licenses, which quickly are given a monetary value in the marketplace. Once transferred, these rights become capitalized, such that any proposed change in a regulation must face bitter advocacy and political lobbying on the part of those whose licenses or quotas might decrease in value with the proposed change.

Because many regulations have been in place for only a few years, the division of responsibilities among different levels within federal nations has not been clearly established. Some areas of regulations are currently shared, and the most appropriate mechanics of cooperation are still being discussed. This is true for many issues in transportation, telecommunications, agricultural marketing boards, and environmental protection.

Regulations present a general problem for the concept of democracy in that most regulations, and their practical interpretations, are developed outside of the legislature and are not discussed in the legislature; many are even developed outside of the executive or cabinet. Both legislative power and executive power have been delegated to non-elected regulatory bodies whose relationships with elected officials leaves these bodies with substantial independence. For this reason, many societies are now examining regulations in terms of the role of elected representatives and of the public. A major issue is how the public interest can best be ascertained, expressed, and included in the decision-making process concerning regulation and regulatory reform.

A growing number of regulations impact international trade and investment. Corporations involved in international economic relations have to pay close attention to these regulations in order to cope with them most advantageously. Increasingly, international negotiations are focusing on regulations that create unfair competition or restrict the activities of foreigners. New international agreements may limit regulations from the perspective of their impact on trade and investment. Concerns for domestic content and domestic ownership have been important, for example, in telecommunications regulations. How can such concerns be reconciled with the desire by foreigners to export telecommunications services and to invest in such activities in other nations? A straightforward evaluation of a regulation's domestic costs and domestic benefits may be unrealistic in the context of international economic agreements.

The pursuit of nationalistic and cultural objectives introduces further complications for cost–benefit analyses. How can these noneconomic criteria be included in the economic evaluations of regulations? What financial value can one place on the achievement of the noneconomic objectives that are often a purpose of regulation? Purely economic evaluations of regulations may not be appropriate in a society's decision about adopting them.

Another difficulty lies in speculating about what would have happened if a particular regulation had not been in place. After a regulation has been effective for a number of years, it may not be clear what would happen if the regulation were removed. So many other factors influence actual outcomes that the isolation of the specific costs and benefits of a particular regulation may involve substantial uncertainty.

Reform and deregulation

In many societies, a general perception has recently developed that the benefits of regulations have not, in practice, been as great as had been hoped when they were first imposed, and, furthermore, that the costs of administration and compliance have exceeded original expectations. Out of this perception, a trend towards deregulation has developed in many societies. A new literature focuses on the anticipated results of particular types of deregulation. Often, this literature emphasizes the degree to which those being regulated have captured the regulatory process so as to benefit the regulated rather than society as a whole. That is, the deregulation argument is based upon the results in practice of particular types of regulation. This illustrates a basic theme of the text, that theory by itself cannot provide adequate answers concerning the optimal balance between collective and individual decision making. Direct analyses of actual experiences are also necessary.

Some have advocated that a formal review process be created for regulations. Regulatory agencies could be required to quantify the costs and benefits of the new regulations which they recommend, before such new regulations could be adopted. Regulations could be reviewed periodically over a ten-year cycle, so that legislators could be sure the regulations continue to be desirable. Regulations could contain a *sunset clause* such that each regulation would automatically cease to exist at a certain date unless the regulation was renewed.

In Canada, the federal government's Economic Council was requested, in 1978, to conduct a thorough analysis of all regulations currently in place. Creating this major review, Prime Minister Trudeau officially acknowledged that "there has developed in Canada a strong concern that increasing government regulation might be having serious adverse effects on the efficiency of Canadian firms and industries and on the allocation of resources and distribution of income."[6] The Economic Council of Canada commissioned seventy-four research studies, including several cost–benefit analyses of particular types of regulations, and in 1981 presented eighty reform recommendations.[7] The basic thrust and purpose of the following recommendations have applicability in other nations as well as in Canada.

First, the Council concluded that Canadian regulations are currently excessive, and are wasting resources and reducing competitiveness. Consequently, many regulations should be eliminated or drastically modified.

Second, after a regulatory agency has been established, the government should continue to provide "policy directives" so that the wishes of the elected representatives of the public continue to be the guiding force in the agency's decisions. Agencies should not be free to develop their own independent criteria for decisions.

Third, appeal procedures for agency decisions should be formalized so that everyone can be aware of these procedures.

Fourth, the public should be brought into the process of formulating and evaluating regulations. Governments should assist in funding private interest groups that wish to be involved in this process.

Fifth, formal cost–benefit evaluations should become a customary practice and should be made available to the public to assist in the development of a reasoned public judgement in regard to the advisability of particular regulations.

Sixth, regulations that restrict entry into economic activities have negative impacts on efficiency, innovation, and income distribution. Consequently, entry restrictions should only be adopted if they are essential for the protection of the public. At present, many occupations require licensing or certification, and many agricultural activities require production quotas. Such entry restrictions should be evaluated with special care.

Seventh, these reform processes require a substantial increase in the time and resources that the legislation devotes to regulatory evaluation and reform. New legislative committees should be created for this purpose. Changing circumstances require that this role be a continual responsibility.

One of the recurring themes emerging from our analysis of different regulatory regimes is the tendency for regulations to outlive their usefulness. In circumstances where technology, economic conditions, and even society's values and preferences are undergoing rapid change, it would indeed be surprising if this were not so. The fact that much of the recent regulation has been in areas where there is still a great deal of scientific uncertainty reinforces the necessity for an efficient process by which regulations can be periodically re-examined and reviewed.[8]

Other nations have also initiated sweeping reviews of their regulations. In the United States, the President's Advisory Council on Executive Organization (the Ash Council) presented a 1971 report in which it expressed many of these concerns.[9] Early in his Presidency, Ronald Reagan established a Task Force on Regulatory Relief, headed by Vice-President George Bush. In the 1981–3 period, this Task Force recommended the reduction and elimination of many regulations. By the time it was disbanded in 1983, George Bush claimed that its initiatives would save businesses and consumers $150 billion over the next decade. This claim, according to Michael D. Reagan, was widely disputed. "An array of consumer and environmental advocates contended that many of the savings were illusory, and that there would be severe costs in terms of health and safety through reduced regulatory protection to the extent that the savings were real."[10]

The theme of deregulation has been a major plank in many political platforms of the 1980s, including those of Brian Mulroney in Canada, Margaret Thatcher in Britain, and Ronald Reagan in the United States. Michael Reagan has developed a list of the principle deregulation actions in the United States over the 1976–82 period, emphasizing that the most notable have been in the areas of communications, financial institutions, and transportation:

1976 – Railroad Revitalization and Reform Act
1977 – Air Cargo Deregulation Act
1978 – Airline Deregulation Act
       Natural Gas Policy Act
1980 – Motor Carrier Reform Act
       Household Goods and Transportation Act
       Staggers Rail Act
       Depository Institutions Deregulation and Monetary Control Act.
       FCC deregulation of cable television
1981 – Oil price decontrol completed by executive order
1982 – Bus Regulatory Reform Act
       Garn-St. Germain Depository Institution Act
       Settlement of AT&T antitrust case[11]

In February 1981, President Reagan issued a formal executive order that would affect all U.S. federal regulation. It "(1) emphasized the importance of measuring the costs and benefits of federal regulations, (2) stressed the significance to be given the resulting analyses, and (3) strengthened the role of the Office of Management and Budget (OMB) to ensure compliance with cost–benefit procedures."[12]

Yet, in spite of the political rhetoric and these specific actions, it appears that regulation in the United States has expanded in the 1970s and 1980s.

Starting in the late 1970s under President Jimmy Carter, and continuing with the quickened pace under President Ronald Reagan, the politically most active part of the regulatory arena of government has been the question of deregulation. There has been more talk about removing regulations than about adding or maintaining them. Yet, in the years 1968–1980, we had the strongest continuous extension of regulation since the 1930s, and perhaps in all of American experience. That twelve-year period saw the creation of the Environmental Protection Agency (EPA), to which new programs have been added as recently as the Superfund in 1980, the Occupational Safety and Health Administration (OSHA), the National Highway Transportation Safety Administration (NHTSA), the Consumer Products Safety Commission (CPSC), and the Office of Surface Mining (OSM), plus a host of statutes establishing even more programs to be distributed among these and other agencies.[13]

Concerns persist about the actual benefits and costs of specific regulations. Analyses and evaluations will continue to result in changes, with the modification and elimination of some, and the imposition and extension of others. One could choose any number of regulatory areas to illustrate the perspectives and recommendations that have been presented in this chapter. The following discussion focuses on five types of regulations: those that restrict and modify international investment; those that control the telecommunications sector and trans-border data flows; those that concern ownership of intellectual property; those that protect the environment; and those that restrict airline entry and pricing.

Regulations affecting international investment

Many countries have been concerned about the possible changes in their economic system that could be caused by foreign investment, and many have established regulations to restrain impacts that are perceived to be negative. This section considers Canada's experiences with the regulation of international investment, and compares these experiences with the practices in other countries. From 1974 until 1985, the Canadian Foreign Investment Review Agency (FIRA) screened investment by foreign firms and attempted to maximize the benefits Canada would gain from foreign investment. FIRA's objectives and processes provide an informative case study of regulations directed specifically at foreign firms. Its problems and inconsistencies – and the difficulties experienced by foreign firms – are found in other nations with similar regulations. The following quotation indicates the concerns about the erosion of national sovereignty, the loss of the best types of jobs, and the shift of those functions considered essential for national growth.

The information revolution may accelerate the erosion of national sovereignty by further increasing the dominance of multinational corporations in the world economy. . . . As a result . . . host countries may experience a serious loss of control over domestic economic activities. . . . The migration of control to head-quarters could cause further reductions in the autonomy of branch plants. Countries such as Canada might evolve from a branch plant economy to a warehouse economy. In such an economy, branch plants would have lost to headquarters, not only jobs, but also important decision-making functions in such key areas as financial control, administration, research and development, planning and marketing.[14]

In examining investment proposals, FIRA staff prepared detailed analyses, based on consultations with federal departments, provincial ministries, representatives of the firms involved, and other interested parties, and these analyses focused on "significant benefit." The factors involved in assessing "significant benefit to Canada" were laid out in Section 2 (2) of the Foreign Investment Review Act:

(a) The effect of the acquisition or establishment on the level and nature of economic activity in Canada, including, without limiting the generality of the foregoing, the effect on employment, on resource processing, on the utilization of parts, components and services produced in Canada, and on exports from Canada;

(b) the degree and significance of participation by Canadians in the business enterprise or new business and in any industry or industries in Canada of which the business enterprise or new business forms or would form a part;

(c) the effect of the acquisition or establishment on productivity, industrial efficiency, technological development, product innovation and product variety in Canada;

(d) the effect of the acquisition or establishment on competition within any industry or industries in Canada; and

(e) the compatibility of the acquisition or establishment with national industrial and economic policies, taking into consideration industrial and economic policy objectives enunciated by the government or legislature of any province likely to be significantly affected by the acquisition or establishment.[15]

In addition to examining investment proposals and soliciting opinions from other government departments, FIRA also took an active role in negotiating with applicants in order to improve the benefits Canada would receive from their investments. The negotiation procedure was sometimes lengthy and could involve any element of the business's op-

erations. The above list of benefits formed the agenda for the negotiations. The evaluation of each proposal included any undertaking to
which the applicant had agreed. The act provided for the obtaining of
court orders to enforce undertakings; it also provided for the citing and
punishment of those who failed to obey such court orders.

A study by Duncan McDowall, *A Fit Place for Foreign Investments:
Foreign Investors' Perceptions of Canada in a Changing World,* surveyed
both actual and potential foreign investors in an attempt to identify
factors that either attracted or deterred investors in deciding on projects
in Canada.[16] The survey attempted, in the words of the author, to reach

not just . . . investors with a proven interest in Canadian investment, but also
those who had considered Canada but had never proceeded with their investment
plans. The questionnaire was mailed during June and July 1983, to a sample
group of companies structured to reflect the overall historical patterns of investment flowing into Canada, according to nation of origin and primary economic activity.[17]

The survey focused on investors' views of Canada over the previous ten
years and found that most potential investors considered Canada to
have an attractive investment climate. However, the study also found
that "a minority of potential investors, 11 per cent of the respondents
[31 firms out of 278] . . . had been deterred from investing in Canada by
the existence of various forms of foreign investment controls."[18]
Furthermore,

those companies and individuals citing government regulation and foreign investment controls as the most important factor in the analysis of their Canadian
investment prospects formed a small but vocal minority. . . . FIRA was criticized
for the principles underlying it and for its bureaucratic operation.[19]

In considering FIRA's processes, a serious concern is that similar
applicants may not have necessarily received similar treatment. Because
FIRA's deliberations were conducted in secrecy, and information pertaining to resolved cases was not available to provide guidelines for
other applicants, a high degree of uncertainty was introduced into the
investment and investment-related decisions of both foreign and Canadian firms. No public documentation exists concerning FIRA's pursuit
of approved cases to ascertain that undertakings given by firms during
review were actually carried out. Not one firm was prosecuted for failing
to fulfil its undertakings, even though the act gave FIRA the power to
do so. The absence of prosecutions does not prove lack of enforcement;
it only raises the suspicion. However, it may have tempted applicants
to make promises in bad faith simply to gain approval. Consequently,
the honest applicant may have been put at a disadvantage. The political

nature of the process added to this concern about inconsistency. FIRA's decisions changed over time as economic and political circumstances changed. Consequently, the timing of one's application could have made a difference in the outcome.

Many nations have regulatory mechanisms to screen foreign investment. A study by Safarian provides a detailed look at the policies of thirteen countries. Safarian finds four basic policies on the treatment of foreign investment, namely,

(1) excluding certain sectors from investments by such companies;
(2) setting rules to control the basis for their establishment and subsequent expansion;
(3) offering incentives for their establishment, often in return for agreement to perform in certain ways; and
(4) treating established foreign-owned firms less favorably than domestically-owned firms.[20]

Safarian analyses the policies of the thirteen countries using these four categories. He discusses the underlying national concerns about foreign direct investment (FDI) and analyses the degree to which regulatory policies fall short of achieving their stated objectives. His recommendation for the future is for countries to avoid unilateral moves and to negotiate multilateral agreements, possibly through GATT or the OECD.[21]

A study by David Anderson contrasts the Canadian and Australian approaches to regulating FDI, specifically in the nonpetroleum-mining sector.[22] Anderson presents a strong case for learning from the Australian approach, particularly for the following reason:

The Australian regulatory apparatus has been largely accepted by the relevant national and international interest groups. In contrast, the Canadian Foreign Investment Review Act and . . . FIRA [have] been the source of widespread domestic and external criticism.[23]

The Australian system, in place since 1976, concentrates on the degree of foreign ownership. Each new mining project must normally have at least 50 percent Australian ownership (75 percent for uranium projects) in order to be approved by the Foreign Investment Review Board (FIRB). There is a *naturalization process,* introduced in 1978, which grants to companies whose actual level of Australian ownership may be as low as 25 percent, prior credit for having 51 percent Australian ownership. "In return they publicly agree to move towards the 51 per cent target and to ensure that a majority of the voting members on their Board of Directors are Australian citizens."[24] Approval must be obtained for each new mining project involving a total investment of $5 million or more (in Australian dollars) or takeover by a foreign firm of a firm with more than $2 million of assets (in Australian dollars).

Like the Canadian system, the Australian system screens FDI in general to ascertain that the proposed investments are not contrary to the national interest. However, the Australian system focuses the regulators' attention on the degree of foreign ownership. In fact, in the mineral sector the Australian approach "is virtually to ignore the national benefits test associated with the general screening mechanism. Instead, it relies on a sector-specific quantifiable test."[25] The "not contrary to the national interest" condition and the 50 percent (or 75 percent for uranium) Australian equity condition must both be met for a project to be approved, with the latter dominating in practice. Thus, in the mining sector the Australians, in effect, use a "fixed-rule" approach. Some features make this an appealing model. Anderson notes that such an ownership requirement for FDI should "reduce the decision time, virtually eliminate the uncertainty faced by proponents, and largely preclude the need to negotiate innumerable performance undertakings."[26]

In 1985, Canada replaced its Foreign Investment Review Act with the Investment Canada Act, whose purpose was cited in the act as follows:

Recognizing that increased capital and technology would benefit Canada, the purpose of this Act is to encourage investments in Canada by Canadians and non-Canadians that contribute to economic growth and employment opportunities and to provide for the review of significant investments in Canada by non-Canadians in order to ensure such benefit by Canada.[27]

Investment Canada continues to monitor foreign investment in Canada. A major focus continues to be the maintenance of cultural sovereignty. Preservation of economic independence also continues as a central objective and is achieved through screening of all large takeovers.[28] In 1983–4, the United States instituted legal action, under GATT, against the sourcing requirements of the FIRA process, which compelled foreign investors to buy from Canadian suppliers. GATT ruled that these requirements were inappropriate, since they placed foreign suppliers at an unfair competitive disadvantage. However, it is quite likely that informal government pressure will continue to influence the sourcing decisions of foreign firms. The death of FIRA has not eliminated the underlying Canadian political objectives. We may expect that the issues discussed above will reappear in Canada as well as in many other nations.

Regulation of telecommunications and trans-border data flows

Throughout the world, governments have increasingly been regulating the telecommunications sector. A list of regulatory interventions has been compiled by U.S. Senator Robert Packwood.[29] These include the targeting of telecommunications for special government assistance, various regulations to protect the privacy of information, tax provisions that treat foreign and domestic firms differently, the licensing of personnel, rules concerning satellites and the leasing of communications channels, equipment standards, the use of government-owned corporations to conduct certain types of activities, and international provisions to enhance the capability of less-developed countries (LDCs) in this sector. Regulatory interventions have been motivated by many objectives, among which the following seem to be most significant: enhancement of cultural sovereignty, provision of domestic employment, and protection of privacy.

The content of telecommunications systems often involves motion pictures, political commentary, and news broadcasts. Each of these can be seen as integral elements of a nation's self-identity. To depend entirely on foreign production and transmission of such programs would be to surrender important decisions about content, interpretation, and scheduling. Foreign perspectives on these decisions could be quite different from the perspective of domestic nationals. Consequently, foreign ownership and operation of telecommunications systems could seriously alter the individual citizen's view of the world and his or her nation's place in it. Many societies share the concerns expressed in the following Canadian quotation:

Canadian sovereignty in the next generation will depend heavily on telecommunications. If we wish to have an independent culture, then we will have to continue to express it through radio and television. If we wish to control our economy, then we will require a sophisticated telecommunications sector developed and owned in Canada to meet specific Canadian requirements. To maintain our Canadian identity and independence we must ensure an adequate measure of control over data banks, trans-border data flow, and the content of information services available in Canada. If we wish to build a Canadian presence in world industrial markets then we will be required to encourage the growth of Canadian telecommunications industries that will be competitive in world terms.

In approaching telecommunications we should realize that its importance demands we view it in a special way. Telecommunications, as the foundation of the future society, cannot always be left to the vagaries of the market; principles that we might care to assert in other fields, such as totally free competition, may not be applicable in this crucial sphere. We must look at it freshly, without preconceived ideas.[30]

Since the telecommunications sector is becoming an ever-greater influence in shaping the attitudes of citizens, we may expect that governments will continually search for new ways to regulate it. These regulations will go beyond a discrimination against foreign corporations. They will include, for example, the setting of rate structures so as to ensure widespread access. Cross-subsidization may be required in rate structures if remote geographical areas and low-income families are to have access. A certain percentage of domestic content may be required if citizens are to be exposed to domestic culture.

Another rationale for telecommunications regulation is the growth of multinational enterprises with their increasing rationalization of production processes, and the fear that this growth will impede job creation in the host country. Faced with such concerns about domestic employment, governments have instituted a variety of regulations. For purchases of hardware, regulations may specify particular product standards that effectively exclude imported equipment, which is built in accordance with different foreign standards. The creation of an indigenous network of radio, television, and movie companies may be seen as providing a mechanism for the cultivation of local talent. As the service sector grows in size and as a higher proportion of jobs are to be found in the telecommunications sector, this issue of employment will become increasingly important. Advances in telecommunications technology are permitting corporations to locate larger segments of their operations anywhere in the world. Customer records and processes of data manipulation can now be accessed across thousands of miles. Inventory control systems can also be monitored far from the actual business operation. A multinational can utilize telecommunication technology to shift jobs from one country to another. Consequently, many societies will continue to impose regulations that protect domestic employment.[31]

To some degree, regulations restricting trans-border data flows may be seen in the context of these domestic employment issues. In addition, privacy has recently become a politically significant issue, and many nations have imposed legislation with the objective of protecting the individual rights of their citizens.

The growth of high technology and the potential for abuse of the vast amounts of personal information being collected in all sectors of society, public and private, is creating a growing awareness of the need for some form of laws to protect the privacy of the individual. Such a movement is becoming well entrenched in some European countries where many data protection (or protection of personal information) laws as they are called, are on the statute books. [In fact] some European laws require a license, issued by a data regulatory agency, to send personal data to another country. If a country to which personal information is being sent does not have similar protective legislative measures, this could be a factor in denying an export licence.[32]

A recent book by Helena Stalson describes this worldwide development.

In 1974, the United States passed the Privacy Act to give its citizens access to information in government files. A few years later, Canada, New Zealand, and seven European countries, including France and Germany, passed legislation protecting the privacy of individuals and in some cases corporate entities. In 1980, the OECD issued nonbinding guidelines of data protection measures, directed at individuals, not legal entities, and 180 U.S. corporations endorsed the guidelines and said that they were conforming to them. In 1981, the Council of Europe's 21 member governments signed a convention similar in many ways to the OECD guidelines but calling for binding application of its principles. Since then, most international firms appear to have learned to live with privacy regulations. Problems seem to have arisen chiefly for financial institutions, which have accumulated large quantities of data on the personal lives and credit worthiness of individuals and institutions, but they too have accommodated to national regulations, and in most cases, have adopted even more rigorous security and confidentiality requirements.[33]

Business systems are being linked more and more with operations in other cities and in other countries. Direct communications with customers, suppliers, and other branches of the same company are becoming increasingly extensive. Costs of selling and warehousing can be reduced, time can be saved, and product modifications can be made easier through telecommunications. The cost of long distance transmission of data and printed materials will likely continue to fall. Frequently, these technological advances will conflict with current regulations and rate schedules. Consequently, societies will continue to see telecommunications regulation as an important decision mode, through which free-enterprise incentives and outcomes can be altered.

Protection of intellectual property

For many societies, today's emphasis on research and education as a high-tech strategy means that the protection of intellectual property cannot be left to free enterprise. Regulations to balance the rights of innovators and the rights of users form an important decision mode shaping the economic system. Advances in any one society depend upon the inventions that have occurred elsewhere in the world and can be limited by restrictions on the international transfer of knowledge. Conversely, the benefits that a society can gain from its own advances in knowledge depend upon the protection that other nations extend to patents, trademarks, designs, copyrights, and other industrial secrets. In view of this, the protection of intellectual property is an international issue with international regulations. The optimal regulations are not obvious; they may differ from one nation to another; and they will no doubt change over time.

On the one hand, developing nations need access to innovation, and their priority is to acquire new technologies. Industrialized nations, on the other hand, owe a large share of their prosperity to innovation and want to receive a fair price for the technology they have developed. Obviously, there is some common ground, because continued access to technological innovation is unavoidably linked to its adequate protection and compensation. The only realistic approach, in my opinion, is to attempt to achieve a fair balance between the rights of innovators and the needs of users.[34]

Intellectual property is being buffeted by several different kinds of changes. In April 1986, the U.S. Office of Technology Assessment (OTA) issued a report describing and summarizing recent changes in the nature and content of information itself.

The changes that new technologies are making in the way that information is created, distributed, and used today are as fundamental as the changes made by the printing press. These changes are undermining many of the mechanisms by which the U.S. intellectual property system has operated in the past.

Originally, the implementation of intellectual property law, and particularly copyright law, was relatively simple. The government granted copyrights to authors and patents to inventors. Rewards were determined in the marketplace. The patent and copyright holders, themselves, monitored infringements and enforced their rights through the courts. Individuals' interests coincided with the public's interest – to profit from copyright, an author had to print his works and sell them; to profit from a patent, the inventor had to disclose his ideas to the public.

Today, technological change is complicating the intellectual property system.[35]

Today, original work may be the result of collaboration among many individuals who live in many countries. Existing legislation, based upon the concept of single authors or inventors in a single country, may no longer be appropriate. Furthermore, science is creating many new types of materials. Original work can often be copied using alternative materials. People who drafted legislation even a few years ago did not foresee the extent of this possibility. Mechanisms for reproducing original work have become more sophisticated and readily available. The printed word, the motion picture, and computer software – all can be copied easily and cheaply without the knowledge of those who created them.

"Pirating" results in commercial sales that deprive the original creator of royalty payments, and it may also directly reduce the sales and profits of an authorized distributor. Television programs can be accessed by satellite and cable in ways that deprive the owners of control, sales, and profits. Domestic regulations concerning such "theft" are difficult to enforce. The ease of trans-border communication means that all nations can be affected by activities of this type anywhere in the world. The failure of one government to police these activities can affect all other nations. A statement by the Office of the U.S. Trade Representative emphasizes the significance of the policing issue.

Piracy thrives even in some countries that have nominally good laws. The causes are simple: inadequate penalties that have no meaningful deterrent effect and a lack of government commitment to enforce the rights guaranteed by law. This problem is particularly acute for such industries as motion pictures, sound recordings and software. Such industries lose hundreds of millions of dollars annually to pirates whose actions, if not encouraged or condoned, are at least not adequately penalized by their governments.[36]

In 1985, a U.S. Council Task Force on Intellectual Property estimated that U.S. companies currently were losing $8 billion in sales annually due to this international piracy.[37] In this situation, where the original creator cannot obtain all the commercial benefits arising from its intellectual advance, the incentive to innovate may be hurt. Future research and development may be retarded.

The main economic rationale for intellectual property protection is to increase the rate of production of intellectual works. In the absence of protection, any enterprising individual could simply obtain a copy of the office work and proceed to manufacture and distribute it to the buying public. Since he would not have to incur the initial costs involved in inventing or creating the work, he could market it at a lower price than the original inventor or creator could. Consequently, the economic incentive to produce intellectual property material would fail. Intellectual property protection is an attempt to overcome this problem.[38]

For both education and entertainment, the individual has greatly expanded his or her desire to own more information in its various forms. The division between reproduction for personal use and reproduction for commercial sale is introducing a new area of difficulty for legislators.

Information is taking new forms which do not automatically fit into existing legal categories. Computer software may be the most dramatic example. Moreover, it is probably fair to say that the design characteristics of many of today's products may not be readily described in ways that are able to exclude substitutes. Yet, with rising incomes and new varieties of products, design characteristics are becoming increasingly important. Specially designed clothing and leather products, for example, are presenting new problems for existing legislation. New manufacturing processes often share this difficulty. It seems that a growing number of original ideas can find multiple uses in today's economy. Often these uses extend far beyond anything dreamt of by the original creator. Where should legislation draw the ownership line in terms of additional uses?

Increasingly, new kinds of information are playing a new role in the educational process. In order to train and retrain people adequately for our information economy, educational institutions need access to patented or copyrighted materials and equipment. Charging royalties and license fees may place the cost for some information beyond the budgetary reach of educational institutions. From the perspective of society as a whole, this may be undesirable.

New technologies can misrepresent or distort original work in ways that are unfair to the intent of the author or inventor. What rights should the author or inventor have over such situations? The OTA report mentioned above emphasizes the difficulties in designing and enforcing appropriate legislation, and it notes that inadequate protection will reduce the private incentive to create and disseminate new ideas and processes.

Information technologies are impeding traditional enforcement mechanisms. They make the copy, transfer, and transformation of works cheaper, faster, and more private, and thus more prevalent and harder to detect and prove. Without effective enforcements of their rights, intellectual property owners may have less incentive to produce and disseminate intellectual works. This, in turn, could jeopardize the benefits society gains from the open dissemination of intellectual works. And, insofar as there are widespread, unimpeded infringements, the legitimacy of intellectual property law might itself be undermined.[39]

Having examined this set of changes in the technology of information, the U.S. Office of Technology Assessment suggests that legislative reforms will have to be an ongoing process. Laws that are most appropriate today may become undesirable at some time in the future, when the technology of information has been altered once again. This need for continual awareness and a constant readiness to modify established practices is an important theme when we shift our attention to other basic changes.

The information economy is increasingly an international economy. Over the years, much of the literature about intellectual property has neglected this international perspective. Economic theory in regard to intellectual property has often been presented as if only one society were involved. Today, each society must realize that developments in other nations concerning the use of information, and other nations' programs to support R&D, will have a direct impact on its own economic activities. In the postwar period, Japan, more than any other country, has been able to copy the technological advances of the United States and Europe. Lower wage rates have combined with this copying of technology to shift the manufacture of many products from the United States and Europe to Japan. Multinational enterprises have taken an active lead in technology transfer, creating offshore subsidiaries to take advantage of lower wage costs.

Many newly industrializing countries (NICs) are in the same circumstances that Japan experienced twenty-five years ago. Singapore, South Korea, Brazil, Mexico, and many others have the capacity to copy the latest in technology and then sell the products into the North American and European markets. Recognition of this new offshore capability is essential when considering legislation that protects intellectual property. Increasingly, domestic legislation, by itself, can offer little protection. In terms of a society's interests, domestic legislation may even be undesirable in that it may simply shove employment opportunities offshore to countries where the protection is not honoured. International cooperation will not be a simple matter, since many societies' interests lie in the rejection of any protection for intellectual property. Why should these countries honour the property ownership of others when their own manufacturers can create jobs and prosperity through piracy and counterfeiting?

An early attempt at fostering international cooperation for the protection of intellectual property was the Berne Convention in 1886. Several succeeding international agreements with regard to this issue have followed. Yet, despite these attempts, there are still problems with piracy of intellectual property. In April 1986, the Reagan Administration in the United States announced that it was considering a new program to combat the piracy of American intellectual property. This program would give duty-free import privileges such as those found in the Caribbean Basin Initiative and the Generalized System of Preference to those countries which protect American patents, copyrights, and trademarks. Many of the developed countries also hoped to create minimum standards of intellectual property protection within the GATT as part of the Uruguay round of trade liberalization.[40]

From this perspective, it is important to see ownership as a public concern rather than solely a private issue. International respect for the patents and copyrights of one's citizens is more than a matter of guaranteeing a fair personal financial reward for their research. It is also a matter of jobs in one's own country as opposed to jobs in other countries. Furthermore, to the degree that public subsidies have paid for the relevant research, this is directly of financial concern to the society as a whole.

An additional complication arises from the process of international dispute resolution. Violation of agreements can not be stopped quickly or easily. Today, a technological advance may offer a competitive advantage for only a few years; it may quickly be overtaken by other advances, or rendered obsolete by changing tastes. By the time an international dispute is resolved through a judicial process, the original creator may have missed the opportunity to profit from the intellectual property.

Government subsidies and tax concessions to support private R&D have become more important elements in international relations, as has government ownership. These can be seen as creating unfair competition, reducing costs below those of unsubsidized, private corporations in other nations. Trade flows can be distorted by these decision modes. Consequently, attention is turning to the competition among societies in this process.[41] In many fields, the pursuit of new knowledge and innovation is becoming a contest among governments. Such sectors include the development of fifth generation computers, new types of aircraft, and a wide range of equipment initially developed for the military.

In the context of these rapid changes, the April 1986 report of the OTA reached a conclusion which is no doubt valid for all countries:

Our understanding of how the system now operates is extremely limited and technology is still changing. It is bringing new parties into the intellectual property debate and making information a critical factor for the economy and for society as a whole. Not surprisingly, the decisions that Congress makes about the intellectual property policy will affect a broad range of other policy areas. . . . In making decisions about intellectual property policy, therefore, Congress will need to take into account new issues and new stakeholders and assure the coordination of policy making among diverse policy areas.[42]

Environmental regulations

The costs imposed by pollution are high. Water pollution damages aquatic life, affecting pleasure and commercial fishing. Both water and air pollution cause aesthetic damages. In addition to these, there are the effects of pollution on health, although the nature and extent of these relationships continue to be debated. As public awareness of environmental problems has expanded, societies have relied increasingly on collective decision making, seeing free enterprise as having failed. In the past twenty-five years, the realm of environmental regulations has grown substantially. In several countries, political parties, such as "The Greens," have adopted environmental regulation as a major component of their philosophy and electoral platform. Pollution involves externalities in that those who cause pollution do not automatically bear the costs of their pollution. Governments have become the intermediaries between those whose activities create pollution and those whose well-being is damaged.

Although the inherent costs and risks in certain types of polluting activities may warrant their absolute curtailment, an overall objective of zero pollution seems unreasonable. Human existence in itself creates polluting wastes, and it is inevitable that a certain amount of pollution will continue to exist. Optimality may not call for the complete elimination of these externalities. Consequently, a particularly difficult aspect of the problem is to determine the level of pollution and the associated environmental damage that is acceptable to society. Henry Peskin, Paul Portney, and Allen Kneese present this as a central issue where public perceptions can change over time.

If, in fact, environmental regulations are an important contributor to our current economic difficulties, it may be because the costs of those regulations were ignored or underestimated when the legislation was passed. There might exist, as a consequence, a bias toward too much regulation. Yet, even if environmental regulations are not a cause of our economic difficulties, the public may perceive them to be so. This perception, and the belt-tightening that can be expected as a result of slow growth and inflation, is already beginning to spell trouble for environmental regulation.[43]

Ronald Coase has suggested that a socially optimal level of pollution can be reached through private negotiations between profit and utility maximizing corporations and individuals. Those hurt by pollution will be prepared to pay the polluter to reduce its pollution up to the amount that reflects the damage they are suffering. Consequently, where private negotiations can take place, government regulation may not be necessary. In order for the Coase Theorem to provide an optimal solution, information and negotiation costs must be small relative to the externality. However, solutions that must be arrived at privately often entail high costs. The burden of these may fall on a few, while the benefits of the final result accrue to many. This problem of free riders often stands as a deterrent to negotiations between the interested parties. For example, it is often difficult and sometimes impossible for consumer groups to organize a common position. People are not accustomed to assigning a monetary value to a safe and clean environment. In addition, there is seldom complete availability or understanding of the relevant information. For example, there is a great deal of uncertainty as to the effects of varying degrees of pollution on the quality of the environment and on human health. One area where individuals appear to have difficulty understanding the implication of an event is in circumstances of very low probabilities. In cases where the probability of an event drops to very low values, many individuals become insensitive to even large potential damages. This limited capability of individuals to attend to rare events can be plausibly viewed as a form of *bounded rationality*.

Thus, in the absence of perfect information and costless negotiations, environmental problems will continue to exist and free enterprise pollution levels will be greater than socially desired. Many societies have sought a solution through regulations. Pareto-optimality implies achieving a pollution control level where the marginal social costs of pollution are just equal to the marginal social costs of pollution abatement. This means that to define a satisfactory solution, it must be possible to determine empirically these marginal costs for each type of pollutant. However, these relationships are generally open to considerable uncertainty and debate.

Apart from the decision about the optimal degree of pollution, a society must also choose among alternative types of regulatory processes. Emission standards, specifying a maximum legal rate of emission, are like a rationing system. The government specifies how much of the environment may be used by each firm for the disposal of wastes, and allows this use at no charge. An emission standard may specify the maximum allowable emissions in terms of absolute density, absolute total rate, or quantity related to the activity in the production process. In general, emission standards are applied uniformly. The effect of this on two dissimilar firms is illustrated in Figure 8.1, which shows the marginal cost curves for pollution control. Without pollution regulations, both firms operate on the basis of zero abatement, and each emits 100 pounds of pollutant per time period. If uniform regulation prohibits emissions greater than fifty pounds per day, both firms must restrict their emissions by fifty pounds per day regardless of their relative costs in doing so. Firm 1 experiences much lower marginal and total abatement costs than does firm 2. For society as a whole, total abatement costs could be reduced by requiring firm 1 to reduce its pollution by more than firm 2's requirement, that is, by imposing different abatement requirements on each firm.

Regulations requiring specific procedures and equipment are frequently used to reduce emissions. Though they are relatively easy to implement from an administrative point of view, there are several drawbacks to this approach. The general uncertainty about future environmental conditions gives support to gradual policies that can incorporate information gathered and that can be modified over time. Once a policy requiring specific equipment has been implemented, the costs of future modification may be excessively large. It is also impor′ant that tech-

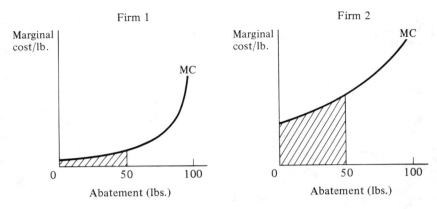

Figure 8.1. Abatement cost with effluent standard.

nological progress in pollution control occurs, but this form of regulation provides few incentives to innovate. Harrington and Krupnick have been critical of the types of pollution regulations that have been imposed in the United States.

The environmental policies with the greatest impact on the national economy are probably those that limit industrial air and water pollution. These policies are now under attack for imposing excessive compliance costs on households, firms, and government, and for retarding innovation and investment. These costs have, in turn, been linked to excessive reliance on technology-based standards and to cumbersome and erratic procedures for obtaining permits for construction of new plant and equipment.[44]

Barry Bosworth has emphasized the importance of choosing the most cost-effective regulations.

One implication of Bosworth's observations is that it would be well for environmental regulators to hasten their search for the most cost-effective policies possible. Carefully designed policies will make fewer demands on what appears to be a limited and slowly growing stock of national economic resources. In addition, such policies will appear less intrusive and thus more politically acceptable.[45]

Many authors argue for economic incentives rather than uniform technological standards. Some governments have, in fact, relied on a considerable variety of market techniques or economic incentives, charging polluters in accordance with the damage they inflict on the environment, or subsidizing polluters who reduce their emissions, or auctioning pollution licenses permitting specified emissions.

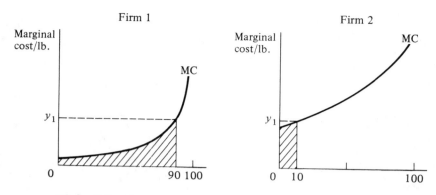

Figure 8.2. Abatement cost with effluent charge.

Effluent charges are prices paid for discharging wastes into the environment. Generally, they are based upon the total quantity of waste discharged. Essentially, they are a form of taxation on environmental damage, encouraging the polluter to reduce the amount of discharge to a level below that which would otherwise have prevailed. If the effluent charge is imposed, all firms may pay the same price per unit. Figure 8.2 shows the behaviour of the two previously discussed firms operating under a uniform effluent charge of y_1 dollars per unit of pollutant. The charge has been designed so that the total pollution reduction for the two firms is 100 pounds per day, the same as under the effluent standard. Their response will be to control emissions until the marginal cost of further abatement is just equal to the effluent charge, so all firms will arrive at equal marginal abatement costs. This minimizes the total cost of pollution control. Firm 1 abates by 90 pounds per day, and firm 2 by 10 pounds per day, for a total of 100 pounds. The cost incurred by each firm for pollution control is the shaded area A under its marginal cost curve. The total cost for the two firms under an effluent charge is lower than under the effluent standard, although the same total abatement is achieved. Thus, the effluent charge may achieve greater efficiency in pollution abatement. This objective of reducing the pollution of firm 1 to a lower level than that of firm 2 could also be pursued through a regime of tradeable emission rights, under which firm 1 might sell a portion of its emission rights to firm 2.

Unit subsidies to induce cutbacks in emissions are an alternative to the use of effluent fees. Suppose a polluting firm under an effluent charge pays x dollars per unit of pollution discharged into the environment. Alternatively, if the environmental authority offers to pay a subsidy for pollution abatement of x dollars per unit, the cost to the polluter per unit emitted is the same as under the effluent fee. For each unit of pollution, it foregoes an x dollars subsidy, so the cost per unit is effectively x dollars. Effluent charges reduce the net profits of a business, whereas subsidies per unit of reduced emissions increase profits. The subsidy will induce a reduction in the emissions per plant like the charge, but by making the industry more profitable than before, it may also generate the entry of new polluting plants. Overall, industry waste emissions in total may be unchanged, or may conceivably even increase. In order to pay polluters according to their reductions in effluents, a government must establish a benchmark from which reductions are measured. Thus, some hypothetical normal level of emissions must be determined for each polluter to serve as the point of reference. As a polluting activity expands, the budget of an effective subsidy program will also have to grow and this can impose an increased strain on the public sector. In contrast, charges on pollution generate public revenues rather than deplete the public treasury. In practice, the use of subsidies has more often taken the form of government grants to assist in investments in pollution control equipment, rather than subsidies per unit of abatement.

Under a pollution permit scheme, the environmental authority determines the aggregate level of waste emissions that is consistent with the community's environmental objectives and then simply auctions off the rights to this limited quantity of emissions. In Figure 8.2, it would be in the interests of firm 2 to bid higher than firm 1 so as to obtain a larger emission right, and in this process total abatement costs would be minimized. Permits avoid some of the shortcomings of effluent fees. In an inflationary period, where the quantity of pollution licenses is fixed, polluters will automatically pay more for each permit as time passes. As population and industrial activity increase, the demand for pollution permits will rise. If the number of permits offered for sale remains the same, their price will be bid up; potential polluters will either have to outbid current permit holders or curb their emissions. Unlike the tax approach, this scheme puts the burden of initiative on the polluters, rather than on public officials. At least in principle, if one area is more vulnerable to pollution than another, this can be dealt with simply by selling a smaller number of pollution permits (which are non-transferrable from one area to another) to the first area than to the second. By setting the level of emissions directly, pollution permits minimize the uncertainty about the rising level of emissions.

Two disadvantages are shared by pollution permits and effluent fees. Neither approach seems to have a high degree of political appeal. In addition, they are only feasible policy alternatives when it is possible to identify the sources of the pollution, and if their emission levels can be monitored effectively. An effective scheme of monitoring and surveillance may be expensive.

Swartzman et al. have emphasized the importance of introducing rigorous analyses in the choice of regulation, but have also indicated the difficulties encountered in the compilation of any economic impact study.[46] Richard Liroff, a contributor to their book, has listed strengths and weaknesses of cost–benefit analysis, where an attempt is made to place a monetary value on all costs and benefits and to compare these values in determining the choice of regulations. Cost–benefit analysis (CBA) provides an analytical framework that increases explicitness in decisions and enhances consistency among decisions.[47] However,

traditional CBA focuses only on efficiency, but other factors, for example, administrability, distribution of impacts, promotion of technological innovation, may be of equal or greater importance in decisions. CBA does not adequately account for impacts on future generations due to difficulties in deriving a present dollar value for future costs and benefits. . . . CBA usually accepts technology as given and cannot anticipate technological breakthroughs. . . . Simple displays of numerical ratios of benefits to costs presented without a guide to assumptions and uncertainties may lend a false air of precision to estimates.[48]

U.S. airline deregulation

The U.S. airline industry provides an interesting illustration of the changing nature of a society's attitude towards regulation: the initial rationale for imposing a permanent regulatory structure; the later evaluation and rejection of certain elements of the regulatory structure; and, most recently, the appearance of new questions about deregulation. Airline industry regulations have been motivated by a variety of concerns, including safety and the environment, as well as by economic issues such as pricing and market structure. In order to pursue this variety of social objectives, price controls have sometimes been combined with non–price regulations.

The U.S. federal government has exercised its regulatory power through three separate agencies. The Federal Aviation Administration (FAA) imposes regulations to enhance safety and to limit noise and environmental damage. In order to operate within the U.S. air industry, personnel, aircraft, and airports all require FAA certificates based upon the attainment of FAA standards. U.S. air traffic control systems are also operated by the FAA.

The FAA is one of the most powerful government agencies. With tens of thousands of employees, a multibillion dollar budget, offices all over the world, its own fleet of aircraft, and an extensive data file on airmen, air-craft, and airports, its influence is tremendous. For anyone even remotely associated with aviation, the FAA touches or intrudes upon their lives constantly.[49]

The National Transportation Safety Board (NTSB) operates within the Department of Transportation. The NTSB has responsibility for investigating air accidents and for recommending safety improvements as a result of these investigations.

The Civil Aeronautics Board (CAB) was responsible for economic regulations, and this is the agency whose activities have been the focus of airline deregulation. Wolfe and Newmeyer summarize the initial rationale for the CAB:

Airline service was too important to leave to the uncertainties of the marketplace and needed to be controlled by the government to insure the public interest. Airlines needed to be regulated to prevent monopoly abuses. It was argued that left unchecked, they would engage in cutthroat competition with the larger, stronger carriers forcing the smaller ones out of the market. The ultimate survivor of this competitive contest would then be in a position to charge whatever price it wanted and exact monopoly profits.

Another argument for economic regulation was that it was needed to ensure adequate service to the public. If there were open competition, carriers would only want to serve the largest markets and leave the small cities without service.

The economic arguments were supplemented by the rhetorical arguments of the airlines themselves, who found it in their interests to be shielded from competition.

The carriers, through their lobbying organization, the Air Transport Association, contended that regulation was needed to ensure stability so that the carriers could obtain financing for their capital needs.[50]

Based upon this rationale, CAB had authority to evaluate the rates charged by any airline on any route and to alter these rates as it believed appropriate. CAB also had the power to allocate routes to alternative airlines, thereby controlling market entry and competition. Furthermore, CAB had supervisory responsibilities that covered all areas of business practices, giving it access and control over corporate accounts and reports, as well as corporate mergers and acquisitions.

Since the 1978 Airline Deregulation Act, government involvement has gradually been diminished and, in 1985, CAB was terminated. Some observers point to improvements in airline efficiency and to decreases in ticket prices as evidence that regulations had been imposing substantial hidden costs. Yet others feel that the objectives of regulations have been sacrificed in the process, indicating that deregulation involves unacceptable trade-offs. An important question is whether the U.S. experiences with airline deregulation can serve as an example or guide for other nations. By comparing the United States and Canada, one can see that even contiguous nations may not face the same balance of shortcomings and advantages when considering an appropriate decision mode.

As part of its studies on regulation, the Economic Council of Canada was optimistic concerning the net benefits of U.S. airline deregulation and concerning the advisability of Canada copying this process. Based on the initial few years of the deregulation experience in the United States, the Economic Council concluded:

> Traffic had grown substantially and productivity in the industry had improved, particularly on dense, short-haul routes where new, competitive carriers entered; Capacity utilization had increased;
>
> Fares dropped substantially on many routes as bargain-priced fares increased popularity;
>
> Subsidies spent to support less profitable services were low;
>
> Domestic trunk carrier service reductions to a number of small stations occurred, but had been offset to some extent by increases in services by local carriers;
>
> New entrants into larger, more dense routes had been fewer than expected;
>
> A number of mergers had occurred;
>
> Safety standards had not declined; and
>
> Destructive competition had not been evident.[51]

Based upon the experience in the United States, the Economic Council recommended Canadian deregulation and was confident that

the self-regulating effects of the market forces will provide a greater choice of fares and services for consumers, increased pressure to keep costs down, and greater opportunity for innovation. Equally important, a more competitive, less protective environment will facilitate the adaptation of the nation's air transportation system to the changing requirements and transportation modes of future generations.[52]

This optimistic view has not been shared by all observers. Some have argued that important differences exist between Canada and the United States, negating the applicability of U.S. experiences: (1) the existence of a linear airline network in the heavily travelled routes in Canada, as opposed to the more distinct hub-and-spoke arrangement in the United States; (2) the reliance by many isolated communities in Canada on air service as their only transportation links with larger centres; (3) the small size of communities in Canada (particularly in the North) and the long connecting distances not experienced to such an extent in the United States; (4) the Canadian market's much smaller size, carrying fewer passengers over longer distances; and (5) differing regional development priorities from those in the United States.

Differences such as these introduce uncertainties as to the results of copying another nation's example. Furthermore, some important implications of deregulation will become apparent only after the passage of a number of years. A wide variety of questions concerning deregulation add to the uncertainties from the perspective of other countries. If increased competition in the airline industry does result from deregulation, does excess capacity exist within existing infrastructure to accommodate increased traffic? Would financial requirements for additional infrastructure be offset by the economic benefits to be derived from a deregulated airline situation? The possibility exists in a more competitive airline industry for travellers to be attracted away from other modes. Would this lead to excess capacity and higher costs in those alternative modes, particularly railways? Would discontinuation of services to remote communities be politically, as well as economically, unacceptable? One of the results of deregulation is to remove rate cross-subsidization. Would direct grants as a means of maintaining service be more desirable?

These questions illustrate the difficulties in predicting the outcomes of deregulation. Many significant effects will become apparent only after a number of years. Differences among countries add to the complexity and uncertainty in evaluating another country's experiences for the purpose of one's own decisions about deregulation. Continual experimentation and modification appear to be necessary as well as continual analysis of practical experiences. Such analysis is complicated, however, by the difficulty of speculating what would have happened in the absence of regulation. Douglas Caves et al. have emphasized this difficulty:

The basic problem with assessing airline deregulation is common to the assessment of many national economic policies: there is no ready control group against which the observed effects of deregulation can be compared. We can observe the course of the industry since deregulation, but it is difficult to say what the course would have been had deregulation not occurred. Some studies have used the period immediately prior to deregulation to gain insight on trends and thereby project what would have happened in the absence of deregulation. . . . Though such an approach has merit, there are pitfalls. Even if trends can be established for the pre-deregulation period, there is no guarantee that such trends would have held in the post-deregulation period.[53]

As Caves et al. have suggested, the evaluation of many regulations is made more difficult by our inability to know what would have happened in the absence of each regulation. This perspective suggests the usefulness of comparing regulations and other decision modes among societies. Societies may differ significantly in important aspects, and so these comparisons – and lessons drawn from them – cannot be precise. Nevertheless, such comparisons may shed some light on the advantages and shortcomings of alternative decision modes.

Essay and discussion topics

1. Compare the use of non–price regulations within two or more economic systems. For each system, indicate the relationship between the reliance on non–price regulations and the attainment of the society's objectives.
2. For two or more economic systems, compare a particular type of non–price regulation. Indicate the advantages and shortcomings of non–price regulations as illustrated by this study.
3. In the 1980s, several societies have introduced major deregulation programs. Choose one deregulation program and discuss its impact on the society's economic system.

CHAPTER 9

Public enterprises

Introduction

Throughout history, societies have chosen to own and operate some economic enterprises on a collective basis. "State-owned enterprises are nothing new in the market economies of the world. The historians of the Roman Empire and the chronicles of the Old Testament offer ample evidence of their ancient origins."[1] The sixteenth century religious Reformation gave moral weight to the free-enterprise process for organizing production and consumption, and the rise of industrial capitalism extended the concept of individual ownership and private decision making. Yet even with the growth of capitalism, societies continued to choose collective ownership and operation for certain activities. Of particular importance were transportation systems. Private investments in roads, canals, and railways exhibited weaknesses or shortcomings of free enterprise, and societies frequently rejected that decision mode in favour of collective ownership.

For the transportation infrastructure, one could argue that the marginal cost of an additional user was negligible. Yet to set price equal to the negligible marginal costs, as efficiency would require, would not yield enough revenue to make the project financially viable. Roads, of course, had the peculiar difficulty that a private owner could not easily exclude use for non–payment of tolls. Tollgates were built, particularly for costly bridges, but individuals could gain access to most private roads quite readily. This pricing issue was made even more difficult because many such projects were in a monopoly position. One road, one canal, or one railway could provide adequately for all the needs of the populace within the geographical area being served. Being a monopolist, the owner would set a price above the marginal cost. Other members of society perceived such monopoly pricing as unfair and inefficient. Rapidly acquired fortunes were seen as concrete evidence of the inappropriateness of free enterprise. Many believed that only government ownership and operation could provide for appropriate pricing.

Transportation infrastructures also demonstrated the problems associated with externalities and private contracts. With a new transportation system, the costs of many products would fall. Local producers could sell their goods over a larger geographical area, and because of scale economies they could experience a reduction in production costs. Items necessary for the production process could be acquired at a lower price, thereby reinforcing this tendency. The ultimate consumer would experience lower market prices for many purchases. In this process, transportation facilities would be able to open up new geographical areas for economic development. Future generations would experience a prosperity that they could not otherwise attain. In theory, a private owner might be able to capture all such indirect benefits. However, this would require price discrimination, charging each user in accordance with his or her gains from the system, and also significant borrowing, to finance the system until future users could pay. Contracts with customers, both present and future, as well as contracts with the lenders of capital were often unable to capture enough externalities and provide adequate financing.

Societies sometimes sought to solve these contract problems by providing subsidies from the collective to the private owner, and/or by lending a portion of the required capital, often at a subsidized rate of interest. Yet these arrangements often failed to be sufficient for the operation to be financially viable under private ownership. The nineteenth century consequently saw a huge expansion of government ownership and operation of roads, canals, and railways. In many cases, governments did not recoup the costs of building or operating these transportation systems. Deficits were paid out of general tax revenue. It is true that taxpayers did not share equally in the resultant benefits. Those closest to a new system might gain far more than those at a distance. Business owners might gain far more than the average citizen. Yet the collective payment, through public revenue, was accepted as appropriate. Collective ownership and operation entailed special problems and shortcomings, but this decision mode was judged, on the whole, to be better, in particular circumstances, than free enterprise.

In the twentieth century, particular activities and investments have been seen as essential for growth, and therefore, as warranting government ownership and operation. With certain activities, the existence of only a small number of producers has caused concerns about the inefficiencies and inequities of monopoly pricing. Thus, the arguments in favour of government ownership and operation of roads, canals, and railways have been extended to airlines, telecommunications, and hydroelectric and nuclear power. Some societies have even accepted these arguments for activities such as iron, steel, and automobiles that are hoped to have a stimulating impact throughout the society, or throughout a particular region within it. Some societies have been more optimistic than others concerning the size of an activity's externalities or have stood in greater need of a solution to particularly high unemployment and slow growth. This perspective emphasizes the need to consider each activity in each society on its own merits, and the need to reexamine each activity as time and circumstances change. This perspective also helps to explain why some societies have chosen collective ownership and operation of a larger proportion of their economy than have others. The objective circumstances have often differed among societies, and the subjective evaluation of these circumstances has also varied.

Henry Parris, in his book *Public Enterprise in Western Europe*, concludes that

the development of public enterprise in Western Europe cannot be related to a single political philosophy consistently applied, and in fact it turns out to be a haphazard affair, with a variety of motives involved.[2]

By the 1970s, the extension of public ownership meant that even in noncommunist nations a substantial portion of aggregate output, perhaps 9–10 percent, was being produced in public enterprise in addition to that percentage produced within the government bureaucracy and the military.

Each society has adopted a wide variety of structures and business relationships for its public enterprises, and these have been modified frequently over time. In these modifications, several basic concerns have been expressed: first, the processes of control by politicians and government over the decisions within the enterprise; second, the achievement in actual practice of society's objectives; and, third, operating costs and efficiency within the enterprise itself. These concerns have permeated the analyses of public enterprise structures and relationships in both the noncommunist and the communist societies. Consequently, although the noncommunist and communist analyses have been developed within separate and distinct bodies of literature, nevertheless, it is interesting and illuminating to consider these analyses together in this chapter. Both bodies of literature have dealt with issues concerning principle–agent relationships, bureaucratic behaviour, innovation processes, incentive systems, and success criteria. In the realm of practical politics, recent debates in both the Soviet Union and the United Kingdom have focused on the appropriate role of the organizational structure of public enterprises. The issues of political control and achievement of objectives, and improvements in efficiency, have permeated debates in the Soviet Union over Gorbachev's decentralization reforms and also debates in the United Kingdom over Thatcher's privatization of public enterprises. Both societies have been concerned about the performance of their public enterprises. Both have evaluated their actual experiences with certain structures and relationships, and both have been instituting significant changes in hopes of improving efficiency, while maintaining a desired degree of control by society as a whole over the decisions within the enterprises.

Today's rationale for public enterprise

In the eighteenth and nineteenth centuries, the societies of Europe and North America wanted a rapid expansion of economic opportunities connected with the extension of commerce. Canals and railroads were an obvious instrument to achieve this objective, and the characteristics presented above were readily acknowledged. In the twentieth century, many of the less developed nations see the iron, steel, or automobile industries in the same light. Construction of huge manufacturing plants will create a new demand for a multitude of smaller domestic firms that can make parts or equipment needed by the basic industry. The unemployed will have jobs. Workers will gain skills and training that they would not otherwise receive. Import substitution may reduce the demand for a scarce foreign currency. Externalities will be substantial, and future beneficiaries will gain – to a degree that the private contracting process cannot adequately provide for. In a less-developed country, each such investment may be the first of its kind. Consequently, the new firm may be a monopolist for the indefinite future. Economies of scale, and low marginal costs, may not be appropriately considered in the monopolist's pricing decisions.

An economically advanced nation may possess such a well-developed capital market that the contracting problems are not severe, even for a huge investment. Competitors, or potential competitors, may exist for many such activities, reducing the likelihood of monopoly. Furthermore, an economically advanced nation may have developed an expertise in the use of other decision modes to achieve collective purposes. Price regulation may be used with less fear of black markets being created. Complex arrangements for subsidies may serve as a viable alternative, incorporating externalities and future beneficiaries into the current economic decisions of the private sector. Experience in the use of non–price regulations may provide confidence that appropriate rules and enforcement mechanisms can achieve some of the same objectives. Consequently, collective ownership and operation may be seen as unnecessary, even though the same society may have considered them appropriate at an earlier time.

Conversely, new circumstances may lead a society to expand its ownership and operation of certain activities. Public research facilities may be seen as a modern form of social overhead capital or public good, necessary for today's entrepreneurship. A precursor of this has been the creation in many twentieth-century societies of agricultural research institutes, and the development of linkages between university agricultural science departments and the implementation of new farming techniques, together with the use of new seeds and new fertilizers. Individual farmers and the corporations supplying the farmers have been able to experiment with new production methods based on the research conducted in these public institutions. Left to themselves, farmers and corporations could not have afforded this level of institutional development, largely because they could not capture all the benefits of the research, and because their organizational problems would have been excessive. Theodore Schultz has emphasized the importance of externalities in this type of research. "Under competition, the reductions in real cost of producing agricultural products realized as a consequence of agricultural research are transferred in large measure to consumers."[3] Such externalities occur through price reductions and they cause the social rate of return in research investment to exceed the private rate of return.

Philosophy and ideology can also be an important element in the choice of public enterprise. Communist societies, in particular, have wanted to perceive themselves as an egalitarian brotherhood within which each member is an equal owner of the means of production. Collective ownership and operation are judged to be morally right, whereas private enterprise is seen as evil exploitation. This view has been the cornerstone of many communist societies and, with the twentieth-century expansion of communism, it explains much of the shift worldwide from private to collective ownership. In Western European nations, a less extreme form of this ideology has focused on the major industries and services, seeing these as too important, for the society as a whole, to be left in private hands. Socialist parties have drawn up lists of industries and services which they have pledged to nationalize if they gain electoral victory. The Labour Party in Britain, for example, nationalized coal, steel, gas, and railways during its 1945–51 government. In 1982, François Mitterand campaigned for the French Presidency on a platform of nationalization, advocating the inclusion of the banking system in his nationalization agenda.

Many societies have been concerned about foreign ownership of key sectors. In some cases, this concern has been grounded on military considerations, with the belief that industries essential for defense should not be controlled by foreigners. In other cases, this concern has to do with a society's cultural or political identity. Some economic activities are particularly important in shaping and defining a society's culture and self-image. Foreign ownership may shift these activities towards the pattern of the foreign national, and so may be rejected for this ideological reason. From a related perspective, foreign ownership of key sectors could alter the growth and development of those sectors in the financial interest of the foreign country. The host country could find its economic future restricted by this situation. These arguments easily lead to advocacy of nationalization as a way of limiting foreign ownership.

In pursuing its objectives in regard to equality, a society may seek to redistribute income and wealth through pricing policies. Some goods and services may be seen as essential for all members, and so their prices should be kept at a level low enough for all to afford. In theory, government could provide subsidies to private firms to cover the gap between the socially desired price and a free-market price. Yet the calculation of appropriate subsidies may be difficult. In particular, a society may feel that different groups should be charged different prices. The elderly or handicapped, for example, should be offered special pricing for housing. Residents of remote areas should pay less per kilometre for transportation services. Collective ownership and operation of public housing or transportation networks may provide more certain outcomes in such cross-subsidization than would a system of subsidies to private firms. If a government operated the facilities, then it could be sure that prices would be set so as to achieve its redistributive objectives.

If the scope of collective ownership and operation increases as a percentage of the total economy, then the economic relationships and outcomes within the remaining private sector lose the attributes which they possess when most of the economy consists of independent, competitive units. Each government enterprise can no longer rely on the private market as a reference scale for determining appropriate prices. Interest, wages, and rents – as well as product prices – are no longer able to perform their function as a means of allocating scarce resources among competing units, since they no longer reflect relative scarcities and marginal productivities. In fact, one of the principal reasons for extending government ownership and operation throughout the economy as a whole is the ideological desire to eliminate this allocative role of market prices. Here the purpose and process of government intervention may change from those described in earlier chapters, in which the focus had been on the most appropriate decision mode to remedy the shortcomings of free enterprise. With widespread collective ownership and detailed central planning, the focus is on the failure of free enterprise as a whole, largely as a result of perceived failures of its price system.

In summarizing and illustrating the twentieth-century rationale for public enterprise, it is helpful to refer to the seven motives described by Henry Parris.

Socialism and consensus: The author indicates that in the United Kingdom, both the Conservative and Labour Parties have altered their positions in regard to public enterprise. The Labour nationalization philosophy of 1945–50 has been replaced by "a shift towards more flexible forms of public ownership, exposed to some degree of competition."[4] The Conservative free-enterprise philosophy did not result in much privatization prior to Margaret Thatcher's electoral victory in 1979. Other Western European countries have also experienced changes in the positions of their political parties. "Nevertheless, ideology does count for something, and in some countries and at some periods it counts for a good deal. The contraction of the public business sector in the United Kingdom since 1979, and its spectacular growth in France since 1981, have both been inspired to a large extent by the ideologies of the parties in power."[5] In the period since Parris wrote these words, it is interesting to note the ideological reversals of President Mitterand when confronted with the business results of some of his earlier nationalizations.

In her book *The Politics of Privatization,* Kate Ascher suggests that a particularly important motivation underlying Thatcher's privatizations has been a philosophical opposition to the monopoly power of public-sector unions. "Competitive tendering and contracting out fit into the Conservative Government's comprehensive and sustained attack upon trade union power."[6] However, for Ascher, the extent of privatization depends not solely upon the ruling party's ideology, but also upon the processes of political lobbying and the strength of those opposed to privatization.

Fiscal monopolies: Societies have frequently created a state-owned monopoly for the purpose of collecting revenue. The monopoly, legally protected from potential competitors, can serve as an effective device for imposing an indirect tax. Many societies have given public enterprises a monopoly on the sale of tobacco, salt, and alcohol.

Natural monopolies: The cost structure of certain activities involves economies of scale and decreasing marginal costs such that a single firm monopolizes the market. Because of the cost structure, no competitors can enter. Particularly when these activities provide necessities, societies have often built them or taken over private monopolies. The phrase *public utilities* is sometimes applied to such cases, particularly with industries such as gas and electricity.

Industrial rationalization: Cost minimization may require standardization of facilities and coordination of supply networks. This motivation is closely linked to the natural monopoly, and some argue that public utilities, such as gas and electricity, would be produced inefficiently at much higher cost if a large number of firms were involved, each with its own local market. The decreasing marginal costs of the potential monopoly may only be realized through a public enterprise.

Regional development: Many societies have created substantial public enterprises in an economically depressed region in the hope that these enterprises will not only provide employment directly, but will also serve as a catalyst for other industries, through a supplier or customer relationship. Parris discusses the Italian state holding company, IRI, which succeeded in stimulating the economic development of southern Italy. In the United States, the Tennessee Valley Authority played a similar role, as did the Cape Breton Development Corporation in Canada's Atlantic region.

Industrial reconstruction: Parris observes that many societies have created public enterprises to deal with special problems that were caused by wars. In 1945, for example, France "confiscated the Renault car company as punishment for collaboration with the German occupying power."[7] At the same time, Austria nationalized

approximately 70 industrial enterprises and three major commercial banks. . . . One motive for this policy was to forestall Russian claims for reparations. More important in the long term was the belief that economic reconstruction following the devastation of war could not be achieved by private capital alone.[8]

Developing national wealth: Pursuing the objective of growth, many societies have invested in basic industries as well as entrepreneurial enterprises. Often these investments have been supported because of a reluctance to rely on foreign capital in essential industries. Recent years have witnessed an extension of public enterprises in response to a belief that high-tech firms must be developed in order to sustain growth and that large enterprises facing financial collapse should be taken over by the state.

In his book *Public Enterprise Economics,* Ray Rees has discussed the rationale for public enterprise under four broad themes:

(1) To correct market failure.
(2) To alter the structure of payoffs in an economy.
(3) To facilitate centralized long-term economic planning.
(4) To change the nature of the economy, from capitalist to socialist.[9]

With regard to market failure, Rees points to monopolies, externalities, and common-property resources, and he also considers "dynamic" market failure where new enterprises cannot be initiated because the capital market is not adequately developed or because private investors are too risk averse. With regard to the structure of payoffs, Rees refers to the distribution of income and consumption and the ability of society to alter distribution through the operation of public enterprises, particularly through pricing policies. With regard to centralized planning, Rees discusses the social perception that certain sectors are essential for growth, especially the infrastructure of transport, communications, energy, and steel. With regard to the socialization of production, ideology can play a role, and the motivation can be elimination of what some people perceive as capitalist exploitation.

In their book *State-Owned Enterprise in the Western Economies,* Vernon and Aharoni have emphasized that, for any one public enterprise, there may be several motivations, and this complexity confuses the simple evaluation of the enterprise in terms of fulfilment of its objectives.

Where the confusion begins is in the fact that state-owned enterprises are usually created with many different purposes in mind, with some parts of the body politic harbouring one main purpose while other parts harbour another. . . . It is in this multiplicity of goals that confusion lies.[10]

Varying degrees of public ownership and control

In addition to the complexity of multiple objectives is the complexity of varying degrees of public ownership and control. In considering the future of public enterprise, Parris has emphasized that "one common factor to emerge from this study of the nine countries is the continuing tendency for the distinction between public and private enterprise to become blurred."[11] In recent years, the belief has grown that the administration of public enterprise can be improved through the infusion of private market forces, and through a distancing from civil servants and politicians. Although still owned by the state, some public enterprises are now acting more like private firms, borrowing capital on private markets, being required to become profitable, and being exposed to private competition.

Parris had divided the varying degrees of state ownership and control into three broad categories:

> *State Enterprises* are those managed directly by a government department.
>
> *State-Sponsored Enterprises* are those with some managerial autonomy from the state, but with a special legal status.
>
> *State-Owned Companies* are those with a substantial degree of managerial autonomy and with the same legal status as private sector firms.[12]

Such classifications, however, are not precise. The choice of public enterprise as a decision mode involves the choice of varying degrees of state ownership, state control, and independent autonomy. In considering these choices, some authors have sought to develop an economic theory of bureaucracy in which they explore the implications of alternative organizational forms. For example, some have applied mathematical analyses to determine the effects of various incentives and controls. Of importance in these analyses are the problems of incomplete information and uncertainty. The government is often unable to know all the relevant business facts concerning the enterprise. Furthermore, the reality that unforeseen circumstances can develop may disrupt the government's expectations. Within this situation of "principal" and "agent," the employees of the public enterprise may have their own interests apart from those of society as a whole. Consequently, various types of *bargaining games* can develop between the state and the public enterprise. In his book *Public Enterprise in Crisis: The Future of the Nationalized Industries,* John Redwood has emphasized that often "the objectives are unclear, and the rewards of success nonexistent."[13] Considering the complexities that arise from alternative objectives as well as alternative organizational structures, Vernon and Aharoni have concluded that "perhaps the most subtle and difficult area of inquiry has to do with the decision-making process."[14] As we shall see later in this chapter, this subject is of particular importance in communist nations where public enterprises form a substantial proportion of economic activities. The framework of detailed central planning, originating with Stalin's Five-Year plans in the Soviet Union, has encountered a series of these problems which merit special attention.

The extent of public enterprise

A number of authors have calculated the extent of public enterprise in various countries and in various time periods. These calculations have been conducted on several bases: the percentage of national output they produce; the percentage of aggregate capital invested in them; and the percentage of total employment they provide. These alternative calculations reveal that public enterprise has been of substantial importance in all modern societies, usually ranging from 10 to 20 percent of national aggregates. In general, the percentages for investment have been higher than the percentages for output or employment, indicating that public enterprises have been more capital-intensive than the private sector. Parris has presented calculations which deal with percentage of output and percentage of investment for nine countries in Western Europe, as well as percentages for a total of seventy-seven economies divided into a group of industrialized countries and a group of developing countries (see Table 9.1). The latter are divided into developing countries in each of Africa, Asia, and Latin America and the Caribbean.

For most societies, the military is one of the largest public enterprises. As Table 9.2 indicates, during the 1972–83 period, the share of defense in total central government expenditure exhibited a downwards trend for both industrial and developing countries, with both groups recording a decrease from approximately 17 percent to approximately 14 percent. Within the industrial countries, substantial variation has persisted, from the United States at well over 20 percent to several countries in the range of 3 to 5 percent. In view of the secrecy connected with most military activity, it is not possible to discern unequivocally the inefficiencies that are apparent with other public enterprises. An important factor in this regard is the ability of the military to rely on the private sector in most countries for the manufacture of a major portion of military supplies. Nevertheless, it is clear that the military in certain countries does form a significant component of the economy, with a considerable impact on the society's economic system.

Communist societies have usually relied upon public enterprise to a far greater degree than have noncommunist countries. Their command systems of central planning are discussed in a later section. Nevertheless, concerns about efficiency and questions about optimal reporting and decision relationships have arisen frequently in most societies.

Table 9.1. *Output and investment shares of nonfinancial
public enterprises*

Averages	Years	Percentage share of	
		Output	Investment
77 mixed economies	1974–7	9.4	13.4
Industrialised countries	1974–7	9.6	11.1
Developing countries:			
Africa	1974–7	17.5	32.4
Asia	1974–7	8.0	27.7
Latin America and Caribbean	1974–7	6.6	22.5
All developing countries	1974–7	8.6	27.0
Individual countries in Western Europe:			
Austria	1970–3	15.8	
	1974–5	15.6	
	1976–7	14.5	19.2
	1978–9	14.5	19.2
Belgium	1970–3		12.4
	1974–7		12.6
	1978–9		13.1
West Germany	1970–3		12.3
	1974–5		14.5
	1976–7	10.3	12.3
	1978–9	10.2	10.8
France	1970–3	12.2	15.4
	1974	11.9	14.0
Ireland	1974–7		13.1
	1978		11.8
Italy	1970–3	7.1	19.4
	1974–7	7.7	17.2
	1978	7.5	16.4
	1979–80		15.2
Netherlands	1971–3	3.6	13.8
	1974–7		14.1
	1978		12.6
Sweden	1978–80	6.0	11.4
UK	1970–3	10.0	16.3
	1974–7	11.3	18.6
	1978–81	10.9	16.8
	1982	11.2	17.1

Source: Henry Parris, *Public Enterprise in Western Europe* (London: Croom Helm, 1987), p. 27.

Table 9.2. *Central government expenditures on defense (as a percentage of total expenditures)*

	1970	1971	1972	1973	1974	1975	1976	1977	1978	1979	1980	1981	1982	1983	1984
World	...	...	**18.52**	**17.11**	**16.46**	**15.18**	**14.35**	**14.15**	**13.91**	**13.93**	**13.71**	**13.78**	**14.12**	**14.27**	...
Industrial Countries	...	...	**19.10**	**17.23**	**16.52**	**15.15**	**14.11**	**13.72**	**13.36**	**13.54**	**13.33**	**13.57**	**14.07**	**14.35**	...
United States E%	...	...	32.20	28.13	26.87	24.64	22.29	◆ 21.88	21.26	21.51	21.16	21.84	23.08	23.69	24.72
Canada G#	...	10.79	...	...	7.57	7.30	7.97	8.00	8.01	7.85	7.70	7.85	7.77	7.98	...
Australia D*	16.77	14.87	14.08	13.14	11.91	10.19	8.86	9.12	8.95	8.93	9.39	9.64	9.86	9.68	9.25
Japan	...	...	...	...	...	...	...	...	...	...	...	...	...	...	...
New Zealand B#	7.89	6.53	5.83	5.20	5.25	4.93	4.96	4.87	4.54	4.61	5.14	5.35	5.32	4.94	...
Austria D	3.67	3.29	3.25	2.95	3.16	3.22	3.15	3.13	3.10	3.13	3.01	2.90	2.92	3.21	...
Belgium A	7.09	7.05	6.68	6.40	6.08	6.27	6.03	5.76	5.85	5.65	5.66	5.47	5.17	...	...
Denmark D	8.00	7.84	7.21	7.06	7.13	7.06	◆ 6.86	6.53	6.36	5.86	6.32	6.09	...	...	...
Finland D	...	...	6.07	6.06	5.07	5.15	4.51	4.60	4.71	4.89	5.63	5.14	5.22	5.53	...
France B	...	...	...	...	...	7.58	7.56	7.13	6.93	7.25	7.50	7.36	7.31	...	...
Germany D	12.60	12.27	12.43	12.09	11.66	10.64	10.20	9.74	9.76	9.64	9.15	9.18	9.09	9.32	...
Iceland D	...	...	—	—	—	—	—	—	—	—	—	—	—	...	...
Ireland A	...	...	...	...	...	...	...	...	...	...	...	...	...	...	...
Italy A	...	...	...	6.27	6.33	4.98	...	...	◆ 3.37	3.51	3.37	3.35	3.56	3.51	3.36
Luxembourg B	2.52	2.39	2.31	2.36	2.35	2.17	2.04	2.04	2.09	2.18	2.14	2.27	2.09	2.12	...
Netherlands A	...	...	...	...	6.84	6.43	5.94	6.25	5.81	5.81	5.54	5.55	5.35	5.30	5.24
Norway C	...	...	9.67	9.38	9.11	9.36	8.50	8.32	...	...	...	8.71	8.50	8.61	...
Spain C	6.77	5.86	6.52	6.30	6.27	5.80	5.70	4.88	4.22	5.17	4.37	3.93	4.30	4.42	...
Sweden E*	13.47	12.93	12.51	12.01	10.91	10.51	9.49	8.60	8.33	7.94	7.72	7.30	7.33	6.87	6.69
Switzerland E	15.64	15.23	15.11	12.87	12.32	10.84	11.02	10.15	10.05	10.38	10.23	10.55	10.48	10.36	...
United Kingdom C	...	...	16.72	16.09	15.43	13.67	14.20	13.78	13.65	14.11	...	...	...	...	...

Table 9.2 (continued)

	1970	1971	1972	1973	1974	1975	1976	1977	1978	1979	1980	1981	1982	1983	1984
Developing Countries	...	...	16.60	16.70	16.26	15.27	15.15	15.57	15.76	15.25	14.98	14.47	14.26	14.02	...
Africa	...	...	...	...	...	...	14.05	14.28	16.77	...	...	...	...	...	...
Asia	...	...	...	23.04	23.52	23.11	22.72	22.75	21.54	20.50	20.38	20.32	20.10	19.57	...
Europe	16.05	15.45	14.97	14.49	15.87	16.42	15.39	20.95	21.11	20.87	21.91	22.18	...	...	...
Middle East	...	...	24.26	26.63	25.50	26.41	26.51	26.03	27.32	25.04	24.38	20.84	19.40	...	...
Western Hemisphere	...	...	9.09	9.26	7.64	6.57	7.34	6.78	6.83	6.86	6.03	5.92	6.25	5.86	...

Notes: Letters A–G following country name indicate percent of general government tax revenue accounted for by central government, where data are available, as follows: A, 95 and over; B, 90–4.9; C, 80–9.9; D, 70–9.9; E, 60–9.9; F, 50–9.9; and G, 20–49.9.
Symbol ◆ indicates break in continuity of time series as described in country notes on coverage of data.
Most recent fiscal years, other than those ending Dec. 31, are indicated as: #, beginning April 1; *, beginning June 30; %, ending September 30; and +, other.

Source: International Monetary Fund, *International Financial Statistics: Supplement on Government Finance,* Supplement Series No. 11 (Washington, DC: International Monetary Fund, 1986), pp. 30–1.

Efficiency within public enterprise

Many studies have attempted to compare efficiency and costs in government-operated enterprises with those of private firms that supply the same products. A general finding of recent studies is that government-operated enterprises are less efficient and their costs are higher. For example, after examining many of the nationalized industries in the United Kingdom, Richard Pryke concluded that

> in the areas that have been investigated, and on the basis of the comparisons which I have made, public enterprise has performed relatively poorly in terms of its competitive position, has used labour and capital inefficiently, and has been less profitable. In most cases the public activities have been losing money over a long period. This is not a comprehensive denunciation but the evidence seems clear.[15]

Such findings are often attributed to the fact that government enterprises do not face the pressures for profit maximization that constantly govern the decisions and efforts of the private firms. Although private firms may have additional success criteria such as sales maximization, or market domination, the need for profit maximization is omnipresent. Profit maximization naturally entails cost minimization, and so the observed relative efficiency of private firms should not be surprising.

For some observers, such cost differentials are not an argument against government operation. Societies choose this decision mode because free-enterprise profit-maximizing, and cost-minimizing, results are not socially optimal. Such observers would not see higher government costs as reflecting waste. Rather, they would see these as the natural result of pursuing other objectives.

Externalities may be particularly important in justifying these higher costs. Provision of services to relatively undeveloped geographical areas may stimulate economic development, as argued earlier, to such a degree that the higher costs may be outweighed by the social benefits. This may be true of transportation, telecommunications, and postal services, for example. Even specific industrial activities, such as steel mills or automobile factories, may experience higher costs if operated as public enterprises, yet higher costs may be justified. One might even argue that current cost patterns will change as development occurs, such that as time passes a government enterprise may close the gap between its costs and those of private firms.

A society may want its government enterprises to cross-subsidize customers, for example, providing services at a lower price to those with lower incomes. Such cross-subsidization may be expected to reduce profits (or increase losses). It may also increase costs if such marginal customers are also high-cost customers, in that they require special assistance, for example, because they are elderly or live in remote areas. A society may expect that its government-operated nursing homes should provide a more intensive level of health care than its privately operated nursing homes.

Apart from these justifications for higher costs, it does appear that government-operated enterprises experience higher labour costs for the same level of achievement. Critics point to this as clear evidence of inefficiency. Employees are able to demand higher wages than equivalent private-sector jobs provide. Politicians see these employees as voters. Consequently, politicians are reluctant to engage in tough wage negotiations that could result in the political alienation of a large group of voters. In a sense, this phenomenon may be seen as a simple income transfer from society to the specific employees. However, it seems that the political strength of such workers may enable them to retard productivity improvements as well. The long-run impact of these attempts to preserve the status quo in job descriptions may entail a substantial gap in costs over those levels attainable under free enterprise.

For many government-operated enterprises, a related element is the fact that close competitors do not exist. In some cases, a society has taken over a privately owned monopoly or oligopoly and has simply maintained that market structure. In some cases, a society has deliberately created a new enterprise because it has felt that only a monopoly could operate successfully and that a privately owned monopoly would not be socially optimal. Transportation and communication systems have frequently been in these situations. For such enterprises, cost and efficiency comparisons are difficult. This absence of competitors also has serious implications for the attitudes of employees towards appropriate compensation, introduction of new technology, personal effort, and customer satisfaction. It also has serious implications for managerial decisions in regard to employee–employer relations on such matters and in regard to the day-to-day operating and investment decisions. In a competitive marketplace, the manager always maintains an awareness of these decisions in other similar firms, but with government-operated monopolies, this yardstick for comparison is missing. If a public enterprise lacks competitors, society and its government are not able to evaluate, with much clarity, the success or failure of public enterprises and their managers.

Modifying public enterprise

From time to time, a society has decided that a particular type of public enterprise should be modified. Of most interest, perhaps, are decisions to distance the enterprise from government officials, while still maintaining public ownership. Traditionally, the bulk of government activities have been directed by a bureaucracy which reports daily to government officials. In some societies, public accountability is seen to be operating when officials must answer, on a daily basis, to a legislature or parliament. Yet this structure can expose the enterprise to daily political pressures which, as noted above, may reduce efficiency, restrain technological improvements, and result in politically motivated income transfers to the employees.

Hence, some observers place considerable faith in the creation of independently operated, yet government-owned, enterprises. These firms may still receive government guidelines in regard to operating and investment decisions. But these guidelines leave a range of judgement to the managers. Periodically, the managers must report to government officials to justify their performance, request investment funds, or request subsidies to cover operating losses. Yet it is expected that this periodic reporting will permit decision making that is more concerned with economic factors and cost–benefit calculations and less concerned with influencing votes.

It should be readily apparent that the nature of these enterprise–government relationships can vary substantially. The content of government guidelines may be general or detailed. Managers may have freedom to borrow from the private sector for investment purposes, or they may have to obtain formal approval for annual investment plans. Managers may have freedom to set the prices for their products, or their prices may require formal approval. To some degree, the independence of the enterprise may depend upon the status of the person who is its chief executive officer; and it may depend upon that person's ability to act independently without being openly chastised or dismissed.

In recent years, an important phenomenon in noncommunist countries has been the tendency for elected officials to intervene in labour–management disputes that involve the threat of a strike and the risk of excessive wage concessions. On the one hand, the public may suffer significantly if a strike occurs. As discussed already, the enterprise is often a monopolist, and so the public will have no alternative source of supply for the product or service. Furthermore, the enterprise is often of an essential type, producing public goods or having substantial third-party effects, and so many members of society may be affected by its shutdown. On the other hand, other employee groups may look to government wage settlements as a guide for private negotiations. Hence, excessive concessions may have negative repercussions throughout the economy, adding to undesirable inflationary pressures. In these situations, elected officials have tended to intervene in an ad hoc manner, legislating employees back to work. They have also intervened with general programs of wage and price controls that restrict the independence of both management and employees.

Producer cooperatives

Some communist nations have created producer cooperatives as a form of public enterprise. Decentralized decision making based on profit maximization can be combined with profit sharing among each enterprise's employees. It is hoped that the creativity and initiative of free enterprise can be stimulated in producer cooperatives. The involvement of all employees in profit sharing may encourage conscientious efforts to improve product quality. Yet the income inequalities and exploitation of capitalist owners can be avoided. To some degree, prices may be allowed to fluctuate in accordance with market forces, and so efficiency may be fostered through individual decisions. The need for central planning could be avoided, even though the majority of a sector's enterprises, or even most of the economy, might consist of public enterprises.

Two communist experiences with producer cooperatives have received considerable attention. In 1928, Stalin's elimination of free enterprise included a shift of most Soviet agriculture from private ownership to *kolkhozy* or collective farms. These producer cooperatives have remained prominent for many decades, as the largest type of agricultural organization. Yet the collective farms have generally been seen as a failure. Any particular worker would not be able to increase his or her income significantly. Each member's share did depend on hours worked, with more hours giving an entitlement to a greater share. Even if the individual laboured with skill and diligence, total farm revenue would not be altered to the extent that individual shares would be much affected. Hence the large number of workers within each enterprise unit appeared to be a factor in the lack of personal incentives. In practice, various principal–agent issues were resolved in ways that also discouraged individual skill and diligence. "The *kolkhoz* is not, in substance, an independent cooperative, for its most important decisions are planned from above."[16] In particular, the collective farm had to provide compulsory deliveries at very low prices that were set by planners, and prior to 1958 it had to pay in kind for services of the Machine Tractor Stations (MTS). This left little surplus to be sold on the free market. Government planners decided on investments and often decided on the crops to be planted. Faced with their disappointing results, the Soviet leadership has replaced many *kolkhozy* with state farms having wage labourers.

Another important communist experience with producer cooperatives has occurred in Yugoslavia.[17] Here each enterprise has had a worker council, elected by all workers. The council has elected a management board with responsibility for enterprise decisions. In practice, each enterprise has had considerable freedom to make its own operational decisions, and prices have generally been set in the market, particularly since 1965. Consequently, central planning has been much less detailed or authoritarian than in the case of USSR collective farms. On the other hand, this Yugoslav model gave government officials a different set of tasks, namely, those discussed in Chapter 4 that arise from free enterprise. Here the failure to control inflation led to severe investment problems, with negative real rates of interest and arbitrary rationing of capital. For this organizational model, a related problem concerns the creation of new firms and investment in entrepreneurial innovations. Group decision making among potential future cooperative members does not seem a viable process for original investments and new firms. The hopes of the period 1950–70 tended to fade with the 1970s and 1980s. These experiences illustrate a basic theme of the text, that each decision mode has its own advantages and shortcomings, and for each society these may change over time.

In the United States, a recent growth in producer cooperatives has occurred in the form of employee stock-ownership plans (ESOPs). The company makes tax-deductible contributions of new stock issues to an employee trust fund, or the ESOP can borrow to buy shares. Special tax concessions encourage this, with the company's sales to the trust being tax deductible and the bank's interest on ESOP loans also being tax deductible. Since they are a post–1970 phenomenon, ESOPs do not yet have enough stock to provide them with control over corporate decisions. It will be interesting to consider their future role and performance.

Privatization

Many societies have concluded that benefits and costs of particular public enterprises do not justify continued government operation. Vigorous political debate has developed as to whether particular enterprises should be sold to private owners. It is important to note that this debate concerns a wide range of possible arrangements for the organizational structure, as well as the terms and conditions of sale. The decision to privatize, or to sell shares to the public, is rarely a simple one. A society may decide to privatize part of the marketplace while maintaining ownership of its particular firm. This may be done by allowing private firms to compete against the government enterprise. Transportation systems, in particular, offer this possibility. Over time, the government enterprise may fill a continually decreasing share of the market, while new private firms become dominant.

A society may decide to sell a portion of the government firm to private shareholders. In this way, the independence of the firm from political pressures may be enhanced. The managers may feel an obligation to the private shareholders as well as to the government officials, and may not be so readily swayed by the arguments of the latter.

In the book *Privatization and Regulation: The UK Experience,* the authors note that privatization can take several forms, including:

> denationalization – the sale of public sector assets;
> deregulation – the opening of state activities to private sector competition;
> tendering – the contracting-out of public provision to private firms.[18]

In Table 9.3, Kay, Mayer, and Thompson indicate the funds raised by the Thatcher administration through the sale of shares, over the period 1979/80 to 1984/5. In their book, Kay et al. include case studies of express coaching, British Airways, British Railways, electricity, airports, telecommunications, and British Gas, examining the impact of these sales on each individual market. Hastings and Levie also examine privatization on a case-by-case basis, but from the perspective of the trade unions involved in each, presenting the various techniques through which the labour movement has opposed privatization.[19] In addition to the impact on individual markets, Mayer and Meadowcroft note that these sales have formed a major segment of total private ordinary-share issues, representing 32 and 55 percent of the latter in 1982–3 and 1983–4, respectively. "Privatization therefore has fundamental financial implications for both the private and the public sectors."[20]

For many communist societies in the 1990s, the shift away from government ownership and operation will involve the issues discussed. Of particular difficulty will be the absence of free-enterprise institutions and practices, as well as the absence of private savings to finance privatization.

Kate Ascher has examined the special circumstances of contracting-

Table 9.3. *Sales of public-sector assets 1979/80–1984/5 (£ million)*

	1979/80	1980/1	1981/2	1982/3	1983/4	1984/5
Sales of shares						
Amersham International			64			
Associated British Ports				46		51
British Aerospace		43				
British Petroleum	276		8		543	
British Sugar Corporation			44			
British Telecom						1,357
Britoil				334	293	
Cable and Wireless			182		263	
Drake and Scull Holdings	1					
Enterprise Oil						380
National Enterprise Board	37	83	2			142
National Freight Company			5			
Suez Financial Company	22					
Total sale of shares	336	126	305	380	1,099	1,930
Sales of other assets[a]	41	279	189	108	43	161
Total asset sales	377	405	494	488	1,142	2,091

Note: Figures shown are net receipts; note that in many cases the tranche of shares sold is less than 100 percent.
[a]"Sales of other assets" includes, for example, the sale of leases on motorways service areas.
Source: John Kay, Colin Mayer, and David Thompson, eds., *Privatization and Regulation: The UK Experience* (Oxford: Clarendon Press, 1986), p. 4.

out. Instead of providing certain services through public servants, governments are increasingly using a procurement process where private firms bid on the terms under which they will supply these services. Ascher notes that "the first signs of real interest in contracting-out as an alternative to direct provision occurred in the U.S."[21] There the 1970s witnessed a growth of contracting-out at the municipal level. In the United Kingdom, the popularity of contracting-out "grew dramatically between 1980 and 1985."[22]

For trade unions, contracting-out is likely to be more serious than the sale of shares to the public. With the sale of shares, the existing union may remain in place, and the employees may keep their jobs. With contracting-out, a private-sector firm taking over the activity may use a completely different group of employees, often without any union affiliation. The wage levels paid by the private firm may be considerably lower than those previously paid to the public servants. Yet, in the pursuit of cost savings, Ascher warns of the "inevitable tension between cost and quality,"[23] and the danger of sacrificing quality in the contracting-out process.

Detailed central planning: The command economy

In a command economy, such as that of the Soviet Union under Stalin, each public enterprise is commanded to achieve certain output levels for a specified product mix and for a specified set of customers, using specified quantities of each input. Central planners may even dictate the technology to be used within each enterprise and may prescribe the production process in considerable detail. Central planners must devise procedures for arriving at their decisions, for communicating their decisions to all workers, and for enforcing their decisions. In some cases, the shortcomings and failures of detailed central planning are an intensification of difficulties that are encountered in other forms of public enterprise. Yet, certain shortcomings and failures in these procedures are unique to this form of public enterprise. It appears that in many respects, the problems appear to vary with the society's stage of economic development, becoming increasingly significant as development proceeds.

People often think of public enterprise in a command economy as being the communist system, and it is true that many communist nations have adopted this decision mode for parts of their economic system. It is also true that, in searching for illustrations of both the successes and the failures of the command economy, we must look to these communist experiences. Nevertheless, communist societies have usually left some of their economic activities outside of the centrally planned process, and in recent years many have been attempting to reduce this centrally planned sphere. The choice as to which activities should come under this planning framework, and which should not, has been a hotly debated topic within communist societies. In the post–1917 history of the Soviet Union, for example, we see many significant changes in this choice, such as the shift from the War Communism of 1917–21, to the New Economic Policy (NEP) of 1921–8, and then to the First Five-Year Plan of 1928–33. In the period since Stalin's death in 1952, several reform periods in the Soviet Union have witnessed the attempt to shift a large portion of economic activity out of the detailed central planning framework. Eastern European countries have been experimenting with various decisions in regard to this, and in recent years China has also implemented this type of reform.

It is possible that a nation's political leaders, operating within this central planning framework, may adopt certain economic policies because they consider such policies to be necessary on the basis of their general ideology or philosophy, even though these policies may reduce the nation's economic efficiency. Of particular importance have been policies related to the concepts of liberty and equality, and the desire to prevent exploitation by private enterprise owners. Many Soviet policies, for example, have been based upon a belief in the labour theory of value, a moral repugnance towards the levying of rent or interest payments, and a conviction that profit and the private ownership of the means of production are immoral. Detailed and comprehensive central planning may facilitate the implementation of such beliefs, and so this planning framework may be preferred for ideological reasons. How can we evaluate the results of such policies? How can we measure the satisfaction received from pursuit of a morally desirable policy? Indeed, should we consider solely the satisfaction of the political leaders, or should we also consider the opinion of the populace? There are no clear answers to these questions. The questions do serve to emphasize the subjective nature of an evaluation of alternative decision modes. Because of political or philosophical considerations, the desirability of this central planning framework varies from one nation to another, depending in each case upon the nation's kind of political system and the ideology and goals of the nation's citizens and political leaders. Similarly, for any nation the desirability of this framework can vary over time depending upon the current political situation and philosophical beliefs.

The centralization of decision making promises a greater certainty concerning the future course of economic development. Without central direction, some industries might produce too little; and the resultant bottlenecks could restrain progress throughout the entire economy. Without central direction, some industries might produce too much; and excessive inventories would accumulate. It is expected that the integration of current production plans and of future investment projects will prevent such a sectorial underproduction or overproduction. It is expected that enterprises will expand in the proper proportion; and that their activities will be synchronized. The government may provide special assistance to enterprises that find themselves in difficulty. It may send more effective management personnel to lagging enterprises, for example. The detailed planning involved in such an economic system could provide for the employment of each citizen. Hence, the danger of an economic depression could be avoided.

Such a planning framework requires that central planners know all the details concerning each production process in the economy, that they coordinate such details, and that they revise their decisions as the production processes change. Can a government be confident that complete and accurate information concerning each production process will, in fact, be transferred from each enterprise – industrial, agricultural, and financial – to its central planners? Even if the central planners can obtain the requisite information, can they reconcile and adjust the production plans of each enterprise so as to achieve the synchronization of all demands for each product with all supplies of each product? These problems of information and coordination are intensified by any change in the circumstances surrounding an enterprise's production process. Any change in such circumstances requires recalculations by the central planners and the issuance of new commands. In practice, can this flexibility be maintained?

In the Soviet Union, the *Stakhanovite* movement under Stalin, and the widely publicized socialist competition of later years, testify that even the Russian Communist Party has believed that a worker can vary output significantly merely by working more diligently or more skillfully. Events of nature such as droughts or floods cannot be predicted and accounted for in the plan. If the economy engages in international trade, the plan can be disrupted by unforeseen changes in export or import prices. One of the most striking features of the Soviet production process as it has operated in the past has been its susceptibility to machinery breakdowns and the difficulties of obtaining spare parts and repairing the equipment. Inevitably, plans have been disrupted. A positive relationship exists between slack and decentralized flexibility, on the one hand, and the ability to overcome such difficulties smoothly, on the other. Soviet leaders have always been reluctant to provide for slack in their planning, believing that the components of a plan should fit together perfectly. They have not seen how inventories of industrial inputs can be productive just as inventories, believing that growth will be sacrificed by increasing inventories.

Decentralized flexibility is limited by this decision mode. Local enterprise directors cannot alter their production plans in conformity with the changing features of their environment. Information must travel to the central planners; the central planners must replan; instructions must go back to the enterprises. Delay occurs. The inability to forecast any particular production function precisely and, consequently, the need for flexibility in planning are major issues in a modern economy where one production function is itself an integral part of production functions of other enterprises. John Montias, in his writings on Poland, states that "in 1955, screws and bolts were so short that they were a limiting factor in the production of boilers – and ships!"[24] Above-plan production can, it is true, be stored as finished inventories, to be allocated in the next plan. Below-plan production, however, means that a firm's industrial or agricultural customers will have their plans disrupted as well.

A modern economy encounters these problems to a greater extent than does a country in the initial stages of its development. As an economy develops, the degree to which production processes are inter-related increases due to increasing specialization in making old products and due to the development of new products whose very nature is increasingly complicated and demands more diverse inputs (the modern aircraft versus the horse-drawn carriage, for example). Thus the pro-duction processes of a nation's enterprises become increasingly inter-related, and the problem of coordinating all production plans becomes more difficult. The flexibility problem also becomes more difficult be-cause an unforeseen occurrence in any one firm may now affect many other firms in a chain reaction whose intensity can increase – as from screws to ships. A simple deterioration of quality or improper assortment of one firm's output can cause another firm's output to be less useful – or even completely useless.

Economic development involves the differentiation of commodities. On the production side, machinery and intermediate products are mod-ified to become more appropriate for the different tasks they perform. On the consumption side, people spend their rising incomes on a wider variety of goods. For the central allocation of commodities, each mod-ification or variety must be considered as a separate product. The in-creasing number of items complicates the three problems of information, coordination, and flexibility. The modern emphasis on quality or ap-propriateness also adds to these difficulties in that many aspects of quality cannot be quantified easily. Successful planning requires that precise information concerning a desired product be conveyed from potential customers to the central planners. The planners must be able to compare this information with information concerning the detailed production possibilities of enterprises that might make the desired item. Finally, the planners must decide which firms should make the item, how much should be produced, and to whom it should be distributed. Involved in this process is a transfer and analysis of information that can be achieved most readily in terms of statistics. If blueprints or verbal description are necessary, as they are with many aspects of quality, then the transfer and analysis of information are greatly complicated.

Changes in technology that can affect both the quality and the cost of a product have become prominent features of all modern economies and appear essential for their progress. An economically less-developed nation can simply copy the technology of more advanced countries. As the technology gap between the former and the latter is closed, however, the framework for central planning must actively foster quality improvements and cost reductions if the nation's rate of economic growth is to be maintained. With the centralization of all decisions concerning the operation of the economy, central planners must obtain detailed knowledge concerning potential innovations, and they must be able to decide whether, in fact, the innovations should be implemented.

Hence, as a nation becomes economically advanced, it experiences at least four trends that complicate the information, coordination, and flexibility problems inherent in this central-planning decision mode. First, products become more complex and require a wider variety of inputs, so the production functions of the nation become increasingly interrelated. Second, both production and consumption goods are provided in a growing number of versions with a wide array of modifications. From the central planners' viewpoint, the number of items to be considered increases. Third, there is a modern emphasis on quality or appropriateness, and many such aspects of a commodity cannot be quantified easily. Fourth, as a nation nears the forefront of international technology, it must foster domestic innovation; and the need to obtain and evaluate information concerning potential innovations presents central planners with an additional complication.

These difficulties may hamper central planning to such an extent that individual enterprises do in fact make decisions concerning their operations. The enterprises may violate centrally issued directives without punishment, knowing that the central authorities are unable to detect such infractions. The enterprises, for example, may ignore repeated pleas by the central authorities for quality improvements. In order to make their future tasks easier, the enterprises may argue for lower production quotas than they think they can attain. The managers of enterprises will consciously engage in such behaviour if their incomes and promotions are based upon attainment of the planned output levels. It is the combination of such a reward system with the information, coordination, and flexibility problems that can lead to energetic deception of central authorities and important violations of central decisions. Yet this reward system may be considered necessary since it provides an assurance that the planned output levels will be attained. Without such a guarantee, the entire set of national economic plans might be meaningless. Hence the attractiveness of this central-planning decision mode is reduced by substantial problems that lie embedded in it.

Political considerations may also affect the desirability of this planning framework. A dictatorship, in particular, may find this economic system extremely appealing since, with it, the political leaders can rapidly impose their will on the populace. This is true, for example, in regard to the nation's savings rate. The decision as to how much of the nation's production should be consumed and how much should be invested is an important factor influencing the nation's rate of economic growth. With detailed central planning, this savings rate can be raised above the level that the citizens would freely choose. The political leaders may also feel that their view of the relative desirability of different consumption products is superior to the view of the citizens. With this planning framework, the leaders can determine the amount of each commodity that will be produced. If they wish, they can ration these commodities in a detailed manner, deciding how much of each should be consumed by each citizen. Or they can permit some freedom in the consumer market by letting each person choose which particular commodities to buy, given the political restriction on the total amount of each commodity that is produced. In the latter case, prices may acquire an important meaning since they must be set so as to clear the market for each commodity; otherwise, the consumer does not have a real choice among commodities.

A final issue that may increase in significance is the possibility that innovations in computers, telecommunications, and information management could facilitate central planning. The rapid pace of improvements in the collection and transmission of data could conceivably enhance the relative attractiveness of this decision mode. Such a possibility illustrates once more a basic theme in this text, that the choice of economic system may change over time because of alterations in economic circumstances, quite apart from alterations in society's objectives.

Central planning in the USSR

The command economy in the Soviet Union did not originate from a clearly articulated or universally accepted philosophy concerning the efficiency and appropriateness of central planning. Rather, the 1917–18 imposition of central planning – with its substitution of administrative allocation of resources and products for the previous market allocation – occurred in response to political considerations: the need to establish order in the midst of military defeat and civil disobedience, and the need to eliminate the decision-making power of formerly wealthy individuals who would oppose the new regime.

The command economy of War Communism established strong central leadership and eliminated the former decision-making processes. In agriculture, the traditional marketing arrangements which had existed under the authority of the landlords were replaced. The spontaneous seizure of land by the peasants was extended and supported with the

Land Decree of November 8, 1917. Six months later, War Communism imposed a system of compulsory requisitions on the peasants, and these requisitions became forced confiscations. The purpose was not to create a central planning structure for agriculture, but rather to ensure an adequate supply of food for the urban centres and the army. In industry, nationalization occurred gradually over the 1918–20 period, again in response to the current realities of the military conflict. The new communist leadership feared that business leaders were siding with the White Russian insurgency, and they wished to control business activities directly to prevent aid to the enemy. Mobilization of labour was deemed necessary to fill the ranks of the army. The military acquisition of necessary industrial supplies was also facilitated by the nationalization.

The military and civil discord created shortages of food and most manufactured goods. In the face of these shortages, the direct allocation of consumer goods through a system of individual rationing appeared necessary. The receipt of wages did not automatically entail purchasing power, since many essential things such as housing, utilities, and much of the food products were provided free. Preferential ration rights became important as a labour-market incentive, instead of higher cash wages. It appears that black markets did develop concurrently with the rationing system and that the planning directives were often violated through direct exchanges by individuals.

The 1917–21 period of War Communism did not establish a national planning structure with an integration of decisions to achieve specific economic objectives. In some sectors, such as mining, a planning structure was established for each of those particular sectors. However, in most cases, these sectorial planners failed to create the information systems that would be necessary to make decisions about the allocation of labour and industrial inputs, and to ensure that these decisions were being carried out. By 1921, the White Russians had been defeated, and this relieved the military need for War Communism. On the other hand, the shortcomings of War Communism were arousing increasing criticism. In agriculture, the forced requisitions did not lead the peasants to produce and supply adequate quantities of food. In industry, wages and rations based upon egalitarianism failed to inspire diligent and creative work. These situations combined with the planning deficiencies to create shortages of many goods and disruptive production bottlenecks.

War Communism did facilitate the achievement of specific political goals: the winning of military victory against the White Russians, the elimination of the landlords and business owners, and the establishment of the Communist Party's domestic power. Yet, confronted with the realities of 1921, the political leadership eliminated much of the War

Communism structure and practices, and it created a New Economic Policy (NEP) under which individual decision making and initiative were encouraged. Whereas War Communism had emphasized egalitarianism both in its elimination of personal wealth and in its provision of equal wages and rations, the NEP permitted the accumulation of personal wealth through the financial incentives of a hierarchy of incomes and the private retention of profit. Free enterprise reappeared.

In agriculture, the forced requisitions were replaced with a single proportional tax applied to each peasant's net produce. Apart from this tax, each peasant could retain the earnings from the sale of products in the free, private marketplace. Prices acquired a new significance in the allocation of goods and services and in production decisions. In industry, each enterprise was now allowed to make its own decisions concerning purchase of inputs, choice of production technologies, and sale of its outputs. Small enterprises were in many cases leased to people wishing to act as business entrepreneurs. Furthermore, foreign investors were permitted to build new firms in the Soviet Union as a means of acquiring advanced technology. Wage differentials were determined through negotiation; and the new role of the marketplace meant that income differentials were meaningful in terms of purchasing consumption goods and acquiring wealth.

The First Five-Year Plan (1928–33) once more eliminated the marketplace as the central mechanism for decision making and allocation. As with War Communism, central planning replaced individual decision making. However, this planning took a far more rigorous and thorough form, with standard practices and enforcement procedures. As with War Communism, agricultural produce was to be forcibly extracted from the peasants. The peasants were forcibly deprived of their landholdings, and these were merged into huge collective farms where cooperative sharing of net revenue replaced private profit making. A greatly increased planning structure, referred to as *Gosplan,* developed detailed material balances to decide upon the appropriate mix of inputs for each agricultural and industrial enterprise, as well as the appropriate production technologies, and the appropriate allocation of outputs. The new central planners were supported in the enforcement of their decrees by a new authoritarian bureaucracy. Dissent and disobedience were met with unrelenting punishment. Millions were killed, millions were compelled to move, and millions were interned in labour camps.

One may regard this new era of central planning as an outgrowth of a widespread philosophical debate in the 1920s concerning the appropriate decision mode for the economy. The Soviet "industrialization debate" was a series of open and often bitter controversies about the optimal rate of capital accumulation; the appropriate allocation of new investment between industry and agriculture; the desired scope for the private marketplace, income differentials, and the accumulation of personal wealth; and the advisability of alternative economic and political relationships with other countries. On the other hand, one can see the new era of central planning as an economic and political structure through which Stalin sought to establish his personal dictatorship. Victory in the "industrialization debate" was not the outcome of superior logical analysis or the development of a popular consensus. Rather the controversies were settled in accordance with the personal decisions of Stalin.

The central planning structure and the economic objectives established in 1928 continued with little change until a decade after Stalin's death. During the period 1928–65, the overall savings rate was maintained at an exceptionally high level. Investment was channelled into industry rather than agriculture. Within industry, the military and producer-goods sectors of mining, transportation, machinery, and steel were favoured, as opposed to the consumer-goods sector. In this way, the average standard of living was restrained in order to maximize the nation's rate of economic growth and in order to strengthen the nation's military capacity. The shortcomings of central planning were clearly exhibited in terms of inefficiencies, distortions, and the lack of incentives. Yet the successes can also be seen in a structure capable of withstanding Germany's invasion, and then of extending its socialist control over the Eastern European countries. Although it destroyed freedom, killed millions, and imposed harsh living standards, nevertheless, the Stalinist central planning system did create economic growth and international power that might otherwise not have been attained.

Reforms in the USSR

In the 1928–53 period, the pattern of investment among different types of industry as well as between agriculture and industry was determined by a few politicians at the summit of the governmental pyramid. At this level, a distinct shift occurred with the death of Stalin, from supreme decision making by one man to a situation where open conflict often took place over such investment decisions. For example, Malenkov's new emphasis in 1963 on more investment in consumer durables was opposed by heavy-industry supporters such as Bulganin and Kozlov, by defense-minded politicians, and also by Khrushchev, who advocated a major shift towards investment in agriculture. Sidney Ploss has emphasized that through the 1950s and the 1960s such controversies were carried from the Presidium and Council of Ministers to the Central Committee of the Communist Party where in vigorous debate and actual balloting the investment policies of the Soviet Union were determined. It was here that the decisions were made to undertake an intensive development of the chemical industry, to shift from steel to aluminum in the construction of many products, and to adopt the Brezhnev program of an expanded investment in land reclamation and the mechanization of agriculture.[25]

Throughout the post–1928 period, a bureaucracy has had responsibility for constructing itemized plans and issuing detailed instructions. The work of these bureaucrats must be coordinated if the activities of each firm are to fit smoothly with those of every other firm. It is clear that the politicians have not been satisfied with the coordination among the central planners. In 1947, the responsibility of formulating plans for the allocation of products among firms and consumers was divided between a newly created State Committee for Materials Supply, known as *Gossnab,* and the older agency known as Gosplan. Responsibilities of Gossnab for consumers' goods were transferred to still another agency in 1951. In 1953, both of these agencies for material supply were merged with Gosplan. This situation lasted for only two years. In 1955, Gosplan was confined to the construction of long-term plans. Responsibility for annual plans was placed in the hands of a new body, the State Economic Commission or *Gosek.* In 1960, responsibilities for construction of long-term plans were this time removed from Gosplan and given to the State Scientific-Economic Council (*Gosekonomsovet*), while for the first time Gosplan was to be responsible solely for annual plans. In 1962, Gosekonomsovet was abolished and once more Gosplan was given responsibility for integrating all national plans. Drastic structural changes such as these have continued, and they illustrate the difficulty the Soviet political leadership has experienced merely in coordinating its central planners.

Until 1957, lower levels of the planning bureaucracy were divided into separate ministries numbering from twenty to thirty. A sweeping reform in 1957 shifted these responsibilities from Moscow to regional *sovnarkhozy.* The reason for the shift was acute dissatisfaction with the previous structure of interindustrial coordination. Each ministry feared that it would not be given adequate consideration in the question of how much material supplies it should receive from other ministries. If it was to perform satisfactorily, each ministry had to be confident that its inputs would arrive, that they would arrive on time, and that they would be of the necessary quality. Consequently, a tendency developed for each ministry to construct informal material balances of its own for the activities for which it was responsible. A principal goal of each ministry was to minimize the inputs which it would need from other ministries. Each ministry provided the central planners with a consolidated estimate of the total output of each commodity which that ministry could produce and of the inputs it needed from other ministries. The planners, however, could not determine the extent to which the ministry was intending to produce for its own use those inputs which other ministries could provide more cheaply – either because some other ministry specialized in certain inputs or because it had a firm nearer to the user than the first ministry did. Examples of excessively long transportation hauls that greater interministry coordination could have avoided have been cited by many Soviet economists. Inefficiency occurred not only because of this type of ministerial independence, but also because by-products useful in other ministries were often discarded.

Aside from the personal interest of ministerial officials, a major problem was that one ministry really could not estimate the cost of its autarky to the economy as a whole. It had no way of knowing how cheaply another ministry could produce or deliver its inputs. Unaware of such costs, each ministry could truly believe that its policy of self-reliance was serving the national interest since this policy was preventing major disruptions due to insufficient or inappropriate inputs; and in some cases this autarky probably was serving the national interest.

The 1957 reform abolished the government ministries and replaced them with over 100 regional planning groups or *sovnarkhozy*. However, the economy still did not run smoothly. In September 1965, in a speech before the Plenary Session of the CPSU Central Committee, Kosygin discussed this *sovnarkhoz* reform.

In the course of time major shortcomings began to appear in the management of industry. Guidance of a branch of industry that was a unified whole in respect to its production technology was scattered among numerous economic regions and ended up totally disrupted. . . . The *sovnarkhozy* do not have the necessary skilled cadres to supervise their many branches of industry.[26]

Economic coordination along regional lines seemed to be even more inefficient than coordination along branch or type-of-industry lines. Now each region tended to become an independent, self-sufficient unit – in order to avoid reliance upon other regional authorities who would place the interest of their own enterprises first. Regional autarky developed in the place of ministerial autarky. To coordinate the economic activities of the regional units, the central planners needed the same type of detailed information they had needed previously, and they experienced the same difficulty in analyzing such information and formulating decisions based on it. In addition, there was now no single group thoroughly familiar with one particular industry and capable of coordinating the activities, such as scientific research and technological innovation, peculiar to that industry. The number of *sovnarkhozy* was cut to forty-seven in an effort to overcome the most obvious inefficiencies caused by a small area trying to fill all its own needs. In 1963, eighteen new councils and planning commissions were created, each responsible for several of the existing *sovnarkhozy*, in a further attempt to improve coordination. In 1965, the entire *sovnarkhoz* system was abolished. In 1965, V. S. Nemchinov, a Russian economist, expressed the following view:

The situation here is analogous to the one that existed with respect to steam engines at the dawn of the Industrial Revolution. In Newcomen's time, before Watt's governor was invented, the movement of steam in a steam engine was controlled by having a person pull the valve by hand at the right moment. Such a situation can no more be tolerated in running an economy than in running a machine.[27]

In the 1960s, a series of decentralized experiments shifted decision-making responsibility from the central planners to the individual enterprises. These experiments provided financial incentives to local managers so as to encourage decisions geared towards improving enterprise efficiency. It was generally thought that to urge or require everyone to maximize profit (or some profit ratio) by reducing costs and increasing output was not enough by itself: Such appeals had to be supported by a system of bonuses for successful performance. Over the years a system of bonus payments developed based on the fulfilment of many indicators, a main one being the fulfilment of the gross-output plan. In addition, the enterprise fund was formed out of profits (or out of savings from reducing unit costs in the case of planned-loss enterprises); and this fund was used to improve cultural and living conditions of the firm's workers.

In the 1960s, the question was raised of replacing the large number of bonus norms by a single index, profit.[28] At one point, Liberman suggested that the incentive norm be based on the level of profitability, but that the bonus could be expressed as a share of the wage fund. For instance, at a profitability rate of 10 percent, an amount equalling 7 percent of the wage fund might be deducted from profits and put into the incentive fund, and at a profitability rate of 20 percent, say 12 percent of the amount of the wage fund might be put into this fund. In any case, "enterprises should have a long-term normative for incentive, which will not be revised every time the enterprise surpasses it. The enterprise should always be sure that a share of its success will be retained by the collective that earned the success."[29]

However, in the early 1970s, these profit reforms were rejected and the former system of detailed central planning was reinstated. It is particularly important to consider the reasons for this rejection, since these difficulties are likely to reappear with the recent decentralization reforms in the USSR and Eastern Europe. The 1960s experiences demonstrated that the shift from a centrally planned system to a decentralized system encounters a number of problems that can frustrate the process. How great will the degree of enterprise independence in plan formation actually be in practice? Will central planners simply add up the intentions of each firm in order to estimate future activities; or will they collaborate in such a way that the rights of the firm will exist on paper only, while the firm repeatedly succumbs to the advice of the planners? In the 1960s, many observers did recognize the importance of these questions, and many hoped for a gradual expansion of each firm's independence. To achieve this, a revision of certain laws would be necessary. This was soon apparent, for example, to Liberman, who in April 1966 wrote,

It is time to think about how to ensure the rights and interests of the enterprises vis-á-vis their ministries. We must foresee the possibility that a ministry official might try by administrative fiat to intervene in matters in which he has no right to intervene, in matters that the enterprise should decide for itself. . . . There may be a dispute. Though the enterprise may be right and the ministry's representatives wrong, the enterprise management will hesitate to enter into a conflict with the ministry to which it is subordinated.[30]

To prevent such an encroachment upon the firm's independence and to bolster the strength of a firm's management in a dispute with central planners, Liberman urged that arbitration machinery be expanded and improved – particularly through creation of a "brain trust" or special staff to concentrate solely on the problems arising in the process of reorganizing the planning and administrative framework.

In practice, the 1960s reform process encountered severe difficulties in regard to the establishment of a new set of "principal–agent" relationships. The 1960s reforms were unable to delineate a satisfactory scope and content for central directives and the appropriate scope and incentives for decentralized decisions. Furthermore, the 1960s reforms were based upon the centralized setting of prices. Chapter 5 has related the Soviet debate as to whether prices should be determined in each marketplace, with contracts negotiated directly between buyers and sellers, or whether prices should be set by central planners. The decision to retain price controls for most products was of major significance, as it exposed the Soviet economic system to the shortcomings discussed in Chapter 5.

The recent Gorbachev reforms may also encounter severe difficulties, even though the need for reforms is widely acknowledged. The shift towards decentralized decision making has been a gradual process that began under Chernenko and Andropov. As early as 1983–4, Western observers commented on this process. For example, John Hardt and Donna Gold noted,

Both in industry and agriculture new laws have been introduced giving workers more say in the day to day functioning of the factory and farm. In industry, worker collectives have been delegated more authority. . . . [i]t [the new law] widened the questions that the working collective was empowered to discuss and gave the collective some rights to decide and supervise the implementation of decisions. In agriculture, a contract system has been introduced whereby the workers contract voluntarily for a portion of the work and are given land and equipment. . . . .

Chernenko has emphasized the importance of both positive and negative incentives and, in keeping with his past concern for popular needs, seems to want to move decisively and quickly in this area.

[As Chernenko states], our chief concern is that the socialist principle of distribution according to one's work be put into effect everywhere once and for all. Those who work with complete devotion should by all means have better pay. Some may say: But we can, even today, punish slackers financially and award bonuses to conscientious workers. This is so. But it seems the penalties still lack strictness, while material incentives lack the proper fairness and sometimes, I would say, generosity. This question should be thoroughly dealt with, and without delay either.[31]

Ronald Amman has emphasized that, in spite of the desire by the party leader and the Central Committee for major reforms, there are "political obstacles to reform." In an article with that title, Amman has pointed to the following five obstacles:

(a) Vested interests of institutions. Reform of the traditional central planning mechanism would remove or dilute several of the most important sources of power of the party apparatus. . . .
(b) The introduction of a market element would produce economic distortions such as regional imbalances and unemployment, which could only be overcome by forms of control which are unfamiliar (and perhaps, culturally alien) to the Soviet leadership. . . .

(c) A far-reaching economic reform could heighten social tensions by (i) increasing income differentials in a general context of decreasing working-class social mobility and (ii) alleviating the problem of labour shortage and, hence, undermining the main bargaining power of workers to bid up their wages. . . .

(d) Political leaders would only contemplate reform if they had confidence in the ability of officials at all levels of the system to carry it out. . . .

(e) Even if they decided to go ahead with reform, Soviet leaders would almost certainly recognize that the economic benefits could only be enjoyed in the long term, whereas the political costs summarized above would be experienced in the short run. This perspective would be bound to make them err on the side of caution.[32]

Writing in 1986, Philip Hanson noted that there were significant inconsistencies in regard to the Gorbachev reforms.

In general, there are striking inconsistencies in the economic measures and pronouncements that have issued so far from the Gorbachev leadership. The occasional use of phrases hinting at market reform, among a much larger flow of non-market messages, is one example. The emphasis on forced growth alongside calls for reorganization is another, and is probably more important. Inconsistency is inherent in practical politics, and not by any means a sign that policies will fail. It does, however, suggest divided counsels, and a leadership that is less decisive than Gorbachev would like the world to believe it is.[33]

Though the final stage of consumer-goods production and sale were to shift to the market mechanism, the transactions between enterprises were still to be based on a central planning mechanism. Furthermore, the problem of quality was not being dealt with by reliance on the market, but rather through the creation of a new group of quality inspectors who would travel from one enterprise to another. Meanwhile, the Party membership retained its responsibility for checking on enterprise performance, often on an ad hoc basis.

Gorbachev's book *Perestroika* has presented general concepts in regard to society's objectives and the processes for attaining them. It is clear that past practices have not been satisfactory, and that the role and administration of public enterprises must be reformed. However, the content of these reforms is not delineated. Rather, Gorbachev has emphasized the need to experiment, to evaluate, and to be flexible.

The restructuring doesn't come easy for us. We critically assess each step we are making, test ourselves by practical results, and keenly realize that what looks acceptable for today may be obsolete for tomorrow.[34]

Communist countries cannot abandon the central planning framework, however, without adopting alternative decision modes. The establishment of alternative decision modes requires new institutions, new laws, and new administrative practices. Although communist nations can look to noncommunist nations for guidance in such a process, their limited experience with these alternatives will pose immense difficulties. As we have seen in earlier chapters, each alternative suffers from its own set of shortcomings. At the present time, as in the 1960s, it appears that, at least in the USSR, reform will entail reliance upon prices that are established centrally rather than in the market. Chapter 5 referred to Oskar Lange's belief that central planners could achieve their goals by setting prices so as to elicit desirable responses from individual enterprises, each making decisions within the centrally determined guidelines.[35] The tasks of central planners are by no means as easy as Lange predicted. The period of transition to this alternative system may be particularly difficult, with central planners becoming acquainted with their new duties and developing solutions to the new problems they encounter. The possibility exists that the Soviet leadership will become discouraged with their reforms and that they will consider the new shortcomings to be even more undesirable than those of their former economic system. The Soviet Union may move, once again, to its traditional planning framework, or onwards to a greater role for the market determination of prices, with even greater decentralization. Future improvements in methods of collecting and analyzing information – innovations in computer technology, for example – may affect the Soviet Union's choices concerning which decision modes to employ.

In order to understand and appreciate the communist reform discussions, it is necessary to realize that the Soviet Union has been involved in a reform movement for many decades, and that this movement has repeatedly explored uncharted paths. At times, the Soviet leaders have adopted a variety of original policies on an experimental basis. It is impossible to predict the economic impact – or the political and social impact – of many new practices. Hence, it is likely that some of today's practices will be discarded, others will be modified, and, in some cases, alternatives will be implemented. The Soviet Union may quite possibly take "two steps forwards and one step back," or may even take one step forwards and two steps back. Basic divergencies of opinion exist in the Soviet Union concerning the best framework for planning and administration. At this point, it appears that the proponents of the various opinions are willing to settle their differences on the basis of practical experience as it accumulates in the future, rather than through resorting to political machinations or overt force. It appears that the USSR is willing to allow other communist nations to make their own choices. Such a development is important not only in the opportunity it is providing for free thought and free discussion within communism, but also in the opportunity it may provide, to other nations as well as the Soviet Union, to ascertain more fully the effects of different decision modes.

Essay and discussion topics

1. Compare the use of public enterprises within two or more economic systems. For each system, indicate the relationship between the reliance on public enterprises and the attainment of the society's objectives.
2. For two or more economic systems, compare a particular type of public enterprise. Indicate the advantages and shortcomings of public enterprises as illustrated by this study.
3. In the 1980s, several societies have introduced major denationalization, or privatization, programs. Choose one such program and discuss its impact on the economic system.

PART III

Choosing objectives and decision modes

CHAPTER 10

Reform and revolution

Introduction

Earlier chapters have analyzed a series of decision modes, each of which is based upon a particular combination of individual and collective decision-making authority. Each has advantages and shortcomings, which theoretical analysis can assist in understanding, but actual experience is also necessary in order to reach judgements about their relative desirability. The decision mode deemed most appropriate for particular economic activities may not be most appropriate for others. Furthermore, for any particular activity, the decision mode deemed most appropriate at one time may not be considered so when circumstances change. Technology may advance; income levels and distributions may alter; consumer preferences may shift; the administrative capability of government may improve; and science may learn to quantify externality impacts with more precision.

At any point in time, each society adopts a combination of decision modes, and this combination forms the society's economic system. This choice involves trade-offs. The judgement involved in such choice must be subjective to some degree, and differences of opinion may develop within each society as to the most appropriate combination and trade-offs. Of importance is the process through which a society arrives at its economic system. To some degree, we can view these choices and processes as experimentation. The use and evaluation of several of the decision modes is relatively recent. Furthermore, rapid economic growth, increases in population, and the spread of urbanization have all combined to increase the significance of externality impacts in ways that have led to greater emphasis on the collective decision modes. So too has the vast mushrooming of human knowledge and the expansion of public involvement in education, research, and technological innovation. Much about the individual–collective decision-making choice has changed. It is only through practical experience that wiser social judgements can be made. Consequently, each society will be continually altering its economic system. From this perspective, the study of com-

331

parative economic systems takes on a new significance: It is not simply an academic exercise; rather it is an essential element in the process of intelligent choice.

At times, a society may choose to alter its economic system so significantly that the word *revolution* is used to refer to the process of change. However, this term has widely varying meanings. Some historians have described agricultural, commercial, and industrial revolutions, whereas others, as well as political scientists and sociologists, have analyzed the violent overthrow of established leaders and administrations. The causes of revolution may vary from one society to another, and may vary over time. Whereas Karl Marx predicted a certain course of events based upon his economic determinism, others have emphasized the role of individuals, and groups, as factors that motivate rebellion, and have discussed the mechanics of the revolutionary process.

Equality and efficiency: The big trade-off

Arthur Okun has written a well-known book whose title is *Equality and Efficiency: The Big Trade-Off*. Okun has made these words an integral part of the literature on the choice of economic system. His concerns deal with equality in legal and political rights and equality of opportunity as well as equality of economic outcomes. An important point, in his view, is that inequality of outcomes can interfere with equality in legal and political rights and equality of opportunity. Unfortunately, money can be used to gain advantages before the courts and through the political system. The rich can hire better lawyers and can finance the costs of a court case. The rich can contribute financially to a political candidate's campaign and can use their personal relationships to influence political decisions. Money can also be used to gain advantages for one's children in terms of the opportunities they face. The rich can purchase a better education for their children, can provide a more useful and varied set of experiences as a preparation for the work world, and can assist in decisions about career choice. Consequently, an economic system that permits inequality of outcomes may limit severely the equality in legal and political rights and the equality of opportunity.[1]

Okun expresses the view that free enterprise provides the maximum economic efficiency. Yet free enterprise results in wide disparities of income and wealth. Any restrictions on these disparities – any attempts to increase equality – inevitably result in a diminution of economic production. Consequently, each society at each point in time must decide on the degree to which it wishes to enforce equality, knowing that at the same time it is reducing efficiency.

Okun acknowledges that the right to survival places a basic level of equality as a necessity for every society. Yet he explains that this notion is "fuzzy" and that it has grown considerably over the past fifty years. Okun suggests that it is wise to keep the "survival" notion fuzzy; otherwise, too many would refuse to work. Those who advocate expansion of social programs must recognize that the incentives to work, to invest, and to innovate will inevitably be damaged. In the extreme, Okun believes that a communist system based on equality would destroy all human motivation to innovate.

Okun concludes that a society will constantly alter its choices, since the equality–efficiency trade-off will be changed as society's objectives change, and as people learn more about the precise dimensions of the trade-off. "A democratic capitalist society will keep searching for better ways of drawing the boundary lines between the domain of rights and the domain of dollars. . . . To be sure, it will never solve the problem, for the conflict between equality and economic efficiency is inescapable."[2]

Other authors have attempted to quantify the trade-off concept. Edgar Browning and William Johnson, for example, state that "identifying the magnitude of this trade-off is probably the most important contribution economics can make to the evaluation of distributional policies."[3] Browning and Johnson have attempted to calculate the extent to which redistribution programs can reduce aggregate output, and have found that these reductions can be substantial. For a certain increase in the disposable income of the poor, the upper income groups will suffer a much larger loss in their disposable income.[4]

Other trade-offs

Each society faces a series of additional trade-offs in its choice of economic system. Though these have not received the emphasis that has been accorded the equality–efficiency trade-off, nevertheless they are also important and they complicate a society's choices. Investment involves the sacrifice of current consumption in order to gain an even greater consumption potential at some point in the future. Free enterprise leaves the bulk of these decisions in the hands of individuals whose decisions shape and are shaped by the market rate of interest. The rate of interest acts as a price paid for the delay in consumption, and for the risks inherent in that delay. Other decision modes provide for some collective decision making in regard to this choice. At the other extreme from free enterprise, the detailed central planning of the public enterprise mode places this decision in the hands of a government which, hopefully, represents the collective will and which, hopefully, gives wise leadership in interpreting and molding that collective will. Stalin decided in 1928 that the Soviet Union should shift to a much higher savings–investment level. His centrally planned economic system enabled him to achieve this. Many observers would point to the enormous human suffering caused by this process of restricting current consumption in order to stimulate industrialization and rapid military buildup. Yet for Stalin this choice of trade-off was presumably rational and optimal.

In recent years, many underdeveloped nations have looked to the Stalinist dictatorial model as possessing the great advantage that it enables a society to maximize its rate of economic growth by maximizing its rate of capital accumulation. Taking the current-consumption–future-consumption decisions out of the hands of individuals enables a society to exercise greater restraint in the interests of a better future.

Other decision modes enable a society to leave decisions in the hands of individuals, but to provide incentives that modify these private decisions. In recent years, economic growth has been based to a major degree on the accumulation of human knowledge and the development of new technology. Innovation has gained greater recognition as a determinant of a society's rate of growth. Many societies have viewed education and research as investments that have important externality impacts, and so these societies have instituted financial incentives to encourage such investments, including subsidies to students, the school system, and private firms that undertake research projects.

One can consider this trade-off from the perspective of intergenerational transfers. To what degree should the present generation sacrifice their consumption levels so that future generations can lead a better life? Recently, many societies have incurred huge fiscal deficits, and as Chapter 7 indicated, these can be a mechanism for transferring a financial burden to future generations. The substantial accumulation of unfunded pension liabilities can also act in this manner. Hence, societies, in choosing their economic system, are able to make a collective decision concerning the trade-off between current and future consumption.

Societies may decide to pursue a number of political objectives where the pursuit entails a cost in terms of consumption goods. Most obvious, perhaps, are expenditures on the military. A political judgement must be made as to how great a sacrifice of consumption and investment should be made in order to protect the society in the event of war. Many societies do choose to devote a substantial portion of their GNP to this purpose. Other collective commitments also are devoted to the maintenance of a national or regional independence. Transportation and telecommunications systems have often been built to link geographical sections of a society more closely in order to diminish the risk that they could break away. Such investments may not be economically optimal, yet they may be seen as worthwhile in terms of national or regional independence. Cultural activities may be supported collectively to foster a political identity. Investment by foreigners may be restricted in order to preserve the domestic ownership of particular economic sectors, such as banking, that are considered important for independence. As Chapter 8 indicated, many societies have established broad policies to limit foreign investment anywhere in the economy and to increase the domestic benefits from any foreign investment that does occur. These trade-offs between political objectives and economic efficiency are very important for society. Yet analysis of these trade-offs is not easy. Many of societies' choices are made on the basis of rhetorical pleas and patriotic emotion. Calculations of risk of war or of foreign economic domination are subject to differences of opinion. What may appear to be a wise trade-off today may turn out to appear foolish within a few years.

In recent decades, most societies have become increasingly involved in collective expenditures devoted to the quality of life. Culture has become a more important aspect of a society's self-image, and a wide variety of activities are supported financially. Ballet, theatre, books, works of art, and even motion pictures are recipients of public funds. National broadcasting systems for radio and television may be owned and operated collectively, with operating losses subsidized by the state. Societies build museums and art galleries, and develop symphony orchestras. Societies are increasingly concerned with their physical environment, establishing more pollution regulation that adds to the cost of production. Societies are opting for a different trade-off between a clean environment and the maximization of output. To some degree, leisure time is influenced by regulations concerning the length of the work week and vacation time. In the twentieth century we have seen a dramatic shortening in the average length of the work week in Europe and North America. Each such choice involves a trade-off between the quality of life and the maximization of GNP as traditionally measured. It is true that one could see the quality of life as being a real component of total production, and one could criticize traditional measurements of GNP as being too narrowly defined. To the degree that one believes the latter, then expenditures on the quality of life may not actually involve a trade-off but rather a measurement problem.

For North America, immigration has been an important economic phenomenon. At times it appears that immigration has stimulated economic development, particularly in the nineteenth century and the early part of the twentieth. Yet at times North America has experienced persistently high rates of unemployment. Should the United States and Canada be seeking to maximize total GNP or rather GNP per capita? This trade-off may bear heavily on decisions about immigration policy, and these decisions may change repeatedly over time as economic circumstances change.

Learning from the British economic system

Robert Bacon and Walter Eltis have argued that, in post–World War II Britain, welfare programs, government ownership, and taxation became so extensive that the economy was seriously weakened. Britain's ability to compete in the world was damaged. The role of the market was severely restricted, and incentives to work productively were diminished. Britain opted for current consumption as opposed to future consumption, and this choice reduced investment and growth potential. These social choices constituted what Bacon and Eltis have referred to as "serious structural problems" and as "the British disease."[5]

Bacon and Eltis warn that other societies may contract the British disease. They point to Canada and the United States where, especially since 1955, "each has diverted a high percentage of employment and investment into the non-market sectors."[6] Fortunately for these countries, unions have not yet been sufficiently organized to raise wages at the expense of profits. "The difference in Britain was that unions had the power to squeeze profits as soon as government spending began to rise rapidly."[7] Bacon and Eltis see the fiscal deficits and mounting national debt as simply a delaying tactic by societies which cannot answer the question, "Who will pay for government programs?"

John Addison and John Burton have supported this view in their book *Trade Unions and Society: Some Lessons of the British Experience.* In Chapter 1, Burton emphasizes that the economic systems of many other countries have been changing in a similar manner:

It is widely thought that the British disease is specific to Britain, the consequence of particular and insular British social or economic characteristics. I shall argue, to the contrary, that the British disease is a common ailment of the body politic, to be observed in many other countries. The United Kingdom is simply in a fairly advanced stage of the "disease."[8]

Addison and Burton link inflationary pressures to the trade-union movement. The authors examine Yugoslavia's practices of worker self-management but reject this as a solution for other nations. The common judgement in these two books is that some societies have shifted their trade-off decisions in the post–1945 period to such a substantial degree that future productive capacity and economic growth potential have been severely damaged. In the case of Britain, one can see Margaret Thatcher's philosophy as based upon a reduction of the collective role, and a revival of free enterprise, so as to reverse these trends.

Learning from the Japanese economic system

In recent years, many authors have examined Japan's conspicuous economic success. Some have sought to isolate particular causes of that success and have discussed whether these elements can be copied by other societies. One of the foremost among these authors is Robert Reich, who has contrasted the Japanese and American economic systems. Reich suggests that rugged individualism – which underlay earlier U.S. achievements – is no longer optimal as the basis for economic growth.

Social investments in citizens' health, education, and welfare are typically seen as comparable to and no less important than private investments in business plant and equipment. . . . Japan's emphasis on community, consensus, and long-term security for its workers – based squarely on traditional communal relationships – appears to have spurred its citizens to greater feats of production than has the rugged individualism of modern America. . . . [9]

The central theme of this book is that in the emerging era of productivity, social justice is not incompatible with economic growth, but essential to it. A social organization premised on equity, security, and participation will generate greater productivity than one premised on greed and fear. Collaboration and collective adaptation are coming to be more important to an industrialized nation's well-being than are personal daring and ambition. And at an even more fundamental level, the goals of prosperity and social justice cannot validly be separated. [10]

Reich emphasizes that social justice and the involvement of everyone in economic decisions are essential for modern technological progress. Within each corporation, all employees must work together in developing new processes and new products. The managerial class by itself does not know enough about production details or customers' needs to be able to innovate quickly and successfully. New organizational structures, reporting arrangements, and financial incentives must be introduced to encourage this internal cooperation. Reich notes that the newly industrialized countries (NICs) are now adopting the mass production technologies of advanced nations. Their much lower wage rates mean that the NICs can enjoy a comparative advantage in standardized products. They are now able to manufacture the products that they used to import and are even able to export these to the advanced nations. These new trade patterns are resulting in the "de-industrialization" of America and Europe.

In order to maintain their high income levels, the advanced nations will have to shift to products that require "precision engineering, complex testing, and sophisticated maintenance . . . custom-tailored to the special needs of particular customers."[11] Such goods and services require short production runs within a flexible system, a labour force that is well-educated and highly skilled, a strong emphasis on quality, and continual advances in technology. In such an environment, "tasks are often so interrelated that it becomes impossible to measure them separately . . . [;] the distinction between those who plan work and those who execute it is inappropriate."[12] Small groups working together and profiting together are an essential key to success in this environment. So too is education. In fact, Reich devotes a large section of his book *The Next American Frontier* to the theme he entitles *The Era of Human Capital*.

Reich believes that the Japanese economic system possesses the features and processes that he advocates. Nevertheless, some authors have raised important questions about the adoption of the Japanese economic system by other societies. It is not certain whether the Japanese system will be able to foster truly original innovation to the degree that Reich anticipates. Until quite recently, Japan has been able to copy the technological advances of other nations. Now, however, Japan's industries are at the frontier of many technologies. The continuation of rapid growth will require greater creativity. How much entrepreneurship the communal atmosphere will actually produce is not yet clear.

Many features of the Japanese system are the result of gradual economic and cultural developments, and are deeply rooted in Japan's history. Whether these can be transferred quickly as the result of conscious public decisions remains to be seen. For example, G. C. Allen has emphasized the role of the *zaibatsu* or huge conglomerates – such as Mitsubishi, Mitsui, Sumitomo, and Yasuda. For over a century, these have been "the chief instruments of economic policy, and their part in Japan's progress can hardly be exaggerated."[13] Harmony in industrial relations is the result of generations of religious and educational teachings. Cooperation may also be, in part, a reaction to military defeat. Furthermore, the Japanese economic system may be supported by the generally recognized need to compete internationally in spite of a weak natural-resource base. A number of these special circumstances may be causes of Japan's exceptionally high savings rate and low wage increases – other key elements in Japan's economic success. Takafusa Nakamura has emphasized the importance of the Second World War in developing

Japan's procedures for economic planning, based on close collaboration between government and industry. Nakamura claims that the wartime processes of decision making led naturally to the postwar cooperative planning, through the Ministry of International Trade and Industry (MITI). "To a great extent, the system which was created during the war was inherited as the postwar economic system."[14]

It is not clear how much weight should be attached to each feature of the Japanese economic system. Some of the noncommunal features may be important. One may point to Japan's very low ratio of public expenditures to GNP as an indication that the role of free enterprise has been essential. One may point to the widespread subcontracting through which the *zaibatsu* obtain components from small firms. These small firms are owned by private entrepreneurs and do not guarantee the famous Japanese lifetime employment. Which elements should a foreign nation try to adopt?

These questions indicate the breadth and complexity of issues in comparative economic systems. Wholesale copying of foreign attitudes and practices would be unwise and often impossible. Yet reflection on the choices of other societies can provide insights into our own choices. For some observers – as with Robert Reich – such reflection can provide helpful guidance in formulating more effective corporate structures and public policies.

Choosing a socially optimal rate of economic change

A society that reforms its economic system to make it more favourable for entrepreneurship may reduce the degree to which the society can achieve other objectives. Conversely, the implementation of new expenditure and taxation programs, and the adoption of new social values, may impair entrepreneurial activity. Within society, particular groups may advocate certain programs in regard to entrepreneurial activities that are in their own interest, and so the trade-off process may spark social and political conflict. Since many of the direct beneficiaries of an entrepreneurial environment do not possess established social, economic, or political power, the proponents of an entrepreneurial environment must wage an uneven struggle against vested interests. Mancur Olson feels that the unevenness of this struggle dooms a nation's progress.[15] Conceivably, a better understanding of the entrepreneurial process and of the trade-offs with other social objectives may lead a nation to a wiser set of decisions that will prevent Olson's gloomy prognostications from occurring.

As Chapter 6 indicated, a myriad of government programs provide subsidies. To finance such programs, government taxation systems are often designed to take funds disproportionately from those with high incomes. To what extent does such redistribution alter economic incentives? The answer to this question is not clear, yet it is obvious that some substantial after-tax incentives must be left if entrepreneurship is to be a pervasive and strong source of progress. Furthermore, it is in the interests of society to design expenditure and tax programs so as to impair such incentives as little as possible. Many such programs are relatively new, and their effects on incentives are relatively unknown.

A society may feel that some regulations over private-sector activity can enhance important aspects of living. Environmental regulations may improve the quality of life. Other regulations may protect people as consumers. Truth-in-advertising and anticombines legislation are examples of such protection. A society may believe that some business circumstances require government to set prices directly. In making choices such as these, a society may often face trade-offs in terms of the long-term impact on innovation. The process for choosing objectives and decision modes involves clarifying the trade-offs that a society will face. Yet, future beneficiaries of change are not able to plead their case as effectively as vested interests. Gains to consumers will be spread across the population. Furthermore, many future beneficiaries of change are unaware of their potential gains.

A society's leaders may improve the public understanding of entrepreneurship, so that people may accept a wiser set of decisions concerning policies that affect the pace of change. Income differentials among individuals, firms, and regions can be seen as incentives for change and as rewards for entrepreneurship, rather than simply as injustices to be corrected by government programs that redistribute income and wealth. With the probable concentration of entrepreneurial success in particular cities and regions, social discord over the substantial differences in opportunities and incomes can only be alleviated if the public appreciates the entrepreneurial process.

An entrepreneurial society requires a cohesive social purpose in which individuals realize and accept two essential elements: first, that entrepreneurial change and adjustment, overall, may help social progress, even though they as particular individuals may not gain and may in fact lose; and second, that the future success and prosperity of their society may be worth the current pain caused by change and adjustment. The first requires that individuals see themselves and their successes as part of a society and of that society's successes; the second requires that individuals see themselves and their children as part of the future society for whose general well-being current sacrifice is desirable. These objectives and values require a social cohesiveness and a personal understanding that seem to vary among societies.

The perspective of Ronald Coase

Ronald Coase has examined the need for public policies from a theoretical perspective rather than through the analysis of history. In theory, individuals should be able to discuss public issues among themselves and should be able to agree on concerted, joint action that is undertaken privately. Does a government structure have to be part of this social decision process? When can interpersonal issues be resolved optimally through direct negotiations, and when can it be necessary for a government to become involved in order for optimality to be attained?

The *Coase Theorem* states that under specific conditions individuals will be able to reach an optimal solution without government involvement. Individuals will be able to discuss the issues that affect some or all of them and will be able to find appropriate solutions. Earlier chapters have placed considerable emphasis on externality impacts. From Coase's perspective, the existence of externalities need not automatically require government intervention. A number of circumstances determine whether private negotiations will fail to attain optimal solutions.

"Transaction costs" may be substantial, particularly if large numbers of individuals are involved. Environmental pollution, for example, may be caused by thousands of corporations and may affect millions of people. In theory, all who are involved might be able to negotiate optimal arrangements for pollution control and cost sharing. In practice, the mechanics for such private negotiations could be so complex and time consuming that costs would be prohibitive. Delegation of responsibility to government can avoid much of these costs.

All individuals affected by the particular issue must be able to participate in the negotiation in order for an optimal solution to be reached. In practice, many individuals lack the requisite time, knowledge, or intelligence to participate wisely. Clearly, future generations cannot express their interest in issues, and yet many issues bear upon their future well-being. Much current investment, for example, will impact the lives of children and those not yet born. Educational facilities, as well as transportation and communication facilities, will be important for them. Current pollution will impact the future environment. Private negotiations may not entail the appropriate representation of future interests, and so the resolution of many issues must involve the participation of a government structure that accepts a responsibility for the society's future.

Prediction and measurement of interpersonal impacts must be possible for each of those affected by a particular issue. Yet the evaluation of alternative scenarios for resolving a particular issue may involve imprecision. Predictions about the outcomes of investment possibilities, for example, may involve a wide range of alternative estimates. Furthermore, measurement may be costly if each party is to negotiate individually. The dimension of time adds complexity, since future impacts must be discounted to compare their present values. The appropriate discount rate and discounting techniques may not be obvious, and these calculations as well may involve uncertainty.

The results of the Coase Theorem depend on a clear assignment of property rights. However, the rights of each participant may be ambiguous. To what degree does each individual have a right not to be affected by the actions of others? To what degree, for example, does an individual have a right to an unpolluted environment? Coase explains that private negotiations will lead to an optimal amount of pollution control. Those individuals whose well-being is reduced by pollution will find it in their interest to pay for pollution control so long as their welfare reductions exceed pollution control costs. But why should those whose welfare has been affected have to pay anything? In practice, how should the costs of pollution control be divided between the polluters (including both shareholders and customers of the polluter) and those individuals whose well-being is affected? For issues like this, a government structure is necessary to decide upon and enforce the right of an individual not to be affected by the actions of others.

The Coase perspective emphasizes that, for some issues, private negotiation may result in optimal solutions. For other issues, the circumstances may cause a failure in private negotiations: The transactions costs may be too great; all individuals affected by the issue may not be able to participate; prediction and measurement problems may be too complex; and the rights of each individual may be unclear. For any particular activity, these factors may vary over time or among societies. Consequently, the most appropriate economic system, or combination of decision modes, may vary over time and among societies.

This perspective becomes even more relevant when one considers that collective decision modes entail their own costs, inefficiencies, and problems of prediction and measurement. As indicated in earlier chapters, many observers lack confidence in the technical competence of the political leaders and civil servants who would be entrusted with making the requisite calculations and judgements. The following section on the theory of public choice considers a number of political factors that distort collective judgements. Collective decision modes depend on political leaders and civil servants who may calculate their own self-interests rather than pursue theoretically optimal solutions. It is not easy to weigh and evaluate the welter of information, arguments, and pressures that are raised by individuals and interest groups. Communication among the participants depends largely on the media, and the interests of the media can foster inaccurate opinions and interpretations. This set of political limitations may also vary among issues, over time, and among societies, depending, for example, on the nature of political institutions and practices and on the experience and skills of the civil service.

The theory of public choice

What is the process through which a society decides upon its economic system? How does a society make its choices or trade-offs among alternative objectives and decision modes? The answer to these questions depends upon the society's political institutions and practices and upon its legal and judicial procedures and precedents. It also depends upon perceptions that are unwritten but generally accepted. Conventional agreement may exist concerning which decision-making modes are fair and equitable, and concerning the degree to which government can make decisions independently of public support. The public-choice literature presents theoretical analyses of the decision-making processes in modern democracies. The underlying assumption is that each member of a society strives for those public policies that will maximize his or her personal well-being. This pursuit of self-interest is true for all who participate in the choice of social objectives and decision modes. Consequently, to understand why and how any society makes public choices, one must analyze the self-interest of the participants. One must also examine the mechanisms available to them for advancing that self-interest. The mechanisms usually entail costs, and each participant weighs these costs against the benefits that he or she may gain. In his book *An Economic Theory of Democracy*, Anthony Downs has analyzed the processes through which political leaders calculate the impact of alternative choices on the electorate.[16] Buchanan and Tullock have also explored this subject in *The Calculus of Consent*.[17]

Faced with particular democratic processes and the costs of participating, individuals may find it most efficient to create "special interest groups" which minimize an individual's costs. Interest groups may also be able to coordinate supportive activities such as public displays of protest. They can concentrate political pressure on individual political leaders. Politicians pursue the goal of reelection. Consequently, their advocacy of a particular economic system depends upon their evaluation of voters' preferences. This evaluation must take into account the peculiarities of the electoral system. Hence a politician will see his constituents not as a homogeneous mass but rather as separate groups. Some constituents may rarely vote. Others may vote consistently for or against the particular candidate and his or her philosophy. These groups of nonvoters and loyal voters may also be given relatively less attention. Greatest weight may be given to swing voters who are aware of the issues, the alternatives, and the possible outcomes. These swing voters usually form a small percentage of the electorate, but they may determine victory and defeat in the electoral process.

A politician confronts a large number of issues over a term in office, and this adds complexity to his or her evaluations and decisions. Each issue may eliminate some swing voters' support at the same time that it pleases others. Voters may consider some issues to be more important than others. The total package of decisions during a term in office must be designed so as to achieve an overall margin of victory. In modifying the economic system, the politician is influenced by professional advisors. A small number of the professional advisors may see their careers as being intimately dependent upon the success of the particular politician. These advisors may develop their recommendations in accordance with the election victory calculus that has just been described. Many advisors, however, enjoy civil service tenure, and so their personal self-interest may not lead to the same set of recommendations. More programs and larger staffs will mean more prestige and income for the bureaucrat. Consequently, bureaucrats may constantly seek a greater role for collective decision modes since that will enhance their personal responsibility.

The media are the major link between the politicians and the voters. In fact, for many people the media are the only link except for election campaigns. The media have their own self-interest. This is based largely upon attracting the attention of the public, since sales of advertising space depend upon the size of the audience. Because of this, the media must portray issues and choices in as dramatic a perspective as possible. Truth and accuracy may not be the only criteria. Nevertheless, the media's interpretations and criticisms play a central role in the process by which societies choose their objectives and decision modes.

Douglas Hartle has described this conception of government decision making as a series of intersecting games: "The term 'game' denotes that each has its own unique set of rules of entry and egress, rules of play, and rules of reward and punishment. Informal rules are often more important than formal rules."[18] A substantial portion of the public-choice literature regards these games as a type of "rent seeking." From this view, public choice may not be aimed at wealth generation for society as a whole; rather it may be motivated by individual self-interest and, in particular, financial gain.[19] Yet these processes of public choice are costly, and so they may be a drain on society's resources. The possible wastefulness of this process is a factor in the relative desirability of alternative decision modes.

Once a public policy has been enacted, many believe that vested interests will tend to "capture" the implementation process. This "capture theory" has received considerable attention since it was first advanced by George Stigler in an article entitled "The Theory of Economic Regulation."[20] Legislation usually provides only broad guidelines, while the actual details are worked out by civil servants. But the civil servants lack adequate knowledge of the economic activities which they seek to influence. The vested interests can lose or gain with a collective decision mode, and so they are prepared to devote substantial resources to affect the implementation process. These vested interests may distort the information about production technicalities and cost implications upon which the government officials depend. They may hire the best experts to convince officials that particular interpretations and decisions are appropriate. They may offer future employment opportunities to government officials. Viewed from this "capture" perspective, the choice of a collective decision mode carries the risk that pursuit of optimality for the general public may, in practice, be supplanted with the pursuit of benefits for special interests. In his book *The Economic Prerequisite to Democracy*, Dan Usher has warned that

the legislature cannot attend to the assignment of income and other advantages, except to a limited extent, without destroying democracy in the process. The preservation of democracy requires a non-political method of assignment.[21]

To allow free reign to the legislature in modifying financial incentives and rewards exposes the society to the risks of capture by vested interests to such a degree that democracy itself may be threatened. Such concerns are somewhat similar to the concerns expressed in Chapter 9 in regard to central planning and its principal–agent problems. Although public choice literature has focused on Western democracies, some of its concepts may usefully be applied to communist nations as well.

Reforming the economic system

Earlier chapters have analyzed the advantages and shortcomings of various decision modes. These analyses have emphasized that theory alone cannot provide adequate guidance in regard to choosing among these decision modes. Only practical experience can demonstrate the actual extent of inefficiencies and distortions, on the one hand, and of beneficial impacts, on the other. And these practical results can vary over time and among societies. Furthermore, each can be modified in countless ways with the hope of tailoring the government involvement to the contemporary needs of a particular society. Consequently, one can regard the various kinds of government involvement in different societies as experiments to be evaluated. Most of these experiments are of recent origin, many having been instituted only after the Second World War. Free enterprise and public enterprise have been in place long enough to have received the most thorough analysis. A myriad of books have been written about each of these, usually focusing on the history of the United States to illustrate the free-enterprise experience and the history of the Soviet Union to illustrate the public-enterprise experience. The other decision modes, however, have so far received much less attention. Over the past few years this situation has been changing. Within many societies, public concern appears to be growing over the costs and benefits of alternative decision modes. Furthermore, in many activities, collective involvement in decision making can alter the price ratios in the marketplace, resulting in "unfair competition" for foreign enterprises. Distortions in patterns of production and trade may affect firms in other political jurisdictions who are not the recipients of similar subsidies or tax concessions. Consequently, international trade negotiations will attempt to limit collective decision making, thereby impacting the signatories' economic systems.

In Chapters 5 and 8, we considered price controls and non–price regulations, examining their wide-ranging ramifications for efficiency, innovation, and social welfare. Regulatory reform has now become a major political issue in many nations. Electoral campaigns in Great Britain, the United States, and Canada have recently witnessed a new advocacy of *deregulation* as a basic principle of the Conservative and Republican parties. The opinion has become generally accepted that for many activities regulation has, in practice, led to severe distortions. Compliance costs have become substantial. Those being regulated have altered their business practices so as to minimize the negative impact of regulations, and these alterations have caused undesirable side effects. Rent controls, for example, have led to widespread deterioration in the quality of rental accommodation. Agricultural marketing boards and various types of nontariff barriers, such as import quotas, have resulted in substantial price increases for consumers. Though public awareness of such indirect impacts has increased, and though some political parties have formally adopted deregulation as a platform plank, nevertheless, it is still too early to predict the degree to which these developments will change the economic system.

It is likely that today's extremely rapid technological change will alter the balance of costs and benefits for the various kinds of government involvement. In particular, the adoption of modern computers and tele-communications will permit a much faster flow of information between economic activities and government officials. Advances in microelec-tronics and software will also facilitate the analyses and evaluations performed within governments.

For nearly all societies, it appears that the basic structure of the economy is shifting, with employment opportunities moving from ag-riculture to industry and, most recently, to the service sector. It is likely that this shift will also have important implications for the choice of economic system. The history of the Soviet Union, for example, has demonstrated that a command economy experiences extremely severe difficulties in planning agricultural activities and considerably less dif-ficulty in planning large industrial complexes. One might anticipate that the burgeoning service sector will present new and significant compli-cations for centralized planning. The service sector depends upon ad-aptation of services to the particular needs of different customers, with quick responses to changes in those needs. It depends upon the personal efforts of employees in their face-to-face dealings with customers. The history of the Soviet Union has demonstrated that these characteristics are not easily planned in a public enterprise economy.

The changing technology and structure of an economy will mean that a type of government involvement that was once considered appropriate for a certain activity will later be considered inappropriate. Chapter 9 suggested that public enterprise may, for certain activities, be most advantageous at early stages of development, for example, for a railway, an airline, a telephone system, a steel mill, or an automobile plant. Externalities may be substantial in the form of stimulus to the growth of other economic activities. Private investors may not be prepared to risk enough of their capital to finance such projects. Initially, these projects may be monopolies, able to charge prices that are higher than would be optimal. As a society grows, its early monopolies will confront greater competition, its capital market will become more sophisticated, and the externalities associated with a particular facility will diminish. Privatization may become desirable as the rationale for a particular government involvement tends to diminish. A major weakness of public enterprise – its difficulty innovating – will become significant only as time passes. Yet new types of economic activities, such as space explo-ration or scientific research, may be viewed in the same light as railways and airlines once were. Hence privatization of some activities may be accompanied by the extension of government ownership and operation to other activities.

Society's objectives concerning the appropriate extent and form of redistribution can also change. Theory by itself can tell us little about the impact of such programs on human behaviour. Examination of actual results has recently provided important information about the impact of welfare programs on incentives to work and to save, and about the impact of taxation policies on those individuals required to pay for the programs. Our understanding of these issues remains at an elementary level.

The process of public choice is also subject to reform. Modifications in electoral systems can reduce the degree to which political leaders must focus on marginal voters. Proportional representation has been adopted in many societies in order to ensure that all voters can have an equal voice in determining government decisions. Many societies have legislation that limits financial contributions to political parties and candidates so as to curtail the influences of donors on the decision-making process. Many societies provide public funds to parties and candidates as a further step in curtailing private influence. In many societies, elected officials are developing new mechanisms for soliciting opinions from the public and for stimulating public awareness and debate. Investigative committees link political leaders with the voters, permitting the presentation of formal briefs as well as the informal questioning of experts and special-interest representatives. Some societies even provide public funds to citizens for the purpose of developing appropriate submissions.

For societies that do not have democratic elections, the theory of public choice requires modification. To some degree, any political leader must retain the support of others – and so must develop policies and programs that ensure that support. Tullock, for example, has stated that

helping the poor is a characteristic behaviour of governments whether dictatorial or democratic. It may well be that democratic governments are more generous in this regard than dictatorial, but we do not really know.[22]

A considerable body of literature and a substantial number of actual political regimes have argued that the absence of universal suffrage may permit a wiser choice of public policies. The absence of regular opportunities for each citizen to influence the process of choice may also have the effect, however, of stimulating revolutionary activity. If the economic system cannot be reformed peacefully and gradually through debate and consensus, then reform may occur through revolution in an abrupt overthrow of the established system.

Revolution

When can we use the word "revolution" to describe the change in a society's choice of decision modes? The answer to this question is not always clear. Predictions about the importance of such a change may differ among observers. Furthermore, what is seen initially as a dramatic and important change may, as time passes, turn out to have less significance than expected.

Some observers have discussed technological change as a revolution, suggesting that many of the established economic relationships have been altered, and they have pointed to a society's agricultural revolution or industrial revolution, analyzing the causes and the effects. Alvin Toffler, author of *The Third Wave,* describes the shift to a postindustrial society based upon microelectronics and robotics, where production processes will be radically altered and new skills will become necessary.[23] Toffler's prognostications resemble those of Robert Reich, who has stressed the implications of such changes for economic relationships and the appropriate decision mode. Within each corporation, and within society as a whole, Reich foresees and advocates a transition towards more collective responsibility and collective decision making.[24] In his book *Stages of Economic Growth,* Rostow has classified periods of distinct economic relationships and has explained why each society moves from one stage to another. Rostow has examined a number of societies and has attributed dates to these transitions.[25]

Some observers may restrict their use of the word revolution to situations where dramatic change involves the acquisition of power by new political leaders and, perhaps, where violence is part of this process. In such cases, one may point to a particular year as the time when the revolution began. History textbooks devote much space to this perspective, chronicling the American Revolution of 1776, the French Revolution of 1789, the 1848 Revolutions in several European countries, the Cuban Revolution of 1960, and many other events of this nature.

Some observers place greater emphasis on the role of particular leaders in the implementation of basic change. They might point to a number of revolutions and say that an individual altered the outcome. Lenin certainly believed that a small elite of determined leaders could play a decisive role and that skills and techniques could be essential in winning the struggle. Some point to the abdication of an existing leader as a major step in some revolutions. In the case of the Shah of Iran, Duvalier in Haiti, or Marcos in the Philippines, the personal decision to flee rather than fight may have altered the course of events significantly.

Political theorists may be inclined to emphasize ideology. The articulation of intellectual criticisms of an existing order and the presentation of new ideals and new philosophical concepts may convince people that basic change is necessary. A revolutionary leader must espouse a cause and must persuade the masses that this cause is just and deserves their support. A society may adopt amendments to its legal constitution on the basis of argument and rational debate, and these amendments may alter existing economic arrangements in significant ways. Weber and Tawny have discussed the role of religious reformation in transforming a society's attitudes towards personal property and material acquisition. In recent decades, revolutionary activity in the Middle East has been linked with the Muhammadan religion and with particular Islamic sects. The belief that one is risking one's life for a supernatural power may give strength to a revolutionary movement. Many revolutions have been aimed at foreign economic domination. Often a society has felt that it should determine its own future and has united to overthrow the foreign control. The American Revolution can be seen in this context, as can the twentieth-century revolutions against colonialism. In each case, basic changes have been made in the economic system as a result of the patriotic ideology.

Some civil wars have involved the attempt by one geographic region in a nation to impose its economic system on a different geographic region, or the attempt by one region to revolt against the domination by another. The North in the U.S. Civil War was determined to change the Southern economic system, which was built upon slavery. In some civil wars, the differences in economic system form only one aspect of basic differences in culture, language, and religion. Hence, noneconomic factors may play a key role in the revolution by one region against another.

Some sociologists concentrate on the attitude of the general populace, discussing those issues which have made the populace amenable to revolution. Why is a group prepared to accept a new leadership and new rules for decision making? The alteration of traditional relationships – for whatever reasons – may create anxiety and the willingness to revolt. Changing social status makes people question their economic system. Ted Gurr, for example, emphasizes what he terms *relative deprivation* in answering the question of "why men rebel."[26]

Revolution involves significant change in the process for making economic decisions: The rights and responsibilities embedded in the economic system are altered. Whether one feels that a particular circumstance should be termed a revolution depends upon one's purpose and perspective. Opinions can differ. Similarly, ambiguity and uncertainty exist as to the relative importance of various elements that underlie a revolution. Some observers may emphasize technological change and economic factors, whereas others may emphasize ideology. The relative weight that one assigns to different motivating forces may well vary from one revolution to another.

Karl Marx and revolution

Much of Marx's writing concerns the subject of revolution. Marx interprets history from the perspective of revolutionary struggles and he describes the nature and causes of these struggles. He begins the *Manifesto of the Communist Party* with a summary of this view.

The history of all hitherto existing society is the history of class struggles.

Freeman and slave, patrician and plebeian, lord and serf, guild-master and journeyman, in a word, oppressor and oppressed, stood in constant opposition to one another, carried on an uninterrupted, now hidden, now open fight, a fight that each time ended, either in a revolutionary re-constitution of society at large, or in the common ruin of the contending classes.[27]

The focus of Marx's analysis, however, is not history, but rather the prediction of future revolution and the description of its causes, its nature, and its outcome. Marx presents an economic determinism: Economic forces shape social and political relationships. Chapter 2 has presented an analysis of Marx's views from a theoretical perspective, whereas here we consider a brief summary of their revolutionary implications. In capitalism, Marx sees that economic forces will lead inevitably to communist revolution. In capitalist societies, some people own the means of production while others do not. Marx believes that modern technology makes large-scale production less costly than small-scale production. Hence ownership will increasingly be concentrated in fewer hands. An ever-larger portion of the population will have to work as wage earners for this ever-diminishing capitalist class. "Society as a whole is more and more splitting up into two great hostile camps, into two great classes directly facing each other: Bourgeoisie and Proletariat."[28]

In his works entitled *Capital*, Marx analyzes the process of wage and price determination. He believes that capitalists will pay their workers less than the value that the workers create. Many readers of Marx have been enraged by this exploitation of the workers, but Marx examines the exploitation process scientifically rather than emotionally. He foresees a time when the capitalists will no longer be able to sell all they produce, since the workers will lack adequate purchasing power. This tendency towards ever-increasing overproduction will lead to increasingly severe depressions with larger and larger numbers of unemployed. In Marx's words,

> It is enough to mention the commercial crises that by their periodical return put on its trial, each time more threateningly, the existence of the entire bourgeois society. In these crises a great part not only of the existing products, but also of the previously created productive forces, are periodically destroyed. In these crises there breaks out an epidemic that, in all earlier epochs, would have seemed an absurdity – the epidemic of overproduction.[29]

Under these conditions, Marx believes that the revolution will inevitably succeed. The ever-smaller capitalist class will not be able to protect itself from the ever-larger proletariat whose rising unemployment will impel them to rebel. The increasingly severe depressions will create such discord and chaos that the need for a new economic system will be generally accepted. Marx foresees a new economic system in which all the means of production will be owned and operated collectively through the government. In the *Communist Manifesto,* he presents a series of ten steps through which the new economic system will be attained and which will define its operation:

1. Abolition of property in land and application of all rents of land to public purpose.
2. A heavy progressive or graduated income tax.
3. Abolition of all rights of inheritance.
4. Confiscation of the property of all emigrants and rebels.
5. Centralisation of credit in the hands of the State, by means of a national bank with State capital and an exclusive monopoly.
6. Centralisation of the means of communication and transport in the hands of the State.
7. Extension of factories and instruments of production owned by the state; the bringing into cultivation of waste-lands, and the improvement of the soil generally in accordance with a common plan.
8. Equal liability of all to labour. Establishment of industrial armies, especially for agriculture.
9. Combination of agriculture with manufacturing industries; gradual abolition of the distinction between town and country, by a more equable distribution of the population over the country.
10. Free education for all children in public schools. Abolition of children's factory labour in its present form. Combination of education with industrial production, etc., etc.[30]

It is interesting to note that the economic systems of many noncommunist nations have incorporated a number of these policies and programs. The economic systems of Europe and North America are now radically different from the free enterprise that Marx had criticized.

Free enterprise has been replaced, to a major degree, by other decision modes in which the people as a whole play a role through their government. It could well be that if Marx were living today, he might look favourably at these modern economic systems. He might even feel that, to a major degree, the revolution he predicted has already taken place in the capitalist world. With political democracy, the proletariat has won substantial victories through the electoral process. Voting has served as a substitute for violence in the transformation of economic systems.

Rostow and the stages of economic growth

Like Marx, Rostow focuses on the economic evolution of societies, and attempts to describe the forces of change. For Rostow, however, the shift from capitalism to communism is not an automatic process. Adoption of communism is a political decision rather than the result of economic determinism. The rejection of one economic system and the adoption of another involves complex ideological and social forces as well as economic causes. Comparing his own analysis with that of Marx, Rostow has emphasized this difference:

The first and most fundamental difference between the two analyses lies in the view taken of human motivation. Marx's system is, like classical economics, a set of more or less sophisticated logical deductions from the notion of profit maximization, if profit maximization is extended to cover, loosely, economic advantage. The most important analytic assertion in Marx's writings is the assertion in the *Communist Manifesto* that capitalism left no other nexus between man and man than naked self-interest, than callous cash payment.

In the stages-of-growth sequence, man is viewed as a more complex unit. He seeks not merely economic advantage, but also power, leisure, adventure, continuity of experience and security; he is concerned with his family, the familiar values of his regional and national culture, and a bit of fun down at the local. And beyond these diverse homely attachments, man is also capable of being moved by a sense of connection with human beings everywhere, who, he recognizes, share his essentially paradoxical condition. In short, net human behaviour is seen not as an act of maximization, but as an act of balancing alternative and often conflicting human objectives in the face of the range of choices men perceive to be open to them.

This notion of balance among alternatives perceived to be open is, of course, more complex and difficult than a simple maximization proposition; and it does not lead to a series of rigid, inevitable stages of history. It leads to patterns of choice made within the framework permitted by the changing setting of society: a setting itself the product both of objective real conditions and of the prior choices made by men which help determine the current setting which men confront.[31]

Despite these protestations, it is tempting to view Rostow's five stages of growth as economic determinism. Historically, each society experiences a long traditional stage when growth in its per capita production is severely limited. For centuries the production technology remains unchanged. Most economic activity is agricultural, and the hierarchical social structure provides little scope for vertical mobility. This *traditional* stage is replaced by a *preconditions* stage in which people become accustomed to change. An expansion of commerce widens the market and brings each society into contact with the practices of others. The landed regional power structure is replaced by a strong centralized government supported by popular feelings of nationalism. The preconditions stage leads naturally to a takeoff into self-sustaining growth. Rostow describes this "great watershed in the life of modern societies" as

the interval when the old blocks and resistances to steady growth are finally overcome. The forces making for economic progress . . . expand and come to dominate the society. Growth becomes its normal condition. Compound interest becomes built, as it were, into its habits and institutional structure.[32]

A key point is that the savings rate rises from 0–5 percent of the national income up to 10 percent or more. This permits rapid capital accumulation and the rapid introduction of new types of machinery and equipment. Inevitably, this process of change results in a new social order and new political structures, in which entrepreneurs acquire new power. During the takeoff in growth, a limited number of economic sectors form the leading component of change. During the fourth stage – *the drive to maturity* – entrepreneurship and progress extend throughout the entire society. Everyone accepts the desirability of innovation and the need to maintain a high national growth rate. People examine their social and political structures critically and are prepared to change any of the established practices if improvements can be made.

The fifth and final stage is the era of *high mass-consumption*. People are concerned about their current living standards, and they want collectively provided social security. They place increased emphasis on collective decision modes. At this stage, society has "ceased to accept the further extension of modern technology as an overriding objective."[33] Although Rostow's book was written over twenty-five years ago, today one may see the current environmental protection programs as an expression of this concern for the quality of life.

Rostow examines a variety of data for several countries, indicating when each passed through particular stages of economic growth. From this perspective, one can see striking similarities in the experiences of these nations. For example,

Russian economic development over the past century is remarkably similar to that of the United States, with a lag of about thirty-five years in the level of industrial output and a lag of about a half-century in per capita output in industry. ...The lesson of all this is, then, that there is nothing mysterious about the evolution of modern Russia. ... In the course of its take-off, it was struck by a major war, in which the precarious and changing balance between traditional and democratic political elements collapsed in the face of defeat and disorder and a particular form of modern societal organization took over control of a revolutionary situation it did not create.[34]

In Rostow's view, the Russian takeoff began in the 1890s and caused changes in social and political relationships. The First World War added greatly to these disruptions. The Communist victory of 1917 was not the logical and inevitable result of economic determinism as predicted by Marx. Rather, the Communist victory was the chance result of political manoeuvring by a skilled and determined cadre who happened to be Communists.

Why men rebel

In his book *Why Men Rebel,* Gurr emphasizes the concept of *relative deprivation.* Each person has a set of expectations about the material possessions and lifestyle to which he or she is rightfully entitled. At the same time, each person sees the capabilities he or she has to achieve or maintain these rightful expectations. Discontent and rebellion are caused by the gap between capabilities and expectations. "Societal conditions that increase the average level or intensity of expectations without increasing capabilities increase the intensity of discontent."[35] People look at the success of others with whom they identify and feel that they should be similarly rewarded. People listen to the promises of new opportunities and feel that they should be able to participate. "Deprivation-induced discontent is a general spur to action. Psychological theory and group conflict both suggest that the greater the intensity of discontent, the more likely is violence."[36]

In Gurr's opinion, relative deprivation causes a deep and enduring frustration which expresses itself in anger and violence. "If frustrations are sufficiently prolonged or sharply felt, aggression is quite likely, if not certain to occur."[37] Gurr links this view to the writings of other sociologists. In *The Natural History of Revolution,* Edwards claims that all revolutions are due to "repression of elemental wishes" in which "people come to feel that their legitimate aspirations and ideas are being repressed or perverted, that their entire property, desires, and ambitions are being hindered and thwarted."[38] In *The Process of Revolution,* Pettee puts this interpretation in terms of feeling "cramped":

People feel cramped when they find that satisfaction of their basic needs for liberty and security is interfered with, and moreover, regard this repression as unnecessary and unavoidable, hence unjustified.[39]

Gurr's phrase "relative deprivation" suggests that people compare their current condition with their own past condition as well as with the experiences of others. A number of factors can cause a shift in one's condition, leading to frustration, anger, and violence. Taxation – particularly taxation that is unexpected and that results from unforeseen changes in the rules – can alter one's income and wealth to a degree that one could consider unfair and objectionable. Shifts in political power can suddenly cause a decline in status for the losers as well as the elimination of financially advantageous opportunities that accompany that power. Economic change can also cause particular groups to suffer while other groups gain. New trade relationships can cause rapid shifts in relative affluence. Technological progress can make some professions obsolete and can make groups of businesses fail, while providing others with opportunities for quick fortunes. Immigration may entail a significant loss in social status for those who enter a new society.

Almost all the literature on collective violence assumes a causal connection between the existence of RD [relative deprivation] or some equivalent concept and the occurrence of violence. A direct relationship between the degree of discrepancy and the intensity of violence is usually implicit, sometimes explicit as it is in the formulation by Ridker, Lasswell and Kaplan, and the Feirabends.[40]

From this perspective, times of economic change automatically bring the potential for revolution. In the traditional society, everyone has an established and clear-cut role. Relationships have become customary and are supported by the society's generally accepted moral values, perhaps even by its religion. For each person, the appropriate code of conduct is unambiguous and receives material rewards in accordance with established practices. The governing elite possess unquestioned status and authority. Times of economic change disrupt all of this. Roles are altered. Relationships are radically new. Moral values and religion seem to lose their ability to provide guidance. The pattern of material rewards creates new winners and new losers. The financial winners acquire new social status and new political power.

The traditional society may undergo little revolutionary pressure in spite of the fact that its citizens live in extreme poverty. On the other hand, the society experiencing economic growth may suffer from revolutionary pressure in spite of its increasing prosperity. This perspective adds further weight to Rostow's discussion of the Russian Revolution of 1917. For seventy years, the preconditions for takeoff, and the takeoff itself, radically altered the established social, political, and economic relationships. The First World War and Russia's military losses added greatly to these disruptions. For hundreds of thousands – perhaps for millions – relative deprivation, frustration, and anger created a willingness to rebel.

Social conflict and social movements

Oberschall focuses on the mechanics and process of revolution. He discusses the competition between the established interests and the revolutionaries as they each seek the support of the masses. In this, he examines the emotional and nonrational elements as well as the conscious calculations by individuals of their risks and rewards. The revolution may be altered by the reaction of the established interests, and particularly by the implementation of reforms. Yet, ironically, the loosening of autocracy may stimulate revolutionary activity, rather than automatically bringing the resolution of conflicts. Revolutionary activity can take a wide variety of forms, ranging from peaceful strikes, demonstrations, and civil protest to spontaneous riots and organized violence. As in all human activity, there are emotional and nonrational factors that shape events. A group protest such as a strike or a riot can gather momentum and a spirit of its own.

Both sides lack full and accurate information about each other; they have misconceptions about each other's strengths and weaknesses; and they respond to concrete problems and choices in complex ways, with a mixture of outrage, anger, puzzlement, and shrewd informed calculation.[41]

Yet logical argument is at the core of a revolution.

In group conflict and social movement situations, the discontented group makes a claim to legitimacy for its goals, program, and actions in the name of ideals and values that have some legitimacy. Both sides compete for public support, for third-party support in the contest. The attempt by incumbents to pin the label of criminal or deviant upon their opponents and the corresponding efforts to paint established elites and their agents as corrupt, illegitimate, and unresponsive, are part of the strategy of conflict as all sides seek to mobilize and increase their human, material, and ideological resources at each other's expense.[42]

Oberschall discusses the individual's calculation of the benefits he or she may gain from a successful revolution and the losses that he or she may suffer if the revolution fails. Each individual weighs these risks and rewards in deciding whether to join the revolutionaries or the reactionaries. Oberschall sees the interaction of these individual decisions as a kind of game. Each individual wants to be on the winning side, and so each is influenced by the decisions of the others.

Any change can hurt some individuals while helping others, and so any change can cause individuals to contemplate revolution. From this perspective, we can view economic progress as potentially being a cause of revolution. Rising incomes may lead to discontent rather than satisfaction. Oberschall points to specific types of change as a source of insecurity, including population change, migration, the growth of cities, and new technology. Some groups, advancing and reaping unheard of profits, seek to speed the process of change and prepare to defend their gains against newer claimants. "Existing institutions and social arrangements are no longer suited to solve new problems of an altogether different order of magnitude. Dissatisfaction mounts; impatience, cramp, hatreds accumulate. Reforms lag behind new needs. . . . Change and conflict are intimately linked."[43] Oberschall emphasizes that the revolutionary forces will grow if the governing elite is unresponsive, prevents protests, and refuses to make concessions. Yet the process of granting reforms may itself cause greater discontent, particularly if the process is erratic, half-hearted, and subject to retractions. Thus, Oberschall discusses the many human elements that enter the mechanics and process of revolution. These various elements make prediction difficult, and they restrict the validity of simple explanations.

The Russian revolution

Since 1860, on several different occasions, the Russian people have abruptly changed their economic system in dramatic and substantial ways. Violence has usually accompanied these changes. Discontent and protest have been met with physical and ideological repression. The 1917 Revolution attracts special attention as the first Communist Revolution and, hence, as a model for future revolutionaries. The 1928 imposition of detailed central planning, agricultural collectivization, and the command economy also stands out as a model for Communist organization processes. But it is helpful in understanding these events to look as far back as the 1860s. The theories of revolution presented earlier find numerous illustrations throughout the century that followed the Crimean War.

Defeat in the Crimean War raised questions about the strength of a feudal, autocratic society in the midst of a modern European world. Seeking to rejuvenate his nation, the tsar abolished serfdom and introduced a series of major reforms. Elimination of the judicial and administrative powers of the landlords created a vacuum which the tsar tried to fill with elected assemblies, an independent judiciary, and a free press. With one sweep, the traditional social and cultural relationships were replaced by the new institutions and new practices of liberal democracy. Lacking experience with these institutions and practices, the Russian people lost their traditional faith in their leadership and became embroiled in debate and acrimony over the optimal path of change. The Crimean War had intruded on traditional relationships, opening the door to change. The pace and extent of reforms left many feeling the relative deprivation described by Ted Gurr.

As the 1860s and 1870s passed, the tsar placed limits on the degree of liberalization. Fearing that the judiciary's legal decisions were favouring the radicals, he withdrew increasing numbers of cases from the regular courts and placed them under the jurisdiction of the police. Opposition leaders were subject to arbitrary arrest. Election to the assemblies was not based on universal suffrage, and the unequal representation meant that the wealthy noble class dominated the assembly decisions. Arbitrary censorship interfered with freedom of the press. From this perspective, the 1860s reforms seem to have actually stimulated discontent and opposition. Bitterly disappointed intellectuals formed radical groups. Bakunin and his followers advocated the violent destruction of the existing regime and its replacement with cooperatives. Lavrov and his followers sought agrarian socialism through a gradual program of education and propaganda.

In 1881, Tsar Alexander II was assassinated and his son, Alexander III, assumed power. He immediately instituted a series of reactionary policies that restricted freedom and gave additional powers to the police and administrators. In the 1890s, the composition of the legislative assemblies, or *zemstvos,* was altered to increase the proportion of representatives from the noble class. Property qualifications became necessary to vote for city councils, or *dumas.* These restrictions intensified the opposition, and each of three broad groups gained widespread support.

The Social Revolutionary Party was established in 1901 as a coalescence of about fifty opposition groups. Their emphasis on an agricultural nation of peasant cooperatives represented the traditional opposition.

The Liberal Party focused on the principles of representative government and the rights of the individual. Its support came only from the recent experiences in the legislative assemblies, and, consequently, it lacked a strong tradition or indigenous philosophical writings. The Social Democratic Party advocated the Marxist revolution and Communism, with an emphasis on industrial workers and a revolutionary elite. Lenin's newspaper, *Iskra,* played an important role in winning popular support for the Social Democrats.

From its birth, *Iskra* was more than a revolutionary newspaper. It became one of the fountainheads of the Russian Social Democratic movement. From *Iskra* editorial headquarters, instructions radiated to hundreds of party cells throughout Russia. The party doctrines formulated in the pages of *Iskra* became the fighting program for groups of party members everywhere.[44]

Lenin felt that the Social Democrats should immediately seek political power and that this revolution could best be achieved through a small party of closeknit and dedicated professionals. Some Social Democrats disagreed, believing that capitalism would have to develop much further prior to a successful revolution and that party membership should be open to everyone. At a 1903 party convention, Lenin and his supporters won the elections for positions as officers of the party, thereby claiming the title of Bolsheviks, or the majority.

On January 22, 1905, a priest named Father Gapon organized a peaceful march to present a petition to the tsar. Father Gapon hoped for gradual improvement in the living and working conditions of the poor and he believed that a liberal, constitutional government could achieve this. His petition pleaded for this, and tens of thousands marched with him. Without warning, the army opened fire, killing hundreds. This outrageous and exaggerated reaction – together with Russia's military defeat by Japan – stirred opposition throughout Russia and inspired a series of revolutionary activities.

The first wave of strikes had hardly subsided when peasant revolts broke out in various parts of the country. The fever spread to the fringes of the Empire. Strikes in the Polish city of Lodz led to an armed rising which lasted nearly a week. Barricades covered the streets and squares of Warsaw and Odessa. In the port of Odessa, the crew of the cruiser Potemkin joined the revolt. In some cities, strikers elected Councils of Workers' Delegates – the first Soviets that emerged from the maelstrom of the popular movement. . . . In October a general strike spread from Moscow and Petersburg throughout the country. All railways came to a standstill.[45]

As a response to this widespread revolutionary activity, Tsar Nicholas signed the *October Manifesto* of 1905 which promised a series of liberal reforms – including acceptance of labour unions, universal suffrage, constitutional government, and a bill of rights. However, as in the 1870s and 1880s, these reforms were gradually limited and withdrawn.

The 1917 Revolution should be seen in the context of these historical events. The pattern of earlier revolutionary activities was repeated. Military defeat caused widespread discontent with Russia's leadership. In 1915 alone, Russia lost two million soldiers. By March 1917, civil disobedience and riots were breaking out across the country and Nicholas resigned as tsar. For the following ten months, the Liberal Party under Kerensky led a provisional government with legislative debate and a constitutional philosophy. Elections were called for November 25. Of the 36 million voters, only 25 percent voted for Bolshevik candidates, whereas 58 percent voted for the Social Revolutionary Party.

When the Constituent Assembly convened on January 18, 1918, Lenin's Bolsheviks physically attacked and dismissed the Assembly, and then decreed that they were in power. Lenin's emphasis on professional revolutionaries proved successful. In fact, the 1905 Revolution can be seen as an invaluable training experience for these professionals. Trotsky's 1905 seizure of power in St. Petersburg, for example, had provided practical knowledge and skills in how to combine mass propaganda with physical violence. Constantly focusing on how to win power allowed the Bolsheviks to be victorious even though they were outnumbered.

The 1917 Russian Revolution illustrates a number of the points made by social psychologists such as Gurr and Oberschall. The period after the Crimean War had witnessed the implementation and reversal of a series of major political and social reforms, as well as a period of substantial economic growth and change. Rapid shifts in the economy, as well as political and social relationships, meant that many groups experienced relative deprivation. Feelings of discontent were aggravated by defeats in the 1905 Japanese war and the First World War. Meanwhile, the Bolsheviks were able to create a skilled and devoted group of professional revolutionaries, trained in the revolt of 1905, and capable of exerting violence when resistance was weakest. Although not based on Marx's predictions of revolution as the final stage of capitalism, the Russian 1917 Revolution does stand out as a dramatic example of radical change in the economic system. As indicated in earlier chapters, however, the War Communism that was established in the 1917–20 period gave way to additional dramatic changes in the economic system. The 1928–33 period, in particular, was marked by violence. Whether these changes and the 1980s communist reforms deserve to be called revolutions is a matter of judgement.

The Lippmann thesis: Public philosophy

Walter Lippmann has discussed the relationships between a society's "public philosophy" and its political and economic system.[46] Lippmann has emphasized that if people are to play a major role as individuals, rather than being directed by a totalitarian government, then these individuals must share certain values and certain approaches to collective decision making. In particular, individuals must respect the right of others to disagree; they must be prepared to compromise; and they must sometimes sacrifice their own interests for the public good. Laws and regulations, by themselves, are not adequate to create a system where individuals act in such ways. It is not possible to graft liberal, free-enterprise mechanisms onto a society that lacks an appropriate public philosophy.

Lippmann's thesis provides an interesting perspective on the recent reforms in process in the USSR and Eastern Europe. Each society confronts limits to its reform process, based upon the society's unwritten social values. These limits cannot be quantified or expressed precisely. Nevertheless, these limits are real and they may impede the smooth operation of market mechanisms and the participation by individuals in both political and economic activity.

For the recent reforms to succeed, the communist nations must adopt a range of institutions and government practices with which they are not familiar. It is likely that these societies will need to make changes in regard to each decision mode discussed in earlier chapters. Yet the adoption of new institutions and practices will not by itself be enough. Unwritten conventions will have to develop if individuals, enterprises, and public servants are to relate with each other as they do in societies that have a long tradition of such decision modes. One can point to a basic level of trust on the part of customers, be they consumers or producers, that the supplier will provide an acceptable quality of product or service. Guarantees and reputations are built only over time. A spirit of compromise must exist if disagreements are to be resolved without violence. There must be some generally accepted concept of fairness in economic and political decisions. A sense of "civility" is necessary in all economic and political activities. How well can the reformed institutions and practices perform when these societies have had no experience with such a public philosophy? How quickly and effectively can an appropriate public philosophy be developed? Such questions are most significant in the context of substantial reforms such as those of the USSR and Eastern Europe in the 1980s and 1990s. Yet to some degree such questions are relevant in regard to gradual modifications as well.

Essay and discussion topics

1. Choose two or more objectives of a particular society and discuss the trade-offs that the society has experienced in pursuing these objectives.
2. Choose a particular reform of an economic system and describe the process through which the society reached its decision to implement the reform.
3. Discuss how the reform process within the USSR has changed over the years since 1917.
4. Choose two or more revolutions in economic systems. Compare and contrast the causes, processes, and impacts.
5. Discuss the reasons why a society may choose revolution rather than gradual change. Illustrate by the use of specific examples.
6. Discuss a particular author's views in regard to the transformation of economic systems from agricultural to commercial to industrial and, finally, to a service economy, and indicate the appropriateness of the word revolution for these transformations.

CHAPTER 11

Constraints imposed by the
new world economy

Introduction

For each society, the choice of an economic system is affected by that society's relationships with other economic systems. This can be seen clearly in cases of military or political domination, where both the ruler and the ruled adjust their economic systems in accordance with the realities of the domination. The existence of the British Empire in the eighteenth and nineteenth centuries meant that, for the many member societies, the choice of economic system was severely circumscribed. The Soviet Union extended its power over Eastern Europe after the Second World War in a manner which limited the options facing societies there. In recent decades, the United States has actively sought to influence the choices of many societies throughout the world, particularly in Central and South America. These cases of military and political intervention illustrate the necessity, when comparing economic systems, to consider each society's choices in the context of that society's relationships with other economic systems.

Relationships that are not military or political can also affect a society's choices. Of special importance are trade and investment. The development of trade relationships can strongly influence a society's economic system, particularly as the domestic structure adjusts to the provision of exports. The characteristics of a principal export, and its production requirements, may affect many features of the economic system and its decision modes, including the nature of employment relationships. The *staple theory,* for example, describes the reliance of some colonial societies in the nineteenth century on exports of wheat, timber, and cotton, and it explains how their economic systems were shaped by these exports. Even in recent decades, many societies continue to rely on the export of a narrow range of natural resources, with significant repercussions on their economic system.

As earlier chapters have indicated, the New World economy has facilitated the mobility of labour and capital, and this has also restricted each society's options. People and corporations may move away from

364

a particular society if its economic system becomes significantly different. Foreign investment can further restrict a society's options by transferring important decisions out of the hands of domestic citizens. Many societies today fear the possibility of such foreign influence, and so they look to collective decision making to play a larger role as a means of counteracting that foreign influence. In recent decades, foreign investment has increasingly occurred within multinational enterprises (MNEs), and it has increasingly been motivated by international differences in technology. Today the MNE links societies in ways that affect the economic systems of its host countries. At the same time, many societies perceive that their growth and prosperity depend upon their international competitiveness, and they look to collective action to stimulate the technological progress upon which that competitiveness is based. From this perspective as well, a society's choices concerning its economic system are not made in isolation from other societies, but rather are shaped by the realities of their relationships.

Although political and military domination have circumscribed many societies' choices concerning their economic systems, the perspective of this book relates more closely to the role of economic relationships. In view of the purpose of this book, this chapter deals exclusively with economic forces, particularly the growing significance of technology as a determinant of trade and investment, and hence as a determinant of the role of government. It also discusses the trade agreements that limit each signatory's choices in regard to decision modes.

The multinational enterprise

There is considerable disagreement on the consequences for the host country of extensive investment by foreigners, particularly by foreign MNEs. As indicated in Chapter 8, many have argued that industries dominated by multinationals consist of truncated branch plants that use inefficient methods of production and that are often limited to an assembly function. Production in these subsidiaries may be oriented to the domestic market with little export capability, while much of the product line is imported as finished products. Production only for the domestic market may mean short production runs that involve high unit costs. It is also believed that most of the key management functions, such as investment decisions, research and development (R&D), market research, and systems development, remain in the foreign country, with the subsidiaries' management role limited to sales and immediate supervision. Nationalists often point to foreign control as a significant factor explaining low productivity in the host country. On the other hand, the multinationalist position has been that subsidiaries improve the performance of industries in the host country through technology transfer that would otherwise occur at a much slower pace and at a higher cost. They also generate substantial employment and tax revenues, and they provide a larger market for materials and services.

According to neoclassical theory, international investment may be motivated by differentials in the interest rates. Capital will move from countries where interest rates are low because capital is plentiful, to countries where rates are high and capital is scarce. However, as Hymer has pointed out, the data on international capital movements do not support this theory.[1] Movements have been concentrated mainly among countries where capital is relatively abundant. There is also considerable cross investment between countries. Almost all foreign direct investment (FDI) is carried out by firms based in the United States, Japan, and a few European countries, and it tends to be concentrated in a fairly small number of industrial sectors, indicating that factors other than interest rate differentials are important determinants of MNE investments.

In Vernon's international product-cycle theory, MNE production and trade are linked to innovation and the international diffusion of new technology. This theory describes the links between trade and investment. In the first stage, a new product is developed and produced exclusively for the market where the innovation has been introduced. If the product is successful, it is exported and foreign direct investment is required to establish distribution and service facilities abroad. In the second stage, the world market for the product has grown and the product becomes standardized but the technology and scale of production continue to create barriers to entry. At this point, the firm may shift production to foreign subsidiaries to take advantage of cost differentials or, as a defensive measure, to retain its share in a market where local competitors could gain an advantage from local production. In the third stage, when the product has become completely standardized, production will be carried out where it is most economical. In cases where foreign production is cost effective, the MNE's home market might be served from abroad, although "the internationalization of production still implies the possibility of continuing exports of components and services or of complementary products by the parent firm."[2]

According to findings by Mansfield, it appears that the product cycle has been compressed in recent years, with the export stage being truncated and sometimes eliminated.[3] Knickerbocker has added to Vernon's theory through his observation of *oligopolistic reaction*. The more highly concentrated an industry is, the more likely it is that rival corporations will decide to establish foreign subsidiaries once the leading firm has pursued that option.[4] Wells, on the other hand, has explained the characteristics of multinationals based in developing countries through his theory of an international *pecking order* where technology, once it has become more or less standardized, is picked up by European or Japanese firms that adapt it for a lower-income market and export it to semi-industrialized countries which in turn will modify the product and sell it to less-developed countries (LDCs).[5]

Magee's *appropriability theory* of direct investment focuses on the returns to specific information. According to this theory, MNEs specialize in the production of information that is most efficiently transmitted intrafirm. The incentive is for MNEs to produce sophisticated technologies because it is easier to appropriate the returns from these.[6] From his review of the theoretical literature, Niosi has derived a set of hypotheses that provide a useful composite framework to study the role of multinationals. The main propositions are as follows:

a. *Capital travels primarily among countries where it is plentiful rather than to regions where it is scarce.* In other words, most foreign direct investment takes place between one developed country and another. Neither orthodox economic theories of the international movement of capital nor classical theories of imperialism explain this essential phenomenon.

b. Some industries breed multinational enterprises more prolifically than others. *Most manufacturing multinationals are found in the most concentrated industries and in those where research and development and technological barriers play the largest role.*

c. *Multinational corporations are most often the largest firms in each industry, the "leaders" of the branches in which multinationalization has occurred.* As a general a rule, they have a "special asset," which is often a technological advantage (new products or processes) but can also be an organizational advantage, better vertical integration, or any other advantage. It is the existence and variety of such advantages that explains cross investment in the same industry in advanced countries. . . .

d. *The products manufactured by large companies follow a cycle* that goes from innovation by a small oligopoly to gradual standardization by firms that by now have become multinational, and then to complete standardization of the product. At this last stage, as writers in the tradition of Vernon see it, the market becomes competitive. Others, such as Harry Magdoff, argue that concentration on a world scale does

not diminish and barriers to entry are not reduced with the standardization of the product. . . .

e. *As late-developing countries undertake the process of industrialization,
    they become home to their own local multinationals.* The main asset of
    these multinationals may be their adaptation of technology developed
    in an advanced country to a smaller market or a more labour-intensive
    production process.[7]

Rationalized product or process investments have formed a trend since
the 1970s, when some MNEs began adopting a centralized, integrated
production and marketing strategy with underlying global objectives.
Rationalized production within MNEs involves the specialization by
each subsidiary in certain products or components that are then exported
throughout the world, often by means of the MNE's distribution networks. Each subsidiary has certain *global mandates*. The specialization
in components has been "prompted mainly by growing differences in
labour costs between the advanced industrial and the developing countries and [it] tends to be concentrated in labour-intensive industries."[8]
End product specialization has benefited from the reduction in tariffs
throughout the world and the increasingly freer access to large, standardized markets. In the case of vertical or component specialization,
the lower labour costs and favourable tax and investment policies in
less-industrialized countries have been important factors, as has been
the reduction of tariffs on intrafirm trade through tariff remission programs in many countries. In the past, import-substituting investments
were often linked to high transport costs or tariffs which were obstacles
to trade. Increasingly today, rationalized product or process investments
"flourish in conditions of free trade and low transport costs."[9]

By 1980, import-substituting activities accounted for about 30 percent
of FDI stock according to Stopford and Dunning.[10] The primary sector
and rationalized investments each made up 20 percent, with the remaining 30 percent allocated to services. The rate of growth of rationalized investments in manufacturing and in services has been very strong
since 1970, while the primary sector has experienced a steady reduction
in international investment.

Multinational enterprises and the transfer of technology

One of the recurring themes in the literature on multinationals is that
of technology. In Hymer's work, the issue of technological advantage
is viewed as one of the main types of firm-specific advantages which, in
the presence of imperfect markets, allows firms to overcome the higher
costs of producing in a host country. Innovation and the process of

diffusion are also central to Vernon's product-cycle theory, whereas the *internalization* of markets in technology is a focus of Buckley and Casson's work.[11] According to Caves, the extent of R&D spending is a predictor of MNE activity in an industry:

> [H]ence, in those industries where most R&D takes place, both the R&D and foreign investments are likely to be concentrated among the larger firms. Just as R&D promotes foreign investment, it is possible that foreign investment promotes R&D. The established MNE has in hand the knowledge needed to predict the payout to innovations in diverse national markets, not just the home market. If the MNE's information network indeed yields an advantage for this purpose, it enjoys both a higher and more certain mean expected return from investments in innovation than a similarly placed single nation company.[12]

It is therefore not a coincidence to find that (1) the bulk of innovations still originate in the United States; (2) the United States accounts for approximately half of the industrial R&D expenditures among OECD countries; (3) the United States is the home country of more MNEs than any other country; and (4) U.S. MNEs invest the most, in aggregate and in comparison to other foreign-based MNEs, in technology-intensive sectors.

The results of a study by Mansfield, Romeo, and Wagner emphasize these technological relationships. First, it appears that the rate of return expected from R&D activities by a firm is directly related to the level of its overseas activities both in terms of exports and foreign subsidiaries. Second, the higher the level of expected return from R&D, the more likely the firm's orientation is towards basic research and long-term projects. Third, if the results of their R&D could not be exploited through their foreign subsidiaries, the firms estimated that their volume of R&D would drop by 12 to 18 percent.[13]

As Caves has indicated, a central issue is whether MNEs allocate R&D activity, as they do their production facilities, in order to maximize net revenue.[14] This issue relates to the transferability of technical knowledge across nations and to the economics of R&D activity.

> Effective execution of R&D requires a continuous interchange of information with the manufacturing facilities of the company for research to be directed to significant economic problems and for the R&D solutions to prove operational. Because of the strategic role of R&D, a similarly close interface with top corporate management is also important. These requirements for close communication and interchange, along with any scale economies in the R&D function itself seem to dominate the decision where to situate R&D activities. They call for centralization at company headquarters, but qualified by the centrifugal pull of manufacturing facilities dispersed to serve far-flung markets.[15]

Because MNEs tend to dominate the development of technology in the United States, they are also perceived as the key vehicle through which U.S. technology is exported.[16] MNE-based technology transfers can be channelled through exports of goods, licensing agreements, joint ventures, or through FDI. The multinational that sets up a subsidiary will transfer technology by training management and labour, by providing technology-specific information to engineers and technicians, by providing product-user services, and by creating incentives for suppliers to upgrade their technology.

In general, firms with adequate capital resources will undertake FDI rather than licensing, for appropriability reasons. The estimated life of the innovation, the level of complexity of the technology, and the concern to protect quality standards will all reinforce this preference. Licensing is more likely to be considered in cases where the foreign market is not sufficiently large, the firm lacks the necessary resources to undertake FDI, or there are expected returns from cross-licensing.

The MNE's role in the supply of technology is indicated by the extent to which this trade is among affiliates of the same parent company, and not on a third-party basis. For U.S.-based MNEs especially, management has strongly preferred to capitalize on their possession of proprietary technology rather than to license it to potential competitors.[17]

Technology transfers through multinational activities have become of major importance. However, the technology transfers appear to impact developed and developing countries differently. As reported by Mansfield, the mean age of technologies transferred to overseas subsidiaries in developed countries, in the 1960–78 period, was about six years, whereas transfers to developing countries occurred only after ten years. On the other hand, the mean age of technologies transferred through channels other than subsidiaries was much higher (thirteen years).[18] According to Stopford and Dunning, the technology strategies of MNEs are quite different between developed and developing countries. In developed countries, the more advanced forms of technology appear to be transferred in accordance with an overall international strategy. However, these transfers do not occur so readily in developing countries. Affiliate technology transfers appear to underlie the international investment by MNEs in the technologically advanced industries operating in developed countries.[19]

Multinational enterprises and employment

Because of the increasingly important role of MNEs, their impact on the level and composition of employment has become a key issue in many countries. In 1981, the 500 leading MNEs employed almost 26 million people. Taking account of home-country, as well as foreign-based, MNE employment, multinationals accounted for more than 40 percent of national industrial employment in nine of the wealthiest industrialized nations. Clearly, MNEs can have a major impact on a society's economic system. There has been some concern even in the United States over the employment impact of U.S. MNE operations. Allegations from American labour unions, for example, have claimed that through their expansion of manufacturing facilities abroad, MNEs have been a vehicle for exporting U.S. jobs.[20] Chaudhuri, in his paper on U.S. MNEs and American employment, proposes a conceptual framework based on the product-cycle theory and its links to FDI to explain the relationships involved. The fundamental issue underlying Chaudhuri's framework is to establish whether the location of production facilities abroad is necessary. Accordingly, it is considered that the foreign activities of MNEs involved chiefly in primary resources or services are not of concern, since location abroad is necessary to either exploit the resources or service the foreign markets. It is in manufacturing activities that employment gains or losses are an issue.[21]

In many cases, MNEs have adopted world product mandates (WPM) to serve the entire world market. There are several kinds of WPMs. These differ in relation to the level of risk to the parent and the level of control maintained by the parent.[22] One variation is full world product mandating in which all functions related to the product are carried out by the subsidiary and control is maintained over product renewal, evolutionary products, growth rates, exports, and other strategic policies. Another variation is partial world product mandating in which the subsidiary will carry out some R&D and total production but where international marketing and remaining policies are under parent control. A third variation is in strictly production mandates, in which the subsidiary carries out production and where R&D, if undertaken, is limited to product or process development and all strategic management occurs at the parent level. For the positive effects associated with a WPM to occur, it is generally agreed that at least a partial type of WPM is required. Because of the risks and costs associated with full WPMs, partial WPMs are also more likely to be implemented. Essentially, the decision to adopt a WPM strategy remains with the parent firm. It is generally agreed that the onus is on the subsidiary's management to promote and justify the feasibility of the WPM as a preferable option for the enterprise as a whole. But corporate headquarters management must also be receptive to the idea, a product line demarcation must be established, and some autonomy must be granted to the subsidiary.

The issue of efficient decentralization of R&D is important. The extent of scale economies involved is undoubtedly a factor, although studies have found that the problem is in keeping the proper balance between autonomy and control and that decentralization obviously complicates the nature of the control relationship between corporate headquarters and R&D.[23] It has also been suggested that although the early stages of R&D may be incompatible with WPMs, the later stages are perhaps more suitable.

Other relevant costs are those associated with restructuring the subsidiary from an import-substituting operation to a rationalized one, as opposed to the costs of closing existing facilities. The relative costs of production, transportation, and communication versus those of other locations will be considered. To the extent that WPMs are incompatible with trade impediments, low tariff rates and duty remission agreements will encourage WPMs. Government incentives may also play a significant role by providing tariff remission schemes, R&D and employment subsidies, tax incentives, and favoured government procurement status. These factors have already come into play in setting up a number of present mandates. As described by Etemad, from the parent company's viewpoint, the WPM could imply a reduction in risk associated with developing new technology, marketing, and investing as well as a reduction in sources, commitments, and responsibility.[24]

Throughout the world, the creation and diffusion of new technology is now perceived as the foundation for future economic growth and prosperity. The newly industrialized countries (NICs) are quickly adopting technologies that were created in the advanced economies of Western Europe and North America. This technology transfer, often through MNEs, has altered traditional patterns of comparative advantage and international trade. Meanwhile, societies with advanced economies have become increasingly concerned about their ability to innovate. This race for more efficient technology has become a major determinant of international competitiveness. As participants in this race, individuals and corporations now look to collective action to help them win, with education and research playing an increasingly important role. Rather than relying on free enterprise, societies are taking collective initiative to develop their technological capability.

The role of labour qualifications as a determinant of corporate location decisions is particularly important. Today's economies each include a wide variety of occupations, requiring different levels of education and skills and paying different levels of wages. A society that wants to attract the activities that offer high wages must develop the corresponding levels of education and skills. Labour is not homogeneous. Capital can be invested in labour so as to increase its economic value. Moreover, a society that ignores this relationship may be destined for the lower end of the job scale in the new world economy. To retain the best jobs and the highest wages, a society must continually educate and retrain its members. Corporations find that their sales mix is constantly changing. This trend has brought about a change of emphasis in production activities from economies of scale to economies of scope, whereby retaining a competitive lead requires the ability to respond to the constantly changing needs of the market. Indications are that this will result in labour requirements that emphasize greater skill level and adaptability. From this perspective, education and research can be seen as the central mechanisms for creative adjustment and competitiveness in an ever-changing world.

Trade composition and R&D

It is clear that nations differ markedly in their trade composition, with some nations consistently demonstrating a comparative advantage in R&D-intensive products. Table 11.1 illustrates this. For each of 1970, 1980, and 1984, manufacturing exports for each OECD nation are divided into three categories: high R&D, medium R&D, and low R&D. The share of each category in the nation's total exports is compared with the OECD average. This "revealed" comparative advantage indicates that the economies of the United States, Japan, and the United Kingdom are geared towards high-R&D exports, whereas the economies of many other nations are geared towards low-R&D exports.

Table 11.2 presents production statistics for eleven OECD nations for 1970 and 1980, indicating the percentage of total OECD output that is produced in each nation. Industries are grouped into three categories based on R&D intensity: high intensity, medium intensity, and low intensity. Within each of the six high-R&D industries, the United States and Japan account for more than half of the OECD production.

Stimulating technological progress in an international context

Should a government assist creativity and originality, or should it assist in the diffusion of innovations developed in other nations? A small country will capture a relatively small proportion of the gains from an original innovation since many of the firms that can exploit it operate in other jurisdictions. For a small country, the current state of international patent protection – which may offer inadequate legal power to capture all these foreign benefits – is an additional incentive for gov-

Table 11.1. *Apparent comparative advantage of manufacturing industry (OECD Average = 100)*

	High R&D			Medium R&D			Low R&D		
	1970	1980	1984	1970	1980	1984	1970	1980	1984
United States	158	156	156	109	106	98	63	64	64
Japan	123	141	147	78	105	101	114	75	68
EEC[1]	93	93	82	105	101	99	97	102	114
Germany	96	93	82	124	117	119	76	82	86
France	85	81	83	94	98	95	110	108	114
United Kingdom	104	121	118	117	108	98	81	80	89
Italy	77	62	56	99	91	90	111	128	141
Netherlands	97	76	62	62	71	74	139	143	156
Belgium-Luxembourg	44	47	37	94	98	101	127	125	137
Denmark	72	75	66	62	63	60	150	154	171
Ireland	71	113	159	21	56	54	192	146	120
Greece	14	17	13	60	35	31	176	211	244
Canada	55	48	43	124	108	127	91	112	100
Australia	17	26	19	66	71	78	160	166	169
New Zealand	4	9	9[2]	9	24	29[2]	233	231	234[2]
Austria	69	73	63	72	79	85	141	137	142
Finland	19	36	30	36	50	48	199	192	210
Iceland	0.6	3	0.5[2]	64	46	76[2]	176	208	183[2]
Norway	28	38	32	90	93	100	139	136	142
Portugal	46	59	49[2]	36	34	40[2]	188	196	199[2]
Spain	37	43	34[2]	62	86	83[2]	165	143	157[2]
Sweden	73	78	67	83	87	88	128	125	136
Switzerland	185	160	128	105	113	114	61	57	64
Turkey	11	9	10	46	35	28	192	218	249

[1]Excluding inter-EEC trade.
[2]1983.
Source: OECD, *OECD Science and Technology Indicators* (Paris: OECD, 1986), p. 71.

ernments and private interests to invest in diffusion. This situation demonstrates a weakness in the common reference to research and development. Basic research, even when it leads to specific innovations, may yield gains that cannot easily be captured by the innovating firm or by others within the country of origin. Development funds that enable an innovating firm to adopt and adapt practices that have already been discovered may provide benefits, of which a much higher proportion can be captured by that firm or by others within the same country.

Private interests may rationally reject certain types of research and development because they correctly recognize their inability to capture an adequate portion of the favourable results. To the extent that such private rejection is based upon the probable capture of favourable results by other firms in the same nation, a society may act collectively to stimulate research and development, knowing that its citizens, as a group, will capture and benefit from all the favourable results. Subsidies to cover part of the costs of innovation may be the only means whereby a society can achieve a technological advance that is financially worthwhile for that society as a whole. A difficult element enters when one attempts to calculate the degree to which the favourable results will be captured by other nations rather than by one's fellow citizens. How can one predict the ability of other nations to copy the advance, the price at which they will market the products that result from it, and the time scale of such responses? These are particularly serious questions in a world where industry is being rapidly restructured and where trade relationships are changing. International agreements to protect patents, together with international flows of trade and investment, tend to counteract these free-rider problems. However, many nations refuse to sign such agreements, and their enforceability is limited.

International trade patterns, and the agreements on which they are based, are affected by entrepreneurial activities which bring down costs and provide new and better consumer products. A nation's entrepreneurial success may create advantages for its trading partners by reducing the prices they pay for their imports. Yet disadvantages may accrue as well, since competitors may have to make adjustments or fall by the wayside. The losses and adjustment difficulties in the noninnovating society lead to even more frustration if the foreign innovation has been helped by a foreign government's financial assistance. With government programs to stimulate entrepreneurship, the total production costs of economic activities diverge from the individual firm's cost. In such cases, export prices may be much less than total costs would be if public funds were included as part of the real production costs. Consequently, the trading partner whose businesses are being compelled to adjust may justifiably regard the entrepreneurial achievements as unfair competition. A government's programs to stimulate entrepreneurship may prompt foreign governments to respond as their domestic producers realize how they are being hurt.

Trade agreements

Many international agreements seek to limit each signatory's freedom to distort relative prices, and hence they tend to restrict each signatory's choices in regard to its economic system. In understanding why societies that once opted for tariff protection have been shifting in recent decades

Table 11.2. *Share of manufacturing industry in OECD output (11 countries), grouped by R&D intensity*

	United States		Japan		Germany		France		United Kingdom	
	1970	1980	1970	1980	1970	1980	1970	1980	1970	1980
High intensity										
Aerospace	80.9	60.6	0.9	1.0	2.5	5.8	4.7	14.3	5.4	10.2
Computers	52.3	48.6	10.5	17.0	10.1	10.3	4.9	5.8	6.4	6.3
Electronics – components	48.4	33.3	21.7	28.8	7.4	9.0	4.3	8.1	8.4	7.5
Drugs and medicine	41.6	33.2	16.6	18.5	10.5	13.9	9.9	13.2	5.9	7.7
Instruments	51.9	44.1	18.9	26.0	12.3	13.0	4.1	4.3	6.8	7.2
Electrical machinery	42.7	31.2	17.8	23.0	11.3	12.4	6.6	9.2	7.7	8.1
Medium intensity										
Motor vehicles	49.8	40.4	13.9	19.6	10.8	13.5	6.0	8.2	6.9	4.6
Chemicals	45.8	43.6	14.1	14.3	12.5	13.0	6.0	7.8	7.8	7.3
Other manufacturing industries	54.3	40.0	16.0	25.5	8.1	8.3	6.3	9.7	5.1	5.9
Non-electrical machinery	46.1	38.1	15.7	17.5	12.3	14.3	6.8	9.8	7.2	7.9
Rubber, plastics	45.3	39.3	17.1	23.8	7.3	7.2	6.9	10.0	9.2	6.9
Nonferrous metals	47.7	46.4	15.2	12.3	11.2	9.9	7.2	9.9	7.2	6.9
Low intensity										
Stone, clay, glass	38.7	31.0	16.5	22.2	11.5	11.0	6.2	10.7	7.6	7.5
Food, drink	46.7	40.0	10.6	16.0	7.2	8.4	9.5	10.6	9.2	8.7
Shipbuilding	34.1	39.6	28.6	22.1	8.1	6.4	5.9	7.2	7.0	6.3
Petroleum refineries	49.1	51.2	10.1	15.1	8.5	3.7	12.3	9.9	7.7	7.4
Ferrous metals	34.5	34.5	20.6	23.2	12.3	11.5	7.9	7.8	6.9	7.5
Fabricated metal products	45.4	42.6	17.7	20.7	11.2	13.0	4.1	5.6	8.8	5.6
Paper, printing	53.6	46.3	11.6	15.8	6.0	7.1	5.3	7.2	7.4	7.0
Wood, cork, furniture	40.7	34.2	20.1	21.8	8.5	12.3	6.2	7.6	6.0	5.6
Textiles, footwear, leather	44.0	37.2	12.5	17.6	11.0	11.6	8.2	10.1	7.8	7.1

Source: OECD, *OECD Science and Technology Indicators* (Paris: OECD, 1986), p. 117.

Italy		Canada		Australia		Sweden		Netherlands		Belgium	
1970	1980	1970	1980	1970	1980	1970	1980	1970	1980	1970	1980
1.3	1.6	2.0	2.5	0.4	0.9	1.0	1.5	0.4	1.6	..	..
10.1	6.0	1.3	0.7	0.2	1.0	2.1	1.2	0.9	1.8	0.7	0.9
2.9	4.6	1.8	1.4	0.6	0.6	1.0	1.8	2.2	3.3	0.8	1.2
8.7	6.3	2.1	1.5	0.9	1.1	0.7	1.0	1.5	1.8	1.1	1.4
2.3	1.4	2.0	1.5	0.3	0.5	0.6	0.7	0.2	0.8	0.08	0.03
6.0	7.4	2.8	2.5	1.1	1.0	1.3	1.5	1.5	2.3	0.8	0.9
3.6	4.3	4.5	4.2	1.3	1.0	1.2	1.7	0.2	0.5	1.3	1.6
5.3	4.3	2.5	2.3	1.1	1.2	0.9	0.8	2.0	3.2	1.5	1.9
4.5	4.5	3.3	2.5	0.9	1.0	0.6	0.7	0.3	0.7	0.1	0.2
5.5	5.1	1.7	1.9	0.8	0.7	1.7	1.9	0.6	1.0	1.0	1.2
6.0	5.0	2.8	2.3	1.5	1.4	1.1	0.9	1.1	1.3	1.2	1.4
3.0	3.0	2.1	1.7	1.9	4.6	1.7	1.6	0.9	1.5	1.4	1.8
9.2	7.2	2.9	2.7	1.6	1.8	1.6	1.3	1.4	1.8	2.3	2.4
4.8	4.6	4.2	3.4	1.9	1.9	1.5	1.3	2.7	3.3	1.2	1.4
3.5	3.8	2.2	2.1	1.1	1.4	4.9	3.8	3.0	4.3	1.1	2.6
3.6	3.5	3.5	3.0	0.4	0.2	0.6	1.4	2.2	3.1	1.3	1.1
6.8	5.7	2.7	2.9	1.5	1.5	1.7	1.5	1.6	0.8	3.1	2.7
3.9	3.2	3.3	3.3	1.3	1.6	1.7	1.7	1.2	1.5	0.9	0.9
3.8	2.9	5.5	5.3	1.1	1.3	2.8	3.2	1.6	2.4	0.8	0.9
4.9	3.3	5.8	6.2	1.6	1.8	3.5	3.8	1.0	1.4	1.3	1.6
8.1	8.3	3.2	3.3	1.1	1.1	0.8	0.6	1.4	1.1	1.4	1.5

towards the negotiation of free trade, it is helpful to focus on the changing interests of producers. A major factor causing changes in producer interests has been the globalization of assets. Many corporations have been losing their identification with a single nation. Many corporate shareholders do not live in, and are not citizens of, the country where their corporate facilities are located. Linked with this is the globalization of production. Traditionally, all MNE decisions were made in the head office, and subsidiaries produced as instructed. Usually, the product mix was identical to the parent's product mix. The subsidiary had short production runs that were high cost. Today, for many MNEs, the head office is a marketplace for evaluating competitive bids for world mandates. Each subsidiary produces for the world market and enjoys economies of scale. In the past, the local enterprise sought tariffs to protect its sales domestically. In recent years, many MNEs have been able to negotiate special duty remission agreements as part of their rationalized production and global mandates. For many countries a major portion of imports and exports are intra-MNE transactions, many of these being intermediate rather than final products. In this way, free trade was established within MNEs prior to international political agreements, and free-trade agreements can be seen as a political response to the changing interests of producers.

Instead of tariffs, today's enterprises often seek alternative government assistance. The growing significance of technology leads more firms to seek R&D assistance. Through innovation, a firm may alter the global market structure for its products. In the extreme, a political entity might achieve a world monopoly, and alter the international terms of trade. A substantial body of recent trade literature deals with competitive behavior when few producers exist, such that decisions of one firm directly affect the welfare of the others.[25] Game theoretic analysis suggests a variety of strategic reactions. Much of this discussion is relevant in considering the use of subsidies by political entities in order to maximize their producers' interests vis-à-vis those of other political entities.[26]

The relatively greater role of services in the production and employment of most modern economies has also changed the interests of producers. Ronald Kutscher has noted that over the period 1959–85, U.S. employment grew by over 42 million. Of this growth, 93.5 percent took place in the service sector. "As a result, over that period very little growth in absolute employment has taken place in the goods-producing industries. Another way of looking at these developments is to note that the service industries' share of employment has risen from 60 percent in 1959 to nearly 73 percent in 1985. In general, these trends are the same as those in most other industrial countries."[27] For services, tariffs offer few benefits. Protection, if it is to be achieved, must be implemented through alternative instruments such as immigration restrictions, professional regulations, or limitations on foreign investment.[28]

Seen together, these changing interests of producers have diminished the relative strength of political support for protective tariffs. At the same time, the growth of services has meant that tariffs, since they affect goods prices only, are an increasingly arbitrary form of taxation. From this perspective, tariff reductions can also be seen as a type of tax reform that may establish a more uniform tax system.

The Uruguay round of GATT negotiations focuses on several sets of issues other than tariffs, and these can be seen as a direct response to new concerns of U.S. corporations. For U.S. companies today, the protection of intellectual property is necessary to prevent counterfeit products from flooding the U.S. market. The recent growth of services has resulted in U.S. corporate demands for freer access by their personnel to foreign markets. The export of services requires a local presence, and so investment policies have acquired a new significance. Corporations in other developed countries share these concerns.

Much of the trade literature has focused on tariffs as the major government instrument of price distortions, and much of the free-trade discussion has focused on the reduction of tariffs. However, many other government activities also distort prices, shifting price ratios from those that would develop in a private market without a government. As earlier chapters have indicated, recent decades have witnessed a vast expansion of these alternative decision modes, and individual interests actively lobby government for a myriad of regulatory policies and subsidy programs. Free-trade agreements will likely focus on the elimination of these sector-specific and region-specific policies and programs, or at least the harmonization of these among the signatories, so that price distortions are similar in the economy of each signatory.

The politics of free trade includes the development of international agreements in regard to these alternative decision modes. There is some disagreement about the provisions that these agreements should make for retaliating against trade-impacting subsidies in other countries. The view of the injury-only school is summarized by Richard Cooper as follows:

[P]erhaps we should not worry so much about government subsidies to economic activity – or rather government intervention of all types – as far as their effects on foreign trade are concerned, provided the interventions are introduced sufficiently gradually so that they do not impose acute adjustment costs on economic activities outside the country in question.[29]

The view of the anti-distortion school, on the other hand, is that subsidies are bad and "that even a very low threshold of trade impact warrants the imposition of penalties, and that the penalty should offset, as nearly as possible, the initial distortion."[30]

As Chapter 6 has shown, the process for analyzing and negotiating subsidy agreements will be complex, lengthy, and difficult. It will involve processes beyond those normally required for tariff negotiations, and it will require a thorough understanding of individual firms, products, and sectors. A special concern is that subsidies may benefit society as a whole if the subsidized investment and production result in benefits that are external to the firm, such as the employment of those who would otherwise be unemployed. Hence an agreement to reduce subsidies may not be in the interests of the signatories.

With the shift to decision modes other than tariffs, the impact on relative prices becomes less clear. It is often the case that the measurement and comparison of these alternatives must be less precise than the measurement and comparison of tariffs. Trade agreements have usually placed the concept of transparency as a basic objective in negotiations. With political agreements to reduce tariffs and with the shift to alternatives, the traditional objective of transparency will likely suffer considerably.

Many of the alternative decision modes are exercised by subnational governments, and so the rights and responsibilities of subnational governments form an essential component of free trade. Richard Simeon has emphasized that "to achieve its minimal objectives, a trade agreement must constrain provincial and state, as well as federal, activities."[31] However, in many federal states the subnational governments have been guaranteed certain powers in a constitution. Included in this politically more difficult sphere could be various kinds of subsidies, sector-specific or region-specific tax concessions, government-owned enterprises, sector-specific regulations, and government procurement policies. With these, subnational governments may have rights and powers that a national government cannot bind in international agreements. Price distortions may be particularly important in a nation's attempt to provide financial assistance to those regions experiencing relative economic privation. A wide variety of assistance programs may be considered essential, and yet these may distort prices in a way that trading partners consider unfair. Some assistance programs may even be embedded in a constitution.

It can be argued that free trade need not involve the complete elimination of price distortions, but only the creation of similar patterns of
price distortions in the signatory countries. What is clear is that the
establishment of free trade requires a harmonization, if not elimination,
of government decision modes in the signatory countries, in order that
similar price ratios will exist. From this perspective, the extent and
nature of free-trade agreements will be determined by the degree to
which potential signatories share common producer and citizen interests.
It appears that such commonalities of interests are most extensive among
countries that are geographically close. Hence we may expect the creation of more thorough agreements on a regional level, rather than on
a global level.

In a very broad sense, similarity of producer and citizen preferences
for the alternative decision modes is an essential determinant of the
extent and nature of free-trade agreements. This includes similar attitudes towards government ownership, toward the regulation of particular sectors such as financial institutions and telecommunications,
towards subsidies for economically disadvantaged regions, and towards
subsidies for new technology and for education and retraining. It is only
with a similar pattern of producer and citizen interests that societies can
agree to a similar pattern of price distortions and consequently a meaningful free-trade agreement covering these alternative decision modes.
Recent popular shifts towards restraining the role of government and
relying on free enterprise make free-trade agreements more feasible.
From this perspective, one can understand the creation of regional free-
trade agreements at the same time as the creation of new GATT agreements to liberalize trade. GATT free-trade agreements may never be
as extensive and meaningful as regional free-trade agreements. Consequently, it is reasonable to expect continual developments both at the
regional level and also at the GATT level. From the perspective of this
text, such two-track negotiations seem inevitable.

Whereas much trade literature has been based upon static analyses
and the calculation of individual interests as currently perceived, the
writings of Olson and his followers have emphasized the dynamics of
economic growth and the importance of continual change in the
growth process. For Olson, the future interests of the society as a
whole may not be attained if vested interests determine political decisions.[32] Olson emphasizes that the creation of free trade can result in
substantial benefits for future generations. It is also likely that the
creation of free trade may significantly alter production processes to
such a degree that historical data lose their usefulness and models
developed on the basis of historical relationships lose their predictive

382   **Choosing objectives and decision modes**

value. It is here that we see considerable scope for the emphasis by
political scientists on the role of political leadership. Individual political leaders may believe and advocate a vision of society's future benefits from free trade that cannot be tested empirically prior to the
implementation of new trade agreements. In fact, the political choice
of free trade may be motivated by such a vision as well as by self-in-
terested short-run calculations.

Recently, many economists have discussed the dynamic gains in economic growth that may result from free trade. Robert Baldwin, for
example, has emphasized the benefits of a higher growth rate for those
societies that minimize government price distortions, particularly those
involving trade barriers.

One of the most significant economic relationships demonstrated with a high
degree of consistency over the last forty years is the greater rate of economic
growth enjoyed by outward-looking countries pursuing liberal, market-oriented
policies than by countries whose governments interfere extensively with domestic
and foreign trade. An impressive body of evidence from both developed and
developing nations supports this conclusion.[33]

Milton Friedman has also stressed the benefits of freer trade for a
society as a whole. He has recommended that economists attempt to
influence public policy, "by analyzing the changes in institutional arrangements that would bring about the desired results and trying to
persuade the public to introduce those institutional changes rather than
trying to influence policymakers directly."[34] Friedman has advocated a
constitutional amendment in the United States as a basic institutional
change to prevent Congress from restricting trade.

In the postwar period, the USSR and Eastern European countries
conducted trade under an agreement known as COMECON. This
agreement provided for planned exchanges of commodities, such that
individual enterprises and ministries had little freedom in responsibility for trade. With the recent reforms, the planning process for trade
is being reexamined, with the possibility that greater freedom will
be given to enterprises and that market prices may be a trade determinant.

The new world economy

This chapter has described a new world economy in which a number of
historical barriers and divisions are disappearing very quickly. The economic integration of separate political entities is clearly a significant
development for comparative economic systems. New international

agreements may tend to erase political boundaries. In our post–1945 world, the General Agreement on Tariffs and Trade (GATT) negotiations have reduced tariffs and have sought to reduce other trade barriers. Regional trade agreements such as those of the European Economic Community have removed political boundaries for a number of purposes. Quite apart from international agreements, a key role in this economic integration is being played by MNEs, which are responsible for a large portion of the industrial investment within most noncommunist countries. As we have seen, the networks of parents and subsidiaries have become mechanisms for rapidly transferring production technology as well as goods and services. The practice of allocating global missions or product mandates among the subsidiaries of MNEs has enabled MNEs to achieve economies of specialization and scale – and the gains from trade – quite apart from political agreements to reduce trade barriers.

The establishment of subsidiaries within large numbers of political entities has enabled MNEs to apply for subsidies from each government and to apply for preferential treatment in government procurement. That is, MNEs have become local residents of many countries, and are therefore able to avoid nontariff barriers that might otherwise distort trade patterns. Regulations designed to assist domestic firms to the detriment of foreign firms can often be complied with by the local subsidiary of the MNE. Within federal states, where state or provincial governments have their own separate subsidies, procurement preferences, and regulations, the national corporation with branches in each state or province can avoid these trade barriers in the same manner as the MNE can on the international scene. In these ways, quite apart from any new political agreements, closer economic integration is occurring automatically among separate political entities.

For the modern economy, change has become a continuous, everpresent feature, with an emphasis on international investment and the diffusion of new technology. Both the process of technological change and the trend towards greater international integration are continually opening up new trade and investment opportunities. At the same time, certain economic activities are being eliminated, together with the accompanying jobs and incomes. Whether a society will be hurt by these developments or will take advantage of them may depend largely on its economic system. The new world economy, with its integration and competitiveness, will impact societies' choices in regard to economic systems, as well as impact the relative success of alternative economic systems.

Essay and discussion topics

1. Discuss the impact of recent trends in globalization on the ability of a society to create an independent economic system.
2. Discuss the impact of one or more trade agreements on the ability of a society to create an independent economic system.
3. Discuss the constraints faced by a provincial or state society in the creation of its distinct economic system within a political federation.
4. Discuss the advantages and disadvantages for an economic system of the growth of multinational enterprises. Illustrate by the use of specific examples.

Notes

Chapter 2

1. Simon Kuznets, *Modern Economic Growth: Rate Structure and Spread* (New Haven, CT: Yale University Press, 1966), p. 72.
2. Ibid., pp. 81–2.
3. Donnella H. Meadows, Dennis L. Meadows, Jorgen Randers, and William W. Behrens III, *The Limits to Growth: A Report for The Club of Rome's Project on the Predicament of Mankind* (New York: Universe Books, 1972), pp. 189–90.
4. James Tobin, "Macroeconomic Diagnosis and Prescription," in Morley Gunderson, Noah M. Meltz, and Sylvia Ostry, eds., *Unemployment: International Perspectives* (Toronto: University of Toronto Press, 1987).
5. Ibid., p. 36.
6. Ibid.
7. Michael Ellman, "Eurosclerosis?," in Gunderson et al.
8. Ibid., p. 47.
9. Kuznets, pp. 352–3.
10. Paul R. Gregory and Robert C. Stuart, *Soviet Economic Structure and Performance* (New York: Harper and Row, 1981).
11. John P. Hardt and Donna L. Gold, "Economic Reform: Soviet Style," in Hans-Joachim Veen, ed., *From Brezhnev to Gorbachev: Domestic Affairs and Soviet Foreign Policy* (New York: St. Martin's, 1984).
12. Ibid., p. 109.
13. Philip Hanson, "The Economy," in Martin McCauley, ed., *The Soviet Union under Gorbachev.* (New York: St. Martin's, 1987), pp. 97–8.
14. For a further discussion of adjustment issues, see Charles Pearson and Gary Salembier, *Trade, Employment, and Adjustment* (Montreal: Institute for Research on Public Policy, 1983).
15. Martin Weitzman, *The Share Economy: Conquering Stagflation* (Cambridge, MA: Harvard University Press, 1984).
16. Ibid., p. 87.
17. Ibid., p. 88.
18. Joseph A. Schumpeter, *The Theory of Economic Development* (New York: Oxford University Press, 1961).
19. Ibid.
20. Mancur Olson, *The Rise and Decline of Nations: Economic Growth, Stagflation, and Social Rigidities* (New Haven, CT: Yale University Press, 1982).

385

21. Dennis C. Mueller, *Public Choice* (New York: Cambridge University Press, 1979).
22. Olson, p. 74.
23. Ibid., p. 76.
24. Ibid., pp. 78–9.
25. Sidney Greenfield, Arnold Strickson, and Robert T. Aubey, eds., *Entrepreneurs in Cultural Context* (Albuquerque: University of New Mexico Press, 1979), p. vii.
26. Schumpeter, p. 83.
27. Ibid.
28. David Landes, *The Unbound Prometheus: Technological Change and Industrial Development in Western Europe from 1750 to the Present* (Cambridge: Cambridge University Press, 1969), p. 545.
29. Ibid., p. 544.
30. Ibid., p. 545.
31. Paul H. Wilken, *Entrepreneurship: A Comparative Historical Study* (Norwood, NJ: ABLEX Publishing, 1979), p. 11.
32. Everett E. Hagen, *On the Theory of Social Change* (Homewood, IL: Dorsey, 1962), p. 11.
33. Ibid., p. 197.
34. Wilken, p. 12.
35. Robert B. Reich, *The Next American Frontier* (New York: Times Books, 1983), pp. 16 and 20.
36. William G. Ouchi, *How American Business Can Meet the Japanese Challenge* (Reading, MA: Addison-Wesley, 1981), p. 50.
37. Anthony G. Athos and Richard T. Pascale, *The Art of Japanese Management: Applications for American Executives* (New York: Simon and Schuster, 1981), p. 125.
38. Moses Shapiro, "The Entrepreneurial Individual in the Large Organization," in Jules Backman, ed., *Entrepreneurship and the Outlook for America* (New York: Free Press, 1983), p. 60.
39. See, for example, Steven Shavell, "On Moral Hazard and Insurance," *Quarterly Journal of Economics* (November 1979), pp. 541–61.
40. Richard G. Harris, Frank D. Lewis, and Douglas D. Purvis, "Market Adjustment and Government Policy," in Douglas D. Purvis, ed., *Economic Adjustment and Public Policy in Canada* (Kingston,: Ont. Queen's University Press, 1984), p. 112.
41. Economic Council of Canada, *The Bottom Line: Technology, Trade and Income Growth* (Ottawa: Minister of Supply and Services, 1983), p. 32.
42. Joshua Ronen, *Entrepreneurship* (Lexington, MA: D.C. Heath, 1982), p. 3.
43. Ibid., p. x.
44. Victor Thompson, *Bureaucracy and Innovation* (Birmingham, AL: University of Alabama Press, 1969), p. 19.
45. Ibid.
46. Ibid., p. 14.
47. Ibid., p. 11.

48. Kenneth J. Arrow, "Innovation in Large and Small Firms," in Joshua Ronen, p. 16.
49. Economic Council of Canada, p. 5.
50. Alice Rivlin, *Systematic Thinking for Social Action* (Washington, DC: Brookings Institution, 1970), p. 120.
51. Ibid.
52. Michael Denny and Melvin Fuss, *Productivity: A Selective Survey of Recent Developments and the Canadian Experience* (Toronto: Ontario Economic Council, 1982), p. 54.
53. John Kenneth Galbraith, *The Age of Uncertainty* (Boston: Houghton Mifflin 1977), p. 7.

Chapter 3

1. John Locke, *Two Treatises of Government* (Cambridge: Cambridge University Press, 1980), p. 341.
2. Ibid., p. 342.
3. Jean-Jacques Rousseau *On the Social Contract, Discourse on the Origin of Inequality, Discourse on Political Economy*, translated and edited by Donald A. Cress (Indianapolis, IN: Hackett, 1983), p. 124.
4. Rousseau, *On the Social Contract*, p. 17.
5. Rousseau, *Discourse on the Origin of Inequality*, p. 145.
6. Rousseau, *On the Social Contract*, p. 24.
7. John Stuart Mill, *Utilitarianism, On Liberty, and Considerations on Representative Government*, edited by H. B. Acton (Guernsey, Channel Islands: Guernsey Press, 1972), p. 139.
8. Ibid., p. 12.
9. Ibid., p. 16.
10. Ibid., p. 7.
11. Ibid., p. 8.
12. Ibid., p. 9.
13. Ibid., p. 73.
14. C. B. Macpherson, ed., *Burke* (London: Oxford University Press, 1980), p. 41.
15. F. A. Hayek, *Law, Legislation, and Liberty*, Vol. 1 (London: Routledge and Kegan Paul, 1960), p. 121.
16. Robert Nozick, *Anarchy, State, and Utopia* (New York: Basic 1974), p. 161.
17. Ibid., p. 151.
18. Milton Friedman, *Capitalism and Freedom* (Chicago: University of Chicago Press, 1962), pp. 8 and 15.
19. Robert Hale, "Coercion and Distribution in a Supposedly Non-Coercive State," *Political Science Quarterly* 38 (1923), p. 604.
20. See, for example,

"Tortious Interference with Contractual Relations in the Nineteenth Century: The Transformation of Property, Contract, and Tort," *Harvard Law Review* (1980), pp. 1510–39.

Isaiah Berlin, *Four Essays on Liberty* Oxford: Oxford University Press, 1969).

Anthony T. Kroniman, "Contract Law and Distributive Justice," *Yale Law Journal* 89 (1980), pp. 472–511.

21. John Rawls, *A Theory of Justice* (Cambridge: The Belknap Press, 1971).
22. Ibid., pp. 302 and 831.
23. Karl Marx, "Capital: An Analysis of Capitalist Production (1867–1883)," in Max Eastman, ed., *Capital, The Communist Manifesto, and Other Writings of Karl Marx* (New York: Random House, 1932), p. 184.
24. Gordon Tullock, *Economics of Income Redistribution* (Boston: Kluwer-Nijhoff, 1983), p. 2.
25. Bradley Schiller, *The Economics of Poverty and Discrimination* (Englewood Cliffs,: Prentice-Hall, 1980), p. 166.
26. Maddison, "Origins and Impact of the Welfare State, 1883–1983," *Banca Nazionale del Lavoro Quarterly Review* 37 (1984), pp. 55–87.
27. Morley Gunderson, *Economics of Poverty and Income Distribution* (Toronto: Butterworths, 1983).
28. Ibid., p. 47.
29. Abram Bergson, "Income Inequality Under Soviet Socialism," *Journal of Economic Literature* 22 (September 1984), pp. 1052–99.
30. For an analysis of this issue in the Canadian context, see Derek P. J. Hum, *Federalism and the Poor: A Review of the Canadian Assistance Plan* (Toronto: Ontario Economic Council), Chapter 5.
31. Charles Murray, *Losing Ground: American Social Policy, 1950–1980* (New York: Basic, 1984).
32. Ibid.

Chapter 4

1. Adam Smith, *An Inquiry into the Nature and Causes of the Wealth of Nations* (Chicago: University of Chicago Press, 1976).
2. Ibid., p. 477.
3. See Henri Lepage, *Tomorrow Capitalism* (LaSalle: Open Court, 1982).
4. Leon Walras, *Elements of Pure Economics,* translated by William Jaffe (Homewood, IL: Irwin, 1954).
5. See Robert Dorfman, Paul A. Samuelson, and Robert M. Solow, *Linear Programming and Economic Analysis* (New York: McGraw-Hill, 1958).
6. John Von Neumann, "A Model of General Economic Equilibrium," *Review of Economic Studies* 13 (1945–6), pp. 1–9.
7. For an English translation see A. Wald, "On Some Systems of Equations of Mathematical Economics," *Econometrica* 19 (1951), pp. 368–403.
8. The following academics have received the Nobel Prize for Economics in part for the significant contributions each made to the development of

equilibrium analysis and growth. Though they have written extensively, an example of their work is cited for reference.

(1969) Jan Tinbergen, *An Economic Approach to Business Cycle Problems* (Paris: Herman, 1937).

(1970) Paul A. Samuelson, *Linear Programming and Economic Analysis* (New York: McGraw-Hill, 1958).

(1971) Simon Smith Kuznets, *Economic Growth of Nations: Total Output and Production Structure* (Cambridge, MA: Harvard University Press, 1971).

(1972) Kenneth Joseph Arrow, *Studies in Mathematical Theory of Inventory and Production* (Stanford,: CA Stanford University Press, 1958).

(1973) Wassily W. Leontief, *The Structure of the American Economy 1919–1929: An Empirical Application of Equilibrium Analysis* (Cambridge, MA: Harvard University Press, 1978).

(1983) Gerard Debreu, *Theory of Value* (New York: Wiley, 1959).

A standard reference for the issues involved in general equilibrium theory is Kenneth J. Arrow and Frank H. Hahn, *General Competitive Analysis* (San Francisco: Holden-Day, 1971).

9. Alfred Marshall, *Principles of Economics* (London: Macmillan, 1961).

10. Jeremy Bentham, *The Principles of Morals and Legislation* (New York: Macmillan, 1948).

11. Smith, p. 112.

12. Franco Modigliani received a Nobel Prize in 1985 for his work on personal and corporate finance. For an explanation of the lifetime consumption hypothesis see:

Andrew Hall, ed., *The Collected Papers of Franco Modigliani* (Cambridge, MA: MIT Press, 1980).

Albert Ando and Franco Modigliani, "The Life Cycle Hypothesis of Saving: Aggregate Implications and Tests," *American Economic Review* 53 (March 1963), pp. 55–84.

13. John Maynard Keynes, *The General Theory of Employment, Interest and Money* (New York: St. Martin's 1970).

14. Dale Jorgensen, *Productivity and U.S. Economic Growth* (Cambridge, MA: Harvard University Press, 1987).
Robert E. Lucas, *Studies in Business Cycle Theory* (Cambridge, MA: MIT Press, 1981).

15. Robert E. Lucas, *Models of Business Cycles* (Oxford: Blackwell Publisher, 1987).
Thomas J. Sargent, *Macroeconomic Theory* (New York: Academic, 1987).

16. Robert Hall, *Inflation: Causes and Effects* (Chicago: University of Chicago Press, 1982).

17. George Gilder, *Wealth and Poverty* (New York: Basic 1981).

———, *The Spirit of Enterprise* (New York: Simon and Schuster, 1984).

18. Robert Bacon and Walter Eltis, *Britain's Economic Problems: Too Few Producers* (London: Macmillan Press, 1978).

19. Arthur B. Laffer and Jan P. Seymour, *The Economics of Tax Revolt* (San Diego, CA: Harcourt Brace Jovanovich, 1979).

20. Friedrich August Hayek, *The Road to Serfdom* (Chicago: University of Chicago Press, 1944).

21. Ibid., p. 93.

22. Ibid., p. 135.

23. Milton Friedman and Rose D. Friedman, *Free to Choose* (New York: Avon, 1980), pp. 56–7.

24. William Simon, *A Time for Truth* (New York: Readers Digest Press, 1978), p. 12.

25. Ibid., p. 27.

26. Ibid., p. 49.

27. John Kenneth Galbraith, *The Affluent Society* (New York: New American Library, 1978).

28. John Kenneth Galbraith, *The New Industrial State* (New York: New American Library, 1979).

29. F. M. Scherer, "Inter-Industry Flows and Productivity Growth," *Review of Economics and Statistics* 64 (1982), pp. 627–34.

30. E. Mansfield, A. Romeo, and S. Wagner, "Foreign Trade and U.S. Research and Development," *Review of Economics and Statistics* (February 1979), pp. 49–57.

31. Ronald J. Wonnacott, "Canada/U.S. Economic Relations: A Canadian View," in Deborah Fretz, Robert Stern, and John Whalley, eds., *Canada/United States Trade and Investment Issues* (Toronto: Ontario Economic Council, 1985).

32. James Brander and Barbara Spencer, "Strategic Commitment with R&D: The Symmetric Case," *Bell Journal of Economics* 4 (1983), pp. 225–35.

33. Martin Holmes, *The First Thatcher Government, 1979–1983* (Brighton: Wheatsheaf, 1985), p. 40.

Additional references in regard to Thatcher's policies include the following:

John Bruce-Gardyne, *Mrs. Thatcher's First Administration* (London: Macmillan Press, 1984).

Joel Frieger, *Reagan, Thatcher, and the Politics of Decline* (New York: Oxford University Press, 1986).

Peter Jenkins, *Mrs. Thatcher's Revolution: The Ending of the Socialist Era* (London: Jonathon Cape, 1987).

Peter Riddell, *The Thatcher Government* (Oxford: Blackwell Publisher, 1985).

34. Additional references in regard to Reagan's policies include the following:

> Micheal J. Boskin, *Reagan and the Economy: The Successes, Failures, and Unfinished Agenda* (San Francisco: The Institute for Contemporary Studies, 1987).
> John L. Palmer and Isabel V. Sawhill, *The Reagan Experiment* (Washington, DC: The Urban Institute Press, 1982).
> Charles F. Stone and Isabel V. Sawhill, *Economic Policy in the Reagan Years* (Washington, DC: The Urban Institute Press, 1984).

35. Additional references in regard to China's economic reforms include the following:

> Neville Maxwell and Bruce McFarlane, *China's Changed Road to Development* (New York: Pergamon, 1984).
> Carl Riskin, *China's Political Economy: The Quest for Development since 1949* (Oxford: Oxford University Press, 1987).
> James T. H. Tsao, *China's Development Strategies and Foreign Trade* (Toronto: Lexington Books, 1987).

36. M. S. Gorbachev, "Report to the 27th Congress of the Communist Party of the Soviet Union, 25 February 1986," in Robert Maxwell, ed., *Speeches and Writings* (New York: Pergamon, 1986), p. 39.
Additional references in regard to Gorbachev's policies include the following:

> David A. Dyker, ed., *The Soviet Union Under Gorbachev* (London: Croom Helm, 1987).
> Mikhail Gorbachev, *Perestroika: New Thinking for Our Country and the World* (New York: Harper and Row, 1987).
> Martin McCauley, ed., *The Soviet Union Under Gorbachev* (New York: St. Martin's, 1987).
> Hans-Hacchim Veen, ed., *From Brezhnev to Gorbachev: Domestic Affairs and Soviet Foreign Policy* (New York: Berg Publishers, 1984).

37. Wassily W. Leontief, *The Structure of the American Economy, 1919–1939* (Cambridge, MA: Harvard University Press, 1941).
Holis B. Chenery and Paul G. Clark, *Interindustry Economics* (New York: Wiley, 1959).

38. Paul A. Samuelson, "Interactions Between the Multiplier Analysis and the Principle of Acceleration," *The Review of Economics and Statistics* 23 (1939), pp. 75–8.
J. R. Hicks, *A Contribution to the Theory of the Trade Cycle* (Oxford: Oxford University Press, 1950).

39. Robert Dorfman et al., p. 209.
40. Ibid., p. 224.

41. R. G. D. Allen, *Mathematical Economics* (New York: Macmillan, 1963).
42. Nicholas Kaldor, "Alternative Theories of Distribution," *Review of Economic Studies* 23 (1955–6), p. 89.
43. Joan Robinson, *An Essay on Marxian Economics* (London: Macmillan, 1942), p. 10.
44. Ibid.
45. Ibid.
46. Fred Gottheil, "Increasing Misery of the Proletariat: An Analysis of Marx's Wage and Employment Theory," *Canadian Journal of Economics and Political Science* 28 (1962), p. 105.
47. Karl Marx, "The Communist Manifesto," in Max Eastman, ed., *Capital and Other Writings of Karl Marx* (New York: Random House, 1932), p. 329.
48. Joseph A. Schumpeter, *Capitalism, Socialism and Democracy* (New York: Harper and Row, 1962), p. 39.
49. Robinson, p. 47.
50. Marx, p. 330.
51. Paul A. Samuelson and Anthony Scott, *Economics,* 5th ed. (Toronto: McGraw-Hill Ryerson, 1980), p. 613.
52. Robinson, p. 63.
53. Edmund S. Phelps, "The New View of Investment: A Neoclassical Analysis," *The Quarterly Journal of Economics* 56 (1962), p. 548.
54. Moses Abramovitz, "Economic Growth in the United States: A Review Article," *American Economic Review* 52 (1962), p. 781.

Chapter 5

1. Gary S. Becker, *Economic Theory* (New York: Knopf, 1971), p. 108.
2. Oskar Lange and Fred M. Taylor, *On the Economic Theory of Socialism,* Benjamin Evans Lippincott, ed. (New York: McGraw-Hill, 1966).
3. See, for example,

> E. H. Chamberlin, *Theory of Monopolistic Competition* (Cambridge, MA: Harvard University Press, 1933).
>
> R. Triffin, *Monopolistic Competition and General Equilibrium Theory* (Cambridge, MA: Harvard University Press, 1940).
>
> G. J. Stigler, "The Kinky Oligopoly Demand Curve and Rigid Prices," *Journal of Political Economy* 55 (1947), pp. 432–49.
>
> W. Fellner, *Competition Among the Few* (New York: Knopf, 1949).
>
> K. W. Rothschild, "Price Theory and Oligopoly," *Economic Journal* (September 1947), pp. 299–320.
>
> R. L. Bishop, "Duopoly: Collusion or Warfare?" *American Economic Review* 50 (1960), pp. 933–61.

4. Frank Stone, *Canada, The GATT, and the International Trade System* (Montreal: The Institute for Research on Public Policy, 1984), p. 182.

5. Richard Arnott, *Rent Control and Options for Decontrol in Ontario* (Toronto: Ontario Economic Council, 1981).
6. Milton Friedman and George Stigler, "Roofs or Ceilings? The Current Housing Problem," in Block and Olsen, eds., *Rent Control: Myths and Realities* (Vancouver: The Fraser Institute, 1981), pp. 87–103.
7. Ibid., p. 90.
8. Ibid., p. 93.
9. Ibid., p. 94.
10. Ibid., p. 101.
11. Sven Rydenfelt, "The Rise, Fall, and Revival of Swedish Rent Control," in Block and Olsen, p. 208.
12. Peter Navarro, "Rent Control in Cambridge Mass," *The Public Interest* 78 (Winter 1985), p. 90.
13. Robert F. Lanzillotti and Blaine Roberts, "Two Years of Wage–Price Controls: The Legacy of Phase II Price Controls," *American Economic Review* 64 (May 1974), p. 86.
14. Jerry Pohlman, *Economics of Wage and Price Controls* (Columbus, OH: Grid, 1972), p. 169.
15. Ibid.
16. Arnold R. Weber, *In Pursuit of Price Stability: The Wage-Price Freeze of 1971* (Washington, DC: The Brookings Institution, 1973), p. ix.
17. Hugh Rockoff, *Drastic Measures: A History of Wage and Price Controls in the United States* (Cambridge: Cambridge University Press, 1984), p. x.
18. Barry Richman, *Soviet Management* (Englewood Cliffs, NJ: Prentice-Hall, 1965), p. 230.
19. L. Gatovsky, "The Role of Profits in Socialist Economies," *Kommunist* 18 (December 1962), pp. 60–72.
20. Ibid.
21. N. S. Khrushchev, "Speech at the Plenary Session of the CPSU Central Committee," *Pravda* (December 15, 1963), pp. 1–3.
22. M. Kuznetsova, "Demand, Quality, and the Plan," *Pravda* (October 4, 1964), p. 4.
23. "Experiment under Examination," *Izvestiya* (October 21, 1964), p. 1.
24. O. Lacis, "A Survey of Business," *Izvestiya* (September 23, 1965), p. 3.
25. V. Lagutkin, "Plan Indicators to Stimulate Greater Production Efficiency," *Kommunist* 5 (March 1964), p. 88–9.
26. Ibid.
27. V. Nemchinov, "Socialist Economic Management and Production Planning," *Kommunist* 5 (March 1964), pp. 74–87.
28. See Y. Liberman and A. Rudkovsky, "A Plant Working Under the New System," *Pravda* (April 20, 1966), p. 1.
29. V. Sitnin, "Price Is an Important Tool of Economic Management," *Pravda* (November 12, 1966), p. 2.

Chapter 6

1. See the collection of papers in Paul R. Krugman, ed., *Strategic Trade Policy and the New International Economics* (Cambridge, MA: MIT Press, 1986).
2. OECD, *National Accounts, 1970–1982* (Paris: OECD, 1983), p. 522.
3. Economic Council of Canada, *Intervention and Efficiency: A Study of Government Credit and Credit Guarantees to the Private Sector* (Ottawa: Ministry of Supply and Services, 1982).
4. P. Davenport, C. Green, W. J. Milne, R. Saunders, and W. Watson, *Industrial Policy in Ontario and Quebec* (Toronto: Ontario Economic Council, 1982).
5. United States General Accounting Office, *The Federal Role in Fostering University–Industry Cooperation* (Washington, DC: U.S. Government Printing Office, 1983), p. 54.
6. Julian M. Weiss, "High-Tech Development," *Business Facilities* 17 (1984), p. H–23.
7. Charles B. Watkins, *Programs for Innovative Technology Research in State Strategies for Economic Development,* National Governors Association Report, Center for Policy Research, Washington, D.C., 1985.
8. Barbara Hollis, State Activities in Capital Formation, *U.S. Small Business Administration Report,* June 1985, p. 56.
9. Carol Hymowitz, "Where High-Tech Is Low Status," *Wall Street Journal* (May 20, 1985), p. C16.
10. Bruce Babbit, "The State and Reindustrialization," *Issues of Science and Technology* (1984), p. 54.
11. Hollis, p. 56.
12. Julian M. Weiss, "High-Tech Development," p. H–10.
13. Charles B. Watkins, *State Programs to Encourage the Commercialization of Innovative Technology,* National Governors Association Report, Center for Policy Research, Washington, D.C., December 1985, p. 32.
14. Hollis, p. 20.
15. Ibid., p. 11.
16. Watkins, *Commercialization of Innovative Technology,* p. 29.
17. United States, Task Force on Technological Innovation, "Technology and Growth: State Initiatives in Technological Innovation," National Governors Association Report, October 1983, p. 97.
18. United States, Task Force on Technological Development, p. 97.
19. OECD, *National Policies and Agricultural Trade* (Paris: OECD, 1987), pp. 51–2.
20. Ibid., p. 61.
21. The World Bank, *World Development Report, 1986* (Washington, DC: World Bank, 1986).
22. United States, Department of Agriculture, *Government Intervention in Agriculture,* Staff Report No. 229, April 1987. Cited in William M. Miner and Dale E. Hathaway, eds., *World Agricultural Trade: Building a Consensus* (Montreal: The Institute for Research on Public Policy, 1988), p. 49.

23. William M. Miner and Dale E. Hathaway, eds., *World Agricultural Trade: Building a Consensus* (Montreal: The Institute for Research on Public Policy, 1988), p. 49.
24. OECD, p. 51.
25. Miner and Hathaway, p. 55.
26. Robert Reich and John Donahue, *New Deals: The Chrysler Revival and the American System* (New York: Times Books, 1985).
27. Ibid., p. 73.
28. Donald Ryder, *British Leyland: The Next Decade,* Report presented to the Secretary of State for Industry, House of Commons, April 23, 1975. Quoted in Reich and Donahue, p. 78.
29. Reich and Donahue, p. 80.
30. Ibid., p. 85.
31. Ibid.
32. David Metcalf, "Employment and Industrial Assistance," in Alexis Jacquemin, ed., *European Industry: Public Policy and Corporate Strategy* (Oxford: Clarendon Press, 1984), p. 93.
33. B. Deacon and C. Pratten, *Effects of the Temporary Employment Subsidy,* Occasional Paper 53, Department of Applied Economics (Cambridge: Cambridge University Press, 1982).
34. J. B. Davies and G. M. MacDonald, *Information in the Labour Market: Job–Worker Matching and its Implications for Education in Ontario* (Toronto: University of Toronto Press, 1984).
35. J. B. Davies, "Training and Skill Development," in W. C. Riddell, ed., *Adapting to Change: Labour Market Adjustment in Canada* (Toronto: University of Toronto Press, 1986), p. 195.
36. Bernard Udis, *The Challenge to European Industrial Policy: Impacts of Redirected Military Spending* (London: Westview Press, 1987), pp. 34–6.
37. Ibid., p. 65.
38. Ibid., p. 59.
39. Ibid., p. 66.
40. Metcalf, p. 93.
41. Ibid.
42. Ronald Wonnacott, "Canada/U.S. Economic Relations: A Canadian View," in Deborah Fretz, Robert Stern, and John Whalley, eds., *Canada/United States Trade and Investment Issues* (Toronto: Ontario Economic Council, 1985).
43. As an example, see the study of the semiconductor industry in Michael Borrus, James Millstein, and John Zysman, *U.S.–Japanese Competition in the Semiconductor Industry* (Berkeley, CA: Institute of International Studies, University of California, 1982).
44. James Brander and Barbara Spencer, "Strategic Commitment with R&D: The Symmetric Case," *Bell Journal of Economics* 4 (1983), pp. 225–35.
45. Warren Schwartz, "Regulation of Industrial Subsidiaries in the EEC, United States, and GATT," in Michael Trebilcock, ed., *Federalism and the Ca-*

nadian Economic Union (Toronto: University of Toronto Press, 1983), p. 401.

46. Canada, Department of Finance, *Export Financing: Consultation Paper* (Ottawa: Minister of Supply and Services, 1985), p. 3.
47. Daniel S. Lyon and M. Trebilcock, *Public Strategy and Motion Pictures: The Choice of Instruments to Promote the Development of the Canadian Film Production Industry* (Toronto: Ontario Economic Council, 1982).
48. Robert Stern, "Canada/U.S. Trade and Investment Frictions: The U.S. View," in Fretz et al., p. 46.
49. Ibid., p. 47.
50. G. Glenday, G. P. Jenkins, and J. C. Evans, *Worker Adjustment Policies: An Alternative to Protectionism* (Ottawa: North-South Institute, 1982).
51. Stern, p. 39.
52. Ibid., p. 52.
53. Hans Mueller and Hans van der Ven, "Perils in the Brussels–Washington Steel Pact of 1982," *World Economy* 5 (November 1982), p. 262.
54. For example, see:

> A. F. C. Beales, *Education: A Framework for Choice* (London: Institute of Economic Affairs, 1967).
> M. Friedman, *Capitalism and Freedom* (Chicago: University of Chicago Press, 1962), Chapter 6.
> C. Jencks, *Education Vouchers: A Report of Financing Elementary Education by Grants to Parents* (Cambridge, MA: Centre for the Study of Public Policy, 1970).
> E. G. West, "Tom Paine's Voucher Scheme for Public Education," *Southern Economic Journal* (January 1967), pp. 378–82.

55. The following are useful references on the subject of health care:

> Robert G. Evans, *Strained Mercy: The Economics of Canadian Health Care* (Toronto: Butterworths, 1984).
> K. H. Friedman and Stuart H. Rakoff, *Toward a National Health Policy* (Lexington, MA: Lexington Books, 1977).
> Christopher Ham, *Health Care Policy in Britain* (London: Macmillan Press, 1982).
> Paul J. Feldstein, *Health Care Economics,* 3rd ed. (New York: Wiley, 1988).

56. Michael Harloe, *Private Rented Housing in the United States and Europe* (London: Croom Helm, 1985), pp. 176–7.
57. Ibid., p. 216.
58. George Sternlieb and David Listokin, "A Review of National Housing Policy," in Peter D. Salins, ed., *Housing America's Poor* (Chapel Hill, NC: The University of North Carolina Press, 1987), p. 29.
59. Ibid., p. 32.
60. John English, ed., *The Future of Council Housing* (London: Croom Helm, 1982), p. 29.

61. Ibid., p. 195.
62. David Whithman, "The First Sixty Years of Council Housing," in English, p. 216.
63. Claire Holton Hammond, *The Benefits of Subsidized Housing Programs: An Intertemporal Approach* (Cambridge: Cambridge University Press, 1987), pp. 106–7.
64. Brian Holmes, "Equality and Freedom in Education," in Brian Holmes, ed., *Equality and Freedom in Education* (London: Allen and Unwin, 1985), p. 2.
65. David Turner, "Education in the U.S.A.: Freedom to be Unequal," in Holmes, p. 121.
66. R. Murray Thomas, "The Symbiotic Linking of Politics and Education," in R. Murray Thomas, ed., *Politics and Education: Cases from Eleven Nations* (Oxford: Pergamon Press, 1983), pp. 9–10.
67. Philip G. Altbach, Robert F. Arnove, and Gail P. Kelly, eds., *Comparative Education* (New York: Macmillan, 1982).
68. Jencks.
69. G. B. J. Atkinson, *The Economics of Education* (London: Hodder and Stoughton, 1983), pp. 98–9.
70. Philip H. Coombs, *The World Crisis in Education: The View from the Eighties* (New York: Oxford University Press, 1985), p. 212.
71. T. N. Postlewaite, "Success and Failure in School," in Altbach et al., p. 201.
72. Irwin Sobel, "The Human Capital Revolution in Economic Development," in Altbach et al., p. 5.
73. Mervyn Matthews, "Long-Term Trends in Soviet Education," in Janusz Tomiak, ed., *Soviet Education in the 1980s* (London: Croom Helm, 1983), p. 5.
74. Roberta Marine, "The Socialization of Children in China and Taiwan: An Analysis of Elementary School Textbooks," in Altbach et al., p. 153.
75. Shi Ming Au and Eli Seifman, eds., *Education and Socialist Modernization: A Documentary History of Education in the People's Republic of China, 1977–1986* (New York: Ams Press, 1987), p. xiii.
76. Bradley R. Schiller, *The Economics of Poverty and Discrimination*, 3rd ed. (Englewood Cliffs, NJ: Prentice-Hall, 1980), p. 165.
77. Robert J. Lampman, "Goals and Purposes of Social Welfare Expenditures," in Paul M. Sommers, ed., *Welfare Reform in America: Perspectives and Prospects* (Boston: Kluwer-Nijhoff, 1982), pp. 5–7.
78. William R. Albrecht, "Welfare Reform: An Idea Whose Time Has Come and Gone," in Paul M. Sommers, ed., *Welfare Reform in America: Perspectives and Prospects* (Boston: Kluwer-Nijhoff, 1982), p. 15.
79. Robert R. Friedmann, "Welfare States: A Summary of Trends," in Robert R. Friedmann, Neil Gilbert, and Moshe Sherer, eds., *Modern Welfare States: A Comparative View of Trends and Prospects* (New York: New York University Press, 1987), p. 288.
80. Ibid., p. 289.
81. In regard to this issue, see also Jeffrey G. Williamson and Peter H. Lindert,

eds., *American Inequality: A Macroeconomic History* (New York: Academic, 1980).

82. Moshe Sherer, "Welfare States: An Overview of Problems and Prospects," in Friedman et al., pp. 296–8.
83. Dorothy Wilson, *The Welfare State in Sweden* (London: Heinemann, 1979), p. 151.
84. Gordon Tullock, *Economics of Income Redistribution* (Boston: Kluwer-Nijhoff, 1983), p. 186.
85. Jonathan Bradshaw and Alan Deacon, "Social Security," in Paul Wilding, ed., *In Defence of the Welfare State* (Manchester: Manchester University Press, 1986), p. 96.

Chapter 7

1. A. B. Atkinson and J. E. Stiglitz, "The Design of Tax Structure: Direct versus Indirect Taxation," *Journal of Public Economics* (1976), p. 74.
2. R. W. Boadway and H. M. Kitchen, *Canadian Tax Policy,* Canadian Tax Papers No. 76 (Toronto: Canadian Tax Foundation, 1984), p. 16.
3. Ibid.
4. Mireille Ethier, "The Underground Economy: A Review of the Economic Literature and New Estimates for Canada," in F. Vaillancourt, ed., *Income Distribution and Economic Security in Canada,* The Collected Research Studies/Royal Commission on the Economic Union and Development Prospects for Canada, Vol. 1 (Toronto: University of Toronto, 1985).
5. J. A. Hausman, "Taxes and Labour Supply," in A. J. Auerbach and M. Feldstein, eds., *Handbook of Public Economics,* Vol. 1 (Amsterdam: North Holland, 1985), p. 249.
6. Samuel A. Rae, Jr., "The Impact of Taxes and Transfers on Labour Supply: A Review of the Evidence," in David W. Conklin, ed., *A Separate Personal Income Tax for Ontario: Background Studies* (Toronto: Ontario Economic Council, 1984), p. 134.
7. Douglas G. Hartle, *A Separate Personal Income Tax for Ontario: An Economic Analysis* (Toronto: Ontario Economic Council, 1983).
8. See Richard Musgrave, Peggy B. Musgrave, and Richard M. Bird, *Public Finance in Theory and Practice* (Toronto: McGraw-Hill Ryerson, 1987).
9. Robin Boadway and Neil Bruce, "Theoretical Issues in Tax Reform," in David Laidler, ed., *Approaches to Economic Well-Being,* The Collected Research Studies/Royal Commission on the Economic Union and Development Prospects for Canada, Vol. 24 (Toronto: University of Toronto Press, 1985), p. 21.
10. See, for example, G. U. Jump and T. A. Wilson, "Inflation and the Taxation of Personal Investment Income: An Appraisal," in David W. Conklin, ed., *Inflation and the Taxation of Personal Investment Income* (Toronto: Ontario Economic Council, 1982).
11. See, for example, Richard M. Bird, *Tax Incentives for Investment: The State*

of the Art, Canadian Tax Papers No. 64 (Toronto: Canadian Tax Foundation, 1980).

12. R. E. Hall and D. W. Jorgenson, "Tax Policy and Investment Behaviour," *American Economic Review* 57 (1967), pp. 391–414.

13. D. G. McFetridge and J. D. May, "The Effects of Capital Cost Allowance Measures on Capital Accumulation in the Canadian Manufacturing Sector," *Public Finance Quarterly* 4 (1976), pp. 307–22.
    F. J. Harman and J. A. Johnson, "An Examination of Government Tax Incentives for Business Investment in Canada," *Canadian Tax Journal* 26 (1978), pp. 691–704.

14. R. M. Solow, "A Contribution to the Theory of Growth," *Quarterly Journal of Economics* 70 (1956), pp. 65–94.
    H. Uzawa, "On a 2-Sector Model of Economic Growth," *Review of Economic Studies* 29 (1961), pp. 40–7.

15. See, for example:

    M. S. Feldstein, "Social Security, Induced Retirement and Aggregate Capital Accumulation," *Journal of Political Economy* 82 (1974), pp. 905–26.
    L. H. Summers, "Capital Taxation and Accumulation in a Life Cycle Growth Model," *American Economic Review* 71 (1981), pp. 533–44.
    David G. Davies, *United States Taxes and Tax Policy* (Cambridge: Cambridge University Press, 1986).

16. A. Deutsch and G. Jenkins, "Tax Incentives, Revenue Transfers and the Taxation of Income from Foreign Investment," in Wayne Thirsk and John Whalley, eds., *Tax Policy Options in the 1980s* (Toronto: Canadian Tax Foundation, 1982), p. 225.

17. See, for example, Robin Boadway and Neil Bruce, "The Personal Income Tax: Implications for Investments," in David W. Conklin, ed., *A Separate Personal Income Tax for Ontario: Background Studies* (Toronto: Ontario Economic Council, 1984).

18. United States, Department of the Treasury, *Tax Reform for Fairness, Simplicity, and Economic Growth,* Vol. 1 (Washington, DC: Office of the Secretary, Department of the Treasury, 1984), p. 4.

19. See, for example, M. Daly, J. Jung, P. Mercier, and T. Schweitzer, *A Comparison of Effective Marginal Tax Rates in Canadian Manufacturing,* Economic Council of Canada Discussion Paper No. 293 (Ottawa: Economic Council of Canada, 1985).

20. Boadway and Kitchen, p. 8.

21. N. Kaldor, *An Expenditure Tax* (London: Allen and Unwin, 1955).

22. United States, Department of the Treasury, *Blueprints for Basic Tax Reform* (Washington, DC: U.S. Government Printing Office, 1977).

23. Boadway and Kitchen, p. 27.

24. United States, Department of the Treasury, *Blueprints.*
25. France St. Hilaire and John Whalley, "Recent Studies of Efficiency and Distributional Impacts of Taxes," in Thirsk and Whalley.
26. J. Davies and F. St. Hilaire, *Income Taxation in Canada: Efficiency and Distributional Effects of Alternative Options* (Ottawa: Economic Council of Canada, 1987).
27. France St. Hilaire and John Whalley, "Recent Studies of Efficiency and Distributional Impacts of Taxes," in Thirsk and Whalley, pp. 28–9.
28. France St. Hilaire and John Whalley, "Reforming Taxes: Some Problems of Implementation," in D. Laidler, ed., *Approaches to Economic Well-Being* (Toronto: University of Toronto Press, 1985), p. 204.
29. A. F. Sheppard, "Taxation Policy and the Canadian Economic Union," in M. Krasnick, ed., *Fiscal Federalism,* The Collected Research Studies/Royal Commission on the Economic Union and Development Prospects for Canada, Vol. 65 (Toronto: University of Toronto Press, 1986), pp. 178–9.
30. John Stuart Mill, *Principles of Political Economy* (New York: Sentry Press), p. 823.
31. Ibid.
32. A. B. Atkinson and J. E. Stiglitz, "The Design of Tax Structure: Direct Versus Indirect Taxation," *Journal of Public Economics* 4 (1976), pp. 55–75.
    J. P. Kesselman, "The BTT, the Tax Mix and Tax Reform," *Proceedings of the Thirty-Eighth Tax Conference* (Toronto: Canadian Tax Foundation, 1987).
    Wayne R. Thirsk, *Indirect Federal Taxes, the Cost of Capital and the Issue of Tax Incidence,* Economic Council of Canada Discussion Paper No. 294 (Ottawa: Economic Council of Canada, 1985).
33. Thirsk, p. 14.
34. J. Carlson and C. E. McLure, "Pros and Cons of Alternative Approaches to the Taxation of Consumption," mimeographed (1984).
35. Thirsk, p. 9.
36. J. M. Buchanan and M. R. Flowers, *The Public Finances* (Homewood, IL: Irwin, 1975), p. 134.
37. Boadway and Kitchen, p. 120.
38. Thirsk, p. 2.
39. Ibid., p. 15.
40. S. Cnossen, "Sales Tax Coordination," in *Proceedings of the Thirty-Seventh Tax Conference* (Toronto: Canadian Tax Foundation, 1985), p. 142.
41. Boadway and Kitchen, p. 282.
42. Ibid.
43. Ibid.
44. Ibid., p. 266.
45. See, for example, M. Daly, J. Jung, P. Mercier, and T. Schweitzer, *A Comparison of Effective Marginal Tax Rates in Canadian Manufacturing,* Economic Council of Canada Discussion Paper No. 293 (Ottawa: Economic Council of Canada, 1985).

46. Although dividend deduction may relieve the double taxation of dividends under the PIT and CIT, the result of these provisions is to effectively tax different sources of capital income at different rates. The net impact is unclear.

47. See, for example, J. Davies, "Reform of the Federal Sales Tax," in *Proceedings of the Thirty-Seventh Conference* (Toronto: Canadian Tax Foundation, 1985).

48. For a modern "Keynesian" view of price adjustment, see R. Lipsey, "The understanding and control of inflation: Is there a crisis in macroeconomics?" *Canadian Journal of Economics* 14 (1981), pp. 545–76. For a modern "non-Keynesian" view of price adjustment, see R. Lucas, "Methods and problems in business cycle theory," *Journal of Money, Credit and Banking* 12 (1980) pp. 696–715.

49. The *IS* curve shows the combinations of interest rates and income levels at which withdrawals from aggregate demand (savings, taxes, and imports) are equal to injections (investment, government spending, and exports). The *IS* curve is negatively sloped because investment is negatively related and savings are positively related to the rate of interest, and savings rise due to an increase in income by more than does investment. The *LM* curve shows the combinations of interest rates and incomes at which money demand is equated to a given money supply. It is positively sloped because money demand falls as the rate of interest rises. The intersection of the *IS* and *LM* curves is the only interest–income combination at which both the money market and the goods market are in equilibrium.

50. Of course, an increase in net wealth also shifts the *IS* curve outwards. For a full presentation of the argument that the end result of all shifts in both the *IS* and *LM* curves due to an increased deficit is likely to be no change in national income, see E. Infante and J. Stein, "Does Fiscal Policy Matter?" *Journal of Monetary Economics* 2 (1976), pp. 473–500.
For an opposing argument, see A. Blinder and R. Solow, "Does Fiscal Policy Matter?" *Journal of Public Economics* 2 (1973), pp. 319–37.

51. The original presentation of the St. Louis equations appears in L. Anderson and J. Jordan, "Monetary and Fiscal Actions: A Test of Their Relative Importance in Economic Stabilization," *Federal Bank of St. Louis Review* 51 (November 11–24, 1968).

52. F. Modigliani and A. Ando, "Impacts of Fiscal Actions on Aggregate Income and the Monetarist Controversy: Theory and Evidence," in J. Stein, ed., *Monetarism* (Amsterdam: North-Holland, 1976), pp. 30–42.

53. The original presentation of this model is to be found in R. Mundell, "Capital Mobility and Stabilization Policy under Fixed and Flexible Exchange Rates," *Canadian Journal of Economics and Political Science* 29 (1963), pp. 475–85.

54. Robert Barro, "Are Government Bonds Net Wealth?" *Journal of Political Economy* 82 (1974), pp. 1095–117.

55. See also Robert Barro, *Macroeconomic Analysis* (New York: Academic 1981).

56. D. Ricardo, "Funding System," in P. Sraffa, ed., *The Works and Corre-*

spondence of David Ricardo, Vol. 4 (Cambridge: Cambridge University Press, 1951).

57. For a critique of the Barro model, see J. Tobin, "Stabilization Policy: Ten Years After," *Brookings Papers on Economic Activity* 1 (1980), pp. 19–71.

58. The most forceful exposition of this view can be found in J. Buchanan and R. Wagner, *Democracy in Deficit* (New York: Academic 1977). These two American economists believe that democratic societies are plagued by a built-in tendency towards money-financed deficits. The work of Buchanan and Wagner is prominently cited by supporters of a balanced budget in the United States.

59. T. Sargent and N. Wallace, "Some Unpleasant Monetarist Arithmetic," *Federal Reserve Bank of Minneapolis Quarterly Review* 5 (Fall 1981), p. 4.

Chapter 8

1. Oskar Lange and Fred M. Taylor, *On the Economic Theory of Socialism,* Benjamin Lippincott, ed. (New York: McGraw-Hill, 1966).
2. See, for example:

> C. Lloyd Brown-John, *Canadian Regulatory Agencies* (Toronto: Butterworths, 1981), pp. 114–24.
> Michael D. Reagan, *Regulation: The Politics of Policy* (Toronto: Little, Brown, 1987).
> Michael Cohen and George Stigler, *Can Regulatory Agencies Protect Consumers?* (Washington, DC: American Enterprise Institute for Public Policy Research, 1971).

3. An authoritative reference is Richard A. Posner, *Economic Analysis of Law,* 3rd ed. (Toronto: Little, Brown, 1986).
4. Albert V. Dicey, *An Introduction to the Study of the Law of the Constitution,* 10th ed. (London: St. Martin's, 1961), p. 188.
5. Ibid., pp. 202–3.
6. Pierre E. Trudeau, Letter to the Chairman of the Economic Council of Canada, July 12, 1978. Quoted in *Responsible Regulation: An Interim Report* (Ottawa: Minister of Supply and Services, 1979), p. 119.
7. Economic Council of Canada, *Reforming Regulation* (Ottawa: Minister of Supply and Services, 1981).
8. Economic Council of Canada, pp. 133–4.
9. For an analysis of the Ash Council Report see:

> R. Cramton, "Regulatory Structure and Regulatory Performance," *Public Administration Review* 32 (July/August 1972), p. 285.
> Roger G. Noll, *Reforming Regulation* (Washington, DC: The Brookings Institution, 1971).
> G. O. Robinson, "On Reorganizing the Independent Regulatory Agencies," *Virginia Law Review* 57 (1970), p. 953.
> L. N. Cutler and D. R. Johnston, "Regulation and the Political Process," *Yale Law Journal* 7 (1984), pp. 1395–418.

A. Kahn, *The Economics of Regulation: Principles and Institutions* (New York: Wiley, 1971).

10. Reagan, p. 72.
11. Ibid., p. 73.
12. Daniel Swartzman, Richard A. Liroff, and Kevin G. Croke, *Cost–Benefit Analysis and Environmental Regulations: Politics, Ethics, and Methods* (Washington DC: The Conservation Foundation, 1982), p. 35.
13. Reagan, p. 1.
14. Shirley Serafini and Michel Andreau, *The Information Revolution and its Implications for Canada* (Ottawa: Department of Communications, 1980), p. 28.
15. Foreign Investment Review Act, 1973. c. 46.
16. Duncan McDowall, *A Fit Place for Foreign Investments: Foreign Investors' Perceptions of Canada in a Changing World* (Ottawa: The Conference Board of Canada, 1984).
17. Ibid., p. 1.
18. Ibid., p. ix.
19. Ibid., p. x.
20. A. E. Safarian, *Governments and Multinationals: Policies in the Developed Countries* (Washington, D.C.: British-North American Committee, 1983), p. V.
21. Ibid., p. 92.
22. David L. Anderson, *Foreign Investment Control in the Canadian Mineral Sector: Lessons from the Australian Experience* (Kingston, Ont.: Queen's University Centre for Resource Studies, 1984).
23. Ibid., p. xiii.
24. Ibid., p. 96.
25. Ibid., p. 123.
26. Ibid., p. 4.
27. S. 2. Investment Canada Act, 1985. c. 20.
28. Bruce Little, "New agency strives to erase FIRA's memory", *Globe and Mail* (July 8, 1985), pp. B1–2.
29. Robert Packwood, *Long-Range Goals in International Telecommunications and Information* (Washington, DC: U.S. Government Printing Office, 1983).
30. Consultative Committee on the Implications of Telecommunications for Canadian Sovereignty, *Telecommunications and Canada* (Ottawa: Minister of Supply and Services, 1979), p. 2.
31. Ibid., p. 28.
32. Tom Riley, "Canada Moves Toward Protecting Personal Privacy," *The Globe and Mail* (February 27, 1984), p. 7.
33. Helena Stalson, *U.S. Service Exports and Foreign Barriers: An Agenda for Negotiations* (Washington, DC: National Planning Association, 1985), p. 74.
34. Michel Cote, "The Importance of Intellectual Property in Trade Between

Canada and the United States," in Renée Chudakoff and David Meany, eds., *Canada-United States Law Journal: Proceedings of the Canada-United States Law Institute Conference* (Buffalo: Case Western Reserve Journal of International Law, 1986), p. 7.

35. United States, Office of Technology Assessment, *Report Brief* (Washington, DC: U.S. Government Printing Office, 1986), p. 1.

36. United States, Office of the U.S. Trade Representative, Department of Commerce, *U.S. High Technology and Competitiveness,* Staff Report, February 1985, p. 3.

37. United States, U.S. Council Task Force on Intellectual Property, "A New MTN: Priorities for Intellectual Property," in *A New Round of Multilateral Trade Negotiations: Recommended U.S. Business Objectives,* United States Council for International Business, April 18, 1985, p. 6.

38. James Keon, "Intellectual Property Protection in Canada: The Technology Challenge," in Renée Chudakoff and David Meany, eds., *Canada-United States Law Journal: Proceedings of the Canada-United States Law Institute Conference,* Vol 11. (Buffalo: Case Western Reserve Journal of International Law, 1986), p. 29.

39. United States, Office of Technology Assessment, "Intellectual Property Rights in an Age of Electronics and Information" (Washington, DC: U.S. Government Printing Office, 1986), p. 98.

40. Willard Alonzo Stanback, "International Intellectual Property Protection: An Integrated Solution to the Inadequate Protection Problem," *Virginia Journal of International Law* 29 (1989) p. 517–60.

41. Ronald J. Wonnacott, "Canada/U.S. Economic Relations: A Canadian View," in Deborah Fretz, Robert Stern, and John Whalley, eds., *Canada/ United States Trade and Development Issues* (Toronto: Ontario Economic Council, 1985).

42. United States, Office of Technology Assessment, p. 1.

43. Henry Peskin, Paul Portney, and Allen Kneese, *Environmental Regulation and the U.S. Economy* (Baltimore: The Johns Hopkins University Press, 1981), p. 1.

44. Winston Harrington and Alan J. Krupnick, "Stationary Source Pollution Policy and Choices for Reform," in Peskin et al., p. 105.

45. Peskin et al., p. 2.

46. Swartzman et al.

47. Ibid., p. 553.

48. Ibid.

49. Harry Wolfe and David Newmeyer, *Aviation Industry Regulation* (Carbondale and Edwardsville, IL: Southern Illinois University Press, 1985), p. 34.

50. Ibid., pp. 48–9.

51. Economic Council of Canada, pp. 27–36.

52. Economic Council of Canada, p. 60.

53. Douglas Caves, Lavrits Christenses, Michael Tretheway, and Robert Windle, "An Assessment of the Efficiency Effects of U.S. Airline Deregulation via an International Comparison," in Elizabeth Bailey, ed., *Public Regu-*

lation: New Perspectives on Institutions and Policies (Cambridge, MA: MIT Press, 1987), p. 285.

Chapter 9

1. Raymond Vernon and Yair Aharoni, eds., *State-Owned Enterprise in the Western Economies* (London: Croom Helm, 1981), p. 8.
2. Henry Parris, *Public Enterprise in Western Europe* (London: Croom Helm, 1987), p. 14.
3. Theodore Schultz, "Knowledge Is Power in Agriculture," *Challenge* (September/October 1981), p. 11.
4. Parris, p. 15.
5. Ibid.
6. Kate Ascher, *The Politics of Privatization* (London: Macmillan Press, 1987), p. 47.
7. Parris, p. 19.
8. Ibid.
9. Roy Rees, *Public Enterprise Economics* (London: Weidenfeld and Nicolson, 1984), p. 2.
10. Vernon and Aharoni, p. 11.
11. Parris, p. 173.
12. Ibid., p. 23.
13. John Redwood, *Public Enterprise in Crisis: The Future of the Nationalized Industries* (Oxford: Blackwell Publisher, 1980), p. 203.
14. Vernon and Aharoni, p. 21.
15. Richard Pryke, *The Nationalized Industries: Policies and Performance since 1968* (Oxford: Robinson, 1981), p. 104.
16. Gregory and Stuart, *Soviet Economic Structure and Performance,* 2nd ed. (New York: Harper and Row, 1981), p. 228.
17. See, for example:

    Martin Schrenk, *Yugoslavia: Self-Management Socialism* (Baltimore: Johns Hopkins University Press, 1979).
    D. Jones and J. Svejnar, eds., *Participatory and Self-Managed Firms* (Lexington, MA: Lexington Books, 1982).
    David Granick, *Enterprise Guidance in Eastern Europe* (Princeton, NJ: Princeton University Press, 1975).
    John P. Burkett, *The Effects of Economic Reform in Yugoslavia* (Berkeley, CA: University of California Press, 1983).

18. John Kay, Colin Mayer, and David Thompson, eds., *Privatization and Regulation: The UK Experience* (Oxford: Clarendon Press, 1986), p. 2.
19. Sue Hastings and Hugo Levie, eds., *Privatization* (Nottingham: Spokesman, 1983).
20. Colin Mayer and Shirley Meadowcroft, "Selling Public Assets: Techniques and Financial Implications," in Kay et al., p. 322.
21. Ascher, p. 14.

22. Ibid., p. 22.
23. Ibid., p. 261.
24. John M. Montias, *Central Planning in Poland* (New Haven, CT: Yale University Press, 1962), p. 107.
25. Sidney Ploss, *Conflict and Decision-making in Soviet Russia* (Princeton, NJ: Princeton University Press, 1965).
26. A. Kosygin, "On Improving the Management of Industry, Perfecting Planning and Strengthening Economic Incentives in Industrial Production," *Pravda* (September 28, 1965), pp. 1–4.
27. V. S. Nemchinov, "Socialist Economic Management and Production Planning," *Kommunist* 5 (March 1964), pp. 74–87.
28. See, for example; V. Shkatov, "What is Useful to the Country is Advantageous for Everyone," *Pravda* (September 1, 1964), p. 2.
29. Y. Liberman, "Once More on the Plan, Profits, and Bonuses," *Pravda* (September 20, 1964), p. 3.
30. Y. Liberman, "Confidence Is an Incentive," *Komsomolskaya Pravda* (April 24, 1966), p. 2.
31. John P. Hardt and Donna L. Gold, "Reforming the Economic System: Economic Reform, Soviet Style," in Hans-Joachim Veen, ed., *From Brezhnev to Gorbachev: Domestic Affairs and Soviet Foreign Policy* (New York: St. Martin's, 1987), pp. 113–14.
32. Ronald Amman, "Political Obstacles to Economic Reform," in Veen, pp. 135–6.
33. Philip Hanson, "The Economy," in Martin McCauley, ed., *The Soviet Union under Gorbachev* (New York: St. Martin's, 1987), p. 116. See also David A. Dyker, ed., *The Soviet Union Under Gorbachev: Prospects for Reform* (New York: Croom Helm, 1987).
34. M. Gorbachev, *Perestroika: New Thinking for Our Country and the World* (New York: Harper and Row, 1987), p. 70.
35. Oskar Lange, "On the Economic Theory of Socialism," in Benjamin Evans Lippincott, ed., *On the Economic Theory of Socialism* (New York: McGraw-Hill, 1966).

Chapter 10

1. Arthur Okun, *Equality and Efficiency: The Big Trade-Off* (Washington, DC: The Brookings Institution, 1975).
2. Ibid., p. 120.
3. Edgar Browning and William Johnson, *The Distribution of the Tax Burden* (Washington, DC: American Enterprise Institute for Public Policy Research, 1979), p. 175.
4. Ibid.
5. Robert Bacon and Walter Eltis, *Britain's Economic Problem: Too Few Producers* (London: Macmillan Press 1978).
6. Ibid., p. 139.
7. Ibid., p. 163.

8. John Addison and John Burton, *Trade Unions and Society: Some Lessons of the British Experience* (Vancouver: The Fraser Institute, 1984), p. 4.
9. Robert Reich, *The Next American Frontier* (New York: Times Books, 1983), p. 16.
10. Ibid., p. 20.
11. Ibid., p. 128.
12. Ibid., p. 135.
13. G. C. Allen, *The Japanese Economy* (London: Weidenfeld and Nicholson, 1981), p. 16.
14. Takafusa Nakamura, *The Postwar Japanese Economy: Its Development and Structure* (Tokyo: University of Tokyo Press, 1981), p. 3.
15. Mancur Olson, *The Rise and Decline of Nations: Economic Growth, Stagflation, and Social Rigidities* (New Haven, CT: Yale University Press, 1982).
16. Anthony Downs, *Economic Analysis of Democracy* (New York: Harper Bros., 1958).
17. James M. Buchanan and Gordon Tullock, *The Calculus of Consent* (Ann Arbor: University of Michigan Press, 1962).
18. Douglas G. Hartle, "The Theory of Rent Seeking: Some Reflections," *Canadian Journal of Economics* 16 (November 1983), p. 545.
19. M. J. Trebilcock, D. G. Hartle, R. S. Prichard, and D. N. Dewees, *The Choice of Governing Instrument* (Ottawa: Economic Council of Canada, 1982), pp. 33–4.
20. George Stigler, "The Theory of Economic Regulation," *Bell Journal of Economics and Management Science* 2 (1971), pp. 3–21.
21. Dan Usher, *The Economic Prerequisite to Democracy* (Oxford: Blackwell Publisher, 1981), p. xiii.
22. G. Tullock, *The Economics of Income Redistribution* (Boston: Kluwer-Nijhoff, 1983), p. 186.
23. Alvin Toffler, *The Third Wave* (New York: Bantam, 1981).
24. Reich.
25. Walt Rostow, *The Stages of Economic Growth* (Cambridge: Cambridge University Press, 1962).
26. Ted Gurr, *Why Men Rebel* (Princeton, NJ: Princeton University Press, 1980), p. 13.
27. Karl Marx, "The Communist Manifesto," in Max Eastman, ed., *Capital and other Writings of Karl Marx* (New York: Random House, 1932), p. 321.
28. Ibid., p. 322.
29. Ibid., p. 327.
30. Ibid., pp. 342–3.
31. Rostow, p. 149.
32. Ibid., p. 7.
33. Ibid., p. 11.
34. Ibid., pp. 93–104.
35. Gurr, p. 13.
36. Ibid.
37. Ibid., p. 37.

38. Lyford Edwards, *The Natural History of Revolution* (New York: Russell and Russell, 1965), quoted in Gurr, p. 38.
39. George Pettee, *The Process of Revolution* (New York: Fertig, 1971), quoted in Gurr, p. 38.
40. Gurr, p. 62.
41. Anthony Oberschall, *Social Conflict and Social Movements* (Englewood Cliffs, NJ: Prentice-Hall, 1973), p. 25.
42. Ibid., p. 24.
43. Ibid., pp. 34–5.
44. David Shub, *Lenin* (New York: New American Library, 1948), p. 30.
45. Isaac Deutscher, *Stalin: A Political Biography* (New York: Random House, 1960), p. 63.
46. See, for example, Walter Lippmann, *Essays on the Public Philosophy,* 1st ed. (Toronto: Little, Brown 1955).

Chapter 11

1. S. Hymer, *The International Operations of National Firms* (Cambridge, MA: MIT Press, 1976).
2. R. McCulloch and R. F. Owen, "Linking Negotiations on Trade and Foreign Direct Investment," in C. P. Kindleberger and D. B. Audretsch, eds., *The Multinational Corporation in the 1980s* (Cambridge, MA: MIT Press, 1983), p. 345.
3. E. Mansfield, "R&D Innovation: Some Empirical Findings," in Z. Griliches, ed., *R&D, Patents and Productivity* (Chicago: University of Chicago Press, 1984).
4. F. T. Knickerbocker, *Oligopolistic Reaction and Multinational Enterprises* (Cambridge, MA: MIT Press, 1983).
5. L. T. Wells, "Third World Multinationals," *Multinational Business* 1 (1980), pp. 12–19.
6. S. P. Magee, "Multinational Corporations: The Industry Technology Cycle and Development," *Journal of World Trade Law* 2 (July/August 1977).
7. J. Niosi, *Canadian Multinationals,* translated by Robert Chodos (Toronto: Between the Lines, 1985), pp. 28–30.
8. J. M. Stopford and J. H. Dunning, *The World Directory of Multinational Enterprises 1982–1983: Company Performance and Global Trends* (Detroit: Gale Research, 1983), p. 31.
9. Ibid.
10. Ibid.
11. P. Buckley and M. Casson, *The Future of the Multinational Corporation* (New York: Holmes and Meier, 1976).
12. R. E. Caves, *Multinational Enterprise and Economic Analysis* (Cambridge: Cambridge University Press, 1985), p. 196.
13. E. Mansfield, A. Romeo, and S. Wagner, "Foreign Trade and U.S. Research and Development," *Review of Economics and Statistics* (February 1979), pp. 49–57.
14. Caves.

15. Ibid, p. 198.
16. I. A. Litvak, *The Canadian Multinationals* (Toronto: Butterworths, 1981).
17. Stopford and Dunning, p. 40.
18. E. Mansfield and A. Romeo, "Technology Transfers to Overseas Subsidiaries by U.S. Based Firms," *Quarterly Journal of Economics* (December 1980), pp. 737–50.
19. Stopford and Dunning.
20. Litvak.
21. A. Chaudhuri, "American Multinationals and American Employment," in Kindleberger and Audretsch, eds., *The Multinational Corporation in the 1980s* (Cambridge, MA: MIT Press, 1983).
22. T. A. Poynter and A. M. Rugman, "World Product Mandates: How Will Multinationals Respond," *Business Quarterly* 47 (October 1982), p. 60.
23. W. Fischer and J. Behrman, "The Coordination of Foreign R&D Activities by Transnational Corporation," *Journal of International Business* 10 (Winter 1979).
24. H. G. Etemad, "World Product Mandating in Perspective," in A. Rugman, ed., *Multinationals and Technology Transfers* (New York: Praeger, 1983).
25. Paul R. Krugman, "Is Free Trade Passe?" *Economic Perspectives* 1 (1987), pp. 131–44.
26. James Brander and Barbara Spencer, "Strategic Commitment with R&D: The Symmetric Case," *Bell Journal of Economics* 4 (1983), pp. 225–35.
27. Ronald Kutscher, "Some Aspects of Service Sector Growth in the United States," in Herbert Grubel, ed., *Conceptual Issues in Service Sector Research: A Symposium* Vancouver: The Fraser Institute, 1987), p. 56.
28. See:

> Herbert G. Grubel, ed., *Conceptual Issues in Service Sector Research: A Symposium* (Vancouver: The Fraser Institute, 1987).
> James J. McRae and Martine M. Desbois, eds., *Traded and Non-Traded Services: Theory, Measurement and Policy* (Halifax: Institute for Research on Public Policy, 1988).

29. Richard N. Cooper, "U.S. Policies and Practices on Subsidies in International Trade," in Steven J. Warmicke, ed., *International Trade and Industrial Policies* (New York: Holmes and Meier, 1978), p. 120.
30. Gary C. Hufbauer and Joanna Shelton, *Subsidies in International Trade* (Cambridge, MA: MIT Press, 1984), p. 21.
31. Richard Simeon, "Federalism and Free Trade," in Duncan Cameron, ed., *The Free Trade Papers* (Toronto: Lorimar 1986), p. 189.
32. Mancur Olson, "The Political Economy of Comparative Growth Rates," in Dennis C. Mueller, ed., *The Political Economy of Growth* (New Haven, CT: Yale University Press, 1983).
33. Robert E. Baldwin, *Non-Tariff Distortions of International Trade* (Washington, DC: The Brookings Institution, 1970), p. 130.
34. Milton Friedman, "Economists and Economic Policy," *Economic Inquiry* (January 1986), p. 73.

Index

411